Advance Praise

Scott Spencer stands out among commentators by accompanying us through the experience of reading Mark with its twists, turns, and subtle hints. Always mindful of Mark as a narrative about Jesus as the embodiment of God's action in the world, Spencer reminds us that Jesus's story is not just about ideas but also about believing, living, and growing in community.

—*Greg Carey*
Professor of New Testament
Lancaster Theological Seminary

Spencer, widely known and respected for his scholarship on Luke, brings his expertise in the Synoptic tradition to this excellent guide to understanding the Gospel of Mark. Truth be told, academic commentaries aren't known for being page-turners, but Spencer defies these expectations with his engaging and witty writing style. When I teach or preach on Mark, this will be one of the first resources I consult.

—*Nijay K. Gupta*
Professor of New Testament
Northern Seminary

Spencer delivers an accessible and thoroughgoing literary and theological reading of Mark. His skillful analysis of the narrative elements and attention to characters' emotions showcase how Mark's story connects with its readers. No one can consult *Reading Mark* and hold this Gospel at arm's length.

— *Elizabeth E. Shively*
St Mary's College
University of St. Andrews, Scotland

In this highly readable commentary, F. Scott Spencer deftly guides readers through the narrative of Mark's Gospel, making clear the beauty and brilliance of this oft underappreciated account of Jesus's life!

—*Matthew Thiessen*
McMaster University

READING MARK

Smyth & Helwys Publishing, Inc.
6316 Peake Road
Macon, Georgia 31210-3960
1-800-747-3016
© 2023 by F. Scott Spencer
All rights reserved.

Library of Congress Cataloging-in-Publication Data

Names: Spencer, F. Scott (Franklin Scott), author.
Title: Reading Mark : a literary and theological commentary / by F. Scott
   Spencer.
Description: First. | Macon, GA : Smyth & Helwys, 2022. | Series: Reading
   the New Testament, second series | Includes bibliographical references.
Identifiers: LCCN 2022029196 | ISBN 9781641733960 (paperback)
Subjects: LCSH: Bible. Mark--Commentaries.
Classification: LCC BS2585.53 .S66 2022 | DDC 226.3/07--dc23/eng/20220808
LC record available at https://lccn.loc.gov/2022029196

Disclaimer of Liability: With respect to statements of opinion or fact available in this work of nonfiction, Smyth & Helwys Publishing Inc. nor any of its employees, makes any warranty, express or implied, or assumes any legal liability or responsibility for the accuracy or completeness of any information disclosed, or represents that its use would not infringe privately-owned rights.

Reading Mark

A Literary and Theological Commentary

F. Scott Spencer

Reading the New Testament
2nd Series

Also by F. Scott Spencer

The Portrait of Philip in Acts: A Study of Roles and Relations

Journeying through Acts: A Literary and Cultural Reading

What Did Jesus Do? Gospel Profiles of Jesus's Personal Conduct

Dancing Girls, "Loose" Ladies, and Women of "the Cloth": Women in Jesus's Life

The Gospel of Luke and Acts of the Apostles (Interpreting Biblical Texts)

Salty Wives, Spirited Mothers, and Savvy Widows: Capable Women of Purpose and Persistence in the Gospel of Luke

Song of Songs (Wisdom Commentary)

Luke (Two Horizons New Testament Commentary)

Passions of the Christ: The Emotional Life of Jesus

To our first grandchild,

Madeline ("Maddie") Marie Webber,

born March 10, 2022,

marking a new generation brimming with love, joy, and hope

Contents

Editor's Foreword xv
Author's Preface xvii

Introduction 1
    The Author's Mark 2
    Marking Times and Places 3
    Mark and Method 5
    Marking the Way of the Lord 7

On Your Mark, Get Set, Go (Mark 1:1-20) 11
    Starting Line Banner (1:1) 11
    Scriptural Forerunners and the Pacesetting Baptist (1:2-8) 13
    Running into Battle (1:9-13) 17
    Outrunning the Baptist (1:14-15) 24
    Running with Jesus and Fishing for People (1:16-20) 26

Remarkable Works of Freeing and Forgiving (Mark 1:21–3:35) 29
    Making Clean (1:21-45) 30
        Demon-possessed man (1:21-28) 31
        Fever-stricken woman (1:29-31) 32
        Skin-diseased man (1:40-45) 33
    Getting Away (1:32-39) 36
    Forgiving Sin (2:1-17) 37
        Healing a paralyzed man (2:1-12) 39
        Calling a tax collector (2:13-17) 41
    Bending Law (2:18–3:6) 42
        Fasting (2:18-20) 43
        Sewing and storing (2:21-22) 45
        Harvesting (2:23-27) 46

  Healing (3:1-6) 48
Getting Away (Again) (3:7-19a) 50
Cleaning House (3:19b-35) 52
  Family conflict (introduced) (3:19b-21) 53
  Scribal controversy (3:22-30) 53
  Family conflict (concluded) (3:31-35) 55

Mark My Words: Jesus's Parables (Mark 4:1-34) 57
Many Things in Many Parables: For Whom and Why?
 (4:1-2, 10-13, 33-34) 57
Bear Fruit: The Parable of the Soils (4:3-9, 14-20) 58
Pay Attention: The Parable of the Lamp (4:21-25) 62
Sleep Tight: The Parable of the Growing Seed (4:26-29) 64
Think Big: The Parable of the Mustard Seed (4:30-32) 66

Remarkable Works of Freeing and Feeding I (Mark 4:35–6:56) 69
Freedom from Fear: Stilling the Storm (4:35-41) 70
  Sound sleeper 71
  Stoic teacher 72
  Storm stiller 73
Freedom from Enslavement: Liberating the "Legion"-Possessed
 Man (5:1-20) 74
  Domination 76
  Negotiation 78
    Plea #1 78
    Plea #2 80
    Plea #3 81
Freedom from Death: Restoring Critically Ill "Daughters"
 (5:21-43) 82
  Life and death 84
  Fear and faith 87
  Isolation and integration 90
Interlude: Frustration (6:1-6a) 91
  Nazareth "takes offense" at Jesus (6:1-4) 91
  Jesus is taken aback by Nazareth's "unbelief" (6:5-6a) 93
Freedom from Limited Resources: Feeding the Multitude
 (6:6b-44) 95
  Funding 96
  Feeding 98
  Feeling 99

Freedom from Fear: Walking on Water (6:45-52) 103
   On the land (6:45-48a) 103
   On the lake (6:48b-52) 104
Freedom from Sickness: Healing "Wherever He Went" (6:53-56) 108

Mark My Words: Jesus's Polemics (Mark 7:1-23) 109
   Washing Hands (7:1-8) 109
   Honoring Parents (7:9-13) 112
   Cleaning Inside-Out (7:14-23) 115

Remarkable Works of Freeing and Feeding II (Mark 7:24–8:20) 119
   Freeing a Demon-Possessed Daughter (7:24-30) 120
      Maternal status 121
      Gender 121
      Ethnicity 122
      Socioeconomic status 122
      Species status 124
   Opening the Ears of a Deaf Man (7:31-37) 127
      Fingers probing in the ears 128
      Spitting on and touching the tongue 128
      Looking up and sighing out 129
      Be Opened 133
   Feeding the Crowds (Again) (8:1-10) 134
   Challenging the Pharisees and Disciples (Again) (8:11-20) 137
      Sign and sigh language (8:11-13) 138
      Yeast infection (8:14-21) 139

Missing the Mark through Blindness (Mark 8:22–10:52) 141
   Healing an Anonymous Blind Man (8:22-26) 143
   Predicting Jesus's Death and Resurrection #1 (8:27–9:1) 146
   Interacting with Moses, Elijah, and a Distressed Father (9:2-29) 152
      On the mountain: transfiguration (9:2-8) 153
      Down the mountain: explanation (9:9-13) 156
      Below the mountain: confrontation (9:14-29) 157
         Desperate Father 158
         Jesus 159
         Disconcerted Disciples 161
   Predicting Jesus's Death and Resurrection #2 (9:30-50) 162
      The way of the cross: not promoting grandiose ambitions
      (9:30-37) 162

The way of the cross: not opposing maverick ministers
(9:38-41) 164
The way of the cross: not obstructing little ones (9:42-48) 165
The way of the cross: not losing its salty worth (9:49-50) 166
Interacting with Pharisees, Little Children, and a Rich Man
(10:1-31)..167
Husbands and wives (10:1-12) 168
Little children (again) (10:13-16) 171
Rich and poor (10:17-31) 173
Predicting Jesus's Death and Resurrection #3 (10:32-45) 178
Healing a Blind Man Named Bartimaeus (10:46-52) 183
Shouting out to Jesus (10:46-49) 185
Throwing off his cloak (10:50a) 185
Springing up to Jesus (10:50b) 186
Asking for renewed sight (10:51-52) 186

Question Marks about Jesus's Wisdom and Authority
(Mark 11:1–12:44)..187
Jerusalem Demonstrations (11:1-25) 188
Jesus enters the city as Davidic king (11:1-11)..........................189
Jesus enters the temple as priest-like prophet (11:12-25) 194
The barren fig tree (11:12-14)..195
The dysfunctional house of God (11:15-19) 197
The withered fig tree (11:20-25) 200
Temple Debates (11:27–12:44)..206
Jesus, John the Baptist, and authority (11:27-33) 206
Parable interlude: violent tenants and the beloved son
(12:1-12) 208
Tenant managers..209
Stone builders..210
Beloved son 210
The "others"...211
Jesus, Caesar, and taxes (12:13-17)...211
Jesus, Moses, and resurrection (12:18-27) 215
Jesus, God, and the commandments to love (12:28-34) 217
Jesus, David, and the Messiah (12:35-37)..................................219
Warning epilogue: exploitative scribes and exemplary widow
(12:38-44) 220

Contents

Mark My Words: Jesus's Prophecy (Mark 13:1-37) 223
    Stay Alert to Destructive Times (13:1-4) 225
    Stay Alert to Deceptive Times (13:5-8) 226
    Stay Alert to Defensive Times (13:9-13) 228
    Stay Alert to Desolate Times (13:14-23) 229
    Stay Alert to Deliverance Times (13:24-27) 232
        Cosmic shake-up (13:24-25) 232
        Coming Son of Humankind (13:26-27) 233
    Stay Alert to Delayed Times (13:28-37) 233
        The fig tree (13:28-31) 234
        The estate "lord" (13:32-37) 235

Making His Final Mark: Jesus's Death and Resurrection
(Mark 14:1–16:20) 237
    Betrayal and Arrest (14:1-52) 237
        Perfuming at the house of Simon the leper in Bethany and being
            betrayed (14:1-11) 239
            Characters 240
            Objectives...241
            Means...242
            E/motives 244
        Preparing and consuming the Passover meal in an upstairs
            room in Jerusalem (14:12-25)...247
            Arranging the event (14:12-16) 248
            Exposing the traitor (14:17-21) 249
            Renewing the covenant (14:22-25) 251
        Praying and being abandoned at Gethsemane on the
            Mount of Olives (14:26-52) 253
            Peter's predicted denial (14:26-31)...254
            Jesus's agonized demurral (14:32-36) 255
            Peter, James, and John's lapsed vigilance (14:37-42) 258
            Judas's enacted betrayal (14:43-49) 260
            The disciples' "naked" desertion (14:50-52) 261
    Jewish and Roman Trials (14:53–15:15) 263
        Sham trial by the high priest and Jewish council (14:53-65)......263
        Shameful denial by the apostle Peter (14:66-72) 266
        Shrewd trial by the Roman governor Pilate (15:1-15).................268
            Pilate questions Jesus (15:1-5) 269
            Pilate questions the crowd (15:6-15).....................................271
    Torture and Crucifixion (15:16-41) 273

- Beaten in Pilate's courtyard (15:16-20) 275
  - Places and actors (15:16) 275
  - Props and gestures (15:17-20) 275
- Crucified on Skull Hill (15:21-41) 276
  - Cross (15:21, 30, 32) 277
  - Cup (15:23) 278
  - Clothes (15:24) 278
  - Inscription (15:26) 279
  - Criminals (15:27-28, 32) 280
  - Taunts (15:29-32) 281
  - Eloi/Elijah (15:33-37) 282
  - Curtain (15:38) 285
  - Centurion (15:39) 286
  - Women (15:40-41) 288
- Burial and Resurrection (15:42–16:8a) 290
  - Joseph of Arimathea lays Jesus's body in a tomb (15:42-47) 291
  - Mary Magdalene, Mary the mother of James, and Salome come to Jesus's empty tomb (16:1-8a) 294
    - Entering the tomb to serve (16:1-5a) 294
    - Encountering a "young man" in the tomb (16:5b-7) 295
    - Fleeing the tomb in fear (16:8a) 296
- Appearances and Commissions (16:8b-20) 304

Works Cited 307

Editor's Foreword

Like its predecessor (Reading the New Testament) and its companion series (Reading the Old Testament), Reading the New Testament: Second Series seeks to help readers—whether students or scholars, ministers or laypeople—gain a greater understanding of and appreciation for biblical texts in their original contexts. To this good end, commentaries in this series attend not only to lexical, historical, and critical concerns but are also attuned to and interested in, as the subtitle of each volume signals, literary matters and theological meaning.

Whereas some commentaries are committed to the necessary and salutary task of commenting on every jot and tittle (see Matthew 5:18), works in this series seek to trace the thought and observe the craft of biblical authors in a less atomistic manner. While attending to various trees, they are also intent on not missing the forest. Relatedly, while technically undergirded and academically informed, the commentaries within this series are intended for and are meant to be accessible and valuable to a broad readership. The seventeen volumes that will make up Reading the New Testament: Second Series, then, are written by scholars but are not exclusively, or even primarily, for scholars.

Contributors to this commentary series are accomplished academics, experienced teachers, capable communicators, and professing Christians who are committed to explicating Scripture thoughtfully, clearly, and sympathetically. To the extent that this series results in people reading the twenty-seven New Testament documents with greater skill, care, insight, devotion, and joy, the contributors and editor of Reading the New Testament: Second Series will be grateful and gratified.

Todd D. Still
Baylor University
George W. Truett Theological Seminary
Waco, Texas

Author's Preface

Although the often neglected, and sometimes denigrated, runt of the four Gospels, Mark has long attracted my interest for its fast-paced energy and raw-edged emotion. I once titled a lecture on Mark, "Jesus in the Raw," which is a tad overdramatic but aims to highlight Mark's simpler (not simplistic), sharper, bolder portrait of Jesus, which Matthew and Luke fan out and tone down to some degree. "Second Gospel" by no means means second rate! Though shortest among the four Gospel narratives, it stands strong and tall on its own merits.

I'm grateful that the New Testament canon provides four rich Gospel accounts (Matthew/Mark/Luke [Synoptics] + John) of the life, ministry, death, and resurrection of Jesus the Christ. The Johannine author aptly concludes his Gospel, "But there are also many other things that Jesus did; if every one of them were written down, I suppose that the world itself could not contain the books that could be written" (John 21:25). No single book can possibly contain the fullness of Christ. No four-volume set can either, but I'm glad we have multiple renderings of Jesus's profound story, including Mark's unique, as well as overlapping, version.

Whereas we have a limited group of canonical Gospels, we have a seemingly endless array of commentaries on each one, with new commentaries written and commissioned every year. So why another commentary on Mark? Why this one? Although many fine commentary series fill the market, I have especially valued Smyth & Helwys's Reading the New Testament volumes ever since I reviewed David Garland's superb work on Matthew (1993) in the first series. Offering "A Literary and Theological Commentary" concentrates on two of the most critical dimensions of biblical interpretation, supported but not overwhelmed by technical grammatical, historical, cultural, and ideological matters. The series strikes a balanced interplay between academic and ministerial interests, which appropriately belong together in interpreting New Testament Scripture for Christian faith and practice. In the same vein, the Reading series stresses readability and relatability to laypersons and ministers as well as professional scholars who have neither the time nor inclination to wade through dense, multivolume, thousand-plus-page tomes on each Gospel. At least some, if not most, biblical commentaries should open doors of understanding for a wide range of God's people, not serve as door stoppers!

The contributions to the second Reading series do not replace or in any way reject the commentaries of the first series, like Garland's volume on Matthew and Sharyn Dowd's on Mark (2000), which may still be consulted with great profit. The newer commentaries are not new editions or revisions of the older ones. Rather, they undertake fresh literary and theological treks through the same scriptural texts in light of developing scholarship and interpretive issues over the past three decades. So, for better or worse, this is my "Reading" of Mark—with a lot of help from preceding readers and writers! The best biblical interpretation is a communal effort of ongoing civil-yet-critical dialogue guided—and goaded—by the dynamic Spirit of God.

In this commentary, while I stay close in touch with the Greek text, I use the NRSV as my baseline English text, unless otherwise specified. Other versions are signaled by their common abbreviations, e.g., KJV, NIV, CEB, NETS. *Reading Mark*

Apart from the numerous writers listed in the Works Cited to whom I'm heavily indebted, I would like more personally to thank Todd Still, dean extraordinaire at Truett Seminary, for recruiting me to write on Mark for this second Reading series and supporting me every step of the way. I'm grateful, too, for the fine staff at Smyth & Helwys who have shepherded this work to publication—in particular, Keith Gammons, Leslie Andres, and Holly Bean. This has been my first publishing venture with Smyth & Helwys. I hope it's not the last.

I have dedicated most of my previous books to immediate family members, individually or together: my beloved wife, Janet, to whom I owe all the really good thoughts I've ever had; our amazing two daughters, Lauren and Meredith, now all grown up with families of their own, including wonderful husbands, Mark Vandevelde and Jimmy Webber, who have become our sons-in-heart, not just in-law.

This year has blessed us with our newest family member, Madeline ("Maddie") Marie Webber, who has completely stolen her parents' and grandparents' hearts. She begins a whole new "third series" for me and gets the dedication all to herself! Though she's already precocious, of course (five months old at the time of this writing), she's not quite ready to read

Grampus's "Reading" commentary. But when she gets around to it, I hope it helps stimulate a lifelong passion for reading and brings a smile to her face as a small reflection of the abundant joy she gives us.

Introduction

Until the modern Enlightenment era, the Gospel of Mark did not leave much of a mark on Christian preaching, teaching, and scholarship. Its canonical placement in the second slot among the four Gospels tended to mark it as "second rate." It played second fiddle to Matthew's virtuoso, first-chair performance, framed by a memorable Christmas story (Matthew 1–2) and Great Commission (28:16-20) and featuring five soaring sermons and teaching sessions of Jesus, headed by the incomparable Sermon on the Mount (chapters 5–7). In pathetic comparison, Mark lacks most of this material—no birth story, no Beatitudes! It seems to offer an abridged "Reader's Digest" version of Matthew for readers who can't handle Matthew's sophisticated and substantial fare.

Mark hasn't fared much better in comparison with the third and fourth Gospels, both also longer than Mark and chock full of additional material: Luke has its own captivating Christmas story and several classic parables of Jesus, including the good Samaritan (Luke 10:30-35) and prodigal son (15:11-32); John has its magnificent opening hymn exalting Jesus as creative-incarnate Word of God (John 1:1-18) and collection of Jesus's dynamic signs and "I am" statements, to say nothing about John 3:16! Mark blends in well enough in the Gospel quartet but doesn't add much distinctive value to the group.

Or so it seemed until scholars began to pay more careful attention to Mark both in comparison with the other Gospels and on its own terms. Careful comparative-historical studies turned the tide in favor of Mark's *priority* as the "first biography of Jesus" (Bond 2020); its secondary canonical status has masked its chronological primacy. Instead of viewing Mark as an abbreviation of Matthew, most scholars to the present day (with a few dissenters) regard this shortest Gospel as the foundational template edited and expanded in Matthew and Luke (with John representing a more independent "maverick" account; Kysar 2007).

Moreover, closer narrative-theological analyses of Mark's text have come to appreciate its own literary artistry and thematic emphases, its legitimate claim to be valued as a coherent, complex, compelling, and challenging story in its own right (Rhoads, Dewey, and Michie, 1999; Iverson and Skinner, eds., 2011). Far from being a "CliffsNotes" version of Matthew, Mark constitutes a well-crafted, astute theological narrative of "the good news/gospel of God" and God's just and gracious rule breaking out anew on earth through God's Messiah (Christ) and Son, Jesus of Nazareth (Mark 1:1, 9, 14-15). If we have "eyes to see and ears to hear" (4:9; 8:18) Mark's incisive message of Christ in its own images and idioms, if we mark this Gospel's words carefully and considerately, we discover a remarkable story worth engaging afresh.

The Author's Mark

Another reason for Mark's overshadowing by the other three Gospels has been the diminished status of its supposed author named "Mark," otherwise known as John Mark but sharply distinguished from the venerable apostle John, the son of Zebedee and presumed author of the fourth Gospel. Mark was no apostle at all, whether one of Jesus's twelve apostles, like Matthew and John, or the great apostle to the Gentiles, Paul. Neither was Luke, but he was esteemed as a close companion of Paul and writer of the book of Acts (as well as the third Gospel), which showcases the apostolic words and acts of Peter, John, and Paul.

The fourth-century church historian Eusebius reports the testimony of Papias, the early second-century bishop of Hierapolis, that John Mark wrote his Gospel as "Peter's interpreter"; though not among Jesus's first disciples, Mark was a "follower of Peter" (Eusebius, *Hist. eccl.* 2.15; 3.39). But while the letter-writer of 1 Peter signs off with a final greeting that includes "my son Mark" (1 Pet 5:14) and Paul sends greetings from "Mark the cousin of Barnabas" to the Colossian congregation, along with "instructions—if he comes to you, welcome him" (Col 4:10), Mark's main claim to fame in the New Testament is more infamous than adulatory. Acts reports that "John, called Mark" deserted the first missionary campaign of Paul and Barnabas in its early stages; when Barnabas later wanted to take Mark along on the second mission, Paul flatly refused and split up with Barnabas as a result (Acts 13:13; 15:36-39). Although much is unknown about John Mark, he had a checkered history in early Christian tradition (see Black 1994).

But Mark's personal history and status matters little for interpreting the message of the second Gospel, not least because we can't be certain that he wrote this story of Jesus. Like *all* the Gospels, the one eventually attributed to Mark was *anonymous*. Unlike letters where Paul, for example, identifies himself as the author *within* the document, the Gospel writers do not reveal themselves. Traditional headings "according to (*kata*) Matthew, Mark," and so on were added to later editions. Papias may well be right about Mark's authorship, but his viewpoint was still colored by apologetic aims to promote *Peter's* authority.

In any case, we must be wary of (over)reading an anonymous text like Mark with a speculative profile of the author in mind determining what we expect to find. A classic case of this fallacy assumes that Dr. Luke wrote the books we call Luke and Acts from an avowedly *medical perspective*, thus launching a concerted hunt in these documents for medical clues—a fool's errand, as Henry Cadbury (1920, 39–72) convincingly demonstrated, but more critically a regrettable distraction from the main source of meaning: the *text itself*. A quirkier version of this same fallacy conjectures a cameo appearance by the (supposed) author John Mark as the young man who flees naked from the scene of Jesus's arrest in Gethsemane, leaving behind his single piece of clothing in the grasp of one of the arresting policemen (Mark 14:51-52). While this is one of the few unique (unparalleled) snippets in Mark and while it fits the profile of John Mark as a deserter (in Acts), it scarcely reveals the identity of the Gospel writer or demands that we read the whole narrative from the perspective of an abashed deserter. The streaking young man is never named, and it's hard to see why the author would choose to cast himself in such an unflattering light. Moreover, the theme of Jesus's desertion by "all" his disciples (14:27, 50) is plain enough within the story without support from extra-textual evidence about John Mark's abandoning *Paul* (not Jesus). Within Mark's narrative, the "young man" seems to function as a symbolic rather than historical figure—representing the full company of Jesus's followers both in their tendency to desert (deny, betray) him in times of crisis and in their opportunity to be restored to fellowship with him, to be reclothed, to obtain a renewed lease on life (see commentary below on 16:7 concerning the white-robed "young man" inside Jesus's empty tomb).

Marking Times and Places

Published books today come with a copyright page at the front with Library of Congress cataloging information identifying not only the author but also the date and place of publication and ISBN number. The earliest available Greek manuscripts of New Testament books have no such page, leaving us to infer a book's provenance from internal clues. Again, however, a Gospel like Mark proves more challenging than a letter from Paul. First Thessalonians, for example, which may have been the first New Testament writing, reveals in the first verse its authorship by Paul (together with "Silvanus, and Timothy") and its audience of "the church of the Thessalonians," that is, the congregation of believers in Christ at Thessalonica in northern Greece. Collating other bits of information within the correspondence with material from Acts (17:1-8; 18:1-18), scholars reasonably estimate that Paul wrote this letter *from* Corinth (in southern Greece) *to* Thessalonica around 49–52 CE (Powell 2018, 387–93). Unfortunately, hints concerning when, where, and to whom Mark's Gospel was composed are more allusive—and elusive.

Complicating the issue is the Gospel narrative's deft interweaving of past and present levels or horizons into one continuous story. All biographical narratives (as opposed to mere chronicles or records) combine two levels: history + interpretation. The interpretive level is inevitably biased: honest historians see and write from their own perspectives and viewpoints (how else could they do it?) but not with intent to distort or deceive. The goal is to elucidate the *significance* of past people and events for present life. In Mark's case, Level 1 focuses on select words and deeds of Jesus of Nazareth set within a constructed course of his career up to his death in the early 30s CE. Level 2 reflects particular concerns and challenges in the time of the Gospel author and audience: what does the story of Jesus *mean* for them now and going forward? Mark's text has no "Level 1/2" markings, and traces of seams are minimal and disputed among scholars. Again, a sophisticated narrative like Mark *interlaces* past and present elements with minimal stitch marks. To use another metaphor, the story *flows* with few jarring breakpoints.

But some signs of Mark's situation may still be detected, not least the "signs" of the coming times within a "generation" (forty years or so) predicted by Jesus within the story (Mark 13:4, 29). Specifically, in the last days before his death, he prepares his followers for an intense period of anticipated suffering and conflict, especially in Judea and Jerusalem culminating in the destruction of the temple (13:1-23). It is historically plausible that Jesus, as a prescient observer of the times (to say nothing of Mark's view of Jesus as Spirit-imbued Son of God [1:1, 9-11]), would warn about coming troubles for his people. But the detailed forecast featuring vivid images of future events suggests particular relevance for Mark's *current times*. This linkage becomes even more compelling in light of its remarkable fit with what we know about terrible upheavals in Roman Judea and Galilee around 40–75 CE reported by the first-century Jewish historian Josephus, cresting in the Roman-Jewish War of 66–70 that left Jerusalem and the temple in ruins. These historical correlations, along with Mark's thematic emphasis on the *suffering* or *Passion* (from *paschō*, "suffer") of Jesus and his followers, have led many scholars to posit a date of composition in the late 60s–early 70s. While "Mark" writes as a fervent "evangelist" of the "good news (*euangelion*) of God" in Christ

(1:14-15), he also writes as a concerned pastor for his struggling people during times of crisis.

As for the place of composition and Mark's primary audience, most church leaders and scholars have opted for Rome, following early tradition going back to the late second-century bishop Clement of Alexandria (cited in Eusebius, *Church History* 6.14). The imperial capital makes good sense as the "heart of a dynamic literary culture" and locus of Nero's persecution of Christians in the mid-60s (including, according to tradition, the executions of Peter and Paul) and Titus's triumphal entry after the conquest of Jerusalem (Bond 2019, 9). More recently, however, some scholars have argued for a provenance more proximate to the theater of the Roman-Jewish War, such as Galilee, the trans-Jordanian Decapolis, or Syria—designated areas of conflict and ministry for Mark's Jesus (chapters 1–10; 5:1-20; 7:24-37; cf. 3:7-8; Wardle 2016; Marcus 1992a). In any case, with its translations of various Aramaic words into Greek (5:41; 7:11, 34; 15:34) and narrative asides for non-Jewish readers (7:3, 19), Mark's narrative assumes a Gentile audience, though not exclusively. The mixed congregation of Jewish and Gentile believers in Christ in the capital of Roman Syria, Antioch-on-the-Orontes (see Acts 11:19-30), would offer a plausible original home for this Gospel.

Pinpointing the date and time of Mark's writing, while informative, is not primarily determinative for meaning—or at least not as determinative as the text, which sets its own narrative coordinates within the social and cultural environment of its era. Though a product of its historical time and place, the Gospel also stamped its internal temporal and spatial signatures on its period and area—and beyond—through centuries and across continents! Our world continues to be shaped by Mark's narrative world of crucial times (e.g., "immediately," Sabbath, Passover) and places (e.g., sea, desert, Golgotha). Mark's remarkable story of Christ "plays in ten thousand places" and myriad moments (Hopkins 2018 [1877], 45; Peterson 2005).

Mark and Method

Academic biblical studies today are marked by an abundance of methodological approaches. While some lament this methodological madness, I think there is valuable method in the madness, provided we engage older and newer, traditional and innovative approaches with critical good sense and not simply swallow them whole. The Bible is a rich, complex collection of writings demanding a well-stocked interpretive toolbox, skillfully applied with humble openness to correction and adjustment.

The present volume is part of the "Reading the New Testament" series, which focuses on providing "Literary and Theological Commentary." On the "literary" side, I pay primary attention to the structure, style, and flow of the text itself. Appropriate to Mark's biographical-narrative genre, this commentary carefully tracks the developing characters, unfolding plot, and key themes and motifs of the story across its various time-space settings. This approach particularly aligns with two modern methods of biblical study: *narrative criticism* (Rhoades, Dewey, and Michie 1999; Malbon 2008) and *reader-response criticism* (Fowler 1991; 2008).

On the "theological" side, I aim to keep front and center "evangelical" themes and issues in the foundational sense of the "evangel" (*euangelion*) as "gospel" or "good news"—not as a (divisive) political or ecclesiastical brand, still less as (insipid) "feel-good" advice, but as inspired, in-Spirited word about the liberating work of God in the world through Jesus Christ. The Gospel of Mark is first and foremost a religious story, a story about God, the very "gospel/good news of God" in Christ (1:14).

To be sure, Mark does not present systematic or dogmatic theology in propositional form. But it is theology all the same—narrative, storied, dynamic theology pulsing in the embodied, lived-out experiences of Jesus and his followers in first-century Roman Judea and Samaria. It is thus inherently "practical theology" designed to nurture and challenge the faith and practice of God's people. One important scholarly trend in recent years has seen a renewed call for "theological biblical interpretation" from various angles (Green 2011a; Treier 2008). I see the present commentary as answering this call in some measure. Accordingly, readers might expect my primary narrative-textual analysis to shade now and again into pastoral and homiletic application. Though I'm no full-time pastor or preaching evangelist (or the son of either), I have done a fair bit of interim church work and supply preaching (enough to be dangerous) and (seriously) value those who commit themselves to vocational ministry.

I also welcome insights from other methods that both enhance and challenge my principal literary-theological approach. In *Mark and Method* (2008), Janice Capel Anderson and Stephen Moore edit and contribute to a superb collection of newer "criticisms" and "studies" of Mark, variously labeled narrative, reader-response, deconstructive, feminist, social, cultural, and postcolonial. To different degrees, I use all these methods in my commentary "critically"—that is, advisedly, discriminately, in the best sense of interpretive *criticism*, with the overriding goal of elucidating Mark's text and illuminating its compelling, provocative story of Jesus. Other methods missing from Anderson and Moore's volume that I also find useful include intertextual engagement with second temple Jewish writings (Blackwell, Goodrich, and Maston, eds., 2018), disability studies (Avalos, Melcher, and

Schipper, eds., 2007; Lawrence 2013), and emotion analysis (Spencer 2017a; 2017b; 2019, 706–32; 2021).

Finally, in terms of intertextual resources, I regard one body of ancient literature not simply as helpful and informative but as necessary and imperative for understanding Mark: the Jewish scriptures in Hebrew and Greek (Septuagint/LXX), which Christians came to call the Old Testament and which "Mark" would simply have regarded as Scripture. As useful and enlightening as second temple, "intertestamental" Jewish literature is for interpreting Mark, along with a range of Greco-Roman materials, these remain secondary to this Gospel's absorption in first testament language and thought, evident in citations (starting in the second verse: "As it written in the prophet Isaiah") and allusions throughout the narrative. Note to reader of Mark's Gospel and this commentary: have your *whole Bible* ready to hand to get the full picture.

Marking the Way of the Lord

Orientations for travel tours lay out the itinerary and provide thumbnail sketches of the main sites to be visited. But there is no substitute for undertaking the journey itself and letting the sights and sounds of people and places strike you as they will and build up along the way. Indeed, starting the trip with too much information can predetermine the experience and dampen the joy of discovery, like an exuberant movie preview/review that gives away the plot and best lines.

Travelling or journeying is an apt metaphor for reading, working one's way through a book, essay, or poem with all senses on high alert. The metaphor works especially well for Mark's narrative, which tracks the "way of the Lord" (1:3) Jesus Messiah treads (and occasionally sails) through Galilee (and bordering regions) and Judea, culminating in Jerusalem. "Way" (*hodos*, also meaning "road," "journey") represents a key image in this Gospel, marking not only travel routes but a *way of life*, the way of God and God's realm trailblazed in the dynamic words and ways of Jesus.

Therefore, I recommend using this commentary as a reading guide *along the way* of a fresh open-eyed, open-eared, and open-minded reading of Mark's story. I don't want to give the game away before it starts, but to spark the reader's interest and spur the reading process, I drop a few "teasers" about some distinctive marks of this commentary:

• ***Formation.*** In the course of tracking the development of characters across Mark's narrative, I pay attention not only to the variable responses of followers, seekers, and opponents of Jesus but also to the formative experiences of *Jesus himself*, as he comes to a fuller understanding of his messianic vocation—including some surprises (5:30-31), limitations (6:1-6), frustrations (9:14-29), and changes (7:24-30) along the way. Jesus is a fully fleshed dynamic (not static) character across the story.

- **Feeling.** Interpreters routinely note without much elaboration that Mark's Gospel has a number of emotional raw edges that Matthew and Luke tend to sand off. I aim to dive in and "feel" my way more intensely through Mark's emotive story, treating emotional elements like anger, anguish, fear, frustration, disgust, and despair as significant facets of characterization, as expressions of what *concerns* and *matters to* the characters within the narrative and to the overall narrative purpose (Spencer 2017a). Mark's "special *affects*" are integral elements of the story, not superficial adornments. And again, the main character *Jesus* thoroughly engages in these affective dynamics rather than floating above them on some artificial hyper-rational, super-spiritual, non-emotional plane. I pay more attention than most commentators to the "emotional life" of Mark's Jesus—a full-fledged, -fleshed, -feeling human being—the incarnate Son of God (Spencer 2021).

- **Freedom.** At least since Ched Myers's pioneering, trenchant commentary, *Binding the Strong Man: A Political Reading of Mark's Story of Jesus* (1988), Mark's ardent commitment to a *liberating* theology with social and political implications in the world has been emphasized. While this interpretive angle owes much to "*liberation* theology" rooted in late-twentieth-century Latin American Catholic communities, Mark's narrative should not be forced into this or any other modern theological category. The first-century author of Mark was not (could not be) a card-carrying liberation theologian any more than an Arminian or a Calvinist theologian, or a Baptist or a Methodist churchman.

But as I worked through this challenging narrative, I found myself impressed anew with the frequency and force of Mark's Gospel message of liberation, emancipation, freedom—or to use a related, more classic religious term: redemption. While most dramatically evident in Jesus's "remarkable works" showcased in Mark 1:21–3:35, 4:35–6:56, and 7:24–8:21, this redemptive/liberative theme pulses in various rhythms throughout the story in contexts of strife and struggle, conflict and combat, with evil, oppressive forces seen and unseen, earthly and heavenly (cf. Eph 6:12). At every turn, Mark's Jesus fights for freedom as the authorized "apocalyptic" agent of God, seeking *not*, however, the *end* of the world or *escape* from the world but rather the *restoration* of the world, the *re-creation* of the universe, setting the cosmos to rights according to God's good purpose. And the liberating "victory" that Jesus wins—by *way of the cross!*—is *not* a triumphal-nationalistic takeover but rather a remedial-holistic makeover on multiple levels: freedom from sin, sickness, enslavement, estrangement, dread, death—anything antithetical to the full, flourishing life God desires for all creation.

I composed this short introduction after completing the commentary that was mostly written during the distressing and disorienting months of a global pandemic—a crisis still at hand, alas—as we work our way through the Greek alphabet of nasty COVID-19 variants. While confined in large measure to my house and home study, I have found no small measure of gracious freedom in pondering Mark's remarkable redemptive Gospel, not for the first time by any means, but in a bracingly fresh, freeing, rejuvenating way this time around.

I hope that all who read Mark and this modest commentary will find a similar formative, emotive, and liberative experience to sustain you and yours through the living of these challenging days as seekers and followers of Jesus the Christ.

On Your Mark, Get Set, Go

Mark 1:1-20

Starting Line Banner (1:1)

As reader-runners aiming to keep up with Jesus's spirited pace along a challenging course in Mark's Gospel, we toe the starting line with hearts racing and minds poised to track every step of the pulsing action. But first we take in the banner advertising the race in a pithy headline: BEGINNING OF THE GOOD NEWS OF JESUS CHRIST, SON OF GOD. That's encouraging. However fast and hard the race ahead will be, we take heart in knowing that it is a worthwhile pursuit full of "good news" (*euangelion*)—an exhilarating "evangelical," "gospelized" race (Bird 2013, 30–31). We can expect "good" things along the way. But such blessing is not wrapped up in personal gain as popularly conceived (prosperity, profits, possessions); we can gain the whole world and lose our best lives (8:36-37). The benefits of this race have little to do with padding a portfolio and everything to do with following a person who travels light and free yet proves to be worth leaving everything for (1:18-20; 2:14; 6:8-11; 8:34; 10:21-31).

This person has a common Jewish name: Jesus or Yeshua/Joshua ("The LORD saves") in Hebrew. But he is no ordinary Josh or even the extraordinary Joshua of biblical history. He embarks on a world-saving mission as the consummate Christ or Messiah of God. "Christ" is not Jesus's surname but rather a Greek title (*Christos*) equating with the Hebrew "Messiah" (*Mashiach*), meaning "anointed one," that is, one anointed by God's Spirit to mediate God's rule and advance God's way. Judges, prophets, and kings could receive this "anointed" commission, even including foreign rulers like the Persian Cyrus (Isa 45:1-7).

But Jesus's messianic vocation climactically fulfills that of his anointed forerunners, that is, it fills and fleshes them out fully. To borrow from another New Testament writer, Jesus runs the messianic race as "the pioneer and perfecter of our faith" (Heb 12:2), the fresh trailblazer and faithful finisher of God's creative and restorative work. What qualifies him for such a herculean mission? The Markan banner concludes with announcing Jesus Christ as "Son of God," according to many solid early manuscripts, though not all. Following a scribal pattern of expanding book titles, it's possible that a copy editor added "Son of God" here (Omanson 2006, 56); yet regardless of the original heading, Jesus's status as God's Son is soon certified by God's voice at Jesus's baptism (1:11; cf. 5:7; 9:7; 12:6-8).

As God anointed other figures for "messianic" service, so God adopted other children into the divine family. Indeed, the people of Israel may be imaged as God's "firstborn son" (Exod 4:22-23; cf. *Joseph and Aseneth*, which repeatedly designates Jacob/Israel's favored son, Joseph, as God's firstborn; Collins 2015, 105), even as "all who are led by the Spirit of God are children of God . . . and if children, then heirs, heirs of God and joint heirs with Christ" (Rom 8:14-17). And if that family circle is not big enough, we may also include the angels among the "sons of God" (Gen 6:2, 4; Deut 32:8; Job 1:6; 2:1; Pss 29:1; 82:1, 6). But the identities of "anointed one" and "son" of God especially crystallize in the singular figure of God's ruling representative on earth—the Davidic king of Israel (Ps 2:1-7; cf. 2 Sam 7:13-14; Pss Sol 17:4, 21-46; Collins and Collins 2008; Spencer 2015). Mark's banner attests to the conviction that Jesus fits this Messiah/Son of God bill more fully and finally than King David himself, now dead for many generations. But how exactly Jesus plays out (runs out) this royal role in Mark's narrative remains to be seen.

One additional part of the heading merits consideration—the first word, "beginning" (*archē*, with no "the" article in Greek). At first blush, that seems like an awkward way to begin, like a shaky writer who plunges in, "Let me start by saying . . . ." A waste of words. But though commentators often critique Mark's simple writing style, I'm willing to give more benefit of the doubt. As it happens, the other Gospels also start with some "beginning" reference. Matthew opens with "a book of the genesis/genealogy (*geneseōs*) of Jesus Christ" (my translation); Luke introduces his "orderly account of the events . . . handed on to us by those who from the beginning (*archēs*) were eyewitnesses"; and John's first words read, "In the beginning (*archē*) was the Word." Significantly, each of these beginning notes refers back to earlier roots for the present narratives: creation of the world (John); call of Abraham and covenant with Israel (Matthew); testimony of first followers of Jesus (Luke). The Gospel stories of Jesus of Nazareth begin *in medias res*, or "the middle of things," continuing God's story of creation and salvation from the beginning of the world, through the biblical era of Israel, up to the Gospel authors' time of writing a generation after Jesus's death and resurrection—and beyond for successive generations of readers and followers of the living Christ.

Though Mark's "beginning" banner is not as precisely marked as the other Gospels', it builds on the foundation of the preceding biblical story as much as they do. Mark bursts out of the starting blocks with scriptural scroll in hand, relayed like a baton from divinely inspired forerunners.

Scriptural Forerunners and the Pacesetting Baptist (1:2-8)

Mark's Jesus, while the patent protagonist of the Gospel, does not run a solo race (except, tragically, at the end); while path-breaking, he's no solitary hero hacking his way through the wilderness or climbing to the snow-capped peak of Mount Hermon. He proceeds on a busy highway filled with forerunners and followers. Chief among the former group are the biblical prophets. These "seers" were no ivory-tower, starry-eyed prognosticators; their future vision for God's people sprouted organically from past tradition and present reality, prodding and pressing the people to renew their covenant bond with God in faithful love and justice (see Davis 2014).

Four prophets set the course for Mark's Jesus: Moses, Elijah, Isaiah, and Malachi (1:2-3). Yet they pave the way not only for Jesus but also for his more immediate prophetic predecessor, John the Baptist (1:4-8), whom we meet before Jesus appears (1:9).

While Mark only credits Isaiah as the source of the citation in 1:2-3, the matter is more complicated. The quoted passage conflates material from Exodus (authored, according to tradition, by Moses) and Malachi with Isaiah. Such blending of sources was a common practice in ancient writing, and some later manuscripts change "in the prophet Isaiah" to the more generic "in the prophets." I cite the relevant Old Testament texts below from an up-to-date translation of the ancient Greek scriptures (NETS = *New English Translation of the Septuagint*), since Mark wrote in Greek and read his Bible primarily in Greek. I italicize the portions that Mark echoes.

> *And look, I am sending my angel* [angelon] *in front of you* in order to guard you on *the way* [hodō] in order to bring you into the land that *I prepared for you* (Exod 23:20 NETS).

> *Behold I am sending my messenger* [angelon], and he will oversee *the way* [hodon] *before me* (Mal 3:1 NETS).

> *A voice of one crying out in the wilderness: "Prepare the way* [hodon] *of the Lord; make straight the paths* [tribous] *of our God"* (Isa 40:3 NETS).

These texts highlight the theme of preparing the way (*hodos*) in the wilderness, a straight path (*tribos*) in a crooked world. This way/path marks the track of God for God's people, momentously blazed in Israel's experiences of exodus and exile. The exodus charts the God-led (through Moses) way out of Egyptian slavery, through the waters of the Red Sea and wilderness of Sinai, and toward the land of promise (Exod 23:20; Isa 43:16-17). The exile envisions a way home from Babylonian exile through a blossoming desert highway (Isa 35:1-8; 41:18-19; 51:3). By evoking these historic journeys, Mark sets the messianic way of Jesus in a similar crisis period of enslavement and displacement (now under Roman rule), moving toward liberation and restoration, yes, but not always freely and smoothly across the rough wilderness terrain.

The way of God—a major theme in Mark and across the Bible—carries heavy ethical and eschatological weight (Marcus 1992a; Watts 2001, 2018). The common word for "way," "road," or "journey" (*hodos*), used sixteen times in Mark, stretches beyond its pedestrian meaning to symbolize a *way of life*. Each of us stands at a fork in the road, confronting diverging ways of righteousness/wickedness, justice/injustice, life/death (Deut 30:15-20; Psalm 1; Prov 12:28; Jer 21:9). Which way will we choose? "Choose life!" (Deut 30:19; cf. Mark 8:34-37), the Bible enjoins, which means choosing to walk not simply in the general direction of God's way but in God's concrete *ways*, living out the covenantal bond with God and one another in faithful love (Deut 6:1-9; Mark 12:28-34). This is much easier said than done. We need a lot help along this way, a lot of "straightening" out.

Here another "way" word comes into play, *tribos*, denoting "a familiar . . . well worn . . . beaten path" (BDAG 2000, 1015). Too often God's people veer off the straight, smooth road into crooked, rutted side paths. Isaiah again proves to be a candid travel guide: "And a way (*hodon*) of peace they do not know, and there is no judgment in their ways (*hodois*), for their paths (*triboi*), through which they travel, are crooked, and they do not know peace" (Isa 59:8 NETS; cf. 40:3). But we need more than a prophet pointing out our waywardness. We need someone to show us the way, to blaze the way through the wilderness, to lead us on the right path by example as well as exhortation. We need Jesus Messiah, who fully embodies (incarnates) this journey for fellow pilgrims.

To what end? What is the goal, the finish line? This is the *eschatological* question, dealing with "end-time" matters in the sense of consummation more than conflagration. The goal is not consigning the broken present world to the ash heap but rather stoking the fire of refinement, (re)forging the "good" world God created, and fueling the runners of God's race with renewed energy to persevere to the end (cf. Heb 12:1-2). The quoted Malachi text goes on to announce that the messenger of the Lord's way will come on a climactic "day" to work "like the fire of a smelter and like the lye of cleaners . . . smelting and purifying as it were silver and as it were gold, and he will purify the sons of [Levi] . . . and they shall be bringing an offering to the Lord in justice" (Mal 3:1-3 NETS). Ultimately Malachi reveals the name of this fiery eschatological messenger as *Elijah* returning to earth to continue his prophetic mission of reformation (Mal 4:4 NETS [4:5-6 NRSV]). Leaving the door open for Elijah at Passover meals reflects this tradition of awaiting Elijah's coming in advance of the Messiah "to restore all things" (Mark 9:12; cf. 9:11-13).

In Mark's view, the Messiah Jesus has already come. Jesus had an Elijah advance man—not the actual Elijah but a prophet named *John* cast in the mold of Elijah. John even dressed the part and set up shop in the same general location of Elijah's final feats. John wore "a leather belt around his waist" (Mark 1:6; 2 Kgs 1:8) and donned a cloak of "camel's hair," which is not quite the same as being a "hairy man," as Elijah was (2 Kgs 1:8), but is close enough since prophets in the ancient world were known for wearing "hairy mantles" (Zech 13:4). But such prophetic garb was far from fashionable (no fancy leather belts or camel-hair blazers); rather it befitted rough-hewn, countercultural men (mostly) of the desert, off the beaten path of crooked, exploitative regimes of avarice and injustice. Likewise, John's diet of "locusts and wild honey," far from exotic delicacies, came from hard living hand-to-mouth off the wilderness land (without the perk, as far as we know, of having ravens bring him meat and bread morning and evening, as Elijah enjoyed for a time [1 Kgs 17:6]).

Elijah's last moments on earth took place in the Judean desert near Jericho and the Jordan River where it flows into the Dead Sea. Here Elijah struck the Jordan with his rolled-up mantle, which parted the waters, enabling Elijah and his protégé Elisha to cross over. When they reached the other side, a whirlwind whisked Elijah away in a fiery chariot and blew off his mantle, which Elisha recovered and then used to reverse the river-rending operation in "the spirit of Elijah" (2 Kgs 2:4-15).

It's clearly no accident or gimmick to draw a crowd that leads John to prepare the way of the Lord in the wilderness by calling the "people from the whole Judean countryside and . . . Jerusalem" to be "*baptized*" by him in the river Jordan" (Mark 1:4-5). John follows in the prophetic train of Elijah/Elisha and Moses/Joshua (also known for parting waters, the Red Sea/Jordan River [Exod 14:21-25/Josh 3:9-17]). But there is a twist. Rather than miraculously opening a dry way through the waters, John goes into the Jordan with individuals, immersing (*baptizō*) and raising each one in a ritual "of repentance for the forgiveness of sins" (1:4; cf. "confessing their sins" in 1:5). The "Baptizer" splits the river, so to speak, *with* the bodies of the baptismal candidates, engulfing them *in* the waters before lifting them back up.

While Paul's image of death-burial-resurrection in and out of a watery grave may spring to mind (Rom 6:3-4), the closer parallel for John's baptismal mission, beyond the prophetic paradigms, is the regular purifications practiced by the people themselves, self-dipping in stone water tubs known as *miqva'oth* or in rivers or streams of running water. These acts were not viewed as means of magically washing away sins but as signs of (re)setting oneself apart for service to God (though some baths were health-related or recreational rather than ritual [Meyers 2021, 45]). The stone pools were stationed throughout the land but naturally clustered in Jerusalem around the temple (Sanders 1992, 222–30; Meyers and Chancey 2012, 47–49, 101–104, 233–36).

John may have been especially influenced by the priestly desert sect established at Qumran on the northwest shore of the Dead Sea near the mouth of the Jordan (Taylor 1997, 15–100). These "covenanters," as they called themselves, established a strict, exclusive community in protest against the corrupt temple establishment in Jerusalem, as they perceived it. They followed a rigorous regimen of water rituals to maintain their purity in preparation for God's imminent, cataclysmic (apocalyptic) judgment on the wicked world, in which they alone would be saved (Vanderkam 1994, 71–119, 168–85; Vermes 1999, 145–69).

In marked contrast, however, to the Dead Sea sect's agenda, John does not aim to build a special enclave or holy retreat center in the desert. While he attracts some "disciples" (2:13), he seems more motivated to send renewed, baptized people back into society as "ticking time bombs" (Crossan 1994, 43–44; Saxby 2015, 87), ready to trigger a fresh explosion of God's rightmaking, path-straightening rule. John sets them on a new course driven by a changed heart and mind—the basic meaning of "repentance," a reentry into the land with renewed commitment to follow God's way mapped out in the Torah (Instruction/Law in Genesis–Deuteronomy; see Josh 1:7-9).

Whatever the full ramifications of John's baptizing campaign and whatever buzz he generates, he is not obsessed with promoting his own interests or reputation. He is God's messenger first and foremost, publicizing the coming of "one . . . more powerful" or the "stronger one" (*ischyroteros*), against whom John doesn't hold a candle. Or to use his vivid servile image, he is "not worthy to stoop down and untie the thong of [this stronger one's] sandals" (Mark 1:7). Matthew and Luke delete Mark's "stoop down" (Matt 3:11//Luke 3:16) as redundant, but in so doing they dilute John's humble, worshipful stance toward the coming one. John will recognize the "strongman" leader of God's people when he sees him, but he makes no pretense to being a powerful figure himself, even by association. This raises the issue of what kind of "strongman politics" the Baptist (and Mark) has in mind (see Obama 2018; Ben-Ghiat 2020). Some oppressed people in first-century Roman Judea and Galilee likely longed for a Messiah Strongman.

In what *ways* will Jesus Messiah fit the strongman model? That remains to be seen as Mark's narrative unfolds, since neither the Bible nor early Jewish tradition provided a full-fledged profile of the expected Messiah. Widespread agreement on the *need* for messianic intervention? Yes. Consensus on messianic policy? Not so much. Yet John the Baptist begins to point in the right direction: "I have baptized you with water; he [the stronger one] will baptize you with the Holy Spirit" (1:8). The superior one coming after John will run in the same baptismal current, even as he infuses it with a fresh flood of Holy Spirit energy. He, too, will be a "Baptist" (see Twelftree 2009), working to change the course of people's lives and establish the renewed rule of God in the land (see 1:15), though his main modus operandi will be in *Spirit* rather than water. Spirit-and-water have flowed tightly together since creation to bring new life/order from death/chaos (Gen 1:1-2; cf. John 3:5-8; 7:37-39), and Jesus will prove quite adept with his own waterworks (Mark 4:35-41; 6:45-52). At present, however, John the Baptist hails the coming *Spirit-filled and -led Strongman* suffused with divine power and authority. As such, this Strongman will be a dynamic *political* figure but one set at diametric odds to the present ruling powers. The desert highway prepared by John marks an alternative path to the Roman road, along which the Spirit-Strongman will march and challenge Caesar's down-treading rule (see Myers 1988).

Running into Battle (1:9-13)

With John's dramatic announcement of the powerful one to come—whom we infer to be Jesus Messiah, the Son of God (1:1)—we expect this one's grand, triumphal entrance into the story. And given the political implications of the way of this Messiah and his baptizing advance man—recalling the liberative (exodus)/restorative (exile) watersheds of Israel's history—we might also expect accompanying militant and miraculous signs. Not for the last time, Mark both fulfills and frustrates our expectations.

In what may be the most banal introduction in the history of biography, Mark states, "In those days Jesus came from Nazareth of Galilee and was baptized by John in the Jordan" (1:9). But "immediately" in this fast-paced narrative Mark injects an exhilarating note of surprise (1:10). Precisely because Mark's story zips along, however, we can easily skip over vital material; careful readers should aim to mark every step, including those that seem pedestrian. Here, I argue, there is a method to the blandness of Jesus's entrance "in those days," setting the basic context of his coming in ordinary time rather than calling attention to "the time of Herod" (Matt 2:1), "the days of King Herod of Judea" (Luke 1:5), or "those days [under the rule of] . . . Emperor Augustus" (Luke 2:1). As I will repeatedly note, Mark is keenly aware of the imperial Caesarean-Herodian impingement on Jesus's mission and the critical time at hand for reinforcing God's kingdom (1:14-15). At the same time, however, Mark's Jesus lived and worked in "those days"—those quotidian "every-days" in which ordinary people live and work.

Aligned with this uneventful chronology is a negligible geography. This Jesus comes "from Nazareth of Galilee," a small, no-account hamlet in the northern sector of the Jewish homeland bordering Syria and Phoenicia. Compared with Jerusalem of Judea—the bustling center of Jewish life, home to God's temple, and historic capital of kings David and Solomon—Nazareth of Galilee was backwater bumpkinville. Reflecting common opinion, an "Israelite" named Nathanael sarcastically quips in another Gospel, "Can anything good come out of Nazareth?" (John 1:46). Certainly no Messiah candidate would come from there (John 7:40-42, 52).

So Mark's Jesus first appears as a marginal figure, not the center of attention with a promising pedigree. And it's even more surprising that Jesus joins the Judean throng in coming *to* John for baptism. Wait! Who's preparing the way for whom? Why is Jesus not merely endorsing but also personally *engaging in* this "baptism of repentance for the forgiveness of sins" (1:4)? As the would-be Messiah, shouldn't *he be the baptizer*, not the baptized? Matthew has John voice this very concern, along with Jesus's reassuring response:

John the Baptist: I need to be baptized by you, and do you come to me?
Jesus: Let it be so now; for it is proper for us in this way to fulfill all righteousness (Matt 3:14-15)

By contrast, Mark briefly narrates the fact of Jesus's baptism by John without further ado and then quickly shifts the spotlight from John to Jesus or, more fully, from John's activity to that of the triune God—Father, Son, and Spirit. Although using no formal "trinity" language, Mark features the *intimate, interpenetrating work* of the three divine persons in one dynamic union (commonly called the "economic trinity"; LaCugna 1991, 211–32, 377–411; Moltmann 1993b, 151–62; Fiddes 2000, 6–7, 71–81), showcased in Jesus's extraordinary baptism scene. After unpacking this scene, we will return to the nagging issue of why Jesus personally submits to (John's) baptism in the first place.

"And just" (*kai euthys*) as Jesus "was coming up out of the water" (1:10), various special effects detonate. Mark uses *euthys* more than any other New Testament writer—some forty-two times—most often, as here, combined with "and" (*kai*) to keep the narrative moving and to keep readers alert to sudden twists and turns. In its common adverbial usage *euthys* denotes "immediately" or "straightaway," though English versions of Mark also opt for "just as," "just then," "soon," "at once," or even omission as a (supposed) throwaway term. Only once does the term function as an adjective, meaning "straight"—in the quotation from Isaiah 40:3 we've already seen: "make his paths *straight* (*eutheias*)" (Mark 1:3).

So what happens "immediately" to the baptized Jesus? He receives an audio-visual epiphany from heaven, a personal visitation by the divine Father and Spirit (there's no indication that John or the crowd witness the phenomena). The experience is explosive and directive. Jesus first sees the "heavens *torn apart*," not merely "opened" as in the Synoptic parallels (Matt 3:16//Luke 3:21) but "torn" (*schizō*) or "ripped," just as the temple curtain will be "torn in two, from top to bottom" at the moment of Jesus's death (Mark 15:38). From beginning to end, Mark's story unfolds in turbulent, fractured space with Jesus at the center of a cosmic battle. The fabric of the universe is being ripped apart by sinful humanity (1:4-5) and satanic hostility (1:13). But the good news from God's side is that this tumultuous rending will ultimately give way to a total *mending of the world* according to God's gracious purpose (Sacks 2005, 71–83).

Indeed, this restorative operation is already underway; there's no time to lose dipping a toe in the water. God rips apart the veil of heaven and rushes headlong to earth on the wings of the Spirit to light upon the Son. As the Spirit-wind hovered over chaotic waters at creation (Gen 1:1-2), so the Spirit now anoints Jesus Messiah after he has split the waters of the Jordan with his body in order to re-create the world—a veritable new heaven and earth. Jesus's propulsive "coming up/ascending" (*anabainōn*) from watery depths and the Spirit's "descending" (*katabainon*) from celestial heights signal a breaking through of cosmic barriers and coming together of embattled realms, where the will of God reigns on earth as it is in heaven (see Matt 6:10).

But isn't this volatile apocalyptic combat language belied by the image of the Spirit as a *dove*, the quintessential symbol of peace and love? In the Bible, the prototypical picture of the pacific dove emerges in the wake of the catastrophic Genesis flood, threatening the world's very existence. The dove represents the hope of beginning anew after the devastating storm. But this hope is no fairytale dream of a magic kingdom over the horizon. After the rain ceases, Noah dispatches the dove three times, at weekly intervals, to gauge the level of standing water: the bird first returns to the ark with nothing, then with an olive leaf, and finally leaves for good to remake its habitat in the natural world (Gen 8:8-12). The going will be tough for the dove and all the creatures in the ark, including Noah and his family. Peace will be restored and the world will be remade, but not by divine fiat (1:3-31). More like the second creation account, though with much more struggle, the postdiluvian world will be forged out of the mud, muck, and mire (2:4-7). Likewise, we might imagine the corrupt world in Jesus's day being reformed out of the "muddy waters" of the Jordan (cf. 2 Kgs 5:12).

Yet the actual world Jesus confronts is haunted by imperial military might more than natural muddy mess. The empire prides itself on bringing peace (*pax*) to its citizens and subjects, but it is a peace gained through violent conquest and sustained through forceful oppression, symbolized by its avian mascot, the *eagle* (Carter 2003 and 2013, 74, 77; cf. Josephus, *Ant.* 17.150–56). One could hardly imagine a bird more antithetical to a dove. We get the first flutter of a hint that Jesus Messiah will not wage war like earthly kings. He will fight under the Banner of the Dove. Make no mistake: he will fight to win; he will fight for justice, righteousness, and peace in the power of the Spirit. But God's Spirit-Dove will not leave a trail of dead and broken bodies in its wake. The Spirit-fueled mission of Jesus Messiah aims solely and wholly to bring life, health, and freedom out of death, brokenness, and oppression.

And what does God the Father say to all this? God's lead "voice (*phōnē*) . . . from heaven" joins John's "voice (*phōnē*) . . . in the wilderness," prophesied by Isaiah, in the symphony of authoritative witnesses to Jesus Messiah (Mark 1:3-4). But God alone strikes the highest note in relation to Jesus: "You are my Son, the Beloved; with you I am well pleased" (1:11). Though Jesus enters the story alone, far from his family and hometown of Nazareth who will struggle to accept him (3:19-21; 6:1-6), he enjoys secure, intimate, loving communion in the family of God. Scriptural echoes resound again, particularly the Lord's declaration to the Davidic king, "my son you are" in Psalm 2:7 (NETS), though without the added "beloved" (*agapētos*), a term of endearment.

Isaiah may also resonate once more. In the Hebrew Bible, Isaiah 42:1 reads, "Here is my servant, who I uphold, my chosen, in whom my soul delights; I have put my spirit upon him" (NRSV). Though the prophet features the Lord's *chosen servant* rather than *beloved son*, the portrait of a Spirit-anointed figure who "delights" or "pleases" the Lord fits Mark's depiction of Jesus at his baptism. The Greek version, however, states, "[Jacob] is my servant; I will lay hold of him; Israel is my chosen; my soul has *accepted* him; I have put my spirit upon him" (NETS). Apart from designating God's collective *people* (Jacob/Israel) as God's chosen servant (the "servant" term *pais* also means "child"), the emotive "delightful/pleasing" aspect of this figure has modulated to a more active notion of being "accepted" or "received" by God.

Mark 1:11 uses the Greek verb *eudokeō*, which literally means "think well of" or "take delight/pleasure in." But as Michael Peppard has demonstrated, in Greek biblical contexts closest to Mark's case *eudokeō* has an *elective* as well as emotive connotation, tethering "pleasing" feeling to "choosing" action, including God's commissioning someone for special leadership (Peppard 2012, 106–12; 1 Macc 14:41-47; Gal 1:15; Col 1:19; in Sir 33:14; 39:18; 41:4, the related noun *eudokia* alludes to "divine ordination or resolve . . . divine choice as the determinative counsel" [Schrenk 1964, 744]). Hence, Mark draws on Isaiah 42:1 to convey that God was *pleased to choose* Jesus the Son as *Servant Messiah*. The baptism scene thus marks not only God's affirmation of the beloved Son but also God's *commission* of the Son to ministry. Jesus is not simply to bask in the warm glow of his Father's love; he has a critical operation to carry out. And he is not to lord his privilege as the divine royal heir over his subjects; rather he is called to *serve* God's people in humility (see Mark 9:34-37; 10:41-45). How does Jesus play out this challenging *Royal-Servant, Messiah-Minister* role, which would strike many as an oxymoron?

In the language of the African American spiritual, the first thing Jesus does is "go down in the river" with sisters, brothers, fathers, mothers—"sinners" all—no doubt "to pray" (though only Luke 3:21 specifies that Jesus prays at his baptism) but also to "study the good old way" of the Lord, to prepare to walk in "straight" paths of righteousness. His uniqueness as God's beloved Son, anointed by the Holy Spirit, does not preclude him from "div[ing] into a fully incarnate and diverse world" (Rohr 2018, 1)—from plunging into the depths of suffering, sinful humanity. Indeed, he is able to guide his errant mothers, fathers, brothers, and sisters in the family of God (Mark 3:31-35) precisely because he *relates to them* from below, under the water; he participates *with them*, drawing them ever closer into the divine communion of Father, Son, and Spirit (Fiddes 2000), into the inner courts of God's realm (1:15). Only a *servant-king* acts that way.

Jesus seems all set to launch his militant messianic mission in the power of the Spirit, except that the Spirit proves to be an unpredictable commander-in-chief. "Immediately"—no time to preen in post-baptismal glory—"the Spirit drove [Jesus] out into the wilderness" for a forty-day battle with Satan to test Jesus's mettle (1:12-13). The verb describing the Spirit's action (*ekballō*) indicates a forceful expulsion of Jesus, "seeming against his will" (Levison 2020, 210–11), into more remote wilds of the desert. Elsewhere in Mark the verb typically designates Jesus's action in *casting out demons* (1:34, 39, 43; 3:15, 22, 23; 6:13; 7:26; 9:18, 28, 38, 47). But first the Spirit casts out *Jesus* to wage war with *Satan*. So much for the Spirit as a gentle dove. Yet this "casting out" scenario may provide our best clue to understanding Mark's brief temptation/testing scene (lacking the famous threefold test in Matt 4:1-11//Luke 4:1-13). As Jesus bore the brunt of human sinfulness in baptism, sinking him into the river's depths in preparation for lifting his burdened people out of the mire and into the way of forgiveness, so he must feel the force of satanic attack in the wilderness in preparation for leading his beleaguered people out of enslavement and into the way of freedom. As one cast out into a withering desert combat zone, Mark's Jesus earns his battle scars and hones his ability to cast out demons that are ruining people's lives. This Messiah is no armchair general or palace-lolling king (cf. 2 Sam 11:1-2).

While Mark does not elaborate Jesus's post-baptismal showdown with Satan, he does offer a few details worth noting:

Forty days. The forty-day period of Jesus's testing in the wilderness readily evokes memory of Israel's forty years of hard trudging through the wilderness after crossing the Red Sea (including the forty-day sojourn at Sinai where Moses received the tablets of the Law as the people indulged in idolatrous worship [Exod 24:18; 32:1-6]). Again, the way of Jesus in Mark's narrative retreads—and redeems—the often wayward way of Israel in the wilderness.

Wild beasts. Although the desert battle between Jesus and Satan is popularly conceived as a one-on-one contest with Jesus emerging as the undisputed victor, Mark's account is both more crowded and less decisive. While the presence of "wild beasts" (*thēria*) naturally fits the desert setting (we might imagine hyenas, jackals, snakes, scorpions), the detail that *Jesus* is *with* (*meta*) these creatures is striking (1:13). We might presume they represent demonic troops aligned with Satan, not with Jesus. So why does he associate with these beasts on the battlefield, as he will soon appoint twelve apostles on a mountaintop "to be with (*meta*) him" (3:14; Levison 2020, 67–68)? Although being with wild animals may reinforce his close grappling with satanic elements, more likely it hints at Jesus's commitment to *creational* restoration, alongside the covenantal renewal with Israel we've already highlighted. Conceptions of beasts as predatory threats to humans don't tell the whole story.

The term *thēria* simply designates "wild animals" as opposed to domesticated ones, and in the Greek version of Genesis these animals are grouped with "quadrupeds and creeping things" among species of "living creatures" brought forth by God's "good" earth on the sixth day just before humans enter the picture (Gen 1:24-26 NETS). The environment has become much "wilder" since the halcyon era of Eden, due in large measure to *human* violence (Gen 6:11). But the hope of re-creation, of a regained Eden, a restored "ecotopia" (Bauckham 2010, 115–29), resounds, especially in Isaiah (again): "The wolf shall graze with the lamb" in the realm of the Spirit-imbued ruler (Isa 11:1-2, 6-9 NETS), consummating the Lord's renewal project.

> Look, I am doing new things that will now spring forth,
>   and you will know them,
> and I will make a *way in the wilderness*
>   and rivers in the dry land.
> The wild animals (*thēria*) of the field will praise me. (Isa 43:19-20 NETS)

In the heat of desert conflict, Jesus Messiah begins to reestablish God's "peaceable kingdom" among all creatures of the earth (Bauckham 2010, 126–29; Gieschen 2009; Marcus 2000, 167–71). Against the primordial backdrop of "the tragedy in the garden of Eden, which led inevitably to the expulsion of the first man and woman, the temptation of Jesus injects hope into [the] story" of humanity's expulsion from the garden of Eden "because Jesus, expelled by the Spirit, lives peaceably with the animals and resists the devil's pressure on him" (Levison 2020, 77; cf. 67–69).

Angels. Jesus engages not only with earthly beasts in the desert but also with heavenly beings as counterparts to the Satan figure, who himself has shadowy biblical origins in the heavenly court as chief "adversary/accuser" of humanity (Job 1:6-12; 2:1-7). As Mark presents it, however, Jesus is not so much with these angelic creatures as they are with him; more precisely they "were ministering to/serving (*diēkonoun*) him" (Mark 1:13 NASB, ESV). The NRSV's "waited on him" is correct as far as it goes, but too limited in scope. "Diaconal" service involves a whole range of sustaining ministry, not only food service, as important as that is. The point here is that the incarnate Christ *needs and accepts help* in his rigorous forty-day boot camp. Although "strong" in the power of God's Spirit, he is not some alien superman.

Extending this reminder of Jesus's true humanity with natural needs and limits, we should register that Mark does not report the outcome of this desert battle. While we have every reason to believe that Jesus will fulfill his messianic vocation, he is not declared absolute *Christus Victor* here. He delivers no knockout blow to Satan, once for all. Satan lives to fight another day, and Mark will narrate several more rounds of conflict (1:21-28, 32-34; 3:11-12, 22-27; 4:15; 5:1-20; 6:7-13; 7:24-30; 9:14-29, 38-40).

Outrunning the Baptist (1:14-15)

Now that the coming one announced by John and anointed by God has entered the Gospel story, what will John's role be? Thus far he has been a prominent prophetic figure in his own right, not simply a publicity agent for Jesus. While knowing his subordinate place under the "stronger" Messiah, he still appears to merit a best supporting actor nomination and maybe even costar billing—if he hadn't been arrested so early by the authorities (1:14). Mark drops this bombshell of John's arrest without elaboration; that will come later in a gruesome incident involving John's severed head (6:14-29)! Mark's first readers likely knew already about the Baptist's decapitation (Josephus, *Ant.* 18.116–19; Mason 2003, 213–25), yet on a *narrative level*, Mark creates suspense about John's fate and, more importantly at present, gets John out of the way to focus on Jesus, who promptly moves beyond John's Judean base of operations back to Galilee (1:14).

Why this separation? As we've already noted, a certain tension, manifest in different ways in all four Gospels, complicates the relationship between John and Jesus. Why did John baptize Jesus, not the other way around? Why did John's mission come first and attract so many adherents? Mark deals with these questions indirectly in a way that magnifies Jesus's superior role as Messiah and Son of God while maintaining sincere respect for John's baptizing work. Recall that John proclaimed "a baptism *of repentance* for the forgiveness of sins" (1:4). It is no accident that as Jesus proceeds to "proclaim the good news of God," he punctuates his message with the imperative "Repent" in tandem with "Believe in the good news" (1:15). He thus reiterates John's marching orders even as he replaces him on the battlefield, while John becomes a prisoner of war. Like John, Jesus aims to resist the forces of evil in large measure by reforming the people of God.

But that's not all. Jesus the Christ also surpasses John the Baptist in degree of Spirit-power (1:10, 12), as John predicted (1:8), and also, as we now learn, in *fuller* and *nearer* engagement with God's kingdom in *time* and *space*. The first words spoken by Mark's Jesus declare, "The time is fulfilled (*peplērōtai*), and the kingdom of God has come near (*ēngiken*)" (1:15). Both verbs have what Greek grammarians call a *perfective aspect*, meaning that they connote completed action with continuing effect and "front-grounded" emphasis (Porter 1994, 23, 302–303), as in "I have loved my wife close to fifty years up to the present moment" in an overall "perfective"—enduring and maturing—sense. In Christ, God's rule has already been inaugurated on earth and is guaranteed to stand. That is incredibly good news, the very "good news of God" (1:14). But much interim work remains to be done between beginning and end, commencement and consummation. Fulfillment unfolds surely but slowly over time, with many twists and turns along the way. Mark's Gospel tracks Jesus Messiah's personification and promotion of God's rule at a level unprecedented in human history. But he will not snap his fingers and zap this kingdom into full-fledged reality.

"Kingdom of God" (*basileia tou theou*) constitutes a key concept in Jesus's mission, perhaps its core organizing principle. Unfortunately, however, "kingdom" language is often used loosely in Christian circles today. The New Testament notion of God's kingdom does not designate some fuzzy idea about divine reality or some fixed area of divine activity with static space-time coordinates in heaven or earth. Rather, it represents the *dynamic realm/ reign/rule of God* in justice and righteousness throughout history and "the heavens and the earth" created by God (Gen 1:1). As the Creator, God rightfully rules the entire universe; nothing is off limits to God.

Yet since God rules over free human subjects on earth, this "worldly" dimension of God's realm does not always reflect God's will for the flourishing of humanity and the environment. Hence the need for messianic involvement at ground level to "set the world to rights" (Johnson 2018, 76; cf. Wright 2008, 72, 93, 133, 137–39, 179, 197, 202), to renew God's "kingdom." But what exactly is this "right stuff" Jesus seeks to establish? Models of human kings and rulers leave much to be desired, including some very "wrong" things done by David and Solomon, Israel's chief royal heroes (see 2 Samuel 11–12, 24; 1 Kings 11).

In a lively imagined dialogue with a serious inquirer dubbed "Clara," the theologian Elizabeth A. Johnson astutely bridges the gap between Jesus and Mark's first-century symbol of God's "kingdom" and our often very different twenty-first-century social and political concerns.

> *Clara*: I have to say that the phrase "kingdom of God" does not stir my heart with excitement today. Besides having patriarchal, hierarchical overtones, it simply does not connect with us who live in democratic societies as something greatly to be desired.
> *Elizabeth*: Understandable. But think of it in this first-century way. In a world made up of many kingdoms where power and wealth reigned to the harsh disadvantage of those without either, the kingdom of God meant wondrous changes. For this was the kingdom of the redeeming, saving God of Israel. Slaves would be free, exiles returned home; springs would flow in the desert, abundance mark the fields; justice would be established and mercy reign. In a word, the symbol refers to a state of the world when

the will of God is finally and fully honored; compassion and kindness will abound, joy and peace will break out, and all creation will flourish. Jesus's use of the symbol was inherently subversive. His announcement turned the usual operations of the kingdoms of the world on their heads. God's way of ruling was the opposite of the empire's Caesar. (Johnson 2018, 74–75 [emphasis original])

Running with Jesus and Fishing for People (1:16-20)

Following Jesus's Spirit-directed baptism and testing (1:9-13), preparing him to proclaim the good news of God's restorative rule (1:14-15), we expect Jesus to plunge into his messianic campaign "immediately." But at first he seems to be in no great hurry, strolling along the beach of the Sea of Galilee and observing two brother pairs of fishermen—Simon/Andrew and James/John—casting and mending their nets, respectively: a thoroughly ordinary scene with Jesus as a casual passerby while others ply their trade (1:16, 19). We learn later that Jesus was a carpenter by profession (6:3), but he's not engaged in that or any other work now. Or so it appears.

But this short, apparent lull in the action discloses a dimension of Jesus's "way" easily missed in Mark's dramatic narrative. Jesus does not begin his mission with some eye-popping demonstration, like parting the sea so he can cross through it (he will later walk on the water [6:45-52]). He first simply "pass[es] along" the water's edge while ordinary fishermen go about their business. Whatever he will do, he will do with them and for them in the course of everyday earthly life on land and sea.

But that doesn't mean Jesus won't upend their lives and propel them in a new direction, as the Spirit had just "thrown" him into the desert. The beachcombing Jesus suddenly issues an audacious order to the first pair of fishermen. Without so much as a "how do you do," he commands, "Follow me, and I will make you fish for people" (1:17); walking "a little farther" down the coast, he also calls the net-mending James and John (1:19-20a). "Follow me!" Where? Why? Who are you? Jesus provides no explanation except for the cryptic proposition that he will make them "fish for people" (Spencer 2005). He connects with these men's fishing occupations only to disrupt them. They caught masses of fish in huge dragnets in order to kill them, sell them, and eat them—a disturbing analogy to catching *people*.

Popular associations of fishing with evangelistic outreach tend to conjure up images of whistling excursions to the local creek, cane pole in hand—which have nothing to do with Simon and company's experience. Their fishing enterprises were commercial and heavily taxed by Roman-Herodian overlords who claimed proprietorship of everything in the Sea of Galilee and all goods ferried across it. Toll booths were stationed around the lake (cf. 2:14). Herod Antipas, Rome's client ruler of Galilee in Jesus's day, built his new capital Tiberius on the southwest coast of the lake, which he treated, as one scholar puts it, as his own private "little Mediterranean Sea" (Sawicki 2000, 173; cf. 27–30, 143–47; Hanson and Oakman 1998, 106–10). The fishing industry symbolized the strangling "net" in which the exploitative Roman-Herodian economy had "caught" it subjects (Hanson 1997). Jesus may thus mimic the language of oppressive empire in order to subvert it (see Smith 2008; Liew 2008): his agents will "catch people" in order to "release" them from stifling, tyrannical rule into the flowing, flourishing waters of God's realm. Again, Jesus dives into the depths of conflicting spheres, challenging the powers that be, aiming to rescue his people from the snare of unjust domination by recapturing them for God's righteous kingdom. And again, it will be a struggle, a battle, not a walk in the park or a stroll on the beach.

The four fishermen, however, take no time to process Jesus's larger plan or to ask any questions of this man they've just encountered and been summoned to follow. The first two brothers "immediately" abandon their nets and follow Jesus (1:18), and when he "immediately" calls the second pair, they follow suit, leaving everything to join Jesus, including "their father Zebedee in the boat" and some hired hands (1:20). We might imagine "Zebedee and Sons" painted boldly on the side of the boat, as the sons suddenly ditch the family business to follow this stranger.

In our easy familiarity with this call of the first disciples, we must not miss its stunning impact. Along with the ordinariness of these first fishermen recruits (Mark does not yet call them "disciples" or "apostles"), we are struck by the limited account of what motivates their wholesale career change. *Why do they drop their nets and leave behind everything—family, friends, livelihoods—to traipse after this mystery man?* The only clue Mark provides is that these men follow Jesus because he *said so*. Somehow Jesus's imperative *word* strikes them as powerful and persuasive, worth staking their lives on. We might also infer Jesus's commanding *presence* and his authoritative *way* of speaking that grips audiences as much as what he says, which Mark will develop in the next scene (1:21-28).

At any rate, these four acolytes of Jesus still have much to learn. All Simon, Andrew, James, and John know at this stage is that Jesus's way leads *away*—away from the familiar and the familial—to a puzzling people-catching vocation. Envisioning the deity as "captain," the first-century Stoic philosopher Epictetus advised his young "voyager" students during their recreational periods on shore to remain alert to the captain's summons: "If the captain calls you, run to the boat and leave all those things without even turning around" (Epictetus, *Encheiridion* 7). "Captain" Jesus demands the same total commitment from his "fishermen" crew in the opposite direction, calling them to leave their boats, businesses, and associates to run after him. At least these four each have a brother to accompany them; but otherwise, like expeditionary sailors they leave behind father, mother, wives, children, and extended family for this unknown venture (see 10:28-29). That's either an act of amazing faithfulness (faith + obedience) and loyalty or of sheer foolishness and irresponsibility. There will be times down the road when they themselves wonder about their choice.

Remarkable Works of Freeing and Forgiving

Mark 1:21–3:35

With four followers in tow, Jesus begins his mission. At this early training stage, the disciples observe Jesus in action. Their time will come soon enough to participate more directly (6:7-13). Starting with a bustling first day (1:21-39), Jesus moves throughout Galilee doing remarkable works of freeing and forgiving, liberation and restoration, via his therapeutic word and touch. Jesus shows, as much as tells, the "good news" of God's benevolent realm. Put another way, he backs up his evangelical (*euangelion*) preaching with practical healing; indeed, his *word* is not merely informative but also transformative. His word works! (See 1:25-27; 2:10-12; 3:5.) Likewise, his *touch* is not only connective, physically and emotionally, but also curative (1:30-31, 41-42).

Although the town of Capernaum on the northwest shore of the Galilean sea seems to serve as a base of operations (1:21; 2:1; 9:33), Jesus does not set up shop there, as John did at the Jordan river, calling people to come to him (1:5). Rather, Jesus operates as an itinerant missionary, traveling from town to town ministering in various venues: homes (1:29-34; 2:1-17; 3:19b-35), synagogues (1:21-28; 3:1-6), "through the grainfields" (2:23), and "beside the sea" (2:13-14; 3:7-12), with brief interludes in the desert (1:35) and on the mountain (3:13-19a). No place is beyond God's loving outreach in Christ. And no time is beyond it either: Jesus even keeps working on the Sabbath (1:21-28; 2:23–3:6) as well as during "ordinary time." He draws some religious teachers' criticism for his Sabbath activity, which he vigorously defends as part and parcel of true Sabbath observance. By no means opposed to the creational vision of Sabbath rest, Jesus aims to realize the fullness of that vision through active *rest*oration.

Continuing to disrupt the sacred rest and wholeness God desires for the world are nefarious spirit-forces under Satan's rule. Jesus's forty-day battle with Satan (1:12-13) was just the beginning of Jesus's campaign for liberating those assaulted by satanic agents (3:22). Framed by exorcism scenes (1:21-28; 3:19b-35), this unit features Jesus's purpose and power to free those suffering various types of oppression, whether from demons, diseases, disabilities, or sins. Mark's Jesus brings deliverance, healing, restoration, and forgiveness from a tangled web of physical, psychological, and spiritual maladies affecting the whole person.

Making Clean (1:21-45)

A concise summary of Jesus's ministry appears in the middle of this section: "And he cured many who were sick with various diseases, and cast out many demons" (1:34). "Many" comprise numerous, distinctive individual cases. Mark highlights three of these beneficiaries of Jesus's therapeutic work: a man afflicted by an "unclean spirit" (1:21-28), a woman bedridden with a fever (1:29-31), and a man suffering from "leprosy" (1:40-45).

The first and last cases feature Jesus's *cleansing* action, countering the deleterious effects of an "unclean spirit" (1:26) and an "unclean" skin disease (1:40-42). It's important from the start to understand the biblical view of "cleansing." Though some New Testament texts emphasize cleansing *from sins* through Jesus's blood sacrifice (Heb 9:14, 22-23; 10:2; 1 John 1:7, 9), that is not the main meaning across the Bible. "Clean" and "unclean" function more as *managerial* classifications than *moral* definitions. They reflect the cosmic order established by God's creational acts of "separating" and "gathering" the various elements into their appointed places (Gen 1:4, 6-7, 9-10, 14, 18). Such spaces exist in juxtaposition, not opposition, to one another. While the sun rules the realm of day, for example, with a blazing light "greater" than the "lesser lights" (moon, stars) of night, that doesn't mean the nocturnal bodies are evil or corrupt. God situates all creation in "good" places (Gen 1:4, 12, 18, 21, 25, 31; cf. Acts 17:26).

A similar order governs "living creatures of every kind" (Gen 1:24), which the Torah sorts into "holy/clean" and "unholy/unclean" groups: "You are to distinguish between the holy and the common and between the unclean and the unclean" (Lev 10:10). "Unclean" elements delineated in Leviticus 11–15 include various animals (e.g., carrion-feeding predators), bodily emissions (e.g., menstrual blood and semen), and skin conditions (various scaly conditions and lesions). Ruptures in bodily boundaries require rituals of wholeness and restoration, not acts of atonement (the Day of Atonement for forgiveness of *sins* is discussed separately in Leviticus 16).

Although "unclean" persons are not morally culpable in the strict sense, they do operate in a moral universe governed by the God of holiness, righteousness, and justice. According to the anthropologist Mary Douglas, who is also an astute interpreter of biblical literature, "In Leviticus the body is the cosmos. Everything in the universe shows forth the righteousness of the

Lord." In this system, forbidden, "unclean" animals serve a dual purpose. On the one hand, violent species who consume blood teach us that "eating is a form of predation" and that "holiness is incompatible with predatory behavior," especially toward weak and poor creatures. On the other hand, not killing and eating vulnerable species reminds us not to exploit suffering creatures, human and nonhuman:

> Consider . . . the ants laboring under their huge loads. Think of the blindness of worms, and bats, the vulnerability of fish without scales. Think of their human parallels, the laborers, the beggars, the orphans and the defenseless widows. Not themselves but the behavior that reduces them to this state is the abomination. No wonder the Lord made the crawling things and found them good (Gen 1:31). (Douglas 1993, 21–22; cf. Balentine 2002, 93–100)

While since Job's day even so-called "friends" have blamed victims for bringing trouble on themselves through their sinful conduct, prompting divine punishment, in Mark 1:21-45 Jesus passes no judgment on the three sufferers and issues no calls for their repentance (he addresses sin and forgiveness in the next section [2:1-27]). He reaches out to "cleanse," to free, to heal; to restore order and wholeness to chaotic and broken lives. Within this overall restorative framework, Jesus tailors his ministry to the particular needs of the three individuals.

Demon-possessed man (1:21-28)
The man in the Capernaum synagogue has become dominated by a vicious "unclean spirit." Again, the text never suggests that he merited or invited this assault, and the fact that he enters the synagogue may intimate his love for God and his hope to find God's help. Yet in response to Jesus's authoritative teaching beyond the level of the local instructors (1:22), the possessed man blurts out, "What have you to do with us, Jesus of Nazareth? Have you come to destroy us? I know who you are, the Holy One of God" (1:23-24). This strange mixing of singular ("I") and plural ("us") pronouns betrays who is talking. The man is not speaking for himself in his "right mind" (see 5:15). A sinister band of alien forces has taken control of his life and voice.

An invasive "unclean" spirit-gang preys on this man's life, aiming to devour it like a vulture (Lev 11:13) or a virus (COVID-19). Mark provides no medical chart of symptoms and ill effects beyond noting that when the spirit leaves the man it convulses his body (1:26). However modern science might diagnose this man's physical and psychological condition, Mark writes within the common worldview of the day, which viewed humanity as being under constant threat from unseen nefarious forces (spirits, demons).

The "unclean" spirits' speech to Jesus bristles with sarcastic irony. "What have you to do with us?"—or, reversing the order as the Greek has it, "What have *we* to do with *you*?" (1:24)—aims to stake out their demonic territory and keep Jesus out of their business. But this is precisely what Jesus "has to do" as the agent of God's liberating, life-giving realm. As God spoke the good created order into being, Jesus speaks to restore order and well-being to the man in the synagogue, putting the tormenting "unclean" spirits in their place, *out of* this man's life.

Their second question "Have you come to destroy us?" also drips with audacious deceit. Destructive victimization is their game, not Jesus'; it's the cruel game they've been playing out on the man whom Jesus comes to save. Jesus calls foul and expels the "unclean" team from the field but does not destroy them (though see 5:13).

Finally, the statement "I know who you are, the Holy One of God" marks a perfectly orthodox confession of Christ! This band of evil spirits knows more about Jesus than the synagogue audience at this stage and even after Jesus delivers the possessed man. The congregation senses something "new" and different in Jesus's authoritative teaching, but they do not yet fully perceive what it means. They're "astounded" and "amazed" (1:22, 27), but such responses do not guarantee faith and understanding. They keep wondering, "What is this? What's happening here?" (1:27). Mark's narrative aims to answer this vital question, to reveal the "holy" Christ who has come to "clean" and reorder a messy world. "The demons [already] believe—and shudder" (Jas 1:19). Mark wants his audience to rejoice and "believe in the *good* news" (1:15) of the liberating Christ.

Fever-stricken woman (1:29-31)

The transition in 1:28-30 from Jesus's dealing with the possessed man in the Capernaum synagogue to the feverish woman in a house happens quickly, reinforced by a triple staccato of *euthys*: "At once (*euthys*) his fame began to spread. . . . As soon as (*euthys*) they left the synagogue, they entered the house. . . . Now Simon's mother-in-law was in bed with a fever, and they told him about her at once (*euthys*)." No time to waste now: Jesus operates on the front lines of God's restorative realm, providing urgent care for the weak and wounded.

The house Jesus enters belongs to Simon and Andrew. Living with extended family, like Simon's mother-in-law, was the norm in this culture. Although Jesus will spark tension within his own family and hometown

(3:19b-21; 6:1-6) and embrace a spiritual family beyond natural kin (3:31-35), he still values family ties. Charity begins at home or at least doesn't neglect one's own.

Having a fever requiring bed rest may seem minor compared with being seized by a vicious spirit. But in the ancient world, long before thermometers and aspirin, fever was a serious and mysterious condition: "For most of human history, an unusually high body temperature was a sign of the supernatural. Fevers were sinister but common, unnatural but real. And without a theoretical underpinning by which to understand them, fevers long seemed to be as nebulous as they were deadly" (LaFrance 2015). Rome had multiple temples dedicated to the goddess of Fever (Febris), where sufferers sought relief from spiked temperatures and purchased amulets to ward off feverish attacks (Tavenner 1918, 100–101; Valerius Maximus, *Memorable Doings and Sayings* 2.5.6).

As Jesus proved himself to be the liberating Holy One of God in the synagogue, he now shows himself to be the divine healer in Simon and Andrew's home. There is no need, however, for shrines or statues dedicated to him or charms or incantations invoking his name. Just as Jesus's word silenced and evicted the man's "unclean" spirit, now his hand lifts Simon's mother-in-law from her bed, relieves her fever, and restores her ability to work.

The note that, once free from her fever, "she began to serve (*diēkonei*) them" (1:31) may seem rather insensitive, if not oppressive. The woman just got out of her sickbed! Yet while reflecting women's customary domestic service roles in this society of cooking, catering, cleaning, and childcare, such "diaconal" work is by no means relegated to women alone in Jesus's movement. Indeed, it is the work of angels, as we've already seen (1:13), and later Jesus commends servant (*diak-*) ministry as the "greatest" work for all disciples—including the twelve male apostles (9:34-35)—under *his* leadership: "For the Son of Man came not to be served (*diakonēthēnai*) but to serve (*diakonēsai*)" (10:45).

Skin-diseased man (1:40-45)

In the biblical world, the condition commonly labeled "leprosy" referred to a wide range of scaly, ulcerous skin disorders (and even moldy walls in houses) (Lev 14:34-53), not only to extreme cases known as "Hansen's disease," like those Mother Teresa tended to in Kolkata. Even this latter malady is easily treatable through modern medicine, and though transmittable in droplets via an infected person's cough or sneeze, it is not communicated by touch (see CDC website). Levitical law pertaining to "leprosy" applied to a wide range of "unclean," scaly, psoriatic conditions (including moldy "diseases" in houses). Inspection of these conditions, including certification of their "cleansing" was undertaken by priestly officials, not physicians (Leviticus 13–14). A person afflicted with "leprosy" was quarantined—"he shall live alone; his dwelling shall be outside the camp" (13:46) until pronounced fit by the priests for reassimilation. The "camp," however, designated the traveling tent community in the desert en route to the promised land. It's unclear to what extent isolating "leprous" individuals occurred in more settled village and urban environments (Shinall 2018). In any case, the priests proclaimed physical and societal *wholeness* (holiness), not forgiveness of sins (atonement) (see Baden and Moss 2011; Pilch 1981).

Moreover, the notion of "clean/cleansed" skin as "whole/healed" skin has less to do with hygiene per se, with washing away dirt and grime, than with maintaining bodily wellness, outside and inside. It's more about border security. Externally, it's like our using sunscreen to block ultraviolet rays; internally, it reflects the natural instinct to stanch the outflow of blood. We humans cannot escape our skins, like snakes; we all have skin in the game of life. As Stanford professor of bioengineering and psychiatry Karl Deisseroth succinctly states, "We sense and define the borders of ourselves with skin. . . . Skin is where we are vulnerable" (2021, 108; cf. 99–121).

When a man with "leprosy" approached Jesus and begged him to "make me clean," Jesus "stretched out his hand and touched him," and "immediately (*euthys*) . . . made [him] clean" (Mark 1:40-42). Although he has no social connection with this man, as he did with Simon's mother-in-law, Jesus extends the same healing touch. But unlike the woman cured of fever, this "cleansed" man is not ready to resume his place in society until an authorized priest says so. Since Jesus is not a priest, he dispatches the man to "show yourself to the priest" (1:43-44). Jesus fully respects Torah purity regulations.

Although uttering no word about repentance or judgment (as the exceptional cases of Miriam [Num 12:10-15] and Gehazi [2 Kgs 5:25-27] elicit), Jesus does not speak softly and tenderly to this man. Jesus sends him to the priest in a huff, "sternly warning" (*embrimēsamenos*) him to "[go] away" (*exebalen*) "at once" (*euthys*) (1:43). The two verbs suggest that Jesus barks, even *snorts*, this "Get out!" command, as if casting out a demon (1:34, 39). Jesus then tacks on a strict gag order to "say nothing to anyone" en route to the priest, which the man violates in his exuberance to "spread the word" of his miraculous cure (1:44-45).

What has gotten under *Jesus's* skin in this scene? (Spencer 2014). To get the full picture of Jesus's irritation, we return to his initial emotional response in 1:41. A quick survey of modern versions, however, reveals a stunning discrepancy. On the one hand, the NRSV says that Jesus was "moved with pity," similar to the NASB's "moved with compassion." But on the other hand, newer versions read "Jesus was indignant" (NIV) or "incensed" (CEB). Having pity/compassion and being indignant/incensed are polar opposite emotions. What gives here? Early Greek manuscripts attest to both readings, leaving textual scholars to determine which variant is more likely the original.

This decision may seem obvious. Surely Jesus was moved with compassion toward the skin-diseased man before healing him. Healing in anger seems unnatural, nonsensical. Yet a core principle of textual criticism stipulates that the *more difficult reading* is likelier to be original; that is, a scribe copying a manuscript would be more inclined to change an awkward reading to a smoother one than the other way around (Metzger and Ehrman 2005, 313–14). In the present text, while we can easily imagine a scribe altering the "indignant/incensed" term he discovered in a manuscript, a deliberate change from "pity/compassion" *to* "indignant/incense" is hard to explain. Accordingly, more recent scholarship has opted for the *harder* reading revealing Jesus's *angry* first response (Ehrman 2003; Spencer 2014, 107–109).

While this vehement response fits with Jesus's stern dealings with the "leper" after his "cleansing," it still begs the question of *why* Jesus seems to be in such a bad mood, especially since he promptly restores the man to health. We may assume a *righteous* indignation on Jesus's part, but for what reason? Proposed explanations include that (1) Jesus is angry at the disease, not the man himself; (2) he's upset that the man has come too close, not maintaining required social distance in seeking Jesus's aid (see Luke 17:12-13); or (3) he already anticipates that the man will broadcast his cure against Jesus's command to keep quiet. I suggest another view, however (Spencer 2014), more directly anchored in the exchange between the man and Jesus, focused on Jesus's *will* or on what Matthew Thiessen calls the "motif of desire" (2020, 64; cf. 59–60, 63).

Although the psoriatic man does not intend to antagonize Jesus, his conditional statement—"*If you want* (*thelēs*), you can make me clean" (CEB)—does exactly that, as Jesus replies indignantly, "*I do want to* (*thelō*). Be clean" (1:40-41, CEB). As we will see, Jesus confronts all kinds of opposition with calm and composure. But one thing he will not tolerate is any questioning of his *indomitable will to foster flourishing life*. "Of course I want to help you! That's the whole thrust of what I came to do!" Jesus's will to power ("you can make me clean" = "you have the power [*dynasai*] to make me clean") operates solely to serve his will to promote fullness of life. In purity terms, "Jesus *desires* to rid people of what causes their ritual impurity.... Jesus is involved in a powerful purification mission" (Thiessen 2020, 63–64 [emphasis original])—reinforcing the ritual-legal system, not repudiating it.

Getting Away (1:32-39)

Preceding this emotionally stirring "cleansing" episode and following the healing of Simon's febrile mother-in-law is an interlude reporting Jesus's attempt at a private retreat amid his expanding public ministry (1:32-39). The three individual cases of deliverance exemplify Jesus's widespread mission extending into the night and across Galilee, "cur[ing] many who were sick with various diseases and cast[ing] out many demons" (1:34; cf. 1:39). But it first appears that Jesus may never get out of Simon's house, as "the whole city" presses on the doorstep into the evening, bringing infirm and infected people for Jesus to heal (1:32-33). Only during an early morning lull, "while it was still very dark," can he escape to a "deserted place" (1:35).

But why does he want to get away, given his driving, life-restoring purpose? Mark reports that Jesus heads to an isolated spot to *pray* (1:35). He balances his public action with private reflection, his ministration with contemplation. We're not told what he prays, but we may assume a close connection with his work. As powerful and perceptive as he is, the resources of Jesus Christ the Son of God (1:1) are not limitless: as a human being, he needs renewed strength and continued guidance to fulfill his Father's will. This will not be the last time he seeks quiet moments with God away from the madding crowd—vital breaks from his breakneck mission (3:7-19; 6:30-31; 7:24; 9:2; 14:32).

Yet more often than not, other people break into Jesus's break time. Here Simon and associates track him down to inform him that "everyone is searching for you" (1:37). It won't be long before the crowds find him and press him for further ministry. But again, isn't this what Jesus wants, for people to seek and find the kingdom of God he embodies? Yes and no: yes, he graciously welcomes and serves needy persons who come to him (1:32-34; 6:33-44, 53-56; 8:1-10; 10:13-16); and no, he also shies away from the imposing throng. He's no publicity hound or self-promoting campaigner and even shows ambivalence about getting the word out: spreading the gospel wherever he can, including moving on "to the neighboring towns, so that I may proclaim the message there also" (1:38), yet also trying to silence others' witness about him. Although muzzling demons is understandable, given their sinister nature (1:25, 34), ordering the cured "leper" to "say nothing to anyone" remains curious, and not simply because the man can't hold his tongue about his wonderful experience (1:44-45). Who can blame him? And why wouldn't Jesus want him to testify openly?

Something more seems at stake than Jesus's desire for rest and renewal, as legitimate as that may be. We begin to sense concern on Jesus's part about being known mainly as a miracle worker, a superhero Messiah people seek to cure all their ills, without embracing the full framework of his mission. Other so-called miracle workers and magic men preyed on desperate people, exploiting them for their own social and financial profit (Acts 8:9-11, 18-24; 13:6-8; 16:16-19; 19:11-20; Spencer 1992, 92–103). Along with never charging for his therapeutic services, Mark's Jesus forges a mission of holistic service to God and humanity grounded in self-giving rather than self-gain.

Forgiving Sin (2:1-17)

Jesus's jam-packed first day of ministry did not focus on sin. Remember that "cleansing" the demon-possessed and skin-diseased persons had nothing to do with washing away their sins. But Mark's Jesus is well aware of humanity's sin problem. Revisiting "Capernaum after some days" (2:1), he addresses the issue of sin and sinners in two dramatic scenes: one featuring a paralyzed man whom Jesus heals; the other a tax collector whom Jesus calls. Various elements link these "sin" scenes together.

	Healing a Paralyzed Man (2:1-12)	**Calling a Tax Collector (2:13-17)**
Setting	"At home" in Capernaum with "many gathered around" to hear Jesus teach	"Beside the sea" and in Levi's home with "many" dinner guests
Sin Factor	"Son/Child, your sins are forgiven"	"I have come to call not the righteous but sinners"
Friends	Four attendants who bring the paralyzed man to Jesus	Fellow tax collectors and sinners
Antagonists	A group of scribes	Scribes and Pharisees
Point of Contention	Jesus's claim to forgive sins	Jesus's habit of eating with sinners
Movements	Carrying, lowering, lying, standing up, sitting	Walking along, sitting, getting up, following, reclining at table

Both incidents spotlight Jesus's ministry in *homes*, although the second one begins on the lakeshore, where Jesus calls another disciple, Levi the tax collector, who then hosts Jesus in his house. The home venue recalls the site of

Jesus's healing of Simon's mother-in-law (1:29-31). When Jesus is now said to be "at home" or to have "come home" (2:1 NIV), he seems to be at Simon and Andrew's Capernaum residence. Yet he is scarcely locked in there, and he hangs no shingle outside, as if establishing a medical office. He remains on the move house to house, village to village, inside and outside, in populated and deserted areas—thereby illustrating an important principle about God's realm. As Crossan and Reed state,

> To settle down at Capernaum and let all come to [Jesus] is against the geography of the Kingdom of God. . . . Peter's . . . house . . . could not be his "home base" as if the Kingdom of God could, like the kingdoms of Caesar Augustus at Rome, of Herod the Great at Caesarea, or of Herod Antipas at Sepphoris and then Tiberias, have a dominant center, a controlling place, a local habitation and a name. (2001, 95)

Jesus aims to challenge oppressive forms of domination by bringing God's liberating, love-lifting power to all God's people (see Wink 1998, 1–12; Bruteau 2005).

Concerning the sin factor, Jesus brings *forgiveness*, in tandem with physical healing, to the paralyzed man and has *fellowship* with Levi and fellow tax collectors labeled "sinners." Before investigating each incident, we need a basic understanding of the biblical concept of "sin." In an incisive study, Gary Anderson distills three main metaphors in the Hebrew Bible: sin as (1) weight, (2) debt, and (3) dirt. Accordingly, alleviating sin involves (1) carrying away the weight or burden of sin; (2) forgiving, remitting, or redeeming the debt of sin that binds (unpaid financial debt in the ancient world was a type of enslavement, resulting in imprisonment); and (3) wiping or washing away the taint of sin. Although the third image holds most sway in Christian thought and practice, probably due to the central baptism ritual, it is the least prominent image in the Hebrew Bible and not even the most salient one in the New Testament.

Sin as *weight* predominates in the Hebrew Bible in polar fashion: on the one end, registering the onerous effects of sin weighing down the sinner with the burden of guilt ("Anyone who curses God shall *bear* the sin," Lev 24:15; "Ah, sinful nation, people *laden* with iniquity," Isa 1:4); on the other end, depicting God's gracious removal of sin's pressure and penalty by lifting it off and bearing it away. The Day of Atonement enacts the full drama, as the high priest symbolically transfers the sins of the people to the head of a live goat, the scapegoat, sent out to the desert and set free: "The goat shall *bear on itself* all their iniquities to a barren region; and the goat shall be set free in the wilderness" (Lev 16:22) (Anderson 2009, 15–26).

Although picturing sin as heavy weight, both borne by sinners and carried away by God through God's sin-bearing, suffering servant (Isa 53:4-7), carries over into the New Testament (Heb 12:1-4; 1 Pet 2:24-25), the main sin image shifts to *debt*, as in the Lord's Prayer: "Forgive us our debts, as we also have forgiven our debtors" (Matt 6:12; cf. Luke 11:4). Multiple parables of Jesus also focus on forgiveness and ethical responsibility through various scenarios of debt management (Matt 18:23-35; Luke 7:41-43; 15:11-32; 16:1-13; Spencer 2019, 399–401).

Healing a paralyzed man (2:1-12)
Jesus's first response again takes us by surprise: "Son, your sins are forgiven" (Mark 2:5). Why would he make this statement in this situation? The man has come to Jesus, carried by others, seeking release from his disability, not from his iniquity, and Jesus makes no causal connection between his paralysis and sin. Perhaps Mark's Jesus aims to draw a subtle, symbolic (not causal) link between the paralyzed man's weighed-down physical disability which he needs lifted and the common heavy weight of sin which drags human beings down, necessitating the release of forgiveness. Fortunately, he has four extraordinary friends who not only haul him to the packed house where Jesus teaches but hoist him to the rooftop, dig through the covering, and lower him into the room so that Jesus might raise him up (2:2-4).

Such effort represents a remarkable display of *faith* (*pistis*)—the first explicit example of faith in Mark—which Jesus *sees*, prompting his pronouncement of forgiveness (2:5). This inaugural case of *believing* (*pisteuō*) the good news (see 1:15) evinces faith in action, a demonstrable, determined turn to Jesus for relief and restoration. Coming through the ceiling—literally, "unroofing the roof"—clawing through wooden crossbeams overlaid with mud and thatch, would have been "a major demolition job" (France 2002, 123). But this faith-filled, burden-bearing work ultimately allowed the man to stand up, take up his cot, and walk out of the house under his own weight (2:12)!

While a tacit connection with sin-as-weight might explain part of Jesus's sin statement, he gives a more direct reason to the scribes (Jewish legal experts) in the audience, who gasp at his audacious claim to forgive sins. In their minds, if anyone is guilty of sin, it's Jesus, and gross sin at that—the sin of "blasphemy" for usurping God's exclusive prerogative to forgive sins. No one "can forgive sins but God alone" (2:7)—an undisputed tenet of biblical theology, which Jesus knows full well and agrees with (Exod 34:6-7, echoed in Num 14:18; Neh 9:17; Ps 103:8-13; Joel 2:13; Jonah 4:2). Jesus uses this public spectacle, literally lifting the roof off the place and raising up a bedridden man, to make a provocative claim of intimate alliance with the forgiving God. Jesus speaks directly *for God*, not only as healing prophet but also as forgiving priest, his non-priestly lineage notwithstanding.

Sensing the scribes' shock at his initial statement, Jesus clarifies his intention but only after raising the stakes with a rhetorical question: "Which is easier, to say to the paralytic, 'Your sins are forgiven,' or to say, 'Stand up and take your mat and walk'?" (2:9). He aims to restore the man to health—his primary need, which Jesus does not neglect. He aims to heal as well as forgive—neither of which is easy! Both are *hard work* (the word for "easy" [*eukopos*] is a compound of "good" [*eu*] + "hard work [*kopos*])—yea, impossible work for ordinary mortals. They are constitutive of the very work of God the Creator and Redeemer, who alone can fully *reconstitute* broken bonds of fellowship severed by sin (reconciliation) and broken bodies unable to function and flourish (restoration). Mark's Jesus has already demonstrated his divine participation in the healing sphere; now he underscores his divine partnership in the forgiveness realm: "so that you may know that the Son of Man has authority on earth to forgive sins" (2:10). He not only has authority to teach students—to speak God's creative and re-creative word of life and well-being (1:22, 27)—but also has authority to lift sins.

Again, by pronouncing the paralyzed man forgiven, Jesus does not brand him as particularly sinful more than anyone else or as deserving his disability. But Jesus does present the man as an object lesson of Jesus's mission to make people *whole*, physically and spiritually, psychologically and morally. As Jesus's reputation as an exorcist and healer spreads like wildfire, against all his efforts to tamp down this celebrity (1:44-45), he stresses his companion role as forgiver and restorer.

In addition to claiming divine authority as Son of God (cf. 1:1, 11, 23), Jesus reinforces his human identity by referring to himself as *Son of Man* (2:10). This is Jesus's favorite self-designation in Mark, always voiced, however, in the third person, hinting at its other-related (not self-centered) significance (2:10, 28; 8:31; 9:12, 31; 10:33; 14:21, 41). The term for "Man" here is the generic *anthrōpos*, "person, human being," not limited to "male" (*anēr*), although Jesus is male, a "son" (*huios*). A clearer rendering of the title would be "Son of Humankind/Humanity" or "Son of a Human Being." Thus, Jesus the Son of Humankind effectively claims solidarity with all persons bearing God's image (Gen 1:26-27), all human children made a "little lower than God" in glory and dignity (Ps 8:4-5)—but also in freedom and vulnerability to sin and suffering. Mark's Jesus welcomes, forgives, and transforms sinners from below, from within the human community, fully sharing the human condition.

But the Son of Man's solidarity with humanity should not blunt his concomitant authority as God's prophetic spokesman, like Ezekiel, whom God addresses over ninety times as "son of man" (obscured as "mortal" in the NRSV) (Wink 2002, 19–34, 267–69), and as God's royal agent, in the mold of Daniel 7:13-14, sent to rescue God's beleaguered people and restore God's righteous rule on earth (Dan 7:9-27). A Jewish work around the time of Jesus, known as 1 Enoch, also envisions a heavenly Son of Man figure, but one who mainly executes violent judgment on earthly sinners without mercy or forgiveness (1 Enoch 46:1-8; 48:1-10; 62:1-16; 69:26-29) (see Collins and Collins 2008, 75–100; Bendoraitis 2018). We remain alert to how Jesus fleshes out his Son of Humankind role in Mark's story.

Calling a tax collector (2:13-17)
After dealing with the paralyzed man in a packed house, Jesus "went out again . . . walking along" the seashore, but not by himself. The crowd follows, and he continues to teach them as he walks. But he also continues to give special attention to certain individuals. Now, while passing by "one Levi, son of Alphaeus, sitting at the tax booth," Jesus summons him to "follow me"; and without hesitation, just like the four fishermen, Levi "got up and followed" (Mark 2:13-14). Again, we're struck by the temerity of Jesus's demand and the alacrity of the call-and-response action.

The action then shifts from Levi's workplace to his residence, as it did after Jesus recruited Simon and Andrew (1:16-20, 29-31). Jesus solidifies his disciples' commitment to follow him with fellowship in their homes. The first explicit "disciples" (*mathētais*) reference now occurs in a dinner party setting in Levi's house (2:15), implicitly including the four fishermen along with Levi. The term designates "one who engages in learning through instruction from another," that is, a "pupil, apprentice" (BDAG 2000, 609). Accordingly, Jesus functions as the disciples' teacher or mentor—not, however, through classroom sessions but via companionship on the road, conveying a comprehensive way of life as the curriculum. Jesus's students are about to learn a vital lesson in Levi's house.

The dinner turns out not to be a cozy master-disciple affair. Levi has invited a bunch of fellow tax collectors to meet Jesus, right in line with the original call to make his disciples "fishers of people" (1:17). Appropriate to Levi's occupation, we might say he's "collecting people." But the people he's collecting are not the most upstanding citizens in this society, so much so that Mark mentions "tax collectors and sinners" as a matched set (2:15).

What accounted for this bad reputation? As mentioned previously, toll booths were set up around the Sea of Galilee to collect various duties on goods extracted from and transported across the lake. The fees went into the coffers of Rome's local client-ruler, Herod Antipas. Thus, Jewish tax collectors like Levi were working to support the interests of exploitative foreign powers. As long as the collectors sent the required quotas to the government, they could (over)charge what they liked and pocket the difference (Carey 2009, 22–26). The system was ripe for economic fraud or, in religious terms, *sin* (cf. Luke 3:12-13; 19:1-8). Here the debt image of sin hews close to material reality: the prime temptation for tax collectors was to squeeze the people financially and burden them with heavier debt loads to imperial creditors.

These are not the kind of people a religious teacher normally seeks out; still less would we expect fishermen to embrace those who tax their catch right off the boat. But here they are: Jesus, his disciples, and tax collectors and other sinners eating together in Levi's home—*reclining together* (*synanekeinto*), as was the dining custom, on couches around the table. Such close fellowship catches the suspicious eye of the scribes again, this time allied with a group of Pharisees (see discussion on Mark 2:18–3:6), who keep monitoring Jesus's behavior. Although they ask Jesus's disciples to explain why he consorts with sinners, Jesus overhears and responds directly: "Those who are well have no need of a physician, but those who are sick; I have come to call not the righteous but sinners" (2:16-17).

Jesus again coordinates his ministries to sick and sinful people. But he now goes further with sinners, *calling* them rather than having them brought to him as the ill and disabled were (1:32; 2:3). But calling them to what? Mark leaves the call tantalizingly open-ended, to which Luke adds, "I have come to call sinners *to repentance*" (Luke 5:32). Although I think Mark implies Jesus's invitation to repentance and receiving forgiveness of sins, consonant with John's baptismal mission (Mark 1:4), the lack of explicit demand allows for Jesus's welcome of sinners and his interest in their well-being *as they are*, before any demonstrable change of heart and mind (see Sanders 1985, 200–11; 1993, 246–48). Mark's Jesus does not guard the door or reserve the table for prechecked guests. It is *through* open table-fellowship that Jesus demonstrates his concern for sinners' transformation. If anyone in the present scene is called to repent and change their attitudes, it's the judgmental religious experts!

Bending Law (2:18–3:6)

Jesus continues to spark conflict with religious-legal experts over food-related issues, though in this section their concern is not about who Jesus and his disciples eat with but rather (1) *that* they eat every day without the discipline of fasting (2:18-20) and (2) *how* and *when* they eat, or, more precisely procure food to eat on the Sabbath (2:22-28). The question of Jesus's commitment to "lawful" behavior (2:24; 3:4) comes to the fore.

Fasting (2:18-20)
The annual Day of Atonement provides a touchstone for fasting and Sabbath observance: "It is a sabbath of complete rest to you, and you shall deny yourselves; it is a statute forever" (Lev 16:31; cf. 23:32; Num 29:7). The act of "denying" or "humbling, afflicting" (*'anah*) oneself implies the practice of fasting (Ps 35:13; Isa 58:3, 5; Kaiser 1994, 1113). Devout people fasted on various special occasions to seek forgiveness of sins, guidance during times of crisis, release and comfort in seasons of mourning, and justice and mercy on behalf of the hungry and homeless (Isa 58:6-7). Some made it a regular habit, like the Pharisee in Jesus's parable who testifies to a twice-weekly fasting regimen (Luke 18:12). According to the Roman historian Suetonius, Emperor Augustus referred to the Jews' common practice of fasting, though he does so only to tout his own supposedly stricter fasting discipline: "Not even a Jew . . . fasts so scrupulously on his sabbaths as I have today" (Suetonius, *Augustus* 76). Although a few hypocrites might flaunt their fasting to boost their pious reputation (Isa 58:3-4; Matt 6:16), most Jews practiced this discipline sincerely, in compliance with biblical law.

Marking out the seventh day every week (between sunsets, Friday–Saturday) as a sacred Sabbath has long been a defining factor of Jewish life. As a time devoted to worship, fellowship, and rest from daily labors, it aligns with fundamental rhythms of creation and redemption inscribed in the Ten Commandments. As God rested on the seventh day after making the whole world, so God's people must rest every Sabbath and reflect on God's gracious blessing of life (Gen 2:1-3; Exod 20:8-11). And as God rescued the Israelites from centuries of enslavement (being worked to death), so every Sabbath they and all people and draft animals in their employ must be released from labor (Deut 5:12-15).

Despite his attendance in the synagogue (Mark 1:21; 3:1) and adherence to Levitical law pertaining to persons with "leprosy" (1:43–44), Jesus appears to be lax in his fasting and Sabbath practices in the view of some members of an influential Jewish group known as Pharisees (2:18, 24; 3:6). Although scribes and Pharisees periodically align in Mark (2:16; 7:1, 5), they remain distinct groups. Unlike the Pharisees, scribes also closely affiliate with the chief priests (8:31; 10:33; 11:18, 27; 14:1, 43, 53; 15:1, 31).

A note on the Pharisees: Before investigating Jesus's side of the fasting and Sabbath cases, it's important to represent the Pharisees and their position fairly (see Sievers and Levin 2021). Unfortunately, much Christian preaching and teaching about this group has been based on caricature, such that "pharisaical" has become synonymous with "hypocritical" (Boys 2000; Salmon 2006; Levine 2021). To be sure, some Pharisees, like some members of any religious group—including Jesus's disciples—could display hypocrisy from time to time. But overall, the Pharisees of Jesus's day commanded respect for their commitment to studying the law and prophets and seeking to apply scriptural principles to daily life. The first-century historian Josephus noted that the Pharisees, with whom he affiliated for a time, were "esteemed most skillful in the exact explanation of their laws" (*J.W.* 2.162; cf. *Life* 191; Marshall 2018, 56–58). And like Jesus, they conducted their teaching and reforming work as lay volunteers, not as professional clergy (priests). The Pharisees had much in common with Jesus, which partly explains why they watch him so closely in Mark's story (3:2).

The conflict between Jesus and the Pharisees in Mark largely represents spirited intramural, in-house debate over scriptural interpretation and application, which both Jesus and the Pharisees cared deeply about. Precisely because of such fervent common concerns, sparks could fly; there's no feud like a family feud. We've already seen that Jesus's table-fellowship with sinners was a sticking point with some Pharisees. It's not that the Pharisees wanted nothing to do with sinners and wished God would eliminate them. They wanted sinners to repent and be forgiven as much as Jesus did, but they advocated a different mission strategy. The Pharisees took pains to model God's righteous standards in everyday life, especially within their homes, treating them virtually as temples and their tables as altars, not for literal sacrifice but for offering themselves to God as "living, holy sacrifices" (Rom 12:1), as Paul—"a Pharisee" (Phil 3:5)—says (Murphy 2002, 233–37; Neusner 1984, 58; 1988, 32–35). Sinners must first seek God's forgiveness and change their ways before communing around the "pure" table—a policy in line with John the Baptist's prerequisites for baptism (Mark 1:4-5; cf. Matt 3:7-10). By contrast, Jesus the "physician" uses a welcoming table as a means of grace for sinners, rather than a conditional end goal to which sinners should aspire.

The Pharisees aimed to adapt biblical law advanced by venerated elder-teachers (rabbis) (Josephus, *Ant.* 18.12; Marshall 2018, 57). But, as later compendia of rabbinic thought (Mishnah and Talmud) demonstrate, these teachers engaged in lively debate among themselves as well as with other teachers like Jesus. For the sake of argument, Mark and the other Gospel writers tend to present a singular Pharisaic position at odds with Jesus's perspective. But they also variously hold the teachings of Jesus and the Pharisees in dynamic tension on the spectrum of "old"/traditional and "new"/progressive viewpoints, depending on the situation.

Sewing and storing (2:21-22)
Jesus was just as devoted to the "old," venerable Jewish scriptures as the Pharisees or any other Jewish teachers. His "new" message entailed reclaiming and renewing, recasting and reforming the "old" tradition—not creating a unique gospel out of whole cloth. Speaking of cloth, Jesus spins two textile analogies relevant to the present conflict: one involving sewing a new patch on an old coat; the other involving storing new wine in an old wineskin, typically fashioned from goat hides. The mix of new and old materials can be dicey: when the new patch shrinks (after washing), it "pulls away" from the old cloth "and a worse tear is made"; as new wine continues to ferment, it produces expanding gas (carbon dioxide) that bursts old, brittle containers (Mark 2:21-22).

In both examples, a thoughtless mix of old and new damages *both elements*. Jesus desires both to preserve and to revitalize the older tradition, to hold old and new together in tension, striking the right balance between shrinking and bursting, contracting and expanding. In terms of rightly applying God's written law in daily life, we must often negotiate between strict (constrictive) and more flexible (expansive) approaches, or what Matthew's Jesus images as "binding" and "loosening" by those who gather with him in his name (Matt 18:18-20; Powell 2018, 134–35).

With regard to fasting and Sabbath observance, Mark's Jesus takes a looser stance than the Pharisees, without cutting loose, however, the main scriptural line. He is by no means opposed to the discipline of fasting for followers of the Baptist and the Pharisees (Mark 2:18) or even his own disciples under normal circumstances. But these are not normal circumstances. It is *wedding season* for Jesus the "bridegroom" and his beloved "bride"-people, and weddings are times of joyous feasting, not serious fasting (Matt 22:1-10; John 2:1-11). In biblical imagery, wedding banquets symbolize the celebration and consummation of the covenantal bond of God and God's Messiah with Israel and the church (Isa 62:1-9; Matt 22:1-14; John 3:28-30; Eph 5:25-33; Rev 19:6-9). But this side of the climactic heavenly "marriage supper" (Rev 19:9), nuptial festivities don't last forever but rather give way to the mixed joys and sorrows of married life, complicated during times of separation, especially in death. Mark's Jesus discloses for the first time that in the coming days he (the bridegroom) will be "taken away" from his friends, and at such a challenging time, "then they will fast" (Mark 2:20). Church practice after Jesus's death bears out this prediction (see Acts 13:2; 14:23; and the early addition "prayer *and fasting*" to Mark 9:29; Omanson 2006, 83).

Harvesting (2:23-27)

The Pharisees in Mark become even more concerned about Jesus's apparent laxity in enforcing Sabbath regulations in two venues: grain fields (2:23-27) and the synagogue (3:1-6). While the Hebrew Bible clearly establishes the core principle of rest and refraining from hard labor on the Sabbath, it provides no catalogue of specific prohibited activities. Various lists appear in later Jewish writings reflecting ongoing debate (see Jubilees 2:29; 50:6-13; Damascus Document 10:14–11:18; m. Shabbat 7:2). In one place the Mishnah admits, "The rules about the Sabbath . . . are like mountains hanging on a hair, for [teaching of] Scripture [thereon] is scanty and the rules many" (m. Hagigah 1:8). In other words, interpreters of Sabbath law walk a thin tightrope.

There was consensus, however, regarding stoppage of basic plowing and reaping fieldwork on the Sabbath (Exod 34:21; m. Shabbat 7:2). Related prohibitions of handling and consuming food hark back to Israel's wilderness era when God instructed the people to gather a double batch of manna the day before the Sabbath (Exod 16:5, 22-30). For example, the sectarian wilderness community at Qumran stipulated, "No man shall eat on the Sabbath day except that which is already prepared. He shall eat nothing lying in the fields" (Damascus Document 10:20-21). The Sabbath was not typically a day for fasting, however, as some outsiders, critical of strange Jewish practices, claimed (see Feldman 1993, 161–67). Some Jewish sources *forbad* fasting on the Sabbath (Jdt 8:6; Jubilees 50:12; Cohn-Sherbok 1979, 35)—a time to enjoy, not procure and prepare, God's gracious bounty with thanksgiving.

One Sabbath, Jesus's disciples walk a fine line through some fields on the edge of unlawful behavior, as they "pluck heads of grain" (Mark 2:23). Some Pharisees, who oddly notice this activity (what are they doing in the fields on the Sabbath?), believe Jesus's followers have crossed the line and demand that he explain why he allows such illicit conduct (apparently Jesus himself is not picking grain) (2:24). Although the Pharisees level no specific charge against the disciples, presumably "plucking" equates with *reaping*; moreover, they doubtless *eat* some of this "harvest" as they proceed through the field. In our Western preoccupation with private property, we might add trespassing and stealing to the disciples' offenses. But biblical law required farmers to leave some uncollected crops at the borders of their fields for the itinerant poor to glean (Lev 19:9-10; 23:22; Deut 24:19-22; cf. Ruth 2:1-23). The problem in Mark's story from the Pharisees' perspective is not what Jesus's disciples do but *when* they do it—on the Sabbath. And their concern is not unreasonable.

So what does Jesus have to say about his followers' behavior under his mentorship? He draws on two sources of authority: *scriptural* and *personal*. Jesus shares with the Pharisees a commitment to the biblical law and prophets. Here he interprets Scripture by Scripture, appealing to an example from the life of David in 1 Samuel (part of the "former prophets") to clarify Sabbath law. He pitches his argument to the Pharisees' wheelhouse: "Have you never read?" (Mark 2:25). They have, but have they fully grasped what they've read?

The case in 1 Samuel 21:1-6 features David's entreating the priest at Nob, named Ahimelech (Mark 2:26 misidentifies him as Abiathar, Ahimelech's son [see Sam 21:1-2; 22:20]), to provide bread for David's soldiers The priest demurred at first because the only bread available was "holy bread," "the bread of the Presence," reserved exclusively for the priests. Although the Samuel story does not mention the Sabbath, Leviticus stipulates that "every sabbath day Aaron [the first high priest] shall set [twelve loaves] . . . before the LORD regularly as a commitment of the people of Israel, as a covenant forever" (Lev 24:8; cf. 24:5-9). David and his men had no right under normal circumstances to receive this bread on the Sabbath or any other day. But again, these were not normal circumstances as David, God's king-elect (1 Sam 16:1-13), was on a military defense "expedition" against the current king Saul who sought David's life. When the priest of Nob received assurance that David's troops had remained celibate during their mission, he gave David the sacred loaves (21:5-6).

This is an exceptional case, to be sure, but Jesus and his followers are also engaged in a critical kingdom mission, though not a military one. The analogy also falters in that Jesus's disciples have received no priestly authorization. But Jesus's main point is that, like David's soldiers, Jesus's men have "*need (chreian*) of food on the Sabbath (Mark 2:25; Matt 12:3// Luke 6:3 omit the "need" factor) to carry out their God-ordained work, which continues on the Sabbath, as does God's redemptive work (see John 5:16-18; 9:4) and priests' ritual work (see Num 28:9-10; Matt 12:5). What better day to meet basic, life-sustaining human needs than the Sabbath commemorating the goodness and wholeness of God's creation? Such is the "intent" of Sabbath law reformulated by Jesus: "The sabbath was made for humankind (*anthrōpon*), and not humankind (*anthrōpos*) for the sabbath" (Mark 2:27; Robbins 1989, 128; Spencer 2010b, 368–74).

Jesus further buttresses this claim with another appeal to his personal, God-given authority as the Son of Humankind (*anthrōpou*), sent to promote the rule of God on earth and meet the needs of God's people: "So the Son of Man (*anthrōpou*) is lord even of the sabbath" (2:28). Jesus has the right and responsibility to rule the Sabbath *for* the benefit of humanity (and all creation).

Mark's Gospel builds a powerful portrait of Jesus Son of God and Son of Man with wide-ranging authority to cast out demons, heal diseases, forgive sins, suspend fasting duties, and permit limited reaping and eating on the Sabbath. As Jesus's authority mounts, it increasingly grates against the traditions of some religious legal scholars like the Pharisees, and it comes to a breaking point with another healing act Jesus performs on the Sabbath.

Healing (3:1-6)

Jesus now gets fed up with these the present group of wary Pharisees, directing anger and grief (aggravation) against their "hardness of heart" (3:5); in turn, they ramp up their resistance to Jesus, plotting with some Herodians (political allies of Herod Antipas) "how to destroy him" (3:6).

Why does this particular Sabbath healing spike the emotional temperature to a fevered pitch? Jesus's previous Sabbath work of deliverance sparked general audience amazement, not anger (1:27). Now, however, the Pharisees and Jesus sharpen their focuses, and neither party likes what they *see*. The already suspicious Pharisees are now "watching Jesus closely (*paretēroun*)" (CEB; cf. NAB) to see if he will cure a man with a "withered hand" on the Sabbath and thus publicly taint Jesus as lax Sabbath keeper (3:2). For his part, as if sensing the Pharisees' wary eyes upon him, Jesus deliberately makes a scene, calling the disabled man to "come forward," literally "in the middle" (*eis to meson*), so the whole assembly might *see* him. The healing incidents thus far have been initiated by the afflicted subjects (1:23-24, 40) or their family or friends (1:30; 2:3-5). Now Jesus takes full charge from the start.

After summoning the man, Jesus turns the tables on the Pharisees, challenging *them* about Sabbath law: "Is it lawful to do good or to do harm on the sabbath, to save life or to kill?" (3:3; cf. 2:24) Put this way, there is only one obvious response, which the Pharisees opt not to voice for obvious reasons; so "they were silent" (3:4). Then Jesus *looks around (periblepō)*, as he often does in this Gospel, taking the measure of an audience before making a serious point or a bold move (3:5, 34; 5:32; 11:23; 12:11). He doesn't meet the Pharisees' gaze as much as melts it "with *anger (orgēs)*" mixed with *anguish* or painful grief (*lypē*) at "their hardness of heart" (3:5). Anthropologists and psychologists observe that emotion registers on people's faces in remarkably common expressions across cultures (Darwin 2009 [1872]; Ekman 2007; Keltner 2009, 16–51). We quickly "read" basic emotions like anger and grief in others' faces before they say a word. Although Mark never describes

Jesus's face, we can imagine the Pharisees seeing and feeling the force of his emotional response.

Scientists and philosophers also study how emotions *motivate* behavior or "action tendencies" (Frijda 1986, 69–93, 231–41; 1988, 351; Lazarus 1991, 92–112) to realize important goals, *what matters most* to a person (Roberts 2003, 60–79; 2007, 11, 14). Directly out of his anger and grief, Mark's Jesus moves to act, enjoining the man to stretch out his hand, which then becomes "restored" (3:5). Here we confront another surprising instance of Jesus's anger (again omitted in parallel passages, Matt 12:12-13//Luke 12:9-10). In contrast, however, with the "leper" case (1:41), here Jesus's anger is not directed at the infirm man but at the religious teachers. Nonetheless, the thrust of the anger serves a similar aim, namely, to reinforce Jesus's driving purpose to restore flourishing life, to "do good," to "save life" (Mark 3:4). The added grief component suggests disappointment and aggravation over what Jesus perceives as these Pharisees' emotionally stunted view of Sabbath practice. As keen students of God's law, they should know its grounding in *love* (Levenson 2016).

Again, however, in our sympathy with Jesus's perspective, we should not resort to derisive caricature of the Pharisees as mean-spirited legalists who cared nothing for disabled persons. Although Mark does not elaborate their position in the present case, they likely advocate refraining from non-emergency medical work on the Sabbath. If someone's life were endangered on the Sabbath, even that of an animal fallen into a pit or drowning in a well (see Deut 22:4; Matt 12:11-12; Luke 14:5), no Pharisee would object to providing immediate life-saving aid. But the man with the withered hand is not in such dire straits. Among other debilitated persons Jesus has helped—the demon-possessed, fever-stricken, skin-diseased, and paralyzed—the man with a disabled hand seems in the least danger of losing his life. He could easily wait one more day for healing.

But Jesus sees no good reason to make the man wait a moment longer. What better day than the Sabbath, set aside to celebrate the goodness of God's whole creation, to "do good" and "save life," to make one of God's people whole? If this is a "looser" interpretation of Sabbath tradition, so be it; in this case the spirit of the law, like the spirits of new wine, needs room to breathe fresh life into a "dried up" (*xēros*) appendage. Apart from providing clinical care, Jesus opens up fresh occupational opportunity for the man. When the new day dawns, he will be able to use his restored hand for meaningful work, which humans undertake the other six days of the week (see Gen 2:15; Exod 20:9; Deut 5:13). One early tradition indicates that the man was a *stonemason* by trade (Gospel of the Nazarenes 4; Miller 1994,

444). Irrespective of his particular occupation, it is likely that he, like most people in the ancient world, depended on manual labor.

Getting Away (Again) (3:7-19a)

As in 1:32-39, Jesus again seeks respite from the throng of desperate people clamoring for healing (1:32-35; 3:7-10) and silences the demons/unclean spirits hounding his steps and harassing the people (1:34; 3:11-12). In the present situation, Jesus has the added motivation of getting away from Pharisees and Herodians aiming to silence him (3:6-7)! Moreover, whereas Jesus earlier retreated to the desert by himself, now he heads *with his disciples* to the *lakeshore*, with plans of boarding a boat (3:7, 9). But yet again the crowds thwart his escape. By now the seekers have swelled into "a great multitude" not only from Galilee but also "from Judea, Jerusalem, Idumea [further south], beyond the Jordan [eastward], and the region around Tyre and Sidon [northwest into Phoenicia]" (3:7-8). However much Jesus tries to shun the spotlight and orders others "not to make him known" (3:12), his popularity burgeons.

Apparently abandoning hope of sailing away in peace, Jesus heads for the hills, climbing a nearby *mountain* and calling a select group of disciples (3:13). This summons is significant. Though Jesus already recruited four fishermen and one tax collector beside the Sea of Galilee (1:16-20; 2:13-14), now, on the mountain—a common biblical site of divine encounter—he formalizes their relationship with him and adds seven others to comprise a cadre of *twelve* disciples, "whom he also named *apostles*" (3:14). Though some Greek manuscripts omit this "apostles" (*apostoloi*) designation, its basic meaning of "sent ones" is conveyed in Jesus's choosing these twelve "to be sent out (*apostellē*) to proclaim the message, and to have authority to cast out demons" (3:14-15). This "apostolic" commission to preach the word and free the bound clarifies the enigmatic call to "fish for people" (1:17). Every step of the way, however, these apostles must remain "with him" (3:14), that is, with Jesus, not necessarily in physical proximity but always in faithful loyalty to him and his example of service (Johnson 2010, 41).

Why does Jesus choose *twelve* emissaries? No doubt he selects this number to parallel the twelve clans of ancient Israel descended from the twelve sons of Jacob/Israel. Jesus thus aims with his apostolic representatives to release "all Israel" (Rom 11:26), all God's people, from oppressive forces and restore them to wholeness. But why enlist *these* twelve men in this significant project? These are hardly A-list exemplars. Nothing commends them for special service. The same could be said for the eponymous Israel, first named "Jacob," meaning "heel-grabber, supplanter," which he amply lived up to before his transformative wrestling match with God (Gen 32:24-32). God chooses, appoints, elects by love and grace, not by lot or merit (Deut 7:7-8).

Mark's list of the twelve apostles begins with the four fishermen in an order that splits brothers Simon and Andrew: Simon, James and John, Andrew (3:16-18). Placing Simon and the two sons of Zebedee at the top foreshadows their importance as Jesus's closest confidants (5:37; 9:2; 14:33). Otherwise, the list includes brief but notable elaborations on several apostles' names.

- Simon, to whom he gave the name *Peter* (*Petros*). This nickname, suggesting "Rock/Rocky" (*petra*), will be his primary name in the rest of the story, reinforcing his first and foundational ("rock") position among Jesus's apostles (cf. Matt 16:18). It remains to be seen how Peter plays out this leading role in Mark.
- James and John, to whom he gave the name *Boanerges*, that is, *Sons of Thunder*. Perhaps this nickname reflects their volatile personalities, as evidenced in their proposal to call down heavenly fire on an inhospitable Samaritan village in Luke 9:54. In their only appearance in Mark apart from other disciples, James and John brazenly petition Jesus for honored places on his right and left sides (10:35-41).
- Another "James," listed in ninth place, is called *the son of Alphaeus* (3:18). Apart from distinguishing him from James the son of Zebedee, this filial note associates this James with *Levi*, also called "son of Alphaeus" (2:14).
- Simon the *Cananaean*, in the eleventh slot, distinguishes this Simon from Simon Peter. "Cananaean" seems to transliterate an Aramaic word denoting religious and/or political "zeal" (cf. "Simon the Zealot" in Luke 6:15; Acts 1:13; Donahue and Harrington 2002, 125; Yieh 2009, 260). Three or four decades after Jesus's ministry, around the time Mark's Gospel was written, a group of Jewish freedom fighters loosely known as "Zealots" revolted against Roman rule in the First Jewish War (66–70 CE).
- Judas *Iscariot* is listed last because of his well-known act of betraying Jesus to the authorities (Mark 14:10, 43-46). The meaning of "Iscariot" remains uncertain. The most plausible explanations are geographical, designating a "man from Kerioth" (Josh 15:25), or reputational, reinforcing his betrayer role (Hebrew *sakar* means "deliver/hand over") (Paffenroth 2001, 4–6; Donahue and Harrington 2002, 125) and associating him with those plotting against Jesus, like the Pharisees and Herodians in Mark 3:6 (Heil 1992, 85).

Cleaning House (3:19b-35)

This unit featuring Jesus's works advancing God's liberating, life-giving rule amid resistance from life-stifling forces concludes with a tense encounter between Jesus and the scribes over his exorcising mission (3:22-30). Mark frames this clash, however, with a report of Jesus's conflict with an unexpected group: his "family" (3:21), specifically his "mother . . . brothers and sisters" (3:31-32). More accurately, Mark *splits* the account of family tension and *splices* Jesus's exchange with the scribes in between, creating a sandwich structure, more formally called "intercalation." The family scene is introduced but not resolved until after the scribal dispute.

Sandwich #1
A Family Conflict (Introduced) (3:19b-21)
  B Scribal Controversy (3:22-30)
A Family Conflict (Concluded) (3:31-35)

This marks the first of six "sandwiches" in this Gospel (also 5:21-43; 6:6b-30; 11:12-25; 14:1-11; 15:40–16:8), representing a major literary pattern. Its effects are threefold:

1. *Interruption*: slowing down the story's rapid tempo by breaking up the flow of one event with another; when the initial event is resumed, the reader must pause, look back, and pick up the first thread.

2. *Intensification*: spiking the suspense of the narrative by breaking off the first event and leaving its resolution hanging until later.

3. *Integration*: spurring the reader to correlate the two distinct events, to probe how they mutually interpret one another through key words and common themes.

In the present case, the language of "house" (*oikos*) forms the main connection, used in three ways: (1) *physical residence*: "Then he went home" (3:19b), or more literally, "into a house (*oikon*)," presumably Simon and Andrew's place in Capernaum (see 1:29); (2) *familial relationships*: *oikos* also means "household"; and (3) *political realms*: dynastic "houses" or "kingdoms" of powerful rulers (3:24-27). The axiom Jesus states, "A house divided against itself cannot stand" (3:25), establishes the central theme of this "sandwich." In restoring God's kingdom—God's house/household—Jesus disrupts both the house of Satan (3:26) and his natural household in different ways. The effects of world-shaking (apocalyptic) war rip through the home front as surely as the battlefield.

Family conflict (introduced) (3:19b-21)
Again a crowd throngs to Jesus and his disciples, pressing in and around the house "so that they could not even eat" (3:20). So much for the mountain retreat. For the first time we meet Jesus's "family" or "relatives" (NAB) gathering with the crowd. They've come from Nazareth (see 1:9) to Capernaum to see the popular Jesus, but not to praise him. They're downright embarrassed (shamed) by him because of the report going around that "he has gone out of his mind" (*exestē*) (3:21). This term (*existēmi*) earlier described the audience's mind-blown amazement at Jesus's healing of the paralyzed man (2:12; cf. 5:42; 6:51); here, however, it refers to Jesus's own supposed out-of-mind state in a bad, crazy sense, having "lost his senses" (NASB), "standing outside" (*ex* + *histēmi*) or "beside himself" (KJV), his sane self, that is. Insanity was commonly attributed to demonic possession in the ancient world (see John 8:48; 10:20; Beavis 2011, 68), which is precisely how certain scribes from Jerusalem characterize Jesus in the next verse (Mark 3:22).

No wonder that his family seeks "to restrain him," or "take charge of him" (NIV), probably to haul him back to Nazareth out of the public spotlight. The verb (*krateō*) is used in relation to Mark's Jesus in two opposite ways: negatively, with Jesus as the *object* of being "arrested" or "seized" by the authorities (12:12; 14:1, 44, 46, 49; cf. 6:17; 14:51), and positively, with Jesus as the *subject* of "taking by hand" an infirm woman, girl, or boy and lifting them up to restored health (1:31; 5:41; 9:47). Shockingly, in the present scene, Jesus's family aligns with his opponents. Yet Mark maintains suspense by not reporting whether they seize Jesus or not. We must wait for the denouement of this conflict, even as tensions ramp up between Jesus and the scribes.

Scribal controversy (3:22-30)
Coming "from Jerusalem," the seat of established religious and political power vested in the scribes (and chief priests), these authorities flatly accuse Jesus of being controlled by "Beelzebul" (an obscure name for Satan possibly associated with the Canaanite storm-god Baal [Stein 1997, 45]) and deriving his power to cast out demons directly from "the ruler of the demons" (3:22). Such slander reflects common "political strategy: neutralize the opposition by identifying it with the mythic arch-demon" (Myers and Enns 2009, 46). These scribes aim to demonize Jesus, literally, and destroy his reputation.

Logic and evidence are irrelevant; for political gain they shamelessly affix the deviant Beelzebul label to Jesus and hope it sticks.

But Jesus will not let such an irrational charge stand. Why on earth would Satan undermine his own realm by driving out the demonic minions serving his diabolical "kingdom" and "house"? Any kingdom/house "divided against itself cannot stand." Vehement internal division brings the house down from within, as surely as violent attacks from outside. Jesus aims to bring down Satan's house all right—without and within—as a liberating invader, not as a satanic ally or scheming traitor. Speaking "in parables" for the first time (3:23), Jesus compares his exorcising mission to that of a robber who "enters a strong man's house," binds him up, and takes his possessions. This parabolic image not only sets the stage for Jesus's extended parable seminar in the next chapter but also, according to Elizabeth Shively, "shapes the literary and theological logic of the rest of the narrative . . . evok[ing] a realm of cosmic conflict, revealing how the world works in the presence of Jesus" (2012, 1–2).

The parabolic image bristles with irony. The Satan "strong man" (*ischyros*) figure more than meets his match in "one stronger/more powerful (*ischyroteros*)," as John the Baptist identified Jesus (1:7). By taking the battle into Satan's home territory and binding him and his evil forces, Jesus *loosens* those whom Satan has bound and brutalized. Satan's domain is thus "plundered" by Jesus, but not for material profit. The "property" (3:27) or "goods, belongings, household property" (*skeuē*; L&N 1988–1989, 1:560) Jesus confiscates are *people* abused by demonic spirit-forces and their counterparts among exploitative human rulers. Jesus reclaims these people to redeem them, to set them free for flourishing life in God's realm.

Further irony arises in the only other use of the "property/goods" term in Mark, when Jesus enters the temple in Jerusalem—God's "house"— and cleans house symbolically by upending merchants' tables and obstructing transport of "anything," that is, any "goods" (*skeuos*) through the temple precincts, which had tragically become, in Jesus's view, a "den of robbers" (11:15-17; Myers 1988, 166–67). Any domain, including the sacred temple served by scribes and priests, can take on the nefarious character of Satan's house. To (re)establish justice and righteousness, Jesus's mission entails "breaking and entering" corrupt environments and "robbing" the captives to restore their freedom. This stunning image of the "robber" Christ associates with his projected role as "thief in the night" at his climactic return to earth (see Matt 24:43; 1 Thess 5:2, 4; 2 Pet 3:10; Rev 3:3; 16:15; Myers 1988, 167; Myers and Enns 2009, 46).

In continuing to dismantle the scribes' calumny that he is in league with Satan, Jesus moves from his mini-parable about divided and plundered houses to a solemn warning ("Truly I tell you") about the so-called *unpardonable sin* (3:28-29). This short statement has caused considerable confusion among anxious Christians wondering if perchance they might commit such an unforgiveable act unawares. What exactly is this mortal sin, and why is it beyond the pale of Christ's grace? As always in biblical interpretation, context is critical. Mark's Jesus particularly addresses the scribes regarding *their* preoccupation with blasphemous conduct, forgiveness of sins, and demonic spirit-possession. Recall that in a previous Capernaum house scene, some scribes charged *Jesus* with blasphemy for claiming divine prerogative to forgive sins (2:6-7). Now they add the accusation that Jesus "has an unclean spirit" (3:30; see 3:22). So Jesus deftly turns the tables on the scribes, challenging *their blasphemy* "against the Holy Spirit" (3:29) who drives Jesus's liberating ministry; thereby *they* have effectively placed *themselves*, as long as they persist in their obstinacy, outside the bounds of God's forgiving work.

The Greek term for "forgive/forgiveness" (*aphiēmi/aphesis*) connotes "releasing" or "freeing" from indebting and enslaving conditions, such as sin or, by extension, domination by demonic and other oppressive forces. Jesus aims to enlarge the scope of God's releasing grace, not constrict it, which is why he prefaces his comment about unpardonable "eternal sin" with the sweeping affirmation that "people will be forgiven for their sins and whatever blasphemies they utter" (3:28). The current position of the scribes is an exceptional case: because they so adamantly resist the forgiving/freeing power of God's rule through Jesus Messiah in the power of the Holy Spirit, they shut themselves off from this redemptive realm.

Family conflict (concluded) (3:31-35)
From narrating this altercation between Jesus and the scribes, Mark resumes the earlier drama in which his "family"—literally, "the ones of him" (*hoi par' autou*), "his own"—attempted to "restrain" him and stop his alleged madness (3:21). Will Jesus now rip into them for accepting the scribes' charges that he's become deranged and demon-possessed? The tension becomes more acute as Mark now identifies Jesus's closest relations as "his mother and his brothers" (3:31) "and sisters" (3:32, though absent in some manuscripts). Further, Mark reports them "standing outside" (*exō stēkontes*) the house (3:31), reminiscent of both the slanderous charge that Jesus was "out of his mind" or "[standing] beside himself (*exestē*)" (3:21) and his counter pronouncement that "a house divided against itself cannot stand (*stathēnai*)" (3:25). In this destabilized situation, it may thus appear that Jesus's own household *cannot stand*. Have his mother and siblings crossed the line into blatant blasphemy?

From their "outside" position, they continue to seek Jesus, as the inside assembly informs Jesus, "your mother and your brothers and sisters are outside (*exō*) asking for you" (3:32). Notably, however, Jesus's response, while not favoring his natural kin, does not exclude or excoriate them. As he's done before in tense situations, Jesus opens with a provocative question, in this case, "Who are my mother and my brothers?" (3:34; see 2:8-9; 3:4). Then, as in the synagogue dispute with some Pharisees, he leaves the question hanging in the air, "looking [around] (*periblepsamenos*) at those who sat around him" (3:34), fixing their attention with his eyes. But instead of looking around "with anger" (3:5), he now surveys the assembly with affirmation, answering his own question: "Look (*ide*), here are my mother and my brothers!" (3:34, CEB). He implores the group inside to match his "look"—at themselves!—and to see themselves as his adoptive or "fictive" kin, his extended family beyond blood ties (deSilva 2000, 194–97).

Jesus then caps off this scene—and the entire unit from 1:21–3:35—with a pronouncement that is simultaneously more expansive and restrictive. He welcomes anyone, "whoever," to be his "brother and sister and mother" in God's household, not just those presently "inside." Yet he lays down clear terms for family membership: "Whoever *does the will of God*" belongs to Jesus's true family. Simply hearing, seeing, and being with Jesus are not sufficient; one must actively follow Jesus's pursuit of God's will (*thelēma*), choosing to walk in the God-directed way Jesus chooses (*thelō*, see 1:41).

Doing the will of God remains an ongoing challenge and opportunity for God's household members, demanding persevering obedience but also allowing for sincere repentance when veering off course. Insider/outsider boundaries are not set in concrete: insiders can fall away, and outsiders can find their way to God through Christ. Jesus's closest disciples can miss the mark, and his natural mother and siblings can change their minds. In the next unit, Jesus clarifies the ins and outs of faithful participation in God's kingdom via a series of parables.

Mark My Words: Jesus's Parables

Mark 4:1-34

Having embraced as his true family "whoever does the will of God" (3:34), Jesus continues to instruct the crowds concerning what God's will entails and how they should respond to it. As a "very large" throng gathers, Jesus moves to an outdoor venue "beside the sea," using a docked boat as a dais where he "sat" in a customary teaching posture (4:1). As well as providing a platform to address the people, the boat also positions Jesus for another getaway after his teaching session (cf. 4:35-36).

Many Things in Many Parables: For Whom and Why? (4:1-2, 10-13, 33-34)

The initial notice in 3:23 that Jesus "spoke to them in parables," followed by a brief vignette about a strong man's plundered house (3:27), sets up the extended block of Jesus's parable instruction in 4:1-34. This unit presents four closely related parables representative of the "many things" Jesus taught in "many such parables" publicly to "the whole crowd" and privately, with further explanation, to his twelve disciples (see the frame in 4:1-2, 33-34; also 4:10). For his apostles alone, Jesus explains and applies the first and longest parable in this unit involving sowing seed on various soils (4:14-20).

A major form of Jesus's communication in the Synoptic Gospels, the parables demand a certain level of higher understanding. Although simple tales drawn from everyday life, like farming—a staple occupation in this agricultural economy—the parables are significant "stories with intent" (Snodgrass 2008) to illuminate God's way, the "kingdom of God" (4:11, 26, 30). To be sure, these stories have profound implications for social, economic, political, and ecological life in the world, but only as part and parcel of the right-making rule of God. Jesus is a preacher and teacher "sowing the seed" of God's "word," not a politician or technocrat. So why then not tell it like it is in clear, straightforward language—"Thus says the Lord"? Why "tell it slant" (Peterson 2008) with these sidebar stories that might take the undiscerning hearer off the main path down a dead-end road?

Jesus appears to "throw out" (*para* + *bolē* = "throw alongside") these basic-yet-cryptic stories precisely to throw his audience off balance, to brush them back, shake them out of their ruts, keep them on high alert. If they simply want Jesus to tickle their fancies and confirm their biases, then he's happy to leave them behind in their naïve states—looking but not perceiving, listening but not understanding, casually tilting but not decisively turning to God's way (4:12, echoing Isa 6:9-10). The parables function as a deliberate test ("so that," Mark 4:12) to weed out mere curiosity seekers until they are ready to receive and respond to Jesus's life-directing "implanted word" (Jas 1:21), as depicted in the parable of the soils (see below). The way of God remains open for "whoever does the will of God" (Mark 3:35); initially missing the mark does not preclude improving one's aim, working through deeper and higher levels of response (4:13-20).

By the same token, however, the Twelve who have taken vital first steps to answer Jesus's call still have much to learn and are not immune to backsliding and misunderstanding, as their confusion over Jesus's parable of the soils attests, prompting his rebuke: "Do you not understand this parable? Then how will you understand all the parables?" (4:13). Jesus proceeds to reveal the "secret" or "mystery" (*mysterion*) (4:11) of the soils to them, but it still remains incumbent upon them to grasp this unfolding mystery and act on it. Jesus's parabolic method resists complacency and self-satisfaction among his closest confidants. To follow Jesus remains a lifelong *challenge*.

Yet discipleship also poses an ongoing *opportunity* to reflect, reconsider, and repent. The overarching aim of Jesus's teaching in various modes is to "disclose" the mystery of God's realm, as the parable of the lamp shows (4:22), not foreclose anyone from the truth. Jesus does not establish some tight-knit "secret" society or in-the-know "gnostic" cadre, such as that to which he reveals 114 "secret sayings" in the apocryphal Gospel of Thomas (Goodacre 2012; Henderson 2013, 346–47). Boundaries between insiders and outsiders (4:11) remain fluid in the family of God.

We now turn to see how Jesus unlocks the "secret/mystery of the kingdom of God" (4:11) in four parables.

Bear Fruit: The Parable of the Soils (4:3-9, 14-20)

As a storyteller, while Jesus primarily engages his audience's sense of hearing (4:3, 9, 15-20), he also paints a vivid picture for people to "see." Accordingly, he calls them to keen audiovisual reception—"Listen! Look!" (*Akouete idou*) (4:3)—not just "Listen!" as the NRSV has it (Snodgrass 2008, 150; 2018,

75). Throughout the Bible hearing and seeing involve more than processing sound and light waves: to hear is to receive and respond; to see is to perceive and understand (4:12).

In this first parable, Jesus delineates four different levels of response to the word of God he proclaims by comparison with the relative harvests of seed sown on four types of ground or soil. Although commonly called the parable of the sower, a better designation is the parable of the soils, focusing on the story's key variable. The sower (Jesus) and the seed (word) remain constant: the soils (respondents) make all the difference.

Type of Ground/Respondent	Result of Sown Seed/Word
Beaten path/Hardened	Eaten by birds/Taken away by Satan
Rocky/Shallow	Sprouts but becomes scorched and withered/Sparks initial acceptance but abandons in time of trouble
Thorny/Cluttered	Sprouts but becomes choked by thorns/Choked by worries, riches, and desires for other things
Good soil/Productive	Produces multiple harvest, 30-60-100-fold/Bears fruit in increasing measure, 30-60-100-fold

Among the four possible responses to Jesus's good news, three are bad, either immediately or ultimately unproductive, a waste of God's word. Some have *hardened* hearts, paying hardly any attention to the word, ripe for Satan's snatching any hope of fruitfulness. Others only muster a brief *shallow* enthusiasm, quickly squelched if the word demands too much effort and discomfort. Still others throttle the word amid their *cluttered* anxieties and preoccupations.

Still, however, the overall picture remains optimistic, as Jesus envisions a group of *productive* respondents in *threefold* measure, realizing the word's dynamic potential in their lives thirty, sixty, and one hundred times over. At a minimum, these three good scenarios balance the three bad ones (Herzog 2012, 190); yet more than that, their multiplicative growth suggests the gospel's greater positive influence.

But Jesus mainly aims to present a dynamic story, not a statistical accounting, of possible responses to God's word and will. The four "grounds" are fluid not fixed, representative not restrictive boundaries, allowing for migration. The hardest hearts can soften, the shallowest can deepen, the most cluttered can disentangle—and yes, the most productive can decline and deteriorate ("go to seed") if not cultivated. The world remains contested territory for good and bad intents and purposes, a battleground where Satan-driven forces persist in launching their destructive air raids, even as Jesus thwarts their deleterious missions (1:13, 21-26, 32-34, 39; 3:11, 23-27), where the way of God's people is impeded by rocky roads and thorny threats.

This combative state of affairs during Jesus's lifetime, eventually coming down on his head in a "thorny" act of malice and mockery (15:17) and claiming his lifeblood on a torturous Roman cross, continues with a vengeance after his death and resurrection into the time of Mark's Gospel. Mark writes in the fog of war surrounding Rome's violent smackdown of the First Jewish Revolt (66–70 CE; see the introduction), crushing the messianic hopes of God's people, not least those who staked their lives on the crucified-resurrected Jesus Messiah, in the "rocky" rubble of a devastated Jerusalem and its temple (13:1-2). Mark's first readers could scarcely avoid a crisis of "cognitive dissonance," a maddening struggle to hold on to cherished beliefs and ideas, to keep hope alive, in the face of devastating contradictory circumstances (Johnson 2010, 21–22, 65–66; Tavris and Aronson 2020, 15–54; Festinger, Riecken, and Schachter 1956).

The liberating ministry of Jesus vindicated in his resurrection signaled the end, or at least the beginning of the end, for evil empires opposed to God's righteous realm. But cataclysmic events forty years down the road seemed to upend this presumed victory, leaving followers of Christ and other Jews at wits' and lives' end. Rome was still going strong in 70 CE with no end in close sight. And to bring matters to our doorsteps, if such dissonance threatened believers in Mark's day, how much more in our own, some seventeen centuries after Constantine's sudden declaration of Rome as a Christian empire, which did not so much solve the problem as swallow it whole. "As a matter of the historical record, sin, death, evil, and sin have gone on unabated and have done very well for themselves in the two thousand years since Yeshua [Jesus] was crucified, a cause to which the post-Constantinian church in particular made no small contribution" (Caputo 2019, 99; cf. 19, 79). How long can we pray, "How long, O LORD" (Ps 13:1-2), with real conviction?

Even so, apocalyptic expectations of a new world order remain notoriously stubborn in periods of crisis; indeed, they are built precisely for these hard times, unveiling layers of reality beneath and beyond what appears to be countervailing evidence. If initial layers only expose part of the picture, just wait a little longer for the grand finale! In standard apocalyptic imagination (Collins 1998), you can count on things to get increasingly *worse* before the victorious end. So a major catastrophe like the fall of Jerusalem may be the necessary big bang to trigger God's last judgment on a corrupt world and ultimate salvation of God's people.

The late first-century Jewish apocalypse known as *4 Ezra* (= 2 Esdras 3-14) adopts this viewpoint, using *sowing and reaping* imagery akin to Jesus's parable of the soils, but in different ways to different ends (Snodgrass 2018, 69–76). The apocalyptic seer, writing under the name of Israel's venerable priest, Ezra, pleads for God to "give us [the people] a seed for our heart and cultivation of our understanding so that fruit may be produced" (2 Esdr 8:6). In turn, God announces, "I sow my law in you, and it shall bring forth fruit in you, and you shall be glorified through it forever" (9:31). But as it happens, this glorious harvest will be severely limited by a lack of receptivity and obedience to God's word: "For we who have received the law and sinned will perish, as well as our hearts that received it" (9:36). At the end of the day, "Only a few shall be saved" (8:3). Most will remain controlled by that diabolical "evil seed . . . sown in Adam's heart from the beginning, and how much ungodliness it has produced until now—and will produce until the time of threshing comes!" (4:30). A predominantly evil world full of bad seeds and rotten crops "without number" will finally get what it deserves on the "threshing floor" of divine judgment (4:32), winnowing out and saving the "few" good apples in the process.

Matthew's collection of seed/harvest parables echoes this severe threshing of "evildoers" "at the end of the age," punctuated with fiery furnaces and "gnashing of teeth" (Matt 13:30, 36-43; cf. 8:12; 13:50; 22:13-14; 25:30, 51). That's one way to deal with the dissonance of persistent, triumphant evil in the present age: kick it down the road into a raging inferno.

But such is not the way of Mark's Jesus, at least not through agricultural analogies. He focuses more on fighting the good fight for freedom and fruitfulness in the here and now in the beaten-down, rocky, and thorny territory of the world, daring to keep believing in, hoping for, and working toward multifold renewal, akin to Jeremiah's bold dream during another devastating siege of Jerusalem that "houses and fields and vineyards shall again be bought in this land" (Jer 32:15). Cognitive dissonance is met with cultivative perseverance (cf. Luke 8:15).

This extended commentary on the parable of the soils is warranted by its strategic position heading the first block of Jesus's teaching in Mark. It functions as "*the* parable about parables" (Snodgrass 2008, 145 [emphasis original]; Herzog 2012, 187–88), the programmatic word about the word of God's way in Christ. It sets the script and stage for Mark's unfolding narrative drama of the spread of God's kingdom in the world, established (sown) with fertile power and purpose by God's Son Jesus. As Mary Ann Tolbert notes,

"The characters, groups, and events [in Mark's Gospel] . . . are all portrayed as the concrete illustrations of these four fundamental kinds of responses to Jesus's word [in the parable of the soils]. Every episode and every character or group can be understood by the audience as an example of one of these four alternatives" (1989, 124). As we keep working through Mark's story, we remain alert to how various character groups—disciples, women, afflicted persons, religious leaders, political rulers, demonic forces—operate within and across these quadrants.

The triad of shorter parables that follow reinforce the paradigm of the soils, particularly its optimistic prospects for growth in dark (Mark 4:21-22, 26-27) and difficult times of limited resources (4:32-33).

Pay Attention: The Parable of the Lamp (4:21-25)

The short parable of the lamp (4:21), which, strictly speaking, shows three images of lamp placement rather than tells a story about them, may seem at first glance disconnected from the farming world Jesus primarily evokes in this parable unit. But the picture of a "bushel basket" (*modios*), "grain measure" (BDAG 2000, 656), or "measuring basket" (Danker and Krug 2009, 236) placed over the lamp (4:21), together with Jesus's commentary about "measure" (*metron*) amounts (4:24), maintains the link to agricultural production. More to the point, Jesus's discussion about responding rightly to God's revealed way—to what God *brings to light* in Jesus's word (4:22-25)— fits the overall purpose of his parables (4:11-13).

A lamp has a singular purpose: to illuminate the darkness. That purpose can be thwarted, however, by mismanagement and misplacement, by concealing the lamp under a basket or a bed. Only if properly positioned, unobstructed and elevated on a stand, can the lamp brighten the room (4:21). In a similar fashion, the word of God proclaimed by Jesus in parables (and other forms) aims to illuminate God's realm and guide the people's way in it (cf. Ps 119:105—"Your word is a lamp to my feet and a light to my path"). God graciously works in a mode of full disclosure and exposure, not foreclosure; of openness and opportunity, not opaqueness. The "secret" is out, the mystery revealed, *if* one will "pay attention to what you hear" or, more literally, "see what you hear" (*blepete ti akouete*), again merging optic and acoustic reception into keen perception. Jesus puts the onus on seers/hearers to quit putting their heads in the sand, to quit hiding under the bed, to quit squelching the word through avoidance or ignorance. In short, open your heart and let the light shine in!

And by extension, let the light that dawns inside shine out to others in faithful word and deed, bearing vivid witness to God's enlightened way (cf. Matt 5:14-16). This outreaching ministry of light is suggested by Jesus's subtle shift from "what *you hear*" to "the measure *you give*," that is, give *out* through proclamation and demonstration for others' benefit (Mark 4:23-24; Collins 2007, 253). Correlated with the parable of the soils, we might invoke photosynthesis language, whereby the creative light of God irradiates the implanted seed of God's word and, if allowed to do its potent work without hindrance, produces a fruitful, multi-"measure" bounty. A stewardship principle obtains: "The measure you give will be the measure you get, and still more will be given you" (4:24)—so that you can give more to others and perpetuate the growing cycle.

But serious consequences, short of hellfire, await those who "have nothing" to show for what they've been given and thus nothing to give others. Regarding such irresponsible stewards, Jesus warns, "Even what they have will be taken away" (4:25). This loaded language drives home Jesus's point about faithful management. Gain and loss, growth and recession are measured in proportion to what one has done with whatever one has, little or much (cf. Luke 16:10-13). Even so, the sharp rhetoric of the "haves" profiting more while the "have-nots" are stripped down closer to the bone seems divisive and insensitive. Is this how the economy of God's kingdom works? How might those struggling to survive, such as tenant farmers and migrant workers, then or now, "hear" Jesus's teaching (Cardenal 2010, 158–62; Herzog 2012, 192–96)? If they managed to produce a bumper, hundredfold crop, wouldn't greedy landlords swoop in and "take away" most of the profits, as surely as birds snatch up scattered seed and Satan "takes away" the gospel word before it takes root (note the same "take away" verb [*airō*] in Mark 4:14, 25)?

But remember who's speaking here. Jesus himself comes from humble roots, circulating among the common people from village to village announcing the good news of God's liberating realm. This Jesus, who owns not a speck of land or single coin of the realm (6:8; 12:15-17), appears as an altogether different "lord" (1:3; 2:28) from Herodian landlords in Galilee. This Jesus advances the redemptive, benevolent economy of God, not the exploitative treasury of Caesar or other earthly rulers. "Take away" is the power game they play, giving precious little in return. To the extent that Jesus uses power language in his symbolic stories, I suspect he does so tongue-in-cheek, implicitly tweaking the system. Here perhaps is the real "secret" of his parables, offering a subtle but sure critique of the powers that be in their own words, a subterranean counterview from below, a "hidden transcript" fueling an underground movement destined to burst forth with fresh life and light for all who embrace God's word and will (Scott 1990; Herzog 1994).

Yes, those who refuse to "pay attention" forfeit their opportunity to flourish in God's realm. But Jesus does not aim to confiscate anything from anyone: "be taken away" in 4:25 marks a passive result, not an active intent. Rather, "his mission is to restore life to its full flourishing wherever life was being diminished, destroyed, or taken away" (Caputo 2019, 97). The kingdom of God revitalized in Jesus promotes giving and growing for all. Whatever people "have" (*echei*) in any sphere of life in any measure (4:25), everyone "has (*echei*) ears to hear" (4:23 NIV, CEB), if they just will!

Sleep Tight: The Parable of the Growing Seed (4:26-29)

This parable constitutes one of the few passages in Mark with no parallels in other Gospels. Whatever accounts for this anomaly, we should not miss this parable's powerful and hopeful message, especially during hard times. Jesus returns to the imagery of planting and growing crops, while also maintaining a link with lamplight in the bedroom through the picture of the farmer sleeping and rising "night and day" (4:21, 27).

The parables of the soils and lamp emphasized hearers' responsibility to give active attention to sewn and shone word, allowing it to sink in and bring forth fruit and light. The accent has been on human decision and dedication. But remember, Jesus advances the gospel and kingdom of *God* (1:14-15), which ultimately depends on God's will and work. The parable of the growing seed shifts the focus from faithful response to trustful rest that God's realm will flourish by virtue of its own relentless creative energy.

As in the Sabbath incidents in 2:23–3:6, the *creational principle* again becomes salient. As it is the nature of the land, formed by and infused with God's dynamic word, to "put forth vegetation: plants yielding seed, and fruit trees of every kind on earth that bear fruit with the seed in it" (Gen 1:11), so it is the nature of God's entire realm (including the land) sustained by God's word to "accomplish that which I [the LORD] purpose, and succeed in the thing for which I sent it" (Isa 55:11; see 55:10 for sowing/sprouting analogy). Consequently, Jesus and his fellow spreaders of God's word can rest confidently in its progressive productivity, irrespective of the quality of "soil" on which it lands.

For maximum effect, Jesus spices his parable with mysterious and even absurdist elements. The mystery factor underlying all parables (4:11, 22) becomes key *within* this parable of the growing seed. As the farmer goes about his daily routines of sleeping and waking, the seed he has sown sprouts and grows through a process "he does not know how" (4:27). He has no power or knowledge to make anything grow; remarkably "the earth produces *of itself*," incubating the seed pod and detonating the creative potential, bursting forth in dynamic stages from seed to stalk to head to "full grain" (4:28). Although modern biology details the evolution and chemistry of the growth cycle, the wonder and mystery of *life*—at its essential root and core—remains (Gould 1989). Just so, the realm of God, encompassing the earth and all creation, pulses with an inexorable and inexplicable divine energy that defies finite understanding. The kingdom of God cannot, will not be managed or programmed. It must be accepted and followed. And especially good news during times of crisis, the kingdom of God cannot, will not be thwarted or stunted, however underground it may appear.

But isn't such good news too good to be true? Isn't the picture of a farmer doing no work between sowing and reaping absurd on its face—no watering, weeding, fertilizing, pest-controlling, pruning, nothing? Even in the lush garden of Eden, God employed the first human "to till it and keep it" (Gen 2:15). And we've become all too aware in our time how human exploitation of the earth threatens its (and our) very survival. Mark's Jesus is not naïve about how both his faithless followers and ruthless resistors can impede God's way in the world. Primary calls to "accept [the word] and bear fruit," to "pay attention to what you hear" (4:20, 24), to participate actively in the growth of God's realm, remain in full force. The lazy sower is a caricature, an fool, if he expects to harvest an uncultivated field; but he's a useful fool for a vital point Jesus makes. The fact is, furthering the rule of God, like farming the land, is hard work in a precarious environment. Even *if* one works as hard as one can, there is no guarantee of success: one violent storm, one withering drought, one devastating assault from an invader—be it a horde of rapacious locusts, Roman soldiers, or demonic forces—can wipe out years of progress.

So how does one keep sowing and working, believing and hoping, in the face of such paralyzing insecurity? By being "foolish" enough to trust the creative power of God's word to break through and thrive—through it all, after all (cf. 1 Cor 1:18-25). By daring to "sleep" in the midst of the storm (see Mark 4:38) and to "rise," with sickle close at hand, still expecting God's persisting underground operation to burst forth in new life. Hope springs eternal.

The final note of wielding a sickle to reap the harvest again echoes prophetic and apocalyptic themes—with a twist. The sharp slash of the sickle represented the final judgment executed against the wicked enemies of Jerusalem in Joel's day (Joel 3:13) or against "those who submit to the Roman imperial cult and the structures of Roman imperialism" in John's time (Rev 14:14-20) (Schottroff 2006, 119). In the story of the growing seed, however, Mark's Jesus envisions no reigning Son of Man and angel lieutenant putting the sickle as a sword to the evil empire, as John sees in Revelation 14. In the parable, an ordinary farmer reaps ripe, full grain from the ground he has planted and trusted to do its productive work. As such, this story offers assurance of the present-and-future, "always but coming" kingdom of God from below and above, on earth as it is heaven (Rauschenbusch 2007 [1907], 338; Evans 2004).

Think Big: The Parable of the Mustard Seed (4:30-32)

Assurance in the midst of dissonance, ballast for a teetering faith, is also provided in this short parable, but from a different angle. Whereas the growing seed deals with the mysterious *process* of growth, the mustard seed focuses on the gracious *proportion*, that is, *disproportion* of growth, considering the mustard seed's proverbial reputation as "the smallest of all the seeds on earth" (4:31). Here size matters—inversely: this tiniest of seeds "grows up and becomes the greatest of all shrubs" or "garden plants" (*lachana*) (L&N 1988, 32), comparable to a tree that "puts forth large branches, so that the birds of the air can make nests in its shade" (4:32). Such is the pattern (exponential flourishing) and purpose (productive sheltering) of God's expansive realm.

Note again that the generative power is in the sown seed, not in the sower or in any type of soil in which it is sown. In contrast with other Gospels' versions, Mark's parable mentions no human agent, no "someone" sowing the mustard seed (Matt 13:31//Luke 13:19); it also places the seed in the most generic environment—the "earth" or "land" (*gēs*)—not in the more specialized "field" (*agros*, Matt 13:31) or "garden" (*kēpos*, Luke 13:19). Moreover, Mark's Gospel has no companion comparison of a mustard grain to a small amount of human faith capable of moving a mountain (Matt 17:20) or a mulberry tree (Luke 17:6). Mark's parallel text about mountain-moving faith has Jesus calling the disciples to "have faith *in God*" (Mark 11:22-23), without specifying any measure of faith on their part and without boosting their hope that "nothing will be impossible *for you*" (Matt 11:20). Imagining and realizing the righteous rule of God across a vast world permeated by evil and suffering have nothing to do with calibrating and applying the right dosage of faith, small or great. Once more, establishing God's kingdom on earth depends on God's creative power. Fast-forwarding to Jesus's later teaching in Mark, "For mortals it is impossible, but not for God; for God all things are possible" (Mark 10:27; cf. 14:36).

In the shadow of the cross and the razing of Jerusalem forty years later, Jesus's followers might be forgiven for thinking the kingdom of God was an impossible dream. On the surface, the parable of the mustard seed only exacerbates the dissonance with its exaggerative depiction: the mustard seed is small, to be sure, but is not *the* smallest of all known seeds; it is typically sown in small plots, not all over the earth; and it does not sprout into the "greatest of all shrubs" sporting "mega"-branches that host nesting birds. Again, Jesus paints a wild caricature to burst open the tunnel vision of a beleaguered people. There is better news—the "good news"—than meets the eye and ear in the daily press. The apparent way of things in the world, the status quo, is not the only or ultimate way.

In the face of obstacles, obscurities, and outright opposition, the way of God finds a way to break through and fan out—but not to gild its own path and feather its own nest. Rather, the realm of God served by Jesus serves to serve others, to provide welcome and secure space "so that the birds of the air can make nests in its shade" (4:32). This avian reference catches us by surprise in the parable cluster of Mark 4, which began with the image of birds gobbling up the sown seed on the beaten path, just as Satan grabs God's word from hardened hearts (4:3, 14). Now stunningly, at the end of this parable unit, the seed sprouts, grows, and hosts these hungry birds in a comfortable nesting environment (only Mark refers to the mustard bush's "shade" [*skia*]) so that they can make more birds! The kingdom of God meets hostility with hospitality, the marauding of enemies with nurturing love for enemies: nothing less than the integration and restoration of all creation. In Paul Beatty's award-winning novel, *The Sellout*, the main character says, "Who was I kidding? I'm a farmer, and farmers are natural segregationists. We separate the wheat from the chaff" (2015, 214). Mark's Jesus is not kidding about bucking the world's segregationist-separatist tendencies.

The parable of the mustard seed also echoes the allegory spun by the exiled prophet in Ezekiel 17—again, with a notable twist. Ezekiel features a "noble cedar" tree (Ezek 17:23) from the Lebanon mountain range rather than a mustard shrub from a local garden. By all appearances, the stately cedar stakes a clearer claim to being "the greatest of all" trees. But it can still struggle to survive in a tumultuous environment. In Ezekiel's story, the cedar represents the "house of Israel" (17:1) in two phases of Israel's convulsive history in the sixth century BCE. First, the cedar portrays a stable, independent people from whom a small portion—imaged as a "topmost shoot," a "seed," and a "twig"—is *removed* and *relocated* to Babylon by Nebuchadnezzar's army under the banner of a "great eagle." The replanted seed sprouts in the foreign land, but only as a "low" vine with limited branches, leaves, and "roots [that] remained where it stood" (17:1-6). Second, however, God pledges to take another "sprig from the lofty top of [Israel's] cedar and transplant it *back* to its native soil on a high a lofty mountain . . . in order that it may [again] produce boughs and bear fruit, and become a noble cedar"

(17:22-23a). As a result, "under it *every kind of bird will live; in the shade of its branches will nest winged creatures of every kind*. All the trees of the field shall know that I am the LORD. I bring low the high tree, I make high the low tree. . . . I the LORD have spoken; I will accomplish it" (17:23b-24).

In Jesus's parable, he appropriates from Ezekiel (1) the blessing of all creatures great and small, (2) the frustrating of predatory superpowers (mighty eagles, Babylon and Rome) in the interest of hospitable, nurturing care (shady nests), and (3) the reversing of worldly high/low hierarchies (cf. Luke 1:52). But Jesus also adapts Ezekiel by sticking with the mustard image, against all odds and all appearances. The miniscule mustard seed does *not* miraculously transform into a magnificent cedar tree or giant beanstalk scraping the heavens. It remains an ordinary, unassuming mustard bush that can only claim greatness within another worldview. The kingdom of God "seeded" by Jesus and his followers envisions an entirely different way of ruling than that of worldly powers: an underground rule of God the Creator, foolish and weak by conventional standards, yet pressing toward new ends of restoration and reconciliation by new means of inclusive love and mercy.

Remarkable Works of Freeing and Feeding I

Mark 4:35–6:56

After his extended teaching in and about parables, Jesus is back on the move. The urgent action narrative of Mark proceeds apace. Remember that Jesus delivered his public parable of the soils from a boat on the lakeshore (4:1-2). Although he soon shifted to instruct his disciples in private (4:10, 34), the boat remains available for getting away. So we're scarcely surprised when Jesus announces in the evening after his day of teaching, "Let us go across to the other side" (4:35). Thus begins a dramatic sequence of events set on both sides of the Sea of Galilee, west and east, this side and the "other side" (*eis to peran*, 4:35; 5:1, 21; 6:45), as Jesus and disciples dart back and forth by boat. Moreover, two of the lake trips become eventful in themselves as frightful storm scenes at the beginning and end of this unit (4:35-41; 6:45-52).

The overall narrative effect extends the range and stokes the intensity of Jesus's conflict with hostile forces on land and sea, at home and abroad, with familiars and "others." The "other side" east of the Galilean lake marks heavily Hellenized, predominantly Gentile territory. Although Jews also inhabited the area (Collins 2007, 267), Mark's story featuring large herds of swine (5:11-14), anathema in the Jewish homeland, accentuates the Gentile character of the region. We may schematize the movement this way:

Jewish Galilean Homeland ↔ ((*Stormy Sea*)) ↔ Gentile "Other Side"

Jesus continues to liberate those afflicted by disease and demons, with the added dimension of saving his disciples from *death* at sea ("We are perishing!" 4:38) and raising a *deceased* young woman to new life (5:41-42). The two seafaring stories highlight Jesus's relieving the disciples' intense fear (4:40-41; 6:50); and the exorcism incident, the longest of its kind in the Gospels (5:1-20), depicts Jesus's deliverance of a deranged man totally possessed, enslaved, "occupied" by a "Legion" of demons. We may thus classify Jesus's redemptive work in this unit under headings of "Freedom from" multiple binding forces: Fear, Enslavement, Death, and Sickness (cf. Rom 8:1-15).

Although Jesus's successful freedom campaign across turbulent waters in death-plagued lands dominates this unit, he also faces opposition in the middle of his journey that he *cannot overcome*. Most surprisingly—"amazingly" *for him* (6:6)—his power to do good falters in his hometown of Nazareth (6:1-6). More predictably, but no less shocking, Herod Antipas executes Jesus's primary witness, John the Baptist, serving his severed head on a platter at the ruler's birthday bash (6:24-28)! This lavish and ghoulish banquet scene in Herod's palace with his cronies jarringly juxtaposes Jesus's feeding the hungry masses with limited resources in a deserted area (6:30-44).

Freedom from Fear: Stilling the Storm (4:35-41)

This unit's first remarkable work, commonly known as the stilling of the storm, pairs with the later walking on water incident (6:45-52) as the only miracles of Jesus in Mark (1) set on water, (2) dealing with "natural" phenomena, and (3) focused on rescuing his disciples (4:36; 6:45-46). In the present scene, Mark also provides an additional bit of information (omitted in Matthew and Luke)—"other boats (*ploia*) were with him" (4:36)—that includes a larger cast of characters. To be sure, the story telescopes on the single boat carrying Jesus and his associates with no further reference to these other sailors, thus appearing to "leave the reader with the distracting question of how they fared in the storm, to which Mark offers no answer" (France 2002, 223). But the multiple boats may be more suggestive than distractive, hinting at a larger group affected not only by the storm but also by the conduct of Jesus and company through the storm. What kind of model does the latter group display in their "lead" boat?

Psalm 107 describes four typical situations in which people "cried out to the LORD in their trouble" and received deliverance "from the distress," including those who navigate "the seas in ships/boats" in stormy conditions that God makes to "be still" (Ps 107:6, 13, 23, 28-29; Collins 2007, 258). Even with four seasoned fishermen, Jesus's disciples desperately plead for Jesus to help *them*, which he does by stilling the whirlwinds. Unfortunately, however, in their panicky self-preoccupation, the disciples prove to be wholly unconcerned with "other boats," throttled in their fearful state of "no faith," which Jesus rebukes as surely as he "rebuked the wind" (Mark 4:39-40). Despite following Jesus for some time now, they still lag behind an anonymous foursome who impressed Jesus the first time they met him with their bold "faith" on behalf of their paralyzed friend (2:3-5).

This episode becomes a profound teachable moment for the disciples, as reflected in their pleading to Jesus as "Teacher" (4:38). This address reveals only the most elementary understanding of Jesus (Matt 8:25-26 upgrades to "Lord" to go with the disciples' "little faith"), but at least they admit their lack of knowledge, their cognitive dissonance in a crisis situation, albeit in critical fashion. When in doubt, blame the teacher! "Teacher, do you not care that we are perishing" (Mark 4:38)?

The learning outcome for this story focuses on revealing *who Jesus is* to his followers, close (the Twelve), near (the other sailors), and more distant (Mark's readers). Another snippet of seemingly superfluous information (again dropped by Matthew and Mark) indicates that the disciples "took him with them in the boat *just as he was*" (4:36). Well, how else could they take him? But this apparently banal observation becomes the whole point of the incident. The disciples *resist* letting Jesus be Jesus, taking him for *who he truly is*, on both the basic level of one who *sleeps* in the midst of the storm and on the higher plane of one who *stills* the storm with his commanding word. Though still "very much afraid" (NASB) or "filled with a great fear" (ESV) (*ephobēthēsan phobon*) at the end, they finally wake up to what matters most: "Who then is this" Jesus (4:41)? Certainly no ordinary teacher!

We may further unpack Jesus's identity in this incident, informed by biblical and Roman parallels, in three portraits: (1) sound sleeper, (2) stoic teacher, and (3) storm stiller.

Sound sleeper

This is the only time Jesus sleeps in Mark's story. Matthew and Luke report Jesus's announcement that the itinerant "Son of Man has nowhere to lay his head" (Matt 8:20//Luke 9:58)—nowhere, as it happens, but in a boat rocked by a terrible storm (Matt 8:24//Mark 4:38//Luke 8:23)! Mark particularly highlights Jesus's sleeping by association with the immediately preceding parable and accentuation of where he sleeps in the boat and what he sleeps on.

Recall that the growing seed story featured the routine sleep cycle of the farmer, calmly trusting that the sown seed would sprout and ripen through the passage of time, "night and day" (4:27). Just so, Jesus rests confidently in the way God has prepared for him, whatever winds may threaten to blow him off course. And he rests soundly, securely in the *stern* of the boat on a *cushion* (4:38), more details that Matthew and Luke delete. But these elements in Mark add more to the scene than extra color. Mark's Jesus happily naps at the *back* (stern) of the boat, feeling no need to put himself out front all the time. And no reason not to make himself as comfortable as possible with a *pillow*

(CEB), which likely refers to a "sailor's cushion" (BDAG 2000, 881) used to pad the rower's seat on the hard wood cross plank. But Jesus is doing no rowing or anything else on this voyage—only resting. Overall Mark's Jesus is no lackadaisical, laissez-faire leader. Jesus normally works diligently and selflessly to advance God's way, with no regard for his own comfort. But he also works in obedient faith, trusting in God's will and power every step of the way—a faith his disciples sorely lack in the present incident.

Jesus's sound sleep contrasts notably with that of the recalcitrant prophet Jonah, who hunkers down "fast asleep" in the hull of a ship heading west *away* from the Gentile mission (to Nineveh) God had assigned him (Beavis 2011, 90–91; Collins 2007, 259–60). In this ancient story, *God* stirs up a great storm to get Jonah's attention and get him back on track. Ironically, however, the Gentile crew has to wake Jonah, encourage him to "call on your god," and determine (by casting lots) that he is the cause of this terrible typhoon threatening their lives (Jonah 1:1-8); they finally throw him overboard, as a last resort, after feverishly rowing against the storm to no avail (1:11-16).

In Jesus's case, however, he sails *to* Gentile territory across the lake "as the faithful prophet who does the will of God (cf. Mark 3:35)" (Beavis 2011, 91), confident that God will sustain him through the storm but also hopeful that his disciples might call on God and work through the ordeal rather than wake him and accuse him of not caring (4:38).

Stoic teacher

As one emotionally involved in his life and work, subject to feelings of anger and grief (1:41; 3:5) and other sentiments, as we shall see, Mark's Jesus ill fits the model of the unflappable Stoic sage (Spencer 2021)—*except* in the present story. He out-stoics one Stoic teacher in a similar situation reported by the second-century educator, Aulus Gellius. In his collection of anecdotes, *Attic Nights*, Gellius recounts a voyage he took across the Ionian Sea beset by a vicious "typhoon." In the height of the storm, Gellius noticed that "an eminent philosopher of the Stoic sect" from Athens showed a "frightened and ghastly pale" countenance similar to that of other terrified crew and passengers, though he didn't shout out in panic or despair. Clearly, however, he was struck with fear, understandable in the situation but very unlike the Stoic ideal of remaining tranquil amid life's disturbances. When pressed later, after the storm subsided, about his fearful reaction, the teacher admitted to experiencing a "brief, but inevitable and natural fear." Stoics are no more immune to such first impressions or "fantasies" (*phantasia*) than anyone else. The key is what one does with these initial mental jolts, whether one gives conscious *assent* to them, allowing them to control one's attitudes and actions. This philosopher claims to have resolutely refused to cede to full-blown fear, which would have done nothing to help the situation (Aulus Gellius, *Attic Nights* 19.1.1; Graver 2007, 85–87; Robertson 2019, 62–66).

While Jesus may be fairly said to show feelings of frustration with his disciples in sharply rebuking *their* crippling fear and "no faith," he himself shows no trace of fear even for a second; his companions—not the storm—disturb his peaceful sleep. Upon being awakened, Jesus first stills the storm, bringing the tempest in line with his even temperament (4:39), only to stir up the disciples again with his tough lesson challenging their fear and faithlessness, which, together with his sudden calming of the storm, further stokes their "great fear" (4:41). If we prefer to say that Jesus exercises "tough love," the stress falls on the *tough* part. The optimism of Jesus's parables seems to be blowing away in the wind. Mark's Jesus shows little sympathy here and elsewhere (9:19-24) with people's struggles with faith in anxious situations, not even allowing a little Stoic grace to feel natural, initial fear, short of full-fledged assent.

It's not that Jesus denies or denigrates the emotional component of human nature. He's no Stoic purist by any means, and even the great Stoic teachers, as Gellius affirmed, were not the utterly dispassionate advocates of pure reason they're often presumed to be (see Graver 2007). But for Jesus, *faith* (*pistis*) marks the fundamental disposition of God's realm, the root and branch of its development, the *first response* of its subjects and the driving force of all subsequent responses ("by faith from first to last," Rom 1:17). And such faith dynamically combines *emotional trust* with mental assent and behavioral action (faithfulness) (Spencer 2017b; Morgan 2015; Tillich 1957). In this vital matter of faith, Jesus brooks no compromise, no coddling—which leaves the disciples speechless, not for the last time. One character (not a disciple) will later voice for readers, then and now, an honest plea: "I believe (*pisteuō*); help my unbelief (*apistia*)!" (Mark 9:24). We will see how Jesus responds in due course.

Storm stiller
Among the Synoptic accounts, only Mark recounts Jesus's direct speech "*to* the sea [and wind]" and places it *before* his comments to the disciples, though presumably they also heard his prior rebuke of the storm (4:39). Jesus's familiar words, "Peace, be still," carried over by the NRSV from the KJV, as beautiful and comforting as they are, unfortunately obscure their strong *sonic* force, focused on silencing the storm's terrible *noise*. The first command (*siōpa*) means "Quiet!" (NIV, NIB) or "Hush" (NASB), reinforced by the

second (*pephimōso*), meaning "Be muzzled" (Collins 2007, 257, 261), the same term used for binding animals' mouths (1 Tim 5:18) and, more to the point here, for shutting up demons (Mark 1:25). Popular mythology often attributed sea storms to turbulent demonic agents (Collins 2007, 261–62), fomenting cosmic upheaval and cataclysmic downfall in the dark abyss. It's no surprise, then, that upon reaching the eastern shore, Jesus is "immediately" met by a wild man infested with a horde of demons, who wind up pile-driving a herd of pigs into a watery grave (5:2, 13).

Jesus continues to engage in a cosmic combat. And most remarkably he "wins" without shedding any blood (well, except for the poor pigs) and without breaking a sweat. He "fights" on a different plane in harmony with the great foundational narratives of biblical faith, restoring the world back to its original good purpose.

- *Creation (Gen 1:1-5)*. Like God's work "in the beginning," Jesus simply speaks the word to the dark, chaotic waters to produce life-sustaining order.
- *Flood (Genesis 6–9)*. Like God's gracious dealings with Noah, Jesus saves his followers through a deluge, transforming his little vessel (and the "other boats," we hope) into an ark of safety.
- *Exodus (Exod 14:1–15:21)*. Like God's guiding the Israelites across the Red Sea to freedom, Jesus leads his followers through troubled waters he tames.

But as with the first human beings, with Noah and family, and with the ancient Israelites, Jesus's journey is far from smooth sailing hereafter. In many respects, the hard way has only just begun.

Freedom from Enslavement: Liberating the "Legion"-Possessed Man (5:1-20)

Beyond the association between storms and demons in ancient thought, several other features link Mark 4:35-41 and 5:1-20 (see pg. 75).

No sooner had Jesus "stepped out of (*exelthontos*) the boat" than a crazed man with an unclean spirit came "out of (*ek*) the tombs" (5:2)—*running* toward Jesus, we soon learn (5:6). An ominous scene: out of one tumult straight into another. Far from rising out of the tomb, as Jesus will ultimately do (16:1-8), this man "*lived among* the tombs" (5:3), roaming across the graveyards "night and day" (5:5). The tombs, mentioned three times (5:1, 3, 5), are his habitat, the dead his only companions, his existence a zombiesque living death. The stage is set "on the other side" (5:1) for a life-and-death battle—on death's turf! As Herman Waetjen comments, this demoniac "is

	Stilling the Storm and Saving the Disciples (4:35-41)	**Stopping a Legion and Delivering a Demoniac (5:1-20)**
Watery Threat	Windstorm on the lake swamping the boat and threatening to drown the disciples	Demonic legion overwhelming herd of swine and driving them to drown in the lake
Desperate and Derisive Plea to Jesus	Disciples: "Teacher, do you not care that we are perishing?"	Demons: "What have you to do with me, Jesus, Son of the Most High God? I adjure you by God, do not torment me."
Jesus's Counterquestion	"Why are you afraid? Have you still no faith?"	"What is your name?"
Jesus's Command	"Quiet! Be still!" (NIV)	"Come out of the man, you unclean spirit!"
Peaceful Result	"Then the wind ceased, and there was a dead calm."	"They came to Jesus and saw the demoniac sitting there, clothed and in his right mind."
Fearful Response	"Why are you [disciples] so afraid? . . . And they were filled with great fear" (ESV)	People: "And they [the people] were afraid."
Political Element	Lake: a commercial waterway claimed and controlled by Roman-Herodian government	Legion: Roman military unit conquering and occupying foreign territory

the embodiment of living death . . . the most dehumanized and wretched individual whom Jesus has yet encountered." Yet, Waetjen hastens to add, he's also "incredibly powerful," a terrible force to be reckoned with (Waetjen 1989, 114; cf. Bird 2018, 80).

This episode, the longest exorcism story in Mark, presents a complex, multilevel discourse of power or strength swirling around fraught events of *domination* and *negotiation*.

Domination

Since Mark does not identify the afflicted man by name, he is commonly called the "Gerasene demoniac" because of his association with the area around Gerasa, one of the ten cities in the Decapolis region (5:20). (Some manuscripts set this story near other similar-sounding towns, Gergasa or Gadara, closer to the lake; see Omanson 2006, 12, 70.) In his maniacal state, the man manifests extreme characteristics of being both dominated and dominating, possessed and powerful, enslaved and untamable. (Note: I use terms like "crazed," "maniacal," and "deranged" in a dramatic-metaphorical rather than diagnostic-clinical sense to stress the man's severe physio-psychological condition; for a thoughtful, nuanced treatment of this story informed by ancient and modern assessments of "mental illness," see Toensing 2007.)

On the one hand, he is totally controlled (possessed) by a "Legion" of malevolent demons that speak collectively through and for him as "I-We/Me-Us" (5:6-7, 9-12). They drive him to antisocial (roaming among the tombs) and self-destructive behavior ("gashing himself with stones," 5:5 NASB). And he's stripped down to the bone, literally naked (5:15; cf. Luke 8:27) and socially bereft of dignity. His life is not his own.

On the other hand, the evil forces dominating his mind and body infuse him with a monstrous power beyond any human capacity to restrain him, even with "shackles and chains." As "no one had the strength (*ischyen*) to subdue him" (5:4), he becomes the very embodiment of the satanic "strong man" (*ischyros*) Jesus pictured in 3:26-27.

Despite his bonds-busting, superhuman power, the Gerasene demoniac is in no position to conquer or rule anyone or any territory, except a cemetery! All his vicious strength turns inward, imploding against him. However, where no one could control him, much less help him, Jesus steps in as the "stronger one" (*ischyroteros*, 1:7), uniquely empowered to eradicate "Legion" and liberate its battered human host, transforming him into a healthy condition of "sitting . . . clothed and in his right mind" (5:15). Jesus uses his superior power for deliverance, not domination. And once again, he wields this power through his *word*, not through weaponry or warfare, on behalf of God's peaceable realm.

Even so, Mark's exorcism story is shot through with military-political *language* (Derrett 1979, 5–6; Myers 1988, 190–94; Horsley 2001, 140–48; Boring 2006, 151–52; Beavis 2011, 93–95; Carter 2014). Although mounting no beach assault with his disciple-soldiers from a tank landing ship, Jesus nonetheless takes command of the situation, ordering the occupying demons to leave the man and finally dispatching these enemy forces into a "herd" (*agelē*) or "company" (Danker and Krug 2009, 3) or "troop" (Derrett 1979, 5) of swine, which then "rush" (*hormaō*) like marauding, charging troops into the depths of the sea (5:8, 12-13)—reminiscent of the Egyptian army's fateful pursuit of the fleeing Israelites into the Red Sea (Exod 14:21-31; 15:1-10; Derrett 1979, 6–8; Horsley 2001, 140–41; Thurman 2003, 148). The theme of emancipative exodus thus carries over from the stilling of the storm.

Contemporary with Mark's Gospel and proximate with the location of the present conflict story, during the First Jewish War, the Roman general Vespasian routed the Jews in Gadara (recall that some copies of Mark 5:1 read "Gadarenes" instead of "Gerasenes") with 500 cavalrymen and 3,000 foot soldiers stampeding through the area "like the wildest of wild beasts." They drove fugitives into the raging current of the nearby Jordan River and took 2,200 prisoners and "mighty spoils" of animals (Josephus, *J.W.* 4.413-36). Vespasian also sent one of his lieutenants to Gerasa, where the soldiers killed 1,000 men, seized their families, and plundered their property (4.487-89).

The telltale military symbol in Mark's exorcism story is the very name of the demonic gang—"Legion" (5:9)—denoting a major division of Rome's vaunted army, composed of 5,000 to 6,000 well-trained and efficiently mobilized troops (Kennedy 1992, 789–91). This Legion's affinity with a large herd of pigs ("Send us into the swine," 5:12) reinforces the Roman martial connection. A boar (wild pig) served as the principal mascot for the Syria-based Tenth *Fretensis* Legion ("Legion of the Sea Straits"), whose image was widely displayed on battle standards, coins, and other media. This Tenth Legion played a major role in defeating the rebel fighters (Josephus, *J.W.* 3.8, 64-65; 5.69-70, 135; 7.5, 17; Carter 2014, 153; Leander 2013, 206–207).

The body of the Gerasene demoniac represents a symbolic site of Rome's violent conquering and colonizing domination, which Mark's Jesus opposes in all its forms—physical, psychological, social, economic. But it is too simplistic to read Mark's account as touting King/General Jesus's victory over Rome and all other principalities and powers, which would be a hard sell to Mark's community during or after Roman legions trampled the Jewish homeland. An exorcism story might buoy flagging spirits for a moment but hardly guarantees some great divine intervention, some mighty blast of wind leading God's people to safety and blowing back to drown their enemies, as in the original exodus. Remember Jesus and his disciples themselves came *through* a lake storm, landing them *in* Legion-dominated land.

Further, Jesus mobilizes no crack special-forces team (his disciples would still be in shock from the storm) and summons no heavenly host. He just keeps sowing the word, seed by tiny seed, letting it do its kingdom-growing work mysteriously, incrementally, like "the invasion of a mustard seed" (Garroway 2009; Mark 4:30-32), amid the rocks and thorns that, in Rome's case, took the form of catapulted boulders and thrust spears. He's establishing an altogether different kingdom, not simply replacing one powerful regime with another. This whole new way of ruling comes "not by might and power" in the conventional sense but by the "spirit" of God's way (cf. Zech 4:6), of "sitting" at the peaceable table, of "clothing" those who have been stripped bare by rapacious conquerors, of bringing the world in line with God's "right mind" (Mark 5:15), God's right way of thinking and acting (cf. Rom 12:1-2).

But that's not the whole story. Along with calming and making whole the deranged demoniac, Jesus allows, if not directly causes, the drowning of 2,000 swine via the Legion of demons he "permits" to inhabit them (5:13). This is the only miracle incident where death and destruction accompany Jesus's saving work. This looks more like real war, securing victory by conquest, by *killing* the enemy. Moreover, this story also constitutes a singular Gospel case in which Jesus *negotiates with terrorists*, that is, with the Legion-demons, and with other affected figures who beg him for some concession, which he grants in two cases. In these respects, Jesus does manifest as the conquering hero, the "strong man" who holds the fate of his subdued subjects in his hands. The question is, how does he work out these negotiations and to what ends?

Negotiation

Three character groups—the Legion-demons, the swineherds and people, and the liberated demoniac—"adjure/implore" (*horkizō*, 5:7) or "beg" (*parakaleō*, 5:10-12, 17, 18) the powerful Jesus to do something for them.

Plea #1. The *Legion-demons* twice lodge a strong plea with Jesus: first, daring him to swear an oath, "In God's name, don't torture me!" (5:7 NIV); second, in two parts: "begging" Jesus "again and again" *not* to expel them from the country (5:10 NIV), then "begging" him *to* send them into the swine (5:12). This demonic band audaciously pushes their luck, since they know full well Jesus's august status as "Son of the Most High God" (5:7; cf. 1:24). They also brazenly dare to ask Jesus not to torment or torture *them*, which is precisely what they've been doing "night and day" (5:5) to the poor demoniac! At this point, Jesus ignores Legion's plea and orders the "unclean spirit" to "come out of the man" (5:8). But when Legion presses further to request a reposting into the nearby herd of pigs, Jesus curiously complies.

Two questions beg for attention: Why does Legion make this request? And why does Jesus grant it, rather than just shut up these demons as he's done before (1:25, 34; 3:11-12)? Warren Carter provides persuasive answers.

Knowing it has been defeated by Jesus, Legion bargains for the best deal it can muster, striving "to maintain [as much] domination" as it can; "along with control of the land, the demon has, with impeccable imperial logic, sought to preserve control over the land's production, particularly animals" (Carter 2014, 148). The logic has a fatal flaw, as the demon-infested pigs promptly dash to their deaths in the depths of the sea. Thereby, Jesus turns Legion's request against itself and all it stands for, "mock[ing] Roman power as . . . out-of-control, demonic, militaristic, and (self-) destructive" (Carter 2014, 140).

Fair enough: Jesus emerges not only as the superior strong man but also the shrewder strategist. In the process, however, he treads close to the edge of imperial means of deception and ends of destruction. Why wipe out 2,000 animals in a violent drowning? The striking parallel with the demise of Pharaoh's army in the Red Sea scarcely dilutes the moral problem of both incidents. God and God's Son are agents of life, not death, we hope and pray. Yes, as the "Holy One of God" (1:23) and "Son of the Most High" (5:7), Jesus stands apart from "unclean" spirits (Legion) and creatures (pigs). But while Jewish law prohibited eating non-kosher pigs (Lev 11:7; Deut 14:8), it never specifically mandated *killing* them (which eating them would require) or eliminating the species from the planet. They have their purpose in creation, just not, in the Jewish worldview, for human consumption.

The latter third of Isaiah, stemming from Israel's postexilic era, denounces *God's rebellious people*, "who sit inside tombs . . . who eat swine's flesh," and yet "who say . . . 'do not come near me, for I am too holy for you'," claiming a perverse sense of their *own righteousness* before and even against God (Isa 65:4-5). If they persist in such blasphemous arrogance, they can expect God to "destine [them] to the sword, and all of [them] shall bow down to the slaughter" (65:12). Thankfully, Isaiah's larger vision, announced in the same chapter, anticipates a blessed creation of "new heavens and a new earth" and a peaceable kingdom (see 65:25), leaving the "former things" in the dust (65:17). Mark's exorcism story seems suspended between the former and latter images of Isaiah 65. While the former tomb-roving demoniac desires to "be with" the holy Jesus (5:19), the "swine flesh" possessed by Legion hurtles to its violent death at Jesus's command. No lying down and feeding together with the lamb (Isa 11:6; 65:25). Creation still groans for full restoration (cf. Rom 8:22-23).

Jesus's indomitable will to life, his bold commitment to all lives—a commitment that will get *him killed* (unjustly)—ill fits this swine-drowning incident, along with a later episode where Jesus "curses" a fig tree to death (11:12-14, 21). What does Jesus have against pigs and figs? Fortunately, these are one-off events for dramatic political effects, in this case symbolically countering the diabolical devastating thrust of Roman (Legion) rule (see Spencer 2003, 100–101, 104–105; and commentary below on 11:12-25). Moreover, technically the demons drive the pigs to their watery grave, not Jesus. But he does "permit" them to do so (5:13), which partly abets their murderous aims. The problem is only exacerbated when the swineherds and people of the region voice their concern.

Plea #2. Upon witnessing their animals' destruction, the *swineherds* "ran off" (are they next?) and report the shocking event throughout the area, city and countryside. A group of curious *people* rush to the scene, wanting to see for themselves. Upon observing the incredible transformation of the wild demoniac and devastation of the tame swine (not wild boars), these witnesses further broadcast the news in the region. But they do not regard this as good news. Their primary response is one of *fear*, not faith, prompting them to "beg Jesus to leave their neighborhood," which he does, again complying with a request from antagonists (5:14-18a).

The Gerasene swineherds and people seem to have little regard for the demoniac's well-being. They might just as soon leave him to roam and rot among the tombs; though harming himself, at least he wasn't hurting anyone else out there. And who is this strange Jesus anyway, who has suddenly invaded their shores and conquered this crazed brute of a man? Not for the first or last time, anxious people wonder about the source and scope of Jesus's power and authority (3:21-22; 6:2-3; 11:27-28). If he commands diabolical forces so easily and thoroughly, what might he do to us if we upset him? Remember, these folk on the "other side" have no prior knowledge of Jesus beyond random reports that might have drifted across the sea. These events hit them cold and hard, particularly when they factor in the material and economic *loss* of the swine. The numbers don't add up. The life of a single man—one who had caused so much havoc and distress, no less—scarcely seems *worth* the lives of 2,000 pigs. Before we decry such calculus too quickly—nothing is more precious than a human being's life, *any* human being's life—we should still try to see things from the Gerasenes' viewpoint: these swine were a big part of *their livelihood*. How many people would such a large herd have fed if they hadn't just plunged to their deaths!

Neither Mark nor Jesus shows any sympathy for the lost herd of swine (this is no happy lost *sheep* story [Matt 18:10-14//Luke 15:3-7) or the people dependent on these animals, though Jesus does promptly leave the area, as requested, before causing any more upheaval. We might posit that destroying the "unclean" swine helps faithful Jews in this largely Gentile region stay "holy," along the lines of Moses' insistence that the Israelites "utterly destroy" everything pertaining to the Canaanites in the promised land, lest God's people be led astray (Deut 7:1-6). But Mark sets the current exorcism incident *outside* the holy land, and Jesus mounts no reverse Joshua-style conquest of this foreign territory (Gerasa is no Jericho).

The "Who is this Jesus?" question does not yield easy answers; it keeps pressing, prodding, and disturbing audiences, including Jesus's disciples, in the Gospel narrative. By the same token, an honest assessment of the present story should carry some shock as well as awe and not a little fear for us readers, as it does for characters within the story. Jesus refuses to be domesticated to our tastes. Yet for all this episode's raw dissonance, its "dominant" note still sounds the good news of liberation—for the demoniac certainly, but also for surrounding region. Jesus does not leave Gerasa and environs bereft and bewildered. He enlists an unlikely but effective witness for him and his ministry throughout the area, as we discover in the final plea.

Plea #3. After his remarkable cure, the *Gerasene demoniac*, now his "right" self, approaches Jesus as he is "getting into the boat" and begs "to be *with him*" (5:18), precisely what Jesus had chosen the Twelve to do (3:14) (Black 2011, 138). He longs to follow Jesus, to be a true disciple. Ironically, this is the one plea Jesus *denies*. We soon discover, however, that he does not reject the man so much as *redirect* his focus back "home, to your friends" and throughout the Decapolis, telling "how much Jesus had done for him" (5:19-20).

This man is the first healed person Jesus encourages to testify (contrast 1:44-45), perhaps because the word will be shared in more remote territory outside of Galilee. In any event, Jesus deploys this delivered demoniac, this former agent of Legion, for missionary service before he sends out the Twelve on a specific assignment (6:7-13).

Perhaps the most amazing aspect of this story, however, is Jesus's simple directive, "Go home to your friends," or more literally, "Go to *your* (*sou*) house to the ones who are yours (*sous*)," in other words, "to your own people" (5:19 NIV, CEB). This statement encapsulates the social-relational aspect of healing, so vital to holistic well-being: illness alienates as much as debilitates; healing integrates with family and friends as much as eliminates disease and demons (Pilch 2000; Green 2011b). Remember, this man had been stripped of everything and everyone; nothing was "his." The only "friends" he had before were corpses; his own people couldn't handle him. But now Jesus restores him to his community, with potential for gaining new spiritual brothers and sisters through his witness to the good news of Jesus (cf. 3:33-35).

Freedom from Death: Restoring Critically Ill "Daughters" (5:21-43)

If Jesus and the disciples hope that returning to their homeland will calm down their lives, they are soon disappointed as new crises erupt. At least the return boat trip is uneventful. But when they arrive on shore, another "great crowd" presses around Jesus (5:21), and another desperate individual "begs" for Jesus's attention and action (5:23). This man, a synagogue leader named Jairus, though as opposite a character from the Gerasene demoniac as one might imagine, is frenzied in his own way, frantic with worry about his critically ill "little daughter" teetering at home on the brink of death; accordingly, he pleads for Jesus to "come and lay your [healing] hands on her" (5:22-24).

En route, however, to Jairus's home, with the crushing throng dogging Jesus's every step, a woman with her own serious malady—a chronic bleeding disorder—pushes through from behind, touches Jesus's clothing, and draws healing power from him, which "immediately" stops him in his tracks (5:24b-30). While sorting out this shocking experience, dealing with the woman he addresses as "Daughter" and sending her on her way "in peace" (5:34), word comes that Jairus's daughter has already died. The services of Jesus "the teacher" will no longer be required (5:35). But we know that Mark's Jesus is no ordinary "teacher" (1:27; 4:38) or healer and are thus not that surprised when he still proceeds to Jairus's house to wake the little girl from her "sleep" (5:39). Even so, raising someone from the sleep of *death* raises Jesus's power to another level, crossing the ultimate threshold between life and death. Becoming "overcome with amazement" (5:42) at this feat seems like an understatement.

The intertwining plots of these two "daughter" miracles form the second Markan "sandwich."

Sandwich #2
A Jesus Heads to the Home of Jairus's Ill Daughter (5:21-24a)
  B Jesus Heals a Hemorrhaging Woman and Calls Her "Daughter" (5:24b-34)
A Jesus Raises Jairus's Daughter from the Dead (5:35-43)

Closer examination reveals numerous points of interconnection between the two stories, both comparative and contrastive. They mutually interpret each other and provide key clues to Mark's emphases in this section (pg. 83).

As the action of the two stories crisscrosses, bleeding into each other, so the movement *within* the stories traverses critical theological, emotional, and

Remarkable Works of Freeing and Feeding I

	Bleeding Woman Healed by Jesus (5:24b-34)	**Deceased Daughter Resuscitated by Jesus (5:21-24a; 5:35-43)**
Daughter Relationship	Jesus affirms his spiritual "daughter"	Jairus pleads for his biological daughter
Social Status	Destitute, likely unmarried, possibly divorced, uncertain family situation	Reasonably well off, loving family
Setting	Public scene amid pressing crowds	Private scene in Jairus's home; only the girl's parents and Peter, James, and John allowed inside with Jesus
Time Span	Twelve years of draining disease and financial loss	At twelve years of age suffers fatal disease
Support Network	Unknown, but acts alone	Father, mother, and synagogue community
Element of Touch	Woman touches Jesus's clothing to secure her healing	Jesus takes the dead girl by the hand and raises her up
Act of Faith	"Daughter, your faith (*pistis*) has made you well"	"Do not fear, only believe (*pisteue*)"
Emotional Impact	Fearing, trembling, going "in peace"	Fearing, mock-laughing, weeping, "overcome with amazement"
Reproductive Issues	Probable chronic uterine bleeding, impairing her ability to have children	Life cut short near age of puberty before she was able to bear children
Wider Connections with Jesus	Bleeding (on the cross) and suffering a terrible "scourge" (*mastigoō*, 10:34; cf. *mastix*, 5:29, 34).	Sleeping and waking (in a perilous storm), dying in a situation of (apparent) divine absence (15:34), yet later being raised from the dead

social boundaries between (1) life and death, (2) fear and faith, (3) isolation and integration.

Life and death

Jesus's urgent-critical mission continues to be embroiled in literal life-and-death matters. The storm at sea hit with lethal force, prompting the disciples' reasonable fear that they might "perish"; and the graveyard-dwelling demoniac was possessed by a powerful force hell-bent on destroying him. Although the present two cases are less volatile, they are no less potentially—and actually, with Jairus's daughter—*fatal*.

The woman's chronic "hemorrhages" (5:25, 29) for a dozen years likely involved a gynecological bleeding disorder. The two diagnostic terms Mark uses—"flow/discharge (*rhysis*)" (5:25) and "fountain/spring (*pēgē*)" of blood (5:29)—apply to a woman's regular monthly period, any irregular bleeding outside the normal cycle, and to the process of giving birth in the Greek version of Leviticus (Lev 12:7; 15:19-33). Leviticus 20:18 includes both terms as synonyms: "A man who lies with a woman who sits apart and uncovers her shame—he has laid bare her spring (*pēgēn*), and she has laid bare her flow (*rhysin*) of blood" (NETS). The language of "sitting apart" describes a woman's set-apart, "unclean" status for seven days during and following her period or any other time of genital emission (Lev 15:19, 28). The issue becomes particularly acute for women with irregular or chronic vaginal discharges: "And a woman, if she flows with a flow (*rheē rhysei*) of blood for rather many days, not at the time of her period, even if she flows after her period, all the days of the flow of her impurity are like the days of her period; she shall be unclean" (15:25 NETS). Thus the bleeding woman in our story would have existed in a more or less constant state of "uncleanness." But what exactly does that mean? (See Levine 1996; 2006, 172–75; 2017, 761; Gench 2004, 28–55, Spencer 2004, 59–60).

Purity laws regulating "flows" of blood placed some restrictions on women's movements and contacts, but notions of tightly confined and corseted women do not fit ancient Jewish society. A lone text in Numbers segregates "*everyone* who . . . has a discharge . . . *both male and female*, putting them outside the (wilderness) camp" (Num 5:1-4; Josephus applies this rule to the "city" in *Ant*. 3.361). The Levitical code, however, only prohibits those with genital discharges—again, men as well as women—from entering the "tabernacle" or "sanctuary" until they have completed their ritual washing and seven-day probation (Lev 15:28-32; cf. 12:4; Josephus applies this law to the "temple" in *J.W.* 5.227) (Haber 2003, 274–80; Wassen 2016,

92–94). Further, sexual intercourse (not all social contact) while the woman is menstruating renders both participants "unclean" (15:24, 33).

The sectarian communities reflected in the Dead Sea Scrolls, hyper-concerned with ritual purity, followed the stricter line of Numbers by quarantining "unclean" women during their periods and after giving birth in isolated quarters outside normal residential and business areas (11QT48.14-17). In Jerusalem, three separate zones were to be cordoned off east of the holy city to confine "[1] the lepers, [2] those suffering from a flux [3] and men who had a (nocturnal) emission" (11QT46.16-18; Vermes 2011, 207). In the same vein, a text in the Mishnah refers to separate "houses for impure women," ritually impure, that is, from vaginal bleeding (m. Niddah 7:4) (Harrington 1995, 45–46; Haber 2003, 177–78).

But such extreme separatist measures—"maximalist" and "expansionist" into regular life beyond religious worship in sacred centers (Wassen 2016, 94, 99)—went beyond the letter of the biblical law and were impractical for most ordinary people. Persons afflicted with severe skin diseases ("leprosy") may have huddled together and kept their distance from "clean" society (Lev 13:45-46; Luke 17:11-13)—but not always (Shinall 2018), as we saw with the individual "leper" who approached Jesus in public; recall that while Jesus took issue with the way the man requested healing, neither Jesus nor anyone else recoiled at the man's presence (Mark 1:40-41). The fact is, given the rather complex purity code, most people (including priests) would have been impure most of time in some respect, not least from regular genital emissions constituting a good and necessary fact of *life*! Those dedicated to observing the law had wide access to bathing pools (*mikva'oth*) in Judea and Galilee (along with the freshwater Sea/Lake of Galilee) for purifying ablutions, as needed, without greatly disrupting their everyday lives (Reed 2000, 45–52, 127–28, 157–58; Sawicki 2000, 23–26, 99–101, 118–26; Evans 2012, 25–27, 51–57, 94–95). Thus women with vaginal bleeding, regular or irregular, "may still live at home and lead relatively normal lives" (Haber 2003, 176).

As we stressed in the section on Mark 1:21-45, we should again note that "ceremonial uncleanness" or "ritual impurity" in the Bible is not moral iniquity; it has nothing to do with sin or setting people at odds with another. It has to do with setting apart order from disorder, with setting and protecting boundaries between Creator and creature, salutary and predatory creatures, life and death—all encompassed within God's good creation. The woman's blood of birthing and menstruating is *lifeblood*, flowing out to create another's life, shedding her blood for her child—possibly to the point of death since childbirth was fraught with considerable risk in the ancient world. And so the woman is set apart in honor, not shame: no one more intimately—or precariously—participates in the holy process of creation and occupies the numinous space between life and death than she. Her periods of designated "uncleanness" and "purification" affirm her vital place in the community. She's not rejected, cursed, or disgraced for her uterine bleeding: nothing is more natural or critical to group survival than her life-giving powers. In ancient Israelite culture, a "barren" woman unable to bear children carried a shameful stigma (Gen 30:22-23; Luke 1:25), not a woman with a normal cycle.

Perhaps most telling for Mark, unlike the story of the man with "leprosy" in 1:40-45, the account of the hemorrhaging woman contains *no* mention of her "uncleanness" or Jesus's post-healing instruction that she should go and complete purification rites. Jesus simply tells her to "go in peace" (5:34) as an antidote to her anxiety (see discussion below), not her impurity. Accordingly, related to the central life-and-death theme, I stress less the bleeding woman's impurity than her *infertility* or *incapacity* to participate fully in creative "fruitful" life (see Gen 1:28) (Wassen 2008, 644; Thiessen 2020, 90–91). In her *chronic* condition, she *cannot* "bear fruit" (Mark 4:20) in the most personal and powerful sense, any more than Jairus's deceased daughter can, as she dies at the typical age of puberty, the onset of menses. By healing the woman with a twelve-year-long abnormal flow and raising the twelve-year-old girl on the cusp of beginning her flow, Jesus restores both to healthy, life-giving life.

Moreover, by way of foreshadowing (prolepsis), the two females remarkably preview Jesus's own death and resurrection. The older woman had "endured/suffered much" (*polla pathousa*, 5:24) throughout her illness, matching the "great suffering" (*polla pathei*, 8:31) Jesus predicts will attend his death. More specifically, Jesus's forecast of his impending "flogging/scourging" by the authorities uses a verb (*mastigoō*, 10:34) related to the noun *mastix*, denoting "scourge/plague," which twice designates the woman's "disease" (5:25, 34) (Reid 1996, 142). Beyond sharing the scourge of suffering, this woman and Jesus are the only characters in Mark who *bleed*, who shed their own life-giving blood. Jesus, however, reverses the flow from death to life, from lethal effusion to life-renewing infusion not only for this woman but "for many" (14:24; 10:45).

The younger girl, Jairus's daughter, relates most proximally with Jesus's *sleeping* and more remotely with his *rising* from the dead, although the connections are disrupted by key distinctions. Jesus slept in the storm-tossed boat as a sign of his peaceful confidence in God's protection and awoke—or rather was awakened by deathly terrified disciples—to calm the tempest and preserve life (4:38-41). In the present incident, Jesus pronounces the (really) dead daughter as "but sleeping" (5:39) to signify not only her placid state ("rest in peace") following her terminal disease but, more importantly, his intention to awaken her to fresh life: to rouse her, to raise her from the dead, as Jesus himself will be resurrected after his crucifixion (16:6-7). The other Gospels include other resuscitative miracles: Luke also reports Jesus's raising a widow's son during his ministry (Luke 7:10-17); Matthew adds in conjunction with Jesus's resurrection that "the tombs also were opened, and many bodies of the saints who had fallen asleep were raised" (Matt 27:52-53); and John features the raising of Lazarus in Bethany (John 11:11-15, 38-44). Mark presents only the raising of Jairus's daughter as a parallel to Jesus's own resurrection. The parallel is not perfect since, unlike Jesus, the girl is destined to die again. Nonetheless, she represents the "firstfruits" of God's life-giving power through Christ (cf. 1 Cor 15:20-23).

Fear and faith
Remember that after Jesus stilled the storm, he questioned his disciples' emotional state, pitting their fearfulness against their faithlessness: "Why are you afraid/cowardly? Have you still no faith (*pistin*)?" The narrator adds, "And they were filled with great awe/fear (*ephoēthēsan phobon megan*)" (4:40-41). Reinforcing this dichotomy between fear and faith—though in a more encouraging *imperative* instead of disparaging *interrogative* mode—Jesus exhorts Jairus in the immediate wake of his daughter's death, "Do not fear (*mē phobou*), only believe (*monon pisteue*)" (5:36). In the case of the bleeding woman, however, Jesus issues a tender *declarative* affirmation of her faith in the midst of her fear and as a means of alleviating it: "But the woman . . . came in fear and trembling (*phobētheisa kai tremousa*) before him. . . . He said to her, 'Daughter, your faith (*pistis*) has made you well; go in peace, and be healed of your disease'" (5:33-34). In their own ways, all three stories feature Jesus's negotiating emotional tensions between fear and faith, tremulousness and trust.

While the disciples' fear of impending death in the storm and Jairus's fear after his daughter's death are understandable responses (though Jesus resists them), the woman's intense "fear and trembling" *in her new healed state* is more puzzling. Why does she become so scared *then*, especially after taking such bold measures to reach out to Jesus in the first place? The intervening variable here is Jesus's reaction to having his "power" (*dynamis*) suddenly siphoned from him by some unknown person in the crowd. "Who touched my clothes?" he blurted, as he stopped, "turned," and "looked all around (*perieblepeto*) to see who had done it' (5:30, 32)—the same "looking around" he had done in anger and anguish at the hardhearted Pharisees in the synagogue (3:5) and in surveying the audience attending his teaching in the house while his family remained outside (3:32-34). In the current situation, though Jesus may not be angry as such, he is taken by surprise, taken aback by this unknown person who took something from him without his permission! This has never happened to Jesus before (and won't happen again); he needs to sort out this strange phenomenon before moving on.

For the woman's part, she seizes with fear upon seeing and hearing Jesus's dramatic response to her incognito tapping of his flow of power to stanch her flow of blood. Following in the venerable tradition of Aristotle, many modern scientists and philosophers view thoughts, feelings, and actions as dynamic intertwined processes within, between, and among embodied persons and their environments (Spencer 2017a; 2021, 9–13). Aristotle's classic analysis of emotion discerns that fear is often caused by perceived "enmity and anger from those with *power to do something*; for it is clear that they wish to, and thus they are *near doing it*" (Aristotle, *On Rhetoric* 2.5.3 [1382a]); in turn, fear prompts swift "deliberation" by the frightened person concerning what to do in response to the sensed imminent danger (2.5.14 [1383a]). Precisely the same *power* that healed the woman is what scares her when Jesus promptly demands to know who touched him and extracted his power. Such an august strong man is not to be trifled with; if offended, no telling how he might retaliate.

Another precarious factor potentially stoking the woman's fear is a cultural mindset of *limited goods*, a closed system of nonrenewable, finite resources for which people compete: a zero-sum contest in which anyone's gain is everyone's loss. As anthropologist George Foster has observed, "peasant society" regards *health* as one key limited commodity, particularly related to the supply of *blood* and other critical bodily fluids (including semen). The physical debility of losing blood is exacerbated by the social-psychological belief that such loss is irrevocable and irreplaceable, "a permanent loss resulting in weakness for as long as an individual lives" (even in modern times with transfusion technology, poorer farming communities tend to be more reluctant to give and receive blood) (Foster 1965, 299–300; cf. Malina 2001a, 81–107). Apart from reinforcing the bleeding woman's weakened state, a limited-goods mentality would also perceive that her catalytic touch diminished or drained Jesus's power in some measure. Her gain is his loss in this economy. Moreover, gender dynamics further disrupts the social order: a poor woman enhances her life at the expense of a powerful man.

While we as sympathetic readers might quickly assure the woman—"No, no, fear not; this is the all-powerful and all-loving Jesus, willing to share his inexhaustible resources and welcome you into his tender arms"—she doesn't feel that assurance yet, and Jesus does not immediately offer it. Briefly, but conspicuously, Mark sustains a moment of high tension between Jesus's power and love, a critical moment in which the woman must act.

To her credit, she does not simply take her healing and slink back into the crowd; she does not flee or freeze, but rather decides to come forward, fall down before (not behind) Jesus, spill "the whole truth," and let the chips fall where they may. She speaks truth as a further act of faith *in and through* her "fear and trembling" (5:33).

To his credit, Jesus, in his surprised emotional state, takes in the woman's truth—irrespective of her low social status and conventional prejudice against women's testimony—gives her a fair and considered hearing, and consequently changes his tone from the testy "Who touched me!" to the tender "Daughter, your faith has made you well; go in peace, and [keep being] healed of your disease" (5:34). Together, Jesus and the woman work through the emotionally fraught situation to a *peace-filled* outcome, coming to a point of *mutual trust* in one another, establishing a *relationship* of confident, assuring *faith* (Spencer 2017b, 228–34, 239–40).

In the other daughter story, father Jairus becomes gripped by that most haunting of human fears—fear of *death*—the price we pay as cognitively advanced creatures capable of contemplating our own and others' demises. Jairus knows that his beloved little girl is "at the point of death" when he approaches Jesus (5:22); but that's not when Jesus urges him to "fear not," however much Jairus might have been scared to death about his daughter's fate. Jesus seeks to move Jairus from fear to faith *after* he learns his daughter has died (5:36). We might think that Jesus should now address Jairus's *grief* or *despair*, not his fear. What's left to fear? Emotion researchers stress the *prospective* function of emotions, that is, their drive to anticipate and stimulate assessment of future outcomes (Seligmann et al. 2016; DeSteno 2018, 77; Barrett 2017, 56–83; 107–27; Spencer 2021, 16–18). Fear is a banner case, signaling danger ahead, around the bend. As Aristotle put it, "Let fear [*phobos*] be [defined as] a sort of pain and agitation derived from the imagination of a future destructive or painful evil," especially when that evil is "near at hand" (*On Rhetoric* 2.5.1 [1382a]).

So what fearful prospects lie ahead now for Jairus and his deceased little girl? The prospect of *seeing* her lifeless body, for one (remember, Jairus is heading home when the tragic news comes); perhaps, too, fear of further disaster (is our family under some kind of "curse"?), fear of surviving a loved one, of trying to live in the thick shadow of their death; fear of what the dead daughter may or not be feeling now, of what her ultimate end might be.

Jewish faith in a *general* resurrection at the end of the age was common (see John 11:24), but what about existence in the murky interim? What kind of *faith* sees one through these eerie deathly shades?

Jesus dares to step across the threshold of death into the dark void on the "other side" *believing* in—trusting in, hoping and longing for—new life *now, near at hand*, not just on the last day. So he takes the dead girl's hand and pulls her back into the land of the living, a first venture into the void that Jesus himself will occupy for three days between his own death and resurrection. In the midst of Jairus's overwhelming uncertainty about postmortem experience, Jesus invites him to fight his fear and join Jesus's journey of *faith*. He permits only a few to follow and witness: his inner circle of disciples (Peter, James, and John) and Jairus, his wife, and their close friends. No mockers allowed (5:37-40).

Understandably, when the deceased daughter comes back to life, the group is "overcome with amazement" (5:42), "utterly astounded" (NAB), "shocked!" (CEB)—no doubt with persisting traces of fear, shading now, however, toward awe and wonder. Again Jesus issues a gag order on reporting this miracle, although it's difficult to imagine containing such blockbuster news (5:43a). But most remarkable is Jesus's final order "to give [the raised girl] *something to eat*" (5:43b)—an order remarkable for being unremarkable, for its ordinariness in this extraordinary context, celebrating basic sustenance of life (cf. 2:23-26). Whatever the girl experienced in her minutes or hours of being dead, it made her hungry! For all his involvement in the deepest mysteries of life and death, Jesus embraces everyday acts of feeding and eating as sacred (sacramental). This last note in Mark 5 portends Jesus's increased attention to feeding and eating matters in chapters 6–8.

Isolation and integration

Feeding-and-eating also constitutes a primary social event—table fellowship with family and friends (see 2:15-17). Death is the great isolator, the stark separator. Jesus's simple instruction to give the girl something to eat reincorporates her into the home, similar to enjoining the Gerasene demoniac to "go home to your friends" (5:19). The deathbed gives way to the dinner table. Moreover, as the girl "got up and began to walk about" in her resuscitated twelve-year-old body (Mark waits to disclose her age until 5:42), she may, on the brink of womanhood, begin to plan for marriage and childbearing (as her culture would expect of her), for bringing new life into the world and extending the family circle.

Likewise, Jesus's final word to the healed older woman he calls "Daughter," bidding her to "go in peace" (5:34), not only integrates her into God's family and alleviates her fear of Jesus's reprisal but also restores her potential for full participation in community life. Her gynecological disorder disabled her from fulfilling traditional sexual and maternal roles; if her bleeding condition had started after marriage, it might well have prompted her husband to divorce her for "something objectionable" or "indecent" (NIV) about her (Deut 24:1). And in her chronically "unclean" state—though not generally ostracized or quarantined (see above)—she would have been barred from entering interior temple courts and engaging in religious rites practiced there. Now, as her faith-full outreach to Jesus "has made [her] well"—has saved (*sesōken*) her (5:34)—she is free to enjoy the full fellowship of God's people without stigma and strictures.

Interlude: Frustration (6:1-6a)

After this run of remarkable deeds on both sides of the lake, Jesus "left that place" where he had just healed the bleeding woman and raised up the deceased girl "and came to his hometown" of Nazareth (6:1). A risky move, given the recent encounter with his family, who had traveled to another town (probably Capernaum) to "restrain" his alleged deranged behavior and curb the dishonor he was bringing on the family (3:21). As it happened, Jesus's mother and siblings failed to stop him or even get a personal audience with him, as he welcomed all who do God's will as "my brother and sister and mother" (3:34-35).

The prospects of a happy family reunion are not good. While the hometown folk are "astounded" at Jesus's teaching in their synagogue (6:2), and while Jesus himself becomes "amazed" at their response (6:6a), we readers are not surprised that such wide-eyed reactions reflect suspicious doubt and bewilderment rather than mutual trust and belief. But what precisely sparks the frustration?

Nazareth "takes offense" at Jesus (6:1-4)

On Jesus's home turf, his relatives and neighbors "took offense" (*eskandalizonto*) at his words and actions (6:3). The Greek verb *skandalizō*, from which the English "scandalize" derives, denoted either a passive response, "to take offense or be offended," or an active move, "to do wrong or sin" (Friberg, Friberg, and Miller 2000). The CEB incorporates both meanings in our text: "They were repulsed by him and fell into sin" (6:3). The latter meaning corresponds to the shallow, "rocky" respondents to the gospel in 4:17 who "fall away" (*skandalizontai*) after an initial spurt of interest (Black 2011, 146). Ironically, when Jesus returns to his hometown roots, the people prove to be rootless in their reception of his message. What sparks the Nazarenes' misunderstanding?

They struggle with the *source* (where) and *substance* (what) of Jesus's ministry. "*Where* did this man get all this?" they wonder, warily (6:2). "This man" (*toutos*) doing "these things" (*tauta*) makes no sense to them; he must have some strange outside "supplier." Their suspicions likely run along similar lines that his mother and siblings earlier heard from some scribes. Has Jesus become possessed by demons under Satan's rule (3:21-22)? How otherwise can they explain *what* he does: the paranormal wisdom (*sophia*) and power (*dynamis*) he exhibits (6:2)?

Mark's narrative has already offered ample evidence that Jesus's wise teaching and wondrous power come from *God*, certifying his vocation as God's Son and Messiah. While we might expect the scribes to take offense at Jesus's ministry, since he lacks the right pedigree and training from their perspective, it's less obvious why his own community refuses to give him the benefit of the doubt or, for that matter, to be proud of his extraordinary work. That's our hometown boy!

We must, however, appreciate the prevailing cultural mindset of the time, steeped in hierarchical honor-shame codes (Malina 2001a, 27–57; deSilva 2000, 23–93). To honor one's family or, conversely, not bring shame on the family in others' eyes, one must know one's place and stay there—not "get above one's raisin'." One must dutifully play the assigned role, maintain "ascribed" honor, and only obtain extra "achieved" honor by acceptable means, such as distinguished community or military service.

Who does Jesus think he is? Sages and prophets, philosophers and potentates don't come from Nazareth! We Nazarenes know that, just like everyone else out there, if they ever deign to think about us (see John 1:45-46; 7:27, 52). "Is not this [Jesus] the carpenter (*tektōn*)," a tradesman for as long as we've known him, Mary's boy with four brothers (all named here) and some sisters—part of a typical, workaday Nazareth family (6:3)? Where does Jesus get off acting all high and mighty? Shame on him!

Jesus by no means flaunts his wisdom and power, lords himself over his own people, curries favor, or craves fame (remember his repeated orders not to broadcast his miracles). But that doesn't stop his parochial home village from becoming offended by his eccentric behavior. If he's going to spurn their homespun values, as they see it, they will spurn him.

The Nazarenes' taking offense at Jesus's odd embodiment of wisdom and power fits a larger pattern of misunderstanding Jesus's mission in Mark, especially as the *cross* comes into view (8:31-34). On a common-sense plane, such misunderstanding is very understandable. A *crucified Messiah* does not make common sense. It veritably defines cognitive dissonance. What is less powerful and less wise than an ignominious death, "even death on a cross" (Phil 2:8)? Or, as Paul explicitly puts it in wisdom-power and "scandal" terms, "For Jews demand [powerful] signs and Greeks desire wisdom, but we proclaim Christ crucified, a stumbling block (*skandalon*) to Jews and foolishness to Gentiles, but to those who are the called, both Jews and Greeks, [the crucified] Christ *the power of God and the wisdom of God*" (1 Cor 1:22-24). An offensive *scandal*, indeed—precisely what his disciples stumble over when he forecasts his looming crucifixion (Mark 8:31-34; 9:30-32; 10:32-45). Grasping the divine wisdom and power of the cross requires keen spiritual discernment and bold trust in the creative-transformative power of God. We must press ahead on Mark's narrative journey to get the full picture of Jesus's wisdom and power, as scandalous as it is marvelous.

Jesus is taken aback by Nazareth's "unbelief" (6:5-6a)

The situation may seem ripe for another justifiably angry reaction by Jesus toward those who restrict or resist his life-giving ministry (cf. 1:41; 3:5). But not here: he does not mirror the Nazareth community's contempt, tit for tat. He does not take their offense personally. At first, he takes their derision in stride as normal for God's messenger: "Prophets are not without honor, except in their hometown, and among their own kin, and in their own house" (6:4). By definition, prophets of God push social boundaries, challenge conventional norms, call people to change their attitudes and actions (repentance)—things a prophet's people don't take kindly to hearing about themselves. It feels as if the prophet has turned against them, and not for their own good. So Jesus accepts his hometown's consternation as par for the course.

But an unexpected corollary of Nazareth's opposition proves not so easy for Jesus to accept, triggering his response not of being angry but rather "amazed" (*thaumazō*, 6:6), a "verb denoting incredulous surprise" (Moulton and Milligan 1930, 284; cf. Mark 5:20; John 3:7). Jesus is typically the object of others' astonishment/amazement, including from his hometown (Mark 6:2). But following close on the heels of his (implied) shocking surprise, as argued above, at the bleeding woman's stealthy discharge of his power (*dynamis*, 5:30), is his current (explicit) amazement in relation to the Nazarenes' questioning his "deeds of power" (*dynameis*, 6:2). As his messianic mission unfolds, Jesus has to work through his own issues of cognitive-emotional dissonance.

Distinct from the incident with the hemorrhaging woman whose stunning faith (*pistis*) elicits Jesus's flow of healing power (5:28, 34), in his encounter with the people in Nazareth, Jesus "could do no deed of power there, except that he laid his hands on a few sick people and cured them," a startling blockage of his healing power that elicits Jesus's amazement "at their unbelief/unfaith (*apistia*)" (6:5-6a). This marks the first time Jesus faces external limits to his God-given power to help the infirm. A more literal translation of Mark 6:5a exposes his jolting power sag (the reverse of a power surge) in Nazareth: "He did not have the power (*edynato*) there to do any powerful act (*dynamin*)" (except for healing a few sick folk). This assessment proves to be more than Matthew can handle, as it edits Mark to read, "And he *did not do* (*epoiēsen*) many deeds of power there, because of their unbelief" (Matt 13: 58). Matthew "corrects" Mark's report of Jesus's surprising debilitation by attributing his limited performance of miracles to a deliberate *decision* he makes in response to the Nazarenes' lack of faith. No unsettling amazement by Matthew's Jesus; he retains full control (Spencer 2021, 159–65).

But must we follow Matthew (and many interpreters since) in sanding off this rough edge of Mark's portrait of Jesus? Must we insist on Jesus's sovereign control of people and events, superseding human free will? As the Son of God become flesh and blood, fully embodying human life, why should he not be *affected by* other human beings, by others' bodies, minds, hearts, and wills, as well as affecting their lives? Is covenantal, "uncontrolling love," freely given, not the essence of the divine-human relationship (Oord 2015)? Such a relationship can only be sustained through mutual *trust/faith* (*pistis*). The Nazarenes' hardened *apistia*, their distrust of/unfaith in Jesus, complicates his ability to *entrust* his empowered self to them. His power/energy is an integral part of his whole being, not some commodity he manages.

Even so, the matter is not so cut and dried that people's unfaith or diminished faith disqualifies them from Jesus's powerful aid. Recall that his frustration with the disciples' faithlessness on the lake did not preclude him from calming the turbulent waters and saving their necks (4:38-41). Faith is not a formula; trust is not a transaction. It does not operate with debit and credit accounts. Faith is *dynamic* and *relational* all the way through, not formulaic and transactional. Mark's *narrative of faith* allows for ebbs and flows, variations and fluctuations throughout the course of Jesus's ministry.

Situated at the heart of the miracle unit in 4:35–6:56, this short interlude—candidly reporting that "could do *no deed of power*" (6:5)—provides critical perspective on Jesus's dynamic mission. Mark's Jesus is not a miracle machine with a magic Midas touch. He takes on special cases of need *as they present themselves,* and he continues to try to limit publicity (except for encouraging the liberated demoniac's witness across the border in the Decapolis [5:19-20]). Moreover, Jesus himself continues to *learn* (cf. Heb 5:8) about the limits of his power in his complex relations with others. As Jesus leads the way of faith in Mark's story, he also "lives by faith" and learns "from faith to faith" (Rom 1:17 KJV, NAB, NASB) along the way.

Freedom from Limited Resources: Feeding the Multitude (6:6b-44)

However taken aback Jesus was by his hometown's chilly reception, it does not stop his mission in other places. He "went about" or "made the rounds" (*periēgen kyklō*) "among [other] villages" in Galilee, continuing his "teaching" (6:6b). By the end of the chapter, he returns to performing benevolent "deeds of power" (6:41-56). Before that, Jesus dispatches the twelve disciples on their first solo mission, delegating "them [his] authority over the unclean spirits" (6:7). They successfully carry out an exorcising and healing ministry (6:13), punctuated by challenging the people to "repent" (cf. 1:15).

Afterward, these twelve "apostles" ("sent ones") return and report back to Jesus (6:30). But Mark postpones narrating this fact, splicing in between an extended account of John the Baptist's beheading by Herod (6:14-29). And so we come to Sandwich #3—served up on a putrid platter! (6:25-28).

Sandwich #3
A Jesus calls and sends out the twelve apostles on their first mission (6:6b-13)
  B Herod beheads John the Baptist (6:14-29)
A The twelve apostles report back and Jesus feeds the five thousand (6:30-44)

On first glance, it's hard to see the interconnections between these events. The titillating account of Herod's birthday bash featuring a dancing girl and a ghoulish beheading seems grossly out of place. Mark's Gospel may have its raw edges, but this is way too raw! Moreover, this story makes no mention of Jesus. While it picks up the loose thread of John's arrest in 1:14, we've all but forgotten about John by this point; and the Herodian royal family has had no role in the narrative (except the "Herodians" briefly mentioned in 3:6).

On closer examination, however, the "sandwich" yields a provocative sweet-and-sour blend of counterpointed characters and actions related to elements of (1) funding, (2) feeding, and (3) feeling—spread across distinct settings of (1) village, (2) palace, and (3) desert.

	Apostles' Mission in the Villages	Herod's Party in the Palace	Jesus's Ministry in the Desert
Funding	Sent out (*apostellō*) with no bread, no bag, no money	A "king's" ransom, the wealth of a "kingdom"	Five loaves of bread, two fishes
Feeding	Voluntary hospitality to apostles	A lavish banquet for Herod and cronies; Herod "sent" (*apostellō*) a soldier-guard to bring John's head on a platter	Dinner plus leftovers for a hungry crowd, though apostles want Jesus to "send them away" (*aperchomai*)
Feeling	—	Herod's fear, perplexity, and deep "grief"; Herodias's hostility	Jesus's compassion

Funding

The two preceding miracle accounts have stressed Jesus's gracious liberating power in the face of limited resources. Regarding the Gerasene demoniac, "no one had the strength to subdue him" (5:4), much less help him, and the deranged man had no means of helping himself. The woman slowly bleeding to death "had spent all that she had" on doctors, to no avail (5:26). Both figures were at the end of their ropes, with Jesus as their last hope. Although these are extreme cases of deprivation, they reflect a common perception of limited world resources for which people must compete. Drawing on the work of anthropologist George Foster, I introduced this worldview above in relation to the woman's limited health and blood supply. Foster extends the concept to other spheres of life:

> Peasants view their social, economic, and natural universes—their total environment—as one in which all of the desired things in life such as land, wealth, health, friendship and love, manliness and honor, respect and status, power and influence, security and safety *exist in finite quantity* and *are always in short supply*, as far as the peasant is concerned. Not only do these and other "good things" exist in finite and limited quantities, in addition *there is no way directly within peasant power to increase the available quantities*. (Foster 1965, 296 [emphasis original]; also 1972)

Applying Foster's work to New Testament social history, Douglas Oakman stresses that the notion of limited goods was not simply a mental construct for small-minded people but also a material reality: "In fact, *limited-good perspectives* are rooted in specific circumstances that regularly yield *actual limited goods* for most people, and such circumstances recurrently conditioned the social and cultural attitudes and values of the Bible" (Oakman 2018, 98 [emphasis original]). Surplus goods and profits that villagers produced and earned on their small farms often went to service debts to landlords, pay taxes to Caesar and client-rulers like Herod, and feed the appetites of elites in urban centers (Oakman 2018; Neyrey and Rohrbaugh 2008). The mission of Jesus and his apostles, disrupted by Herod's brutal bacchanalia, presents the starkest of contrasts between commoners and potentates, villagers and upper-crust city dwellers.

On the one hand, Jesus does not merely accept his and his followers' limited-resource status but affirms and accentuates it. His twelve emissaries have already left their homes and businesses, and now he sends them out with virtually *no* material support: "He ordered them to take *nothing* for their journey (*hodon*) except a staff; *no* bread, *no* bag, *no* money in their belts; but to wear sandals and not to put on two tunics" (6:8-9). They must depend on the voluntary (not coerced) hospitality of others (6:10-11), many of whom could be strapped villagers themselves.

When the Twelve return from their mission, Jesus leads them to the desert for a restful retreat "by themselves" (6:31-32), which again proves futile as the crowds rush ahead to the site (6:33). After his all-day teaching session with no meal breaks, the apostles urge Jesus to "send away" the hungry people to get their own food. He has other plans, however, insisting, "You [twelve] give them something to eat" (6:34-37a). The disciples reveal their limited-good mindset, which, it must be said, seems to fit the facts. They are in a literal food desert and muster only a measly five loaves and two fishes among the crowd (no one had planned a big picnic). Someone estimates it would take 200 denarii, about a half year's earnings for a common laborer, to buy bread for everyone—money neither Jesus nor the apostles have (6:37-38)!

On the other hand, "King Herod" Antipas sits atop the economic ladder in Galilee and exploits the people for his and his cronies' benefit. Headed by Antipas, the cadre of noblemen—"courtiers" or "great men" (*megistanes*), military officers, and "leading/first men" (*prōtoi*) (6:21)—controlled the means of production (land and tenant farmers) and flow of goods throughout the region, including levying taxes and tolls to pad their coffers and the treasury of the Roman Empire, which they served as broker-agents (Hanson and Oakman 1998, 63–130). Antipas built the city of Tiberias—named after the Roman emperor Tiberius—on the southwest shore of the Sea of Galilee and established it as the capital and commercial center of his "kingdom."

The extravagant birthday party Herod throws flaunts his abundant, if not unlimited, resources. His flippant offer of "even half of my kingdom" to the dancing daughter who pleased him (6:22-23) demonstrates his cocky pride in his surplus wealth. Life in the Tiberias palace couldn't be more different from that in the surrounding villages and countryside that funded Herodian dominance; or in the desert, where the ascetic prophet John had baptized sinners and denounced Antipas's illicit marriage to "his brother Philip's wife," Herodias (1:4-6; 6:17-18; Spencer 2003, 59; Crossan 1991, 236–37) and where Jesus teaches and feeds the multitude.

Feeding

Although the "banquet" term (*deipnon*) used in Mark 6:21 can refer to an ordinary supper, the main meal of the day, in the New Testament it usually designates "an elaborate dinner celebration" with guests (BDAG 2000, 215)—a "feast" (CEB). Thus, while Mark provides no menu for Herod's party, we can assume a lavish affair stocked with the finest foods and drinks. Furthermore, we can bet Herod doesn't lift a finger except to wag it while barking orders to cooks, servants, and soldiers, culminating in the horrid order to bring in John's severed head on a platter (6:27-28)! The banqueters are not planning to cannibalize John, but the grisly dish does showcase the profligacy of the occasion and the decadence of the Herodian court.

This bloody "wooden platter" (*pinax*) (Friberg, Friberg, and Miller 2000) offers a stark contrast to the nourishing table service provided by Jesus and the Twelve (Anderson 2008, 140). At first the apostles are not sent out to feed the needy but rather to free the demonized and heal the diseased (6:7, 13); still they themselves need feeding, which, per Jesus's instructions noted above, must come from gracious hosts they encounter on the way (6:9-10). He's not advocating mooching off others or demanding food as payment for spiritual services rendered. He does, however, take seriously an economy of *voluntary hospitality*, a *shared community of goods*, material and spiritual, involving "all of the desired things in life" (to reprise Foster 1965, 296; cf. 1 Cor 9:11). And he cuts no slack to inhospitable resistors, directing his emissaries to "shake off the dust that is on your feet" as a public sign of protest against closed-door households (Mark 6:11; cf. Luke 9:5; 10:11; Acts 13:51). This perspective views all goods, of whatever type and measure, as *gifts of God for the common good*.

After benefiting from others' hospitality, however, the apostles prove to be reluctant hosts themselves to the visiting crowd in the desert (Mark 6:35-37), until Jesus takes charge in executing a huge "dinner on the grounds," organizing the five thousand "men" (*andres*, 6:44) (presumably with their families) into manageable units (6:39-40) and enlisting the Twelve as waiters and busboys (6:41-43). Jesus provides the main course, a sumptuous bread-and-fish feast with enough to "fill" everyone's belly plus twelve baskets "full" of leftovers (one for each disciple to pick up) (6:41-43).

This wondrous feeding in the desert recalls God's giving manna and meat (quail) during Israel's wilderness trek (Exodus 16; Numbers 11)—but with a notable twist. This occasion features no divine raining down of bread or blowing in of birds (and no zapping desert rocks into bread; see Matt 4:1-4// Luke 4:1-4). Here Jesus uses ordinary available resources, meager though they are. He does not create out of nothing (*ex nihilo*) but rather out of the "five loaves," which he takes, blesses, breaks, and gives to the Twelve who distribute to the people, and out of the "two fish," which he "divide[s] among them all"—all five thousand-plus who eat their fill (6:41-44)!

A multiplicative miracle occurs, transforming limited goods into a bountiful supper. But it is a *shared* miracle worked out through multiple hands: from those of the original donor(s) of bread and fish → the Twelve → Jesus → (back to) the Twelve → the people. Jesus makes it all happen, but he doesn't work alone. He works at the crosspoint of heavenly and earthly axes (cf. 6:41), mediating divine and human activity. Some have suggested that the "real" miracle is Jesus's persuading a crowd with limited resources, who otherwise might zealously guard their scarce resources, to share generously with their neighbors, thus creating enough to go around (Theissen 1989, 106; Spencer 2003, 141). Or even more remarkably, this Jesus who bears rightful claim to be the Son of God works *with* the poor masses as *one of them*—having no money, no surplus of goods, no stockpile of food—foreshadowing the offering of his broken body and shed blood as *redemptive food and drink* "for many" (14:22-24; cf. 10:45; Spencer 2004, 57; Anderson 2008, 133). Jesus Messiah represents the very antithesis of Herod Antipas.

Feeling

Although John the Baptist says and does nothing in this scene, his past denunciation of Herod's taking his (living) brother's wife, in violation of Jewish law (Lev 18:16; 20:21), and his forceful presence behind the scene, even in prison, drives the emotional action in this story. Mark tightly joins Herod and his wife and daughter—both named Herodias (6:17-19, 22, though the daughter is named Salome in Josephus, *Ant.* 18.136)—in common Herodian cause against John, fueled by strong feelings. Mrs. Herod smolders with bitter hostility toward John for threatening her place at court; hence she "wanted (*ēthelen*) to kill him" (6:19). Her anger toward the "righteous and holy" John (6:20) has no trace of "righteous" anger about delimiting a robust will to life, as Jesus expressed to the man with "leprosy" ("I do choose/want [*thelō*]" to heal you [1:41]). Herodias feels nothing but resentment toward John (L&N 1988, 761), a deeply "internalized hostility" (Danker and Krug 2009, 129), "nurs[ing] a grudge against (*eneichen*)" him (6:19 NIV), a murderous vendetta at that, which she soon satisfies.

But she can't operate unilaterally without her husband's authorization, and his feelings toward John are more complicated. First, even after incarcerating John, Herod *fears* (*phobeomai*) John precisely because of his "righteous and holy" character and courage to speak truth to power (6:20a). Like a lot of unscrupulous strong men, Herod remains internally weak and insecure, ever on the lookout for threats to his position and exposures of his flaws. Josephus, who commends John as a "good man" with a "righteous" mission, reports that Herod especially feared John's popularity with the people who might be rallied into an outright rebellion against the ruler (*Ant.* 18.116-19; Mason 2003, 213–25; Taylor 1997, 5–6, 217; Meier 1994, 19–24). Mark mocks Herod Antipas's jealous and precarious hold on power by calling him "king" (6:14, 26) when he was only a *tetrarch*, ruling a mere quarter of father Herod the Great's realm. When Antipas, again spurred by his ambitious wife, pressed Gaius Caesar to give him a full kingdom, the emperor promptly stripped him of his tetrarchy and banished him to Gaul! He thus was never a legitimate "king" (Josephus, *Ant.* 18.240-55; *J.W.* 2.183 [here Antipas is exiled to Spain]; Culpepper 2011, 154).

Beyond fearing the prophetic punch and popular stir of John's preaching, Herod also fears John's posthumous power beyond the grave, reincarnated in *Jesus's* mighty deeds (*dynameis*, 6:14). As Douglas Geyer notes, the so-called "king" "is a prime actor in a melodrama about fear of retaliation due to political violence through assassination. When Antipas hears about the miracles of Jesus, he does not think of beneficial acts in the countryside. Instead he thinks of the prophet whom he had violently killed. In his mind, the miracles indicate a response from his victim" (2002, 207; cf. 207–23). Such paranoia about assassination plots is typical of megalomaniacal tyrants (Smith 2006, 271–72). Mark prefaces his story of Herod's past execution of John with Herod's present "hearing" (mentioned twice [6:14, 16]) about John's "powers . . . at work" *in Jesus*, prompting Herod's conclusion: "John, whom I beheaded, has been raised" (6:16). Thus Mark both stitches the report of John's execution to the preceding accounts of Jesus and the apostles' mission of proclaiming repentance (6:12) and performing miracles (6:2, 5, 7, 13) and prefigures Jesus's own "passion" and resurrection at the end of the Gospel (McVann 2008). The word and work of God through authorized prophets cannot be bound or killed; one way or another, it eventually bursts forth with renewed life and boomerangs back on those who oppose it.

The second emotion Herod experiences involves being "greatly *perplexed* (*ēporei*)" by John's preaching, which nonetheless Herod still "liked to hear" ("gladly/with pleasure" [*hēdeōs*]), even while John was in prison (6:20b). Herod's fear of John includes a measure of respect for the Baptizer's insight and influence that fall short, however, of true understanding and commitment. Herod takes the "rocky" road of response (4:16-17). Though he "enjoyed listening" to John (6:20b CEB), he doesn't take John's message to heart; in his perplexed state, he remains "at a loss . . . very much disturbed" (BDAG 2000, 119), but not disturbed enough to change his heart and mind (repent). He has a birthday bash with his best buddies to orchestrate!

But the party turns sour for Herod, hitting him with an unexpected third emotion: "The king was *deeply grieved* (*perilypos*)" at Herodias's (mother and daughter's) demand for John's beheading (6:25-26). It's hard to know how seriously to take Mark's language here. One suspects an ironic dig at Herod in suggesting his capability of feeling any sadness, much less deep grief, for executing a troublemaker threatening the stability of his family and reign. The fact that he has a "soldier of the guard" (*spekoulatōra*, 6:27)—that is, a "bodyguard" and "executioner" (Smith 2006, 273–74; BDAG 2000, 936–37)—ready to hand belies any genuine compunction about killing suspected enemies. Mark's only other use of the intensive term *perilypos*, denoting "a condition of deep inward pain and disappointment" (Danker and Krug 2009, 280) applies to *Jesus's* roiling anguish in Gethsemane on the eve of his crucifixion, which he confesses to Peter, James, and John ("I am deeply grieved [*perilypos*], even to death," 14:34) before pleading with his Father to "remove this [lethal] cup from me" (14:35-36). Jesus maintains his irrepressible will to life to the end, surmounted only by God's overarching will for him to drink the cup of human suffering to the dregs (cf. 10:38-39; 14:23-24). And so Jesus prays—"Not what I want (*thelō*), but what you want" (14:36)—and "give[s] his life a ransom for many" (10:45; cf. 14:24).

Again, the contrast between Herod's and Jesus's *desires* could not be starker. Herod wants to do "whatever" the dancing girl who "pleased" him might "wish/want (*thelēs*)," up to half his realm (6:22-23), and does "not want (*ēthelēsen*) to refuse her" (6:26), even when she makes her gruesome request for John's head on a platter. It's even possible that Herod indulges some sexual desire or "pleasure" aroused by the daughter's dancing (Culpepper 2011, 157; 2007, 204; McVann 2008, 154); elite banquets were often erotically charged affairs featuring courtesan entertainers (Corley 1993, 24–79,

93–95). But Mark's account does not play up the titillating nature of the girl's dance or Herod's response (Spencer 2004, 55–56; Bach 1996, 108–11). More than feeding his sexual appetite and wanting to appease his wife and daughter, Herod wants to preserve his honor-standing before his male guests; after making his rash public oath to the girl, he has to stand by it to save face (6:26). As Herod's polar opposite, Jesus wants to do his Father's will, even at the cost of his own life; he seeks to serve and save others, not himself.

Though ostensibly grieved at the prospect of decapitating John, Herod quickly gives the execution order and carries on with his party. But in Jesus's case, truly grieved by his pending execution, he accepts his fate and offers up his life in solidarity with John and all who suffer unjustly at the hands of capricious authorities. King Herod in Galilee, like Governor Pilate in Judea (see 15:1-15), may feign an interest in compassion and justice, but they ultimately wield the tyrant's sword to preserve their turfs. Jesus Messiah, the true King and Lord of God's gracious, redemptive realm, yields his life in order that "many" others brutalized by ruling powers may live (see Spencer 2014, 124–28; Smith 2008, 202; 2006, 277–87).

We don't have to jump ahead to the end of Mark's story, however, to see Jesus as Herod's emotional opposite. In the desert teaching-and-feeding scene following John's beheading by Herod's henchman and burial by John's disciples (6:27-29), Jesus, though again seeking respite from the pressing crowds, nonetheless has "compassion for them, because they were like sheep without a shepherd"—sheep who need to be led and fed (6:34). The Bible often compares leaders of God's people to shepherds (pastors) and is not shy about denouncing false shepherds who both neglect and exploit their flocks (Jer 23:1-4; 25:34-38; Ezekiel 34; Zech 10:3; 11:4-17; John 10:1-13; Acts 20:28-30; 1 Pet 5:1-5). Herod, his officers, and their Roman imperial overlords were antitheses of tender, compassionate shepherd-rulers, leaving the Galilean masses effectively "without a shepherd."

The verb denoting Jesus's being "moved with compassion" (*splanchnizomai*) correlates with the plural noun *splanchna*, referring to "inner parts of the body, especially the intestines" (L&N 1988, 101), or "the viscera, inward parts, entrails" (BDAG 2000, 938), "bowels," or "guts." As strange as it sounds to our ears, in the Greek biblical world, "bowels" functioned, like "heart," as a metonym of emotions, something akin to our "gut feelings," especially intense feelings of *love*. "I love you with all my bowels" had a similar ring to "I love you with all my heart." Jesus is moved on a visceral affective level that in turn moves him to take pastoral active measures to guide and provide for the common people (Spencer 2021, 184–94).

Herod's "gut," apart from being literally filled with party food and drink, is consumed with fear and anxiety about protecting his own little quarter-kingdom, which, as noted above, the emperor stripped from him rather than granting his expansionist request. Such is the final fate of cruel and greedy tyrants. Another notorious example in Israel's history concerns the Greek-Syrian ruler Antiochus IV, who tortured and killed many Jews in the Maccabean era; consequently, he "justly" received a retributive gut punch in the view of one writer: "As soon as [Antiochus] stopped speaking he was seized with a pain in his bowels (*splanchnōn*), for which there was no relief, and with sharp internal tortures—and that very justly, for he had tortured the bowels (*splanchna*) of others with many and strange afflictions" (2 Macc 9:5-6; cf. 9:7-12). Whereas Antiochus literally and maliciously eviscerated his victims, Jesus, moved with deep compassion (*splanchnizomai*), "refreshed the bowels," to borrow a Pauline image (Phlm 7, 20 KJV), and stomachs of the peasant throng who "flocked" to him in the desert.

Freedom from Fear: Walking on Water (6:45-52)

Mark's story continues to elicit déjà vu: after a long day of ministry into the evening, Jesus again seeks respite apart from the crowd; the disciples struggle in their boat against a raging storm; Jesus calms the turbulent winds and the terrified disciples, and they continue misunderstanding Jesus's identity and mission. But for deft storytellers like Mark, the prime significance of otherwise parallel accounts often lies in their distinctive elements. Unlike in the previous storm story (4:35-41), this time Jesus does not go with the disciples in the boat but rather sends them ahead while he remains "alone on the land" (6:47); he does not sleep but remains alert throughout the night both to God and to the seafaring disciples; and he stills the storm by his *presence* rather than by any pronouncement, although he conveys his presence in an extraordinary manner!

Mark structures this narrative topographically, featuring Jesus's activity on *land* (6:45-48a) and *sea* (6:48b-52). We must not rush to Jesus's big splash event without appreciating the preparatory activity on land.

On the land (6:45-48a)

After dismissing the crowd to return to their homes and dispatching the disciples to the "other side" of the lake (to Bethsaida, on the northeastern shore), Jesus ascends a mountain located near the shore in order "to pray" alone (6:45-46), as he previously did in a "deserted place" (1:35). The present mountain site near the sea recalls the place where Jesus "called to him" twelve apostles, appointing them "to be with him, and to be sent out to proclaim the message" (3:13-14). Now, however, Jesus does not want their company, sending them "ahead" while he communes with God by himself. While appreciating Jesus's longing for private contemplation, we may not expect the *force* of his current desire to be apart. Whereas he bid a standard, "formal farewell" (*apotassō*; BDAG 2000, 123) to the masses (6:46), he "made (*ēnangkasen*) his disciples get into the boat" and leave. The "made" term is "surprisingly strong" (France 2002, 270), typically meaning "force, compel," though here perhaps in a somewhat "weakened" sense of "strongly urge/invite, urge upon, press" (BDAG 2000, 60). Either way, Jesus strongly insists, rather than casually invites, his disciples to launch out on their own and leave him alone.

It's not clear what motivates this forceful order. John Paul Heil suggests it reflects an "aura of suspense" building up to the storm surge (1992, 147). Richard France floats the intriguing explanation that "Jesus packs the disciples off in a hurry to get them away from the contagious atmosphere" of the five-thousand-strong multitude (mob) with possible revolutionary designs to overthrow Roman-Herodian rule and make Jesus king (cf. John 6:15). But France also concedes that Mark may simply use "vivid" language to highlight Jesus's urgent intention to pray (2002, 270–71). He may also set up a training exercise for the disciples, thrusting them into the deep end to bolster their faith and courage, since they won't always have him around to help (cf. Mark 14:7).

But given his followers' fragile, fledging state, Jesus keeps a watchful eye from his mountain perch, taking special notice of how much "they were straining at the oars against an adverse wind" (6:48). Seeing, noticing, paying attention to the disciples' struggle motivates his protective action. Unlike the previous storm scene told from the perspective of the distraught disciples who roust Jesus from sleep, here the story is presented from Jesus's vigilant viewpoint (Fowler 2011, 247), scanning across the nighttime vista of the sea and locking in on the beleaguered oarsmen battling the gusty winds. Their "straining" against or "being tormented" (*basanizomenous*) by the cyclonic conditions ominously matches the experience feared by the demonic Legion who pleads with Jesus—"Do not torment (*basanisēs*) me" (5:7)—before Legion's violent drowning in the sea. Again Mark stages a storm event as a cosmic battle against chaotic forces, with Jesus in command.

On the lake (6:48b-52)

Rather than being met by the tumultuous demoniac on the shore (5:1-2), now Jesus comes out to his distressed disciples on the troubled waters. He's no ivory-tower or mountaintop general sending troops into harm's way and monitoring them from afar. Upon seeing his men's perilous predicament, he abandons his private prayer retreat and dives into the fray, or rather strides into battle, remarkably "walking *on* the water" in the wee morning hours, technically the "fourth night watch" between 3:00–6:00 AM (Fowler 2011, 247; Collins 2007, 333). The language evokes security concerns, the work of night watchmen alert to danger. Again, this time Jesus does not sleep on the job. He presses through the raging elements to reach his associates.

But one might wonder, from the disciples' strained vantage point, if Jesus doesn't make the situation worse before helping them. At first, they have no idea that Jesus is the eerie figure they see floating across the tempestuous lake. And why should they? They're engulfed in a terrible night storm with limited vision, and Jesus is not shining like a personal lighthouse or shouting an assuring message through a foghorn. Who or what is this spectral creature drifting into their orbit? "For they all saw him and were terrified" (6:50)—I should think so.

Apart from his strange mode of sea travel and initial silence, Jesus further complicates the situation by his plan to "pass by (*parelthein*) them," as most versions have it, or as the NRSV opts, "pass them by" (6:48), putting a slightly greater stress on leaving the disciples in the lurch. Either way, Jesus's "coming to" them shifts course to "passing by" them, as if he wants to rubberneck but not rescue them. They need to work through this crisis on their own. Yes—but not entirely on their own. They need reassurance of Jesus's supportive presence in the *midst* of the chaotic storm, indeed, on *top* of it!

While he does not (yet) hop into the boat to take over the oars or tame the surging winds and waves (as in 4:39), he comes into the picture embodying the Lord of the storm and all creation (see Job 9:8; Ps 77:19; Isa 43:16; Hab 3:15; Wis 14:1-4; Vegge 2017, 261; Collins 2007, 333) and the heroic "divine man" conquering the torrential elements. Adela Yarbro Collins comments, "The motif of walking on the water had become proverbial for the (humanly) impossible and for the arrogance of the ruler aspiring to empire," like Antiochus IV Epiphanes (2 Macc 5:21; Collins 1994, 220; Cotter 1999, 155–60). Mark's Jesus operates, however, not out of aspiration and arrogance but out of assurance of his intimate relationship with God and his purpose to instruct his disciples. His walking on water is no stunt. His evasive maneuver evokes God's "passing by" Moses in the cleft of the rock and by Elijah in the mountain cave as a sign of divine "goodness" and protective care (Exod 33:17-23; 1 Kgs 19:11-13). By necessity, the sign is shadowy, since no can survive full exposure to the "face" of God's glory (Exod 33:20). But God's near, nurturing presence is no less real and vital, "'pass[ing] by'

God's servants precisely at their point of deepest desperation" (Henderson 2006, 227; cf. 225–29; Black and Collins 2006, 1736; Heil 1992, 149).

Nevertheless, for all his intentions to offer his disciples a divine epiphany, they don't pick up the signals in their distressed state. Far from "seeing" the misty image of their mighty Lord, they perceive the murky outline of a malign *ghost* (6:49), an ominous phantasm (*phastasma*), the walking dead threatening their lives. Put another way, they perceive a fearsome *demonic stalker* against whom they are helpless. How quickly they forget the authority Jesus had given them over evil spirits (6:7, 13; Henderson 2006, 204–24)! This water-gliding figure is no ghost or demon—a fact the apostles should have known even while not recognizing it was Jesus. As Jason Roberts Combs uncovers in a fascinating study of ancient ghost mythology, spook behavior *never involved walking on water*. Quite the opposite, ghosts couldn't handle the high seas, as in the case of "the Hero," the phantom of a deceased member of Odysseus's party who had been stoned to death by citizens of Temesa for the crime of rape. In retaliation, his ghost goes on a killing spree of the townspeople. Finally, however, the great Olympic boxer Euthymus stops the murderous Hero (Pausanias, *Description of Greece* 6.6-10). As a result, "'The Hero disappeared, sinking into the sea' [6.6.10]. In this instance, the ghost's submergence in water signifies its destruction" (Combs 2008, 353).

We're not told why the disciples believe the "absurd" (Combs 2008) notion that the sea-striding figure is a ghost. Maybe they're just waiting for this figure to plummet into the sea and drag them down with him! Or more likely their impulsive emotions overwhelm their deliberative minds. The disciples suffer cognitive lapses about (1) theological doctrine applied to Moses and Elijah, (2) mythological data about gods and ghosts, and even (3) recent historical experience "about the loaves [and fishes]," which Mark cites as evidence of their persistent misunderstanding (6:52).

Further, Mark chalks up their confusion to their *hardened hearts* or "cardioporosis" (*kardia pepōrōmenē*), reminiscent of Pharaoh's notorious obstinacy leading to his and his army's drowning in the Red Sea (Exod 7:3, 22; 8:15, 19, 32; 9:7, 12, 35; 10:1, 20, 27; 11:10; 13:15; 14:4, 8, 17). The book of Wisdom stigmatizes the ancient Egyptians as "captives of darkness and prisoners of long night . . . terribly alarmed, and appalled by specters . . . and dismal phantoms (*phasmata*) with gloomy faces" (Wis 17:2-4). They become gripped by irrational "ridiculous fear" that "prefers ignorance of what causes the torment (*basanon*) . . . driven by monstrous specters . . . [that] paralyzed their souls' surrender; for sudden and unexpected fear (*phobos*) overwhelmed them" (17:8-15).

Without a doubt, the disciples have a long way to go to understand and trust Jesus fully. But is this the time to pile on them? It would take high-level cognitive processing to link Jesus the Crowd-Feeder with Jesus the Sea-Walker, particularly since his identity is far from clear in the night maelstrom; and it would be hard to imagine conditions less optimal for rigorous reasoning than rowing like mad for your life! Moreover, in this case, Jesus *does not expect* his students to know better. He does not chide them for their fearful or faithless reaction, as when he was previously with them in a storm-tossed vessel (4:40). Here Mark "show[s] the cosmic power of Jesus being vulnerable to the needs of the disciples . . . respecting their limitations and helping them" (Cotter 2010, 252). Here in the face of their terror—which he plays no small part in causing—Jesus "immediately," upon reaching earshot, announces, "Take heart, it is I; do not be afraid" (6:50). In succinct language, he frames two reassuring exhortations—"Take-heart (*tharseite*)"/"Fear not" (*mē phobeite*)"—around a self-revealing declaration, literally, "I am" (*egō eimi*), that is, "I am here; it is I in your midst," with strong echoes of the divine I AM disclosed to Moses (Exod 3:13-14). And then Jesus steps "into the boat with them and the wind ceased" (Mark 6:51). Whatever his primary teaching goal through this ordeal, Jesus ultimately exhibits non-accusatory pastoral care toward his distressed disciples via his compassionate counsel and personal presence. As he came ashore to shepherd the shepherd-less crowds in the barren desert (6:34), he comes aboard to captain the captain-less sailors on the chaotic lake.

Although no doubt relieved by the abated winds and demystified "ghost," the disciples remain "utterly astounded" (6:51), "completely amazed" (NIV) or, closer to the Greek, "sore amazed in themselves beyond measure" (KJV), or "so baffled they were beside themselves" (CEB). As Ivar Vegge puts it, "they were completely at the extreme outside of themselves," suffering from a "heart" condition better described as "petrified" rather than "hardened," in a state of "extreme cognitive affective distress" more than willful obstinacy. "They 'freeze up' *emotionally* with numbness and insensibility, *cognitively* with blindness and obscurity . . . and *bodily* with stone-like feeling" (Vegge 2017, 260–61 [emphasis original]). In short, they become overwhelmed with the terrifying-mesmerizing (petrifying) *vastness* of this Christ-centered cosmic event. "Mark 6:45-52 dramatically illustrates the Second Gospel's uncanny ability to involve its readers in endless and expansive wonder and awe concerning the identity of Jesus, who simply cannot be contained with narrow, rigid schemas and categories" (Vegge 2017, 262). Suzanne Watts Henderson also stresses Mark's challenge to know Jesus through multilevel, holistic experience: "For Mark 'understanding' is more than a matter of cognitive affirmation of propositional truth; it is a matter of life-orientation, trust, and the new reality of God's dominion evinced in and through Jesus" (2006, 211).

Freedom from Sickness: Healing "Wherever He Went" (6:53-56)

Following the second sea-storm incident, Jesus and the disciples "land at Gennesaret" (6:53), not Bethsaida as originally planned (6:45). Evidently, the strong winds had blown them off course. Gennesaret was a fertile plain on the western edge of the Sea of Galilee (called the "lake of Gennesaret" in Luke 5:1) between Tiberias and Capernaum (Edwards 1992; Rousseau and Arav 1995, 109–10; Josephus *J.W.* 3.506-21). Here Mark notes that they "moored the boat" (6:53), signaling the end of their bumpy back-and-forth sailing ventures in chapters 4–6. Jesus and his followers stay on terra firma through the rest of the narrative (until Jesus is hoisted up on the cross).

Upon coming ashore, Jesus again attracts an enthusiastic audience (see 5:21). Here Mark stresses that "people at once (*euthys*) *recognized* him" (6:54), in pointed contrast to the disciples' recent *mis*recognition on the lake. The people's vision is not obscured by wind and darkness. What do they experience in their encounter with Jesus? This unit began with the pivotal question, "Who then is this, that even the wind and the sea obey him?" (4:41). It now concludes with a succinct summary of Jesus's continuing dynamic ministry (6:55-56). Four facets stand out.

- Jesus's work focuses on healing "the sick" (6:55) or, more literally, those suffering in a "bad" way or "having a bad condition" (*kakōs echontes*) (cf. 1:32, 34; 2:17).
- Jesus's primary means of healing here is by *touch*, including those who "touch the fringe of his cloak" (6:56), specifically recalling the outreach of the hemorrhaging woman (5:27-30).
- A sense of desperate *urgency* continues to imbue Mark's story; here the Galilean people who recognized Jesus "rushed" or "scurried about" (NAB) the area in order to "bring the sick on mats to wherever they heard [Jesus] was" (6:55). While Jesus remains on the move, the people seize every opportunity they can to access his healing touch.
- The *scope* of Jesus's healing mission encompasses the "whole region," rural and urban, from "villages [and] farms" to "cities [and] marketplaces" (6:55-56). His salutary influence cuts across social and territorial boundaries. Its impact is felt "wherever he went" (6:56).

Mark My Words: Jesus's Polemics
Mark 7:1-23

Mark again breaks up a run of Jesus's miracle-working with a block of his teaching. The dynamic activity of Jesus's liberating word is balanced by the trenchant analysis of his enlightening word. In 4:1-34, Jesus explained the process of receiving and responding to the word of God's kingdom through a series of parables drawn from the agricultural world. In the present unit, Jesus focuses on the priority of attending to the written "word of God" over "tradition"-based modifications (7:13). Although the disciples ask Jesus to interpret a "parable" he offers in this segment (7:17), the material in question (7:14-15) does not fit the typical parable mold. Here Jesus uses multiple examples to illustrate his argument, but no parables per se.

As producing food (farming) forms the backdrop for the parables in Mark 4, consuming food (eating) informs Jesus's teaching in Mark 7, aptly placed between instructive feeding stories (5:43; 6:14-44; 7:24-30; 8:1-21). In addition to addressing the crowds in public (7:14-15; cf. 4:1-9) and the disciples in private (7:17-23; cf. 4:10-34), Jesus first responds to another query from the Pharisees and scribes about what they regard as his followers' improper, "impure" dining habits (7:1-8; cf. 2:15-20, 23-28). Jesus thus engages again in polemics (disputation) with religious teachers, in this case defending what we might call a "strict constructionist" view of biblical interpretation. And once more, food plays a critical symbolic role in marking legal, social, and moral boundaries.

The debate and discussion unfold around three related issues: washing hands, honoring parents, and cleaning inside-out.

Washing Hands (7:1-8)

As an increasingly popular Galilean prophet, teacher, and miracle-worker, Jesus draws the attention of Pharisees and scribes "from Jerusalem." We don't know whether they make a special trip to encounter Jesus or just happen to be in the region on other business. In any case, they "gathered around him" or, more precisely, "gathered together with him" (*synagontai pros auton*) in a kind of informal "synagogue" fellowship (7:1). Although these teachers use the occasion to question Jesus about his disciples' behavior, they do not appear to be particularly hostile, like some Pharisees who conspired with the Herodians about "how to destroy" Jesus (3:6). In the present scene and elsewhere in Mark, the Pharisees take Jesus seriously, even as they challenge him. They choose to be around him although they practice different dining rituals.

Here the Pharisees observe and object to the disciples' manner of "eating with defiled [common (*koinais*)] hands, that is, without washing them" (7:2; cf. 7:5). Apparently, Jesus himself complies with requisite hand-washing, but he is also presumed accountable for his followers' negligence. In the framework of ritual purity, washings have nothing to do with hygiene (washing away germs) or salvation (washing away sins); instead they reinforce the sanctity or set-apartness of God's people for faithful service to God. Naturally, temple priests in frontline service to God undertook many special ablutions; and the Pharisee and scribal legal scholars sought to extend priestly purity practices to the wider community as a "kingdom of priests and a holy nation" (Exod 19:6 NIV; cf. 1 Pet 2:9; Harrington 1995, 47–54).

The obligation of washing one's hands before eating, however, lacks scriptural support. A priest must immerse his entire body in water before consuming a sacred offering *if* he has recently become "unclean" by touching a leper or a corpse or by emitting semen (Lev 22:1-7). And any persons who have physical contact with a man in a state of "uncleanness" due to his bodily "discharge" will themselves "be unclean until the evening," *unless* they "rinse their hands . . . wash their clothes, and bathe in water" (Lev 15:11). But the Torah lays down no rule about washing hands before meals.

The Pharisees' endorsement of ritual hand-washing before eating any food coincides with widespread Greco-Roman practice (Athenaeus, *Deipnosophistae*. 9.408-409; Furstenberg 2008, 192–93) but more particularly derives from the Pharisees' aim to embody the priestly spirit of biblical law in the habits of daily life. Such interpretive traditions and debates surrounding them are recorded in rabbinic writings. On the hand-washing issue, one text from the Mishnah denounces Eliezer son of Hanoch for resisting the duty to purify his hands. It goes as far as suggesting that he was excommunicated from the community forever, symbolized by laying a stone on his coffin as if he had been stoned to death! (m. 'Edduyot 5.7). Another text recounts a debate between the houses of Hillel and Shammai over when hand-washing should occur (before or after pouring wine and sweeping floors) and where the towel should be placed (table or couch) (m. Berakot 8.2-4; Furstenberg 2008, 192; 2021, 204–206). A later commentary concedes that washing hands before eating is optional only to insist that washing *after* eating is mandatory, so much so that "the sages have said, 'Whoever does not wash his hands after the meal is like one who takes a life'" (Numbers Rabbah 20.21).

It's hard to know the currency and extent of such views among first-century Pharisees, but Mark claims in a parenthetical note for Gentile audiences that "the Pharisees, and all the Jews, do not eat unless they thoroughly wash their hands" at mealtime and immerse (*baptizō*) food they purchase at the public market along with cookware and dinnerware they use (7:3-4). Mark seems to forget here that "all the Jews" would include Jesus's disciples. Matthew, generally better informed about Jewish practice, omits this note (Matt 15:1-2), which exaggerates the habit of "all the Jews." Josephus indicates that the Sadducee party did not allow Pharisee traditions that exceeded the written Torah. He also reports, however, that the Pharisees enjoyed greater popularity among the common people (*Ant.* 13.297-98). Still, washing rituals before meals were not universally practiced by Jews. The Pharisees' emphasis on such washings may have reflected their particular concern to bring practices from the holy temple into their ordinary homes (Wills 2017, 84) in "an egalitarian move" (Levine 2021, 418) that involves laypeople in the service of God's "priestly kingdom and holy nation" (Exod 19:6; cf. 1 Pet 2:5).

The term rendered "thoroughly" or "carefully" (CEB) to describe how hands should be washed literally means "with a clenched hand, fist" (*pygmē*), like that of a boxer (L&N 1988, 99). The image may reflect the extent of the washing (entire hand up to the wrist joint) or the amount of water used (fistful). One tradition stipulated using a "quarter log" of water (m. Yadayim 2.1), a small measure of a cup or cupped hand, perhaps due to the limited supply of water (Hooker 2001, 172, 175; Omanson 2006, 75; Boring 2006, 199). Be that as it may, such rules stem from human *commentary* on Scripture, not from divine *commandment* within Scripture. Jesus presses this critical distinction in exposing the Pharisees' hypocrisy: "You abandon the commandment of God and hold to human tradition" (7:8).

Biblical interpretation is necessary to understanding and application; simple quotation of commandments is insufficient. For example, does "You shall not murder" apply to all people in all situations, including war? Are there "degrees" of murder? But not all interpretations are equally valid or convincing. Although some traditions faithfully adapt scriptural principles to various circumstances, other developments unduly compromise or complicate. In the present case, Jesus flatly regards the Pharisees' hand-washing tradition as antithetical to inscribed Torah, not because they're breaking a specific commandment but because they're making a mandate out of a ritual practice loosely implied in the law. In so doing, they run the risk of elevating their own requirements over those stipulated in Scripture, of valuing external regulations over internal motivations, of placing mechanical operations over heartfelt worship of God. (Christians can run the same risk; biblical interpretation is risky business.)

Jesus buttresses his point by appeal to the prophets, the authoritative commentators on Torah *within* the Bible. Like Jesus and most Jews, the Pharisees accepted "the law and the prophets" as God's written word (see Matt 5:17; 7:12; 11:13; 22:40). As in the parable discourse, Mark's Jesus challenges his hearers with the words of Isaiah, this time marking the hypocritical Pharisees as an extended target of the prophet's critique (Mark 7:6-7; Isa 29:13; cf. Mark 4:11-12; Isa 6:9-10). The Pharisees' problem in this case is that their "lip" service to God proves to be a sham, given the callous condition of their "hearts"—"far from [God]" (Mark 7:6; cf. 6:52). True worship does not consist in perfunctory performance of external words and acts but flows out of integral, internal devotion to God. This crucial tenet reverberates elsewhere in Isaiah and other prophetic literature (1 Sam 15:22-23; Isa 1:10-17; 66:2b-4; Hos 6:6; Amos 5:21-24; Mic 6:6-8).

And "heart"-centered knowledge and practice of God's law is firmly grounded *in the law* as well as the prophets. The classic Torah text recited daily by faithful Jews, known as the *Shema*, reads, "Hear, O Israel: The LORD is our God, the LORD alone. You shall love the LORD your God with *all your heart*, and with all your soul, and with all your might. Keep these words that I am commanding you today *in your heart*" (Deut 6:4-6; cf. Mark 12:29, 33-34). Moreover, Moses reinforces the connection between internal desire and external demonstration by exhorting the people to display signs of God's commandments on their heads, their houses—and their *hands* (Deut 6:7-9). There's nothing wrong with the Pharisees' hand-washing rituals *if* these acts flow out of sincere love for God and for others, not out of duty for duty's sake and not simply to score points against those who fail to measure up, as the Pharisees judge Jesus' disciples. Such conduct is tantamount in Jesus' book to "abandon[ing] the commandment of God and hold[ing] to human tradition" (Mark 7:8).

Honoring Parents (7:9-13)

Jesus's second plank in his argument that prioritizes Scripture over tradition juxtaposes one of the Ten Commandments—"Honor your father and your mother" (Exod 20:12; Deut 5:16) and related injunctions not to speak ill of one's parents (Exod 21:17; Lev 20:9)—with the tradition known as "Corban," related to "gift" or "offering," which some Pharisees, Jesus claims, "have a fine way" of exploiting to weasel out of providing financial support for their parents (Mark 7:9-11). Jesus uses "fine way" as an ironic dig against the Pharisees' *wrong* way of serving God (and parents), as "Isaiah prophesied *rightly*" about them. "Fine way" in Mark 7:11 and "rightly" in 7:6 render the same Greek adverb (*kalōs*). Or perhaps Jesus poses a more direct challenge: "Are you doing the *right thing* in rejecting God's commandment?" (BDAG 2000, 506). Either way, Jesus effectively charges the Pharisees with "abuse" of parents (Derrett 1970, 367).

While the Torah has numerous regulations governing offerings, the Corban tradition falls outside the Bible, connected with sworn vows that dedicate some sum of money or property exclusively to God for the temple treasury. Josephus reports Theophrastus's observation that the Jews in the ancient world swore a Corban oath declaring "a thing devoted to God" (*Ag. Ap.* 1.167). There's nothing wrong with dedicating funds to God; the problem comes when people manipulate such pledged offerings to God in order to deprive others of support demanded by God—a scheme that effectively uses God's name to circumvent God's word.

Jesus's concern for superfluous and misguided vows was shared by other Jewish teachers, including rabbinic heirs of the Pharisaic tradition. Saul Lieberman nicely summarizes this concern:

> Generally speaking, popular oaths and vows are an expression of piety. . . . But the natural tendency to swear was carried to excess. . . . The learned Rabbis were confronted with a double task. On the one hand they had to emphasize the sacredness of the oath, the necessity of avoiding it and the evil consequences of transgressing it. On the other hand they had to keep the unbridled zeal of the populace in check, to teach them to distinguish between valid oaths and meaningless outbursts of supposedly holy words. (Lieberman 1994 [1965], 115; Baumgarten 1984/1985, 6–7)

It's hard to know the extent to which some Pharisees or other Jews used the Corban tradition *particularly* to avoid supporting needy parents. Respect for parents and other elders was highly valued, regardless of social class and partisan differences on other matters. Rabbinic discussion concerning vows that sons might make to deprive their parents of funds and benefits typically focused on whether the sons could be *released* of such vows voluntarily (a change of heart) or compulsorily. Vows made to God or in God's name, even rash, ill-considered vows, were taken seriously (Num 30:1-2; Deut 23:21-23; Judg 11:29-40; Pss 50:14; 76:11; Eccl 5:4-6). Accordingly, the Jewish sages admitted that any schemes to dissolve vows "fly in the air and have nothing to support them" (m. Ḥagigah 1:8; see Mishnah, *Sefaria*). Nonetheless, in judging a debate between Rabbis Eliezer and Zadok, the sages seem to favor Eliezer's argument for nullifying a vow that detracted from honoring his father and mother (m. Nedarim 9:1). The particulars of the case remain vague, however.

Elsewhere, this tractate on "Vows" (Nedarim) considers another case in more detail. Apparently, a son who had denied his father access to the son's property through a Corban oath wanted to lift the ban so that the father could attend his grandson's wedding feast. Accordingly, the son ceded his property's courtyard to a friend so that the father could celebrate the feast. This friend, however, threw a wrench into the whole scheme by rededicating the courtyard to God and restoring the initial restriction on the father! The friend wanted no part of any ploy to renege on the original vow, even in the interest of family reconciliation. Neither did the sages. They ruled that by definition a vowed gift comes with no strings attached; the beneficiary of the gift, whether God or a friend or anyone else, should manage the gift as they will (m. Nedarim 5.6; see Derrett 1970, 367–68; Baumgarten 1984/1985, 11–12; France 2002, 287).

The Jewish philosopher Philo of Alexandria provided some way out of keeping oaths, but only in exceptional cases. He urges people only to make sworn vows with "sober reason and deliberate purpose . . . under the guidance of wisdom, and justice, and holiness" (*Spec. Laws* 2.9-12). If for some foolish or perverse reason, however, a person vows to commit patently wicked acts such as adultery, rape, and other violent acts, these vows must be renounced or at least never enacted (2.13-15). In another writing Philo staunchly defends the permanence of dedicatory vows made to God, contending that violation amounts to robbing God. Regarding vows that affect support for wives, sons, or servants (Philo doesn't mention parents), these may only be annulled by the high priest or by some (unspecified) compensatory settlement (*Hypoth.* 7.3-5).

It's easy to get bogged down in loopholes and minutiae governing oaths and vows (consider modern oaths of office or wedding vows). The main point for Jesus is adherence to "the word of God" (Mark 7:13). It's no accident that he uses an example related to human words certified by solemn appeal to God through the Corban tradition. Words matter to Jesus—beginning with the creational and commanding word(s) of God in Scripture. Responsive words from God's people must faithfully accept and act upon the divine word(s), without distortion or evasion. Human speech must honor God's word, not least God's command to honor one's parents. Still, the interpretive factor cannot be avoided. Whereas Jesus took a more lenient view about healing on the Sabbath than did some Pharisees, he now resists relaxing obligations to honor parents. Not for the last time in Mark, we see that Jesus (and the Pharisees) do not fit strict "liberal" or "conservative" labels.

Although not spelled out in Mark, Jesus's position on oath-taking and vow-making might imply that he would rather they not be taken or made in the first place—which is precisely where Jesus comes down in Matthew's Sermon on the Mount. No need for "swearing" as a performance-enhancing maneuver: "Let your word be 'Yes, Yes' or 'No, No'; anything more than this comes from the evil one" (Matt 5:37; cf. 5:33-36; 23:16-22; Jas 5:12). "Yes" to the commandment to honor parents, period. "No" to extraneous commentary, especially that which twists God's name to subvert God's word.

Cleaning Inside-Out (7:14-23)

Jesus then "called the crowd again" (7:14), more specifically, "called" the people "to himself" (*proskalesamenos*) for special instruction, as he had previously summoned the twelve disciples (3:13; 6:7) and the scribes (3:23). The present assembly presumably includes the disciples and the Pharisees/scribes (they haven't been dismissed). But now Jesus takes a wide-ranging focus, targeted to "all of you" (7:14), and makes a broad-based point via a pithy aphorism: "There is nothing outside a person that by going in can defile, but the things that come out are what defile" (7:15).

Jesus shifts from discussing particular cases of tradition (hand-washing/vow-making) to declaring a universal principle of life. The links between these matters are more allusive than obvious. The issue of "defilement" or "making common/vulgar" (*koinoō*) harks back to the Pharisees' objection to Jesus's disciples' habit of "eating with defiled/common (*koinais*) hands" (7:4), although one's hands don't exactly qualify as something "*outside* a person" that goes *into* the body. Technically, it's the *food* that the hands put into the mouth that goes into one's system; but nothing has been mentioned yet about kosher or non-kosher fare. The inside-outside dichotomy evokes the distinction between internal worship of God from the heart and external practices that "make void the word of God" (7:6-13). But Jesus's axiom about defilement in 7:15 does not quote the law or prophets per se and has no direct connection to serving God or fulfilling vows.

It's hardly unreasonable, then, that the disciples ask Jesus in private to explain further this aphorism or axiom (somewhat mislabeled a "parable"), although Jesus again chides them for "fail[ing] to understand" (7:17-18). Yet he proceeds to provide much-needed clarification, tying together this instructional block around the call to heart-rooted devotion to God manifest in honorable attitudes and actions. Jesus now brings food into the picture to illustrate his inside-outside principle: food enters into the stomach (*koilian*)—"not [into] the heart (*kardian*)"—and is excreted out of the body into the latrine or sewer. This natural process—moving from outside the body into its digestive system and out again in waste—"cannot defile," since it bypasses the heart, the seat of human will, thought, and feeling *out of which* come defiling "evil intentions" that prompt a raft of evil actions, twelve of which Jesus rattles off, from "fornication" to "folly" (7:19-22).

Jesus thus caps off this polemical discourse with an emphasis on *moral* purity rather than ritual purity as such. Better put, he stresses a holistic perspective on matters of purity and impurity, "cleanness" and "uncleanness." As I've previously noted, "uncleanness" deriving from consuming various meats or secreting bodily fluids did not make one sinful or iniquitous, as did immoral acts of unfaithfulness and injustice against God and neighbors. Nonetheless, so-called ritual and moral regulations go hand in hand (and heart in heart) in biblical law, as Deuteronomy 6:4-9 makes crystal clear. The same holds true for the extended purity legislation in Leviticus, as Matthew Thiessen avers: "Ancient readers . . . would have read Leviticus as a unified work and would have therefore understood this priestly book to emphasise *both* ritual and moral purity" (2020, 193, emphasis original). As for dietary laws in particular, which seem so arcane to modern readers, there is a *moral* method underlying proscriptions against eating the flesh of certain creatures.

The Hellenistic-Jewish Letter of Aristeas insists that Levitical bans on consuming certain "unclean" animals have nothing to do with some quirky, "excessive preoccupation" Moses had with mice, weasels, wild fowl, or other polluted species (Letter of Aristeas 144–45; see Shutt 1985). Instead, such food "regulations have been made with righteousness in mind . . . to the intent that through the whole of our lives we may also practice justice to all mankind" (168). Eating predatory birds is forbidden because they represent rapacious creatures "which dominate by their own strength." Accordingly, "by calling them impure," Torah reinforces the "solemn binding duty . . . to practice righteousness . . . and not achieve anything by brute force, nor lord it over anyone . . . nor deprive [anyone] of anything" (146–47). Likewise, mice, weasels, and related animals should not be eaten due to their "mischievous," exploitative natures as much as their physically dirty (unclean) habits (163–65) (Whittle 2018).

Although Jesus would doubtless affirm the interlinked ritual and moral dimensions of dining practices, he is not primarily concerned with the classification of pure/impure meats but rather with "the direction impurity travels" (Thiessen 2020, 195; cf. Furstenberg 2008, 181, 196). We might imagine that "unclean" comestibles contaminate the body outside-in through ingestion. So conceived, impurity invades or penetrates the body. Jesus, however, follows the biblical line of "unclean" substances *emitted or discharged from* the body, such as blood, menstrual fluid, semen, and pus. As for food, pollution inheres in the process of defecation, not ingestion. Feces—the waste product of all food, "clean" as well as "unclean"—are obvious taboos of human diets, kosher or unkosher.

Jesus's concept of purity focuses on output rather than intake, specifically output from the *heart*—the willing-thinking-feeling producer of good and evil acts and attitudes, deeds and dispositions. So conceived, the heart is the moral center and generator of human character—not the stomach or other parts of the digestive system (mouth, esophagus, bowels) necessary for physical survival. In and of itself, food is morally neutral, as Paul says in another context: "'Food will not bring us close to God.' We are no worse off if we do not eat, and not better off if we do" (1 Cor 8:8). This perspective is likely what Mark has in mind in the parenthetical comment, "Thus [Jesus] declared all foods clean" (Mark 7:19). That is, foods in themselves are what they are and what they should be according to God's "good" creative purpose: "God saw *everything* that he had made, and indeed, it was *very good*" (Gen 1:31). That includes human beings and "creeping things and wild animals of the earth of every kind" (1:24), to which God gave "every green plant for food" (1:30).

Although the creation accounts in Genesis 1–2 presume a vegetarian diet (see also 1:29; 2:4b-17) with no consuming of animal flesh and thus no need to classify meats as "clean" or "unclean," most Israelites (and other peoples) became omnivorous, prompting various purity regulations. Such laws remain pervasive in modern cultures, including the US where the Department of Agriculture carefully monitors all stages of meat production to guard against harmful contamination, though without religious implications. But again, whatever the context—ancient or modern, religious or secular—the critical component of food consumption is not the foodstuff itself but the *use of food*, not what is eaten but *how food affects* personal and social life. From a biblical perspective, including Jesus', the core issue is ethics, not dietetics (see Barnhill, Budolfson, and Doggett 2016; 2018; Gross, Myers, and Rosenblum 2020; Yanklowitz 2019).

The bottom line regarding Jewish food rituals and practices promotes "liberty and justice for all." Long before Thomas Jefferson, the prophet Isaiah applied this principle to fasting, which he observed some people practicing merely as a show of piety to boost their spiritual reputations. Speaking for God, Isaiah challenges such supercilious performers with pointed rhetorical questions: "Is not this the fast that I choose; to loose the bonds of injustice . . . to let the oppressed go free . . . to share your bread with the hungry? (Isa

58:6; cf. 58:1-14). Likewise, never allowing a single "unclean" morsel to pass one's lips is pointless if one's lips routinely slander or demean other people or if one never shares a kosher crumb with the needy.

Then there's the matter of dealing with non-Jews, which became a critical issue as more and more Gentiles joined the earliest Jesus congregations. Leading Jewish apostles like Peter and Paul had to be persuaded by dramatic divine revelations to relax their strict compliance with biblical food laws when it clashed with the supreme law of love toward all people, including Gentiles to whom kosher regulations did not apply (see Acts 9:1-19; 10:1–11:18; 15:7-11; Gal 1:13-16; 2:11-14; 5:14). Among fellow Jews, keeping kosher was well and good, but such habit should not hinder sharing the gospel with Gentile seekers or strengthening communal fellowship (*koinōnia*) with Gentile believers.

And what of Jesus's practice? As a devout Jew, he doubtless conformed to kosher guidelines. If he had routinely eaten non-kosher food or patently abolished food laws, it's hard to imagine why his followers would continue to debate the matter for decades. Thus far Mark's story has mainly confined Jesus's ministry to Jewish Galilee. His lone venture into the Gentile region of the Decapolis involved no eating or feeding. His visit resulted in the destruction of two thousand swine, an "unclean" species (Lev 11:7-8; Isa 65:4; 66:17; 1 Macc 1:47; Josephus, *Ant.* 12.53); and he refused to permit the local man formerly possessed by a horde of "unclean spirits" to accompany him back to Galilee (Mark 5:1-20).

Boundaries, however, between Jews and Gentiles are about to be relaxed in the next unit, particularly in relation to *eating and feeding* (7:24–8:21)—a development that Jesus seems to prepare for in his polemic with the Pharisees and scribes over hand-washing and other traditions and his instruction to the crowds and disciples regarding ritual and moral pollution (7:1-23) (Boring 2006, 196). But what he (and we readers) may *not* be prepared for is the further understanding *Jesus himself* gains in the next incident (7:24-30), impelling him toward fuller table fellowship with Gentiles (see 8:1-10).

Remarkable Works of Freeing and Feeding II

Mark 7:24–8:20

After a teaching session in Galilee, Jesus again heads across the border. This time, however, he travels by foot as well as by boat and stays longer in "foreign" territory. He first goes overland to the north into "the region of Tyre" (Syria-Phoenicia) (7:24), then southeasterly "towards the Sea of Galilee, in the region of the Decapolis" (7:31)—the general area where he encountered the Gerasene demoniac (5:20)—into the desert (8:4), and finally sailing (not walking) on the lake toward Bethsaida on the northeast shore via Dalmanutha (8:10, 22). The journey is oddly circuitous, moving further north in Phoenicia to Sidon before arcing south and east into the Decapolis (7:31). But all of it maps outside of Galilee with greater likelihood of dealing with Gentiles.

Jesus's itinerary again reflects a desire to get away for a spell from the rigors of his mission. He seems more determined than ever to have a private retreat. Instead of heading out to a "deserted place" (1:35), however, or hopping into a boat for a sailing excursion (4:35-36), Jesus enters an unspecified house near Tyre incognito. Mark stresses that Jesus "did not want anyone to know he was there." He even seems to have left his closest disciples behind. Still, as usual, he "could not escape notice" altogether (7:24).

On this occasion, neither the disciples nor the crowds impinge on Jesus's privacy but rather a lone local woman, a "Syrophoenician" mother who pleads for him to deliver her demon-possessed daughter (7:24-26). And as it happens, this persistent mother not only disrupts Jesus's immediate plans but plays an implicit role in shaping his continuing mission to Gentiles: first to another individual, a hearing- and speech-impaired man (7:31-37), and then to another hungry crowd, totaling "about four thousand people" (8:1-10). Thereafter, Jesus engages in further debate with a group of Pharisees and his disciples, respectively (8:11-21).

Food motifs remain prominent in this unit, ranging from crumbs that fall from the family table (7:28) to basketfuls of leftovers for an outdoor banquet (8:8, 20) to yeast used in bread-making (8:14-16). Again, dietary and culinary elements illustrate key social and moral issues that Jesus wants his followers to "perceive or understand" (8:17).

This quest for thorough understanding of God's way continues to demand alert senses and active responses, such as hearing (7:25, 33-34, 37; 8:18), seeing (8:18), speaking (7:28-29, 35-37), sighing (7:34; 8:11), and perceiving from the heart (8:17). Nothing less than full-bodied engagement with God's word and God's world is required to "open" blind eyes, deaf ears, and hard hearts (7:34-35; 8:17).

Freeing a Demon-Possessed Daughter (7:24-30)

Even though "great numbers from . . . the region around Tyre and Sidon"—commercial ports in the coastal province of Syria-Phoenicia—earlier came to hear Jesus in Galilee (3:8), it's somewhat surprising that he now chooses to enter their territory. Although the biblical prophets roundly denounced the opulent, exploitative, idolatrous domains of Tyre and Sidon (Isaiah 23; Ezekiel 26–28; Joel 3:4-8; Zech 9:2-4; cf. Ps 45:12-13), Israel continued to foster economic ties with its northern neighbors. In Israel's golden age, Kings David and Solomon used Phoenician materials and craftsmen in constructing the royal palace (David) and temple (Solomon) in Jerusalem (2 Sam 5:11; 1 Kgs 5:1-18). In Jesus's era, Herod the Great undertook building projects in Tyre and Sidon, and Jews were required to pay the annual temple tax and transact temple business in Tyrian coins, due to their high content of pure silver, notwithstanding their image to the god Melkart/Heracles on one side and an inscription touting Tyre as the holy city on the other (Reed 2007, 85–86; Rousseau and Arav 1995, 326–28; Theissen 1991, 73). In turn, poor farmers in upper Galilee served as a "breadbasket" for the wealthy Phoenician cities, fomenting resentment and ill-will on the Galilean side (Theissen 1991, 79; Gench 2004, 19; cf. Acts 12:20). Josephus reports that conflict between Syrian Tyre and Galilee persisted during the Jewish-Roman War of 66–70 CE (*J.W.* 2.458-59, 478, 588; cf. *Ag. Ap.* 1.70; Carter 2019, 191).

So why does Mark's Jesus go into this region? Certainly not to conduct any commercial business, and not initially to level any prophetic critique or launch any preaching or healing mission. Rousseau and Arav suggest a competitive motive vis-à-vis Eshmun, the god of healing worshiped in a Sidonian temple: "Jesus wanted to show Gentiles the supremacy of the God of the Jews, even in a domain in which the power of another god was recognized" (1995, 328). That may have been the happy result of Jesus's presence in the area, but it is not his original intention in the narrative. Mark simply notes Jesus's desire for seclusion: he wants *no one* (*oudena*) to know his whereabouts

(7:24; omitted in Matt 15:21). While we might presume that Jesus schedules a personal spiritual retreat from his fast-paced activity, we're not specifically told that he goes away to *pray* (as in 1:35).

Whatever motivates Jesus's plans to be alone, they crumble when a woman "immediately heard about him" (see 1:45; 3:21; 5:14, 27; 6:55) and abruptly shows up "bowed down at his feet," begging him to heal her "little daughter" suffering from demonic possession (7:25-26). Dwellings in the ancient Mediterranean world commonly allowed open access without locked doors or gates. Nonetheless, Mark portrays this woman as an unwelcome *intruder* on Jesus's privacy. She does not start off on the right foot (or knee) seeking Jesus's aid.

In addition to her maternal status, Mark identifies this anonymous seeker by gender and ethnicity: "Now the woman was a Gentile, of Syrophoenician origin" (7:26). These multiple "intersectional" character markers (she is not a "flat," one-dimensional figure) compare and contrast with those featured in recent episodes in Mark 5–6 (on intersectionality, see Crenshaw 1989; Collins 1998; Schüssler Fiorenza 2009; Carter 2019, lviii–lvix, 187–93; Collins and Bilge 2020; Yee 2020; on "flat" and "round" characters in biblical narrative, see Resseguie 2005, 123–26, 147, 152–53, 253–54).

Maternal status

A parent imploring Jesus to help an afflicted child most directly recalls Jairus's plea on behalf of his dying "little daughter" (5:22-23). A notable contrast emerges, however, in Jesus's initial response: whereas he promptly accompanied the distraught father to his daughter's bedside and, after an unexpected delay, raised the deceased girl to new life (5:24a, 38-39), he first balks at the mother's request and makes no house call, even when he decides to heal her child (7:27, 29-30). Parents and daughters also came into play metaphorically in the therapeutic encounter between Jesus and the hemorrhaging woman (5:34) and literally in the schemes of the Herodian royal family resulting in John's death (6:22-28) (Marcus 2000, 367, 466).

Gender

The pair of recent "daughter" incidents links with the present story of a mother's concern for her bedeviled daughter in presenting determined, persistent women often characterized pejoratively as "pushy." The bleeding woman pushed through the crowd to touch Jesus's clothing and trigger his flow of healing energy (5:27-29); Herodias and her daughter manipulated Herod to order John's beheading (6:24-28); and now the Syrophoenician woman keeps pressing Jesus until he cedes to her demand for help (7:28-30). Toward different ends, for good (bleeding woman's restoration and Syrophoenician daughter's deliverance) and ill (John's death), these women get their way in a man's world (Spencer 2004, 47–75).

Ethnicity

The Syrophoenician woman's non-Jewish or Gentile identity associates her with the Gerasene man in the region of the Decapolis, who, as it happened, also came upon Jesus suddenly and "bowed down before him" (5:6). This man, however, was infested himself with a "Legion" of demons, in contrast to the Syrophoenician woman who intercedes on behalf of her demon-possessed daughter. As a Gentile mother, she also stands in contrast to the Jewish Jairus, the other parent who secured Jesus's help for a desperately ill daughter.

The language Mark uses to portray this non-Jewish woman suggests a more precise ethnic profile. Though translated as "Gentile" in various versions of Mark 7:27 (NRSV, NASB), the term *Hellēnis* more properly denotes "Greek" (RSV, CEB, NIV) language, ideas, and culture advanced by Alexander the Great and successors. Numerous people across the ancient Mediterranean world had become "Hellenized" to one degree or another; for centuries Greek functioned as the common commercial and literary language (*lingua franca*). At the same time, many also maintained "native" identities to one degree or another. Many Jews of the era, such as Philo of Alexandria and Saul of Tarsus who wrote in Greek and adapted Greek concepts, were "Hellenized" Jews. By the same token, the woman who approached Jesus was a "Hellenized" Syrophoenician, that is, "Greek by ethnicity and Syrophoenician by location of birth" (Cadwallader 2008a, 120–22), someone with a mixed, "hybrid identity" (Leander 2013, 225; cf. 226–30).

Socioeconomic status

As an anonymous woman who comes to Jesus alone (possibly single/unmarried; Betsworth 2010, 134), the Syrophoenician supplicant again contrasts with Jairus, who stands out as a named, married synagogue leader with numerous friends and supporters (5:22, 35-40). Otherwise, Mark provides no clear indicators of the woman's position in her community, her financial resources, or other social markers. But that has not stopped some scholars from filling out her profile with clues from the text hinting that the woman represents a prominent "Greek 'lady'" (Donahue and Harrington 2002, 233; cf. Acts 13:50; 17:12) and/or prosperous Tyrian merchant, part of "a dominant, oppressive group" (Boring 2006, 209) making her bed of ease at the expense of poor Galileans (Ringe 2001, 84–86; Gench 2004, 18–20). The literal bed (*klinē*) on which her ill daughter lies (7:30) may designate a fancier structure than a simple cot or mat (*krabattos*) (Theissen 1991, 71–72), a sturdy raised bed allowing for underneath storage (see 4:21) rather than a flimsy floor pallet (Leander 2013, 224).

Or maybe not. Mattress terminology is not much to rest on. Both terms are used in the Synoptic Gospels for the paralyzed man's "bed/mat" (*klinē* in Matt 9:2, 6; Luke 5:18; *krabattos* in Mark 2:4, 9, 11), and together in Acts 5:15 for the "cots and mats (*klinariōn kai krabattōn*)" (the first term is a diminutive form of *klinē*) bearing sick folk brought to Peter for healing. Why the woman does not carry her afflicted daughter to Jesus most likely has to do with the risk of moving a severely weak, sickly child (as with Jairus's daughter) rather than the size of the bed (too cumbersome for transport). And we're told nothing about the property value of the woman's "home," although calling it "*her* house/home" (*oikon autēs*, 7:30 CEB, NASB) suggests that she owns it. Overall, Mark casts the Hellenistic-Syrophoenician figure as an ordinary mother, not a businesswoman or community leader, still less a rapacious urban exploiter of rural Galilean peasants. She wants to press Jesus into serving her daughter's need for healing, but she scarcely wants to oppress Jesus financially or make him her permanent servant.

Addressing interpreters who align this woman with dominant economic oppressors, Hans Leander offers an important corrective. Although he grants the woman a "more affluent status" than that of Jesus and most Galileans (2013, 224), Leander also stresses their *shared subordinate status* under Roman rule: "Jesus as well as the woman represented the dominated—they are both Roman subjects. . . . A story about subjected peoples—a Syrophoenician Greek and a Jew—who overcome enmity without a Roman intervention therefore suggests an incipient universalism beyond Roman control." The Roman historian Livy judged Greeks from Syria and Asia to be "worthless . . . peoples . . . born for slavery" (*History* 36.17.5); likewise, the Roman statesman Cicero regarded both Syrian Greeks and Jews as "peoples born to slavery" (*On the Consular Provinces* 10) (Leander 2013, 238).

Peoples subjected to imperial domination do not automatically become allies; historical social and political tensions die hard. In the first century CE, Jewish memory was still strong and painful regarding the brutal attempt by the *Greek-Syrian* tyrant, Antiochus IV (175–164 BCE), to Hellenize Jews in their homeland and eradicate Jewish faith and practice (1 Maccabees 1–2). And at the outset of the Jewish-Roman War (66–70 CE), Jews rebelled against Greeks in Caesarea (the Roman-Herodian provincial capital) to whom Emperor Nero had given control of the city (Josephus, *J.W.* 2.284-88). Thus, whatever common social ground Jesus and the Syrophoenician woman may inhabit as Roman subjects, their distinctive familial, gender, ethnic, and (possibly) financial statuses—along with the woman's ill-timed intrusion on Jesus's privacy—present potential for conflict.

Species status

Even with these grounds for frustration over the Syrophoenician mother's petition, Jesus's first response is particularly jolting, as odd as it is off-putting: "Let the children be fed first, for it is not fair to take the children's food and throw it to the dogs" (7:27). The woman is not asking for food, has not said anything about food or feeding, and does not interrupt Jesus's dinner. While Jesus's interest in food suits Mark's theme in chapters 5–8, it seems ill-suited to the present scene. Moreover, Jesus speaks *at* the woman more than *to* her, advancing a general principle of food distribution rather than a specific assessment of the woman's case. As Alan Cadwallader comments, "Jesus secretes himself, not only behind closed doors (v. 24b) but also behind a universal policy (v. 27)" (2008b, 265). At the outset, Jesus seems to give this woman less direct, personal attention than he does other seekers and even demons who address him (1:24-25, 40-41; 2:4-5, 9-11; 5:6-9, 32-34).

To be sure, Jesus's comment about "children" links with the woman's concern for her daughter's well-being, prioritizing children's nutritional needs ("Let the children be fed *first* [*prōton*]" over those of "dogs"—a rather innocuous prizing of human survival above that of nonhuman animals, without denying divine and human care for other creatures (cf. Matt 6:25-26//Luke 12:22-24). But Jesus's meaning seems to cut below this surface, at least as the woman interprets it. She feels a personal slight. She hears a "dog whistle" of exclusion not acceptance, of discrimination not acceptance. She presumes that Jesus classes her and her daughter among the dogs. So in her "downward dog" position "bowed down at his feet" (7:25), she barks back at Jesus—with all due respect (!) from a dog's viewpoint: "Sir/Lord, even the dogs under the table eat the children's crumbs" (7:28).

Does she mishear, misunderstand Jesus's meaning as others have done and will do, like some scribes, Pharisees, and Jesus's own disciples? According to Matthew, one of Mark's earliest interpreters, Jesus prefaces his statement about feeding children before dogs with a more favorable animal image for his own people: "I was sent only to the lost sheep of the house of Israel" (Matt 15:24). Here *ethnicity* marks the main dividing factor: Jewish (Israelite) "sheep" vs. Gentile (Canaanite) "dogs" (Matthew 15:22 uses the archaic label "Canaanite" for the woman). I think Matthew has read Mark rightly, making explicit what Mark's Jesus implies. Jesus recently taught and fed a large crowd of fellow Jews out of "compassion for them, because they were like sheep without a shepherd" (Mark 6:34). He does not yet regard himself as the shepherd-caretaker of Gentiles, his ministry to the Gerasene demoniac notwithstanding, which was pretty much forced upon him and scarcely embraced the wider Gentile populace, especially the swineherds! While happy to take on a pastoral-shepherd role (6:34), Jesus never envisioned himself as a pig-farmer or dog-minder, giving his "holy" service to dogs or throwing his "pearls" of wisdom to pigs (Matt 7:6). Thus his association of the Syrophoenician woman, her child, and her people with dogs appears derogatory and degrading (Cotter 2010, 152–53), prompting one modern commentator's striking assessment that Jesus gets "caught with his compassion down" (Ringe 1985, 69).

But wait! Not all dogs were or are wild, filthy curs. Dogs have a noble history as family pets and work dogs—and not just in modern times where we dote on our beloved pooches. Ancient funerary inscriptions, sculptures, and reliefs attest to the valued place of dogs in Roman society (Harrison 2012; Ferris 2018; Brewer, Clark, and Phillips 2002). On the work side, the Roman scholar Varro classified dogs into two groups: "the hunting-dog suited to chase the beasts of the forest, and the other which is procured as a watch-dog and is of importance to the shepherd" (Varro, *De re Rustica* 2.9.2; Grout 2021). So dogs have long helped humans care for sheep!

But that is not the primary Jewish biblical image of dogs and not what Jesus has in mind when responding to the Syrophoenician woman; for her part, even though she's not Jewish, she's close enough to the border to pick up on the ethnic slur. The Bible typically views the canine species (Heb *keleb*/Gk *kyōn*) as a "vile and contemptible animal . . . the scavenger *par excellence*" (Thomas 1960, 414). Mosaic Law stipulates, "You shall be people consecrated to me; therefore you shall not eat any meat that is mangled by beasts in the field; you shall *throw it to the dogs*" (Exod 22:31). As predatory carnivores, dogs will eat any "unclean" bloody flesh thrown their way and thus do not merit "clean" food from "consecrated" human tables. They will even lick bloody and suppurating sores on human bodies (Luke 16:20-21) and gnaw human flesh. In a particularly grotesque scene, Queen Jezebel of ancient Israel was *thrown down* from her lofty palace window, her blood spattering the wall below, her body trampled by horses, and her corpse mauled by dogs (2 Kgs 9:30-37; cf. 1 Kgs 21:19-24; 22:38; 2 Kgs 9:10). Jezebel's horrible fate hits a little too close to home with Mark's story, as Jezebel represents a polluted, foreign *Phoenician* (Sidonian) princess (1 Kgs 16:31; cf. Rev 2:20-23; 22:15), a distant ancestress of Mark's Syrophoenician woman, though the latter has no royal position.

When the woman begs Jesus to "cast/throw out" (*ekbalein*) the "unclean spirit" from her daughter, Jesus suggests that "it is not fair" to "throw" (*balein*) any decent thing to "unclean" dogs, like her and her kind (7:25-27). Without doubt, this is one of the most shocking scenes in all Gospel literature, the closest Jesus comes to treating a human being with contempt, as if they were a disgusting animal (Spencer 2021, 133–37). Some have suggested that Jesus mitigates his canine image by using a diminutive term (*kynarion*), meaning "little dog, doggie, puppy." But apart from the fact that the word may denote any "house-dog [irrespective of size] in contrast to a dog of the street or farm" (BDAG 2000, 575), comparing the woman and her child to a little dog may be taken as further evidence of *belittlement* (Pokorný 1995, 324; contra L&N 1988, 44), to say nothing about the offensiveness in many cultures of applying female-dog language (little or big) to women or girls (Burkill 1967, 172–73; Cotter 2010, 148–51). Further, proposing that Jesus delivers his dramatic line with a wink and a nod, a "twinkle in the eye" (France 1987, 247), or "a bit of tongue-in-cheek" (Camery-Hoggatt 1992, 150), as if toying with the woman, teasing or testing her before granting her request, doesn't help much. Trifling with this desperate mother's feelings for her afflicted daughter would be even crueler than playing on longstanding ethnic conflicts. She had nothing personally to do with historic oppression of Jesus's people by Greek, Syrian, and Phoenician authorities and armies. From multiple angles, it remains hard to gloss over Jesus's "hard saying" (cf. 10:21-24) to this woman.

But precisely because Mark lets Jesus's "dog" comment stand in all its sheer rawness, it sets in sharp relief the next responses of both the woman and Jesus. For her part, the Syrophoenician woman doesn't skip a beat: "If Jesus wants her to play the dog she will do so with dogged persistence and dexterous panache" (Spencer 2021, 138). In her retort about scavenging dogs lapping up scraps under the table, she throws Jesus's canine quip back to him in order to convince him to meet her need even as she confesses faith in his life-giving power: a few crumbs from him will suffice to save her daughter (compare "crumbs" to tiny "mustard seed" in 4:30-32; Luke 17:6).

For his part, far from being offended by the woman's "sassy" backtalk (Smith 2016), Jesus acknowledges her bold word and accedes to her plea without further delay: "On account of this word" (*dia touton ton logon*), you may go [to find that] the demon has gone out of your daughter" (7:29, my translation); or "Good answer! . . . Go on home. The demon has already left your daughter" (CEB) (see Schüssler Fiorenza 1992, 10–15). This Jesus—this Lord, Messiah, Son of God, Son of Humankind—who has repeatedly demonstrated the authority of his word to teach, heal, and save now remarkably heeds *this word* of *this woman*, this "foreign" woman. She holds him to account as one committed to using his power to free all persons, all children of God suffering possession by nefarious forces.

Whatever the intention of Jesus's opening rejoinder, he quickly recognizes that it can be (mis)construed in a harmful, prejudicial way. So he *changes* his tone, his mind, and the course of his mission *because* of his encounter with this wise Syrophoenician woman. If Jesus gets caught in any measure with his compassion down, he instantly pulls it up again when challenged by this persistent mother. Jesus's compassion thus aligns with humility as marks of the true Lord and Son of Humankind (see 10:42-45).

Opening the Ears of a Deaf Man (7:31-37)

Elizabeth Struthers Malbon aptly states that "Mark 7:31 has got to be the strangest geographical reference" in this Gospel (2002, 48). It maps Jesus's route from the Mediterranean coastal area around Tyre, located northwest of Galilee, to the Decapolis region on the southeastern side of the Sea of Galilee. But apart from going the long way around the lake on foot rather than transecting it by boat, Jesus starts this southward excursion by heading twenty miles further *north* up the coast to Sidon. Jesus thus appears to be wandering about more than usual, trying perhaps to sort out further the jarring encounter with the Syrophoenician woman. In any event, he opts for the time being to remain in predominantly Gentile territory (with the "dogs") rather than return to his Galilean homeland. And most oddly, he returns to the Decapolis where he had dealt with the "Legion"-possessed man and a bunch of upset citizens and swineherds who begged him "to leave their neighborhood" (5:17, 20). In the course of revisiting this hostile place, he brings physical healing to a hearing-and-speech-impaired man (7:32-35) and social healing to the people in the area, who affirm his "well"-doing (7:37).

Initially, however, Jesus again seeks isolation, as "he took [the disabled man] aside, in private, away from the crowd" (7:33a). Mark's Jesus continues to be wary of publicity, particularly the kind that touts his miracle-working to the neglect of the way of painful suffering and lowly service he will tread (8:31-35; 9:30-32; 10:32-34, 41-45). Ironically, after he restores the man's hearing and ability to speak clearly, Jesus's command to the audience "to tell no one" once more falls on deaf ears and fuels more testimony: "the more he ordered them, the more zealously they proclaimed" his astounding feat (7:36).

The dramatic core of this incident, however, is not its broadcast by witnesses but rather Jesus's odd means of performing the event. As Thomas Long comments on these "strange bits," "We don't get a tidy Jesus. We get a sweaty, embodied, guttural Jesus. We hear the brute physicality of the gospel being performed. We hear him groan and grunt as he works" (2015, 33–34). Such "brute physicality" may be one of the reasons no other Gospel includes this episode. More particularly, we see and hear the embodied Christ thrusting his fingers into the man's ears, spitting (on) and touching the man's tongue, looking heavenward and sighing, and speaking a powerful word (*Ephphatha*) of "opening" (7:33-34).

Fingers probing in the ears

Jesus has previously used a therapy of touch but never like this! He took the hand of Simon's feverish mother-in-law and of Jairus's deceased daughter and raised them up (1:31; 5:41-42), and he reached out his healing hand to a skin-diseased man (1:41). But here he takes more intense, invasive action by inserting his fingers into the man's ear canals. The verb (*ballō*) can signify "forceful motion" ("throw, hurl"; BDAG 2000, 163), reminiscent of the scraps "thrown" to the dogs and the demon "thrown (out)" of the daughter in the preceding story (7:26-27). In the present case, the term may simply mean "put, place" but likely carries a stronger nuance of *thrust*. As Jesus puts his finger (literally) on the man's problem, his poking, piercing action suggests attacking the problem with direct force, as if in a battle against deafness in all its forms, physical and spiritual. It is mission critical in Mark to *hear* the gospel message (4:9-20; 6:11) and the Gospel narrative, the main medium of reception in an oral culture (Shiner 2003; Botha 2012, 163–90; Dewey 2013).

Spitting on and touching the tongue

If Jesus doesn't shock our modern sensibilities by sticking his fingers in the man's ears, he certainly does by spitting and touching the man's tongue (treating the speech impediment associated with deafness). Whether Jesus spits directly on the man's tongue and rubs in the saliva or spits on his fingers and applies it makes little difference: either way, the same fingers he plunged into the ears he now puts into the man's mouth—mixed with spittle! Physicians and healers have always been granted special license to transgress bodily boundaries in treating their patients. And as it happens, saliva was thought to have medicinal properties in the Greco-Roman world, especially the saliva of divinely anointed persons.

Pliny describes various therapeutic uses of spittle for ailments ranging from leprosy, cancer, epilepsy, and blindness to a "crick in the neck" or an insect lodged in one's ear. In the latter case, spitting into the ear would expel the pest. Further, placing a saliva-moistened finger behind an anxious person's ear was thought to soothe his "disquietude of mind." As for mouth-to-mouth operations, some claimed that spitting into the open maw of venomous serpents made them explode! But not just any saliva would do the trick. "Fasting spittle"—produced in the early morning before breakfast—was preferred, and Pliny references one special Cypriot family "endowed with remarkable [curative] properties" in their bodies, including sweat and spittle "possessed of remedial virtues" (Pliny, *Nat.* 28.5-7; Collins 2007, 370–71).

The Roman historian Suetonius recounts a tale in which the new emperor Vespasian, saddled by his humble origins, boosts his fragile status in Egypt as a "new-made emperor." Two men—one blind, one lame—approach him and claim that the healing god Serapis appeared to them in a dream and urged them to seek Vespasian's medical aid. Serapis specifically indicated that the blind man would receive his sight when Vespasian "spit upon" his eyes. Although Vespasian was skeptical, his advisors pushed him to give it a whirl, and lo and behold, his spittle restored the man's vision and demonstrated the emperor's divine power (Suetonius, *Lives of the Twelve Caesars, Vesp.* 7.2-3; Eve 2008, 2–12; Mark 8:22-26).

Although a general audience familiar with these cases might regard Jesus's use of spit as a sign of his divine might and majesty, personal glorification is not his prime motivation. Remember that Jesus performs this miracle in private, away from impressionable crowds, and attempts to tamp down publicity even as he ironically enhances the man's ability to speak. Jesus does not seek imperial fame and power but rather promotes a selfless, servant-centered vocation as Messiah antithetical to Caesar's way (10:42-45). Alternatively, we might think that Jesus applies saliva to the man's tongue as a tangible aid to faith; but faith is not a factor here as it is in other healing incidents (2:5; 5:34; 9:23-24; 10:52).

Whatever prompts Jesus to incorporate his spittle into the man's treatment, the action displays intimate contact with a disabled person. It also blurs boundary lines and emission norms, although the Torah does not label saliva as "unclean." Jesus recently stressed that "it is what comes out of a person that defiles," though chiefly focusing on what comes out of the "human heart" (7:20-21). At any rate, it strikes us modern readers as odd, if not offensive, to picture Jesus secreting a bodily fluid *out of* his mouth *into* the man's mouth to help make him whole.

Looking up and sighing out

As Jesus combines actions of spitting and touching, so he conjoins looking up and sighing out—sight and sigh (7:34a). "Looking up to heaven" (*anablepsas eis ton ouranon*) matches what Jesus did before blessing, breaking, and distributing the loaves to the five thousand (6:41). But this is the first time Jesus *sighs* (*stenazō*)—the only time he sighs in the four Gospels, except for one additional occurrence in Mark 8:12. Mark places these two instances of sighing close together, flanking a second feeding incident (8:1-10). What does Jesus's sudden urge to sigh signify?

Sighs may be impulsive or deliberate, expressing a range of positive or negative feelings, including pleasure (Aaah!), relief (Whew!), calming down (Whoa!), pain (Ow!), or frustration (Ach!), among other emotions. Sound makes all the difference in distinguishing types of sighs. Oral presenters of Mark's story would supply their vocal interpretations. The written text, however, proves less revealing. Commentators have proposed various explanations for Jesus's sighing in the present context (Collins 2007, 371–72), including association with (1) prayer or supplication (Meier 1994, 713), (2) compassion or sympathy (Blackburn 1991, 216–18), and (3) preparation for and execution of an exorcism through "mystical magic" (Dibelius 1935, 86; cf. Bonner 1927, 172–74).

Each of these options is possible but not wholly satisfying. Jesus's heavenward look may signal prayer, but he is not explicitly reported as praying to God here (or in 6:41), unlike John 11:41 which quotes Jesus's heaven-directed thanksgiving to the Father. In Romans 8:26, Paul speaks of the Spirit's intercessory prayer for us "in our weakness . . . with sighs (*stenagmois*) too deep for words" or "wordless groans" (NIV). Paul indicates, however, that we need such spiritual aid because "we do not know how to pray as we ought"—a deficiency that Mark would not ascribe to Jesus.

Jesus's sigh might echo the sounds that the speech-and-hearing-impaired man was capable of uttering, thus expressing a kind of fellow-feeling for him. But again we cannot be certain without an audio version; moreover, Mark says nothing in this episode about Jesus "having compassion" (*splanchnizomai*) on this man, as he does for the crowds in the nearby feeding scenes (Mark 6:34; 8:2). John Hull extends the sympathy element into the realm of "sympathetic magic," suggesting that Jesus's sigh both imitates the man's speech impediment and the expulsion (exhalation) of an evil spirit that had "bound" his tongue (1974, 84; Collins 2007, 372). Although Mark highlights the freeing dimension of the man's healing—literally, "the bond/chain (*desmos*) of his tongue was loosened (*elythē*)," 7:35 (my translation)—this does not mean that Jesus uses magical exorcising techniques. Evidence from ancient Greek magical papyri focuses on inflicting *curses* that tie tongues and throttle one's ability to speak (Deissmann 1978 [1927], 304–307). By contrast, Jesus lifts the curse (if there were one) and loosens the bound organ of speech.

As for specific spells and incantations, one example involved an elaborate concoction of sighing with special words, incense, and gestures designed to lure a faraway person into one's presence (*Papyri graecae magicae* IV.2491-95; Bonner 1927, 172–73; Betz [ed.] 1986, 83). Another magical recipe combined "bellow-howling" with sighing and hissing (*Papyri graecae magicae* XIII, 941-46; Betz [ed.] 1986, 193; Collins 2007, 371–72). Neither example fits the sighing Jesus who calmly speaks a single word of healing (no shouting or howling) and deals with a man brought to him by others (no summoning from a distance).

The cluster of Greek terms related to sighing derives from the root *sten-* meaning "narrow, constricted." English terms based on this root include "stenography" (*short*hand, compact writing) and "stenosis" (as in spinal stenosis, compacted vertebrae). Applied to the physical process of sighing, *sten-* reflects the bursting release of compressed air in the lungs, perhaps combined with sensations of tightness in the chest and throat. Likewise, physical sighing signals emotional release in "tight" situations. Such release may result from pain or pleasure: venting frustration in a time of crisis or expressing relief at a successful escape (Teigen 2008, Vlemincx et al. 2010b, Lewis 2013). The former would be heard as a guttural groan, the latter as a blissful moan.

On the painful side, a passage from the Hellenistic-Jewish story of Susanna succinctly illustrates the connection between constrictive (stenotic) sighing and circumstances: "Susanna groaned (*anestenaxen*) and said, 'I am completely trapped (*stena*). For if I do this, it will mean death for me; if I do not, I cannot escape your hands'" (Sus 1:22). The trap has been set for Susanna by two unscrupulous elders who force upon her a terrible choice between two evils: either submit to their sexual pressure or suffer the lethal consequences of their false testimony about her (nonexistent) adulterous affair with a young man. Susanna's sighing/groaning erupts out of her dire straits, her strangled sense that "things are narrow for me on all sides" (Sus 1:22 NETS).

Paul speaks more generally of his personal ministerial struggles through "troubles (*thlipsesin*), hardships, and distresses (*stenochōriais*)" (2 Cor 6:4 NIV), while he also claims that despite being "hard pressed (*thlibomenoi*) on every side, [we are] not crushed (*stenochōroumenoi*)" (4:8 NIV). Even more broadly, Paul senses the "whole creation ... groaning/sighing (*systenaxei*) in labor pains" and all God's children who "groan/sigh (*stenazomen*) inwardly" with the world both in frustration and in hope for the ultimate release (liberation) and restoration of all things (Rom 8:22-23; cf. 8:18-30).

In advising his students concerning how they should deal with those grieving the loss of a precious child or piece of property, the Stoic teacher Epictetus counsels them "not to be carried away by the impression that [the bereaved] are in dire external straits" but to realize that "what is crushing (*thlibei*) these people is not the event (since there are other people it does not crush [*thlibei*]) but their opinion about it." Here Epictetus stresses the familiar Stoic principle that what one thinks about a disruptive "event" should override what one feels about it. Rational judgment trumps emotional impulse. Yet Epictetus allows for some emotional engagement with others, provided it's not taken too far: "Don't hesitate, however, to sympathize with [the bereaved] in words and even maybe *share their groans/sighs* (*synepistenaxai*), but take care not to *groan/sigh* (*stenaxēs*) inwardly as well" (*Encheiridion* 16).

Mark's Jesus and the apostle Paul both enter more passionately, more wholeheartedly, into others' suffering than Epictetus allows; they are deeply affected to the point of sighing/groaning *inwardly, within themselves* in sympathy with fellow sufferers (Mark 8:12; Rom 8:22), even as they persist in hope of salvation (Rom 8:24). But while falling short of the Stoic ideal of cool tranquility, Mark and Paul share with Epictetus a common metaphorical concept of affliction as a "crushing, hard-pressing" (*thlibō/thlipsis*; Mark 3:9; 4:17; 13:19, 24; Rom 5:3; 8:35; 12:12; 2 Cor 4:8; 6:4) experience eliciting "sighing, groaning" (*sten-*) out of the intense pressure (see also the synonymous parallel of *sten-* and *thlib-* in Matt 7:14—"For the gate is narrow [*stenē*] and the road is hard [*tethlimmenē*, from *thlibō*] that leads to life").

Taking this tight association of sighing with crushed, constricted, straitened, squeezed conditions—together with Jesus's look to heaven as he faces an afflicted man on earth—I propose that Jesus groans (1) primarily to vent the increasing cosmic tension between heavenly and earthly realms pressing hard upon and stirring hot within him; and (2) to "reset" his attention to deal with the matter at hand of a man in need. It's about *mission*, not magic.

Mark's Jesus is now well into his urgent battle to establish God's righteous, restorative reign against evil, destructive forces. While he has made significant inroads, his mission is not completed. Opposition remains strong, and if anything, Jesus's vocation has become more demanding as it has extended beyond his homeland. The respite Jesus sought in a private house across the Galilean border has brought more exposure for him, more engagement with more sufferers, more evidence that life on God's good earth is not as good as it should be. As Son of God and Son of Humankind, Jesus stands at the nexus between heaven and earth, at the epicenter of apocalyptic conflict between good and evil. No one feels more keenly and stands more deeply in the "gap between aspiration and reality" than Jesus, the "'tragic gap' that . . . forever separate[s] what *is* from what *could* and *should* be" (Palmer 2011, 26 [emphasis original]). It is out of this gap that Jesus groans.

In his research on the phenomenon of sighing, psychologist Karl Teigen has observed, "In the prototypical case, a sigh expresses a mismatch between ideals and realities. A belief is disconfirmed, a hope has to be abandoned, a wish is disappointed, a dream or some other cherished possession may be lost" (2008, 55). Sighing is a natural response to the cognitive dissonance of shattered hopes. And so Jesus sighs or groans in understandable pain and frustration—but *not* as one who has lost all hope. Rather he sighs as a sign of "creative tension-holding" (Palmer 2011, 26), pressing on to bridge the tumultuous gap between heaven and earth.

In this mode of (re)creative tension, Jesus may further sigh to prepare himself for restoring the man's speech and hearing. Again, he prepares for ministerial action, not a magical act. His sighing might be broadly compared to breathing exercises (including sighing) that musicians, athletes, and other performers employ to steady their nerves and reset their focus before undertaking a difficult action, like singing a solo, shooting a game-deciding free throw, or giving a big speech (Guyon et al. 2020; Vlemincx et al. 2010a; Lewis 2013). Yet Jesus does not seem to suffer performance anxiety as such. He's not entertaining anyone; he shuns the spotlight, particularly regarding his miracle-working. His focus falls squarely on mediating God's life-giving, whole-making strength to the infirm and the impaired and to releasing those bound by constrictive forces. He needs all the concentrated attention he can muster amid the din of demonic disturbance and disputations of religious critics (see 8:11-13).

Be Opened

After touching, spitting, looking heavenward, and sighing, Jesus's final therapeutic gesture reprises his tried-and-true method of *speaking the liberating word*. As Mark cited Jesus's restorative command to Jairus's daughter in both Aramaic (*Talitha cum*) and Greek (*To korasion egeire*, "Little girl, get up!") (5:41), we again "hear" Jesus's native Aramaic (or possibly Hebrew [see Rabinowitz 1962]) "voice"—*Ephphatha*—"Be opened" (*dianoinchthēti*) (7:34). Some interpreters detect yet another sign of magical influence, since "Ephphatha" has a kind of abracadabra sound, and magicians routinely used foreign terms for effect (Smith 2014 [1978], 286). While alien to Mark's Greek audience, however, the term was not foreign to Jesus himself. Moreover, the basic "Be opened" meaning of "Ephphatha" is perfectly appropriate to the case at hand without adding some esoteric "Open sesame" energy.

Jesus addresses either the hearing-impaired man, whose ears are functionally closed, or the heavens as the source of outpoured blessing (Mal 3:10; Borg 2006, 147)—or both. In his state of frustrated tension between heavenly ideals and earthly realities, Jesus utters his word of release, reinforcing his sighed relief from cosmic tension, (re)creating breathing room, opening space for flourishing life for all who have "ears to hear," for all who remain "open to God's word" (Owens 2013, 256, 258) in all its forms—therapeutic, prophetic, didactic—revealed in the person of Christ, the text of Scripture, the mind of humanity (reason), and the created world (nature). The narrative effect of Mark's bilingual report of Jesus's restorative word is to draw his non-Jewish (Greek-speaking) hearer/readers into the scene, arrest their attention, and make them sense that they are hearing Jesus's actual voice calling *them* to open *their ears* to his gospel. The good news of God in Christ opens out to all people (Jew and Gentile) and all creation.

The creational panorama is affirmed by the people's exuberant affirmation of Jesus's benevolence: "He has done everything well (*kalōs panta pepoiēken*)" (Mark 7:37)—echoing God's assessment of the whole world in the beginning: "And God saw all the things (*ta panta*) that he had made (*epoiēsen*), and see, they were exceedingly good (*kala*)" (Gen 1:31 NETS; cf. Sir 39:16; Owens 2013, 255; Collins 2007, 376; Marcus 2000, 475–76). Moreover, unstopping "the ears of the deaf" and untying "the tongue of the speechless" fulfill Isaiah's hopes of liberating captive Israel in the "wilderness/desert" on the "Holy Way" home to Zion (Isa 35:5-6, 8, 10). In making the speech-and-hearing-impaired man whole, Jesus signifies free, flourishing life in a "new heaven and a new earth" (Isa 66:22; cf. Mark 13:24-27, 30-31).

Feeding the Crowds (Again) (8:1-10)

Reinforcing the theme of openness, Jesus now opens out his mission from two Gentile individuals in "private" settings "away from the crowd" (7:33; cf. 7:24-37) to extended engagement with the public and renewed instruction of his disciple (Owens 2013, 259). The transitional phrase "in those days" (8:1) marks a continuing period of Jesus's activity in the Gentile-majority Decapolis. Mark particularly focuses on a three-day retreat Jesus leads in the desert with a "great crowd," some having traveled "a great distance" to be with him (8:1-4). While we may presume that Jesus again teaches the people, here Mark fast-forwards to the final feeding. First announced by the narrator (8:1) and then immediately echoed in Jesus's voice (8:2), a dire situation faces the crowd: they "have nothing to eat." Whatever "spiritual" benefits they might receive from Jesus do not compensate for their physical needs. And Mark's Jesus does not promote some artificial divide between body and spirit. Physicality is spirituality and vice versa. Jesus will not send the crowd away with empty bellies.

This second mass feeding incident (8:1-10) exhibits many parallels to the first (6:30-44). Yet the two stories are not mirror images; they have certain distinctive elements that stand out amid the similarities.

Mass Feeding Incidents in 6:30-44 and 8:1-10

Similarities	Differences
Jesus's "compassion" (*splanchnizomai*) for the multitude (6:34/8:2)	Multitude of "five thousand men (*andres*)" (6:34) vs. "four thousand people (*tetrakischilioi*)" (8:9)
Desert/wilderness (*erēmos/erēmia*) setting (6:32, 35/8:4)	Desert setting in predominantly Jewish territory (Galilee) vs. desert setting in predominantly Gentile territory (Decapolis)
Disciples question Jesus about the food supply and function as food servers (6:37-38, 41-42/8:4-8)	Five loaves and two fish (6:38, 41) vs. seven loaves and "a few small fish" (8:6-7)
Crowd ordered to sit down (6:39/8:6)	Crowd sits down "in groups [of fifties and hundreds] as though they were having a banquet on the green grass (*chlōrō chortō*)" (6:39 CEB) vs. crowd sits down unorganized on the "ground (*gēs*)" (8:6)
Jesus blesses/gives thanks for bread, breaks the loaves, and gives to the disciples to distribute to the crowd (6:41/8:6)	[No special blessing for the fish] (6:41) vs. Jesus blesses the fish separately from the bread (8:7)
The people eat their fill, and multiple baskets of leftovers are gathered (6:42-43/8:8)	Twelve baskets of leftovers (6:43) vs. seven baskets of leftovers (8:8)
After the meal, Jesus and the disciples cross the lake by boat toward Bethsaida (6:45/8:10, 22)	After the meal, though sailing toward Bethsaida, Jesus and disciples come ashore at Gennesaret (6:45, 53) vs after the meal, Jesus and disciples sail first to "the district of Dalmanutha" and then on to Bethsaida (8:10, 13, 22)

The key differences have to do with settings and statistics. Although both incidents take place in the desert—recalling the divine feeding of God's people in the wilderness—they do not occur in the same desert regions. The first feeding takes place on the western side of the lake in Galilee, the second on the eastern side in the Decapolis, the same area where he healed the deaf man (7:31). (Following this second feeding, Jesus and the disciples sail north to Bethsaida [8:22] through "the district of Dalmanutha" [8:9], a location otherwise unknown.) The feedings also differ in ambience. Though situated in a "deserted place" (6:32, 35), the Galilean episode has the feel of an organized banquet with guests seated in "groups on the *green grass* (*chlorō chortō*)" (in the desert!) headed by *men* (*andres*, "males") (6:39-40, 44); by contrast, the Decapolis feeding appears to be a more rough-and-ready affair, an impromptu dinner on the grounds—literally, on the "ground" or "earth" (*gēs*)—for an undifferentiated mass of "about four thousand *people* (*tetrakischilioi*)" (8:6, 9).

While the difference in crowd size between four and five thousand seems relatively insignificant (both represent a large assembly), the numbers *twelve* and *seven* carry more symbolic weight. In the first event, the twelve disciples take up "twelve baskets full" of leftovers (6:43), an amount befitting the people of Israel descending from twelve sons of Jacob/Israel. The number seven can be tallied from the five loaves plus two fishes (6:41) but is more central to the second incident involving "seven loaves" and "seven baskets full" of leftover pieces of bread and fish (8:6, 8).

The "perfect" number seven reflects the wholeness and completeness of God's good creation capped off by the divine Sabbath on the seventh day (Gen 2:1-3). Within this created order, human beings made in God's image have special dignity and responsibility as partners with God in managing the world and maintaining the Sabbath rhythm (Exod 20:8-11). The Table of Nations in Genesis 10 identifies *seventy* (a super-multiple of seven) groups populating the post-flood, re-created world, signifying "a natural extension of the creation account . . . a theological witness to a common humanity shared by all" (Fretheim 1994, 409), "the unity of the human race" (Blenkinsopp 2011, 156). Blenkinsopp further comments that "this seventyfold macrocosm corresponds [to] the microcosm of the 70 Israelites in Egypt (Gen. 46:27; Exod. 1:5; Deut. 10:22) and their 70 elders (Exod. 24:1; Num. 11:16). The symbolic resonance is strengthened by the frequent arrangement of the names [in Genesis 10] in groups of seven." Overall, then, in biblical numerology, seven/seventy transcends "ethnic identity with a universalist perspective, implying a sense of shared moral obligation" between Israel and the nations (Blenkinsopp 2011, 156).

In sum, Jesus's double feeding in Mark 6 and 8 signifies the inclusion in God's right-making, flourishing realm of all people, Jew and Gentile, rich and poor, but with a particular "preferential option for the poor," the hungry, the oppressed, as liberation theologians stress (Gutiérrez 1988, xxv–xxviii; Groody and Gutiérrez [eds.] 2014). In the "new math" of God's economy, 12 + 7/70 = Humanity, the total number of people, past, present, and future. (Jesus's double sending of missionaries in Luke—twelve in 9:1-6 and seventy in 10:1-20—makes a similar point.) Following the Syrophoenician woman's plea (Mark 7:28), Mark's Jesus reaches out to a multitude of Gentiles with an abundance of food beyond the few "crumbs" she requested. And following Jesus's own sigh (7:34), he "opens" the heavenly storehouse of resources on the "ground/earth" for another mass of people, reminiscent of raining manna in the desert.

Yet Jesus does not call down heavenly bread in either incident. He uses the meager loaves at hand, thanks God (Heaven) for them, blesses them, and breaks them open, even as he opens human hearts and hands to share bread with one another and conserve leftovers for others' benefit. An amazing miracle to be sure, but one that remains rooted in earth and on earth, that affirms heaven coming down to earth and commingling with earth, that bears witness to a robust creational and incarnational eco-liberation theology (Boff 1997). The two feedings mark *normative*, rather than exceptional, events—how God's world *should* operate.

Challenging the Pharisees and Disciples (Again) (8:11-20)

While Mark no doubt hopes his readers will take to heart everything he writes about Jesus, he especially wants them to dwell on the dual crowd feedings. Notice Jesus's test(y) questions to his disciples: "Do you not remember? When I broke the five loaves for the five thousand, how many baskets full of broken pieces did you collect? . . . And the seven for the four thousand, how many baskets full of broken pieces did you collect?" Although they spout the correct answers, "twelve" and "seven" respectively, the disciples do "not yet *understand*" the full significance of Jesus's feeding missions (8:18-21). Their "hearts" remain just as "hardened" or petrified (*pepōrōmenē*) as they were after the first feeding (6:52; 8:17) and their spiritual ears as dysfunctional (8:18) as were the deaf man's physical ears before Jesus opened them (7:31-37). Jesus has a harder time opening his own followers' ears—and eyes and hearts and minds (8:17-18).

And he's not having any more success convincing certain Pharisees who continue to hound him and challenge his authority. When Jesus disembarks in Dalmanutha, the Pharisees press him for an authenticating "sign from heaven" (8:10-11). They prove completely oblivious to or just plain obstinate about accepting the many signs God has already provided through Jesus's hands, not least the recent feedings of thousands. Deep into his mission now, Jesus continues to battle not only aggressive forces of harm and evil but also obstructive strains of ignorance from religious scholars and his own followers. What's a frustrated Messiah to do?

Sign and sigh language (8:11-13)

Jesus first responds to the Pharisees' request for a heavenly sign with another sigh like the one he expressed between looking heavenward and restoring the impaired man's hearing and speech (7:34). He now sighs or groans, however, more intensely, as suggested by the compound form of the verb and the added emphasis on internal "spiritual" distress: "he sighed deeply (*anastenaxas*) in his spirit" (8:12). Moreover, Jesus's sighing here has nothing to do with preparing himself to perform a miraculous act, since he flatly refuses to grant the Pharisees' plea for some heavenly demonstration: "Truly I tell you, no sign will be given to this generation" (8:12).

Jesus seems to mean that this generation will receive no *more* signs. Notice that he deflects attention away from the Pharisees' special interests to the common interests they share with Israel's present "generation" (*genea*)—the wider populace reflecting the general spirit of the age (*zeitgeist*) (BDAG 2000, 191–92). Mark's Jesus increasingly contemplates the totality of his mission, the big global and cosmic picture, becoming more and more frustrated with "this generation," which he soon dubs as "adulterous and sinful" (8:38) and "faithless" (9:19). He has performed plenty of dramatic signs, not least the pair of abundant feedings, signaling fulfillment of God's restorative rule. If the Pharisees and their compatriots haven't gotten the message by now, they are unlikely to be convinced by additional spectacles. Unfortunately, miracles tend to be addictive, sign-seekers insatiable: enough is never enough. As for Jesus's miracles in Mark, wonderful as they are for those healed and freed by them, they tend to divert others' attention from a much less obvious sign of God's grace and power—the sign of the *cross*—which Jesus soon reveals (8:34). He will continue to work a few more wonders (8:22-26; 9:14-29; 10:46-52), but they will not be his top priority in the second half of this Gospel.

While not "opening" re-creative space between heaven and earth, Jesus's present deep-sighing still reflects further venting of the tension he feels (incarnates) between the divine and human spheres. As the Pharisee legal experts put the squeeze on Jesus to prove himself, they continue to impede the flourishing of God's kingdom. The situation partly recalls Susanna's sighing/groaning (*anestenaxen*), pleading and protesting, as two legal officials (elders/judges) responsible for safeguarding God's righteousness and justice, pressed around her with illicit intent, making "things . . . narrow (*stena*) for [her] on all sides" (Sus 1:22 NETS).

But unlike Susanna, Jesus is not a woman trapped in a gated garden and a patriarchal society. Weary of certain Pharisees' pesky pursuits, Jesus has no patience this time for debate. He promptly gets back in the boat and leaves them, sailing to "the other side of the lake" (8:13 CEB). Whatever plans he had for Dalmanutha, he abandons. He shakes the dust (sand) from his feet against the Pharisees and moves on (cf. 6:11).

Yeast infection (8:14-21)

Back in the boat with his disciples, Jesus once more takes the opportunity to gauge their progress and teach them further. In this third and final boat scene, thankfully no storm erupts on the lake, as in the previous voyages (4:35-41; 6:45-52). But the disciples remain just as confused in their understanding of Jesus's mission. This scene also marks the third and final time the disciples struggle over Jesus's perspective concerning bread, Mark's "third disciples-fret-about-lack-of-bread story," as Robert Fowler quips (2011, 253). As they twice miscalculated the adequacy of available loaves to feed the multitudes as Jesus commanded (6:37-38; 8:4-5), they now misconstrue Jesus's metaphorical statement about bread, filtered again through their limited-good mindset.

Jesus uses the preceding argument with the Pharisees as an object lesson for the disciples: "Watch out—beware of the yeast of the Pharisees and the yeast of Herod" (8:15). Clearly the point focuses on the threat of certain Pharisees who conspire with the Herodians against Jesus (3:6; 12:13). The disciples, however, fixate on the "yeast" reference in its literal-agential function in bread-making and misapply it to their current situation: they had only brought "*one* loaf" on board to sustain them during the trip (8:14, 16). Once more the numbers don't add up.

But math is not their main problem. They continue to suffer spiritual dimness, deafness, and hardness in their eyes, ears, and hearts (8:17-18). After all their time with Jesus, they still do not comprehend the logic of God's realm revealed in Christ's *logos*, the divine word that overwhelms the limited logic of lesser realms. Since Mark first diagnosed the disciples' hard/petrified heart condition after Jesus walked to them on the storm-tossed lake (6:52), they have received further evidence of Jesus's "vast" capacity as one "who simply cannot be contained with narrow, rigid schemas and categories" (Vegge 2017, 262). Remember that Jesus sighs in frustration, as I've suggested, to break through (breathe out) the constricted space between heaven and earth. Jesus does not sigh in response to the disciples' narrow mindset, but his questioning serves the same function: "Do you still (*oupō*) not perceive or understand?"/"Do you not yet (*oupō*) understand?" (8:17, 21; cf. 4:40—"Have you still [*oupō*] no faith?). Still stuck in your straitened condition? Ach!

In this case, the disciples are trapped in a literalist frame of thought, as if they've never heard Jesus speak in parables and images before. The metaphorical value of yeast plays on its concentrated infective power to permeate and expand a lump of dough. Just so, a little misguided teaching (Pharisees) and ruling (Herodians) can either be *converted* by Christ's correct curriculum and right rules to advance God's kingdom, or it can *corrupt* Christ's gospel mission. The prospect of *transformative* growth from a tiny, unlikely source fits with Jesus's parable of the mustard seed (4:30-32), which, as it happens, is paired with the parable of the *yeast* in Matthew 13:31-33//Luke 13:18-21, featuring a woman who mixes a small amount of yeast into fifty pounds of flour to produce a hundred loaves of bread. In the present Markan scene, however, Jesus focuses on yeast as a symbol of the Pharisees'/Herod's potential corruptive influence. This negative image of yeast may evoke the Exodus drama, in which the Israelites removed all traces of leaven (yeast) from their homes and ate unleavened bread the night they fled to freedom. There was no time to waste, no time to let their bread rise (Exod 12:1-20; 13:3-10). On that historic evening, yeast represented the past era of bitter enslavement now left behind with all due haste; unleavening became associated with releasing. Annual commemorations of that original Passover/Feast of Unleavened Bread sustain the people of God's ever-urgent commitment to freedom.

In different ways, some Pharisees and Jesus's disciples both need to "beware" getting stuck in limiting, un-liberating perspectives. Jesus previously challenged the former group for allowing certain traditions to restrict the way of God's dynamic word (Mark 7:6-9), as he presently chides his disciples for their superficial, literalist mindset that obstructs the way of God's restorative kingdom embodied in Jesus Messiah (8:14-21). "Do you not yet understand?" Jesus presses, knowing the answer (8:21). No, they don't, sadly—not yet. But Jesus is not yet through with them either.

Missing the Mark through Blindness
Mark 8:22–10:52

Jesus's pointed questions to his disciples exposing their failure to *see* with their eyes, *perceive* with hearts, and *understand* with their minds (8:17-21) provide a perfect setup for the short incident that follows in which Jesus restores sight to a blind man. By now we know that Jesus's miraculous acts carry symbolic as well as somatic significance, affecting spiritual as well as physical life. In short, Jesus works to make people *whole*. The blind man, while important in his own right, also "clearly" (8:25) represents the dim-sighted disciples struggling to apprehend the full scope of Jesus's mission. Given this continuing vision motif, some commentators take the blind man case in 8:22-26 as concluding the previous unit rather than beginning a new one.

While I grant the close connection between the disciples and the blind man in 8:14-26 (and also between the deaf man in 7:31-37 and the blind man in 8:22-26—both benefiting from Jesus's spittle), I see a larger picture in 8:22–10:52 *framed by two cases of healing blind men*: the first involving an anonymous man near Bethsaida (8:22-26), the last a man named Bartimaeus near Jericho (10:46-52).

These two stories that sharpen the focus on seeing/perceiving/understanding bracket *three instances in which Jesus predicts his imminent death (and resurrection)* (8:31; 9:31; 10:33-34). Jesus voices each prediction privately to his disciples, who in turn continue to miss the mark, to misconstrue Jesus's message. Their (in)sight remains partial at best.

Spliced between the three predictions are *two segments of interactions* between Jesus and multiple characters: Moses, Elijah, and the father of a spirit-seized boy (9:2-29); and Pharisees, little children, and a rich man (10:1-31). In various ways, mostly unflattering, the disciples participate in all these encounters with Jesus. Moreover, the distressed father in the first segment (9:14-29) and the rich man in the second (10:17-31) are both sincere men of faith positively disposed toward Jesus but who nonetheless fall short of Jesus's demanding standards (9:23-24; 10:21-22), just as the twelve disciples do. The path of discipleship proves rough and rigorous as well as rewarding (10:28-31).

The full sequence of events in this unit may be charted as follows:

Healing an Anonymous Blind Man (8:22-26)
Predicting Jesus's Death and Resurrection #1 (8:27–9:1)
Interacting with Moses, Elijah, and a Distressed Father (9:2-29)
Predicting Jesus's Death and Resurrection #2 (9:30-49)
Interacting with Pharisees, Little Children, and a Rich Man (10:1-31)
Predicting Jesus's Death and Resurrection #3 (10:32-45)
Healing a Blind Man Named Bartimaeus (10:46-52)

Befitting a unit that unpacks what it means to follow the way of Jesus Messiah, Mark keeps Jesus on the move in his longest journey, extending over a hundred miles north to south. We may track the main stops as follows:

- Jesus and the disciples arrive by boat in *Bethsaida*, also known as Bethsaida-Julius, on the northern tip of the Sea of Galilee (8:22).
- They then head about twenty-five miles further north to *Caesarea-Philippi* in the region of Paneas (8:27).
- Jesus takes Peter, James, and John up to a *high mountain* in the area (9:2).
- Jesus and the larger company of disciples reverse course, heading south to *Capernaum* on the northwest shore of the lake (9:33).
- They then travel sixty or so miles further south into "the region of *Judea*" (10:1) where Jesus has not been before in Mark's story (people once came from Judea to see and hear him [3:7], but he only now ventures into their territory).
- The travel party comes to the Judean city of *Jericho* (10:46), about fifteen miles from *Jerusalem*, their final destination (11:1; cf. 10:32).

The way of Mark's Jesus now moves inexorably and climactically to Jerusalem, the holy city of God, the capital established by King David. Though we would most naturally say that Jesus goes down to Jerusalem from Galilee in the north, biblical geography, or what we might call "theography," views Jerusalem as the central apex of the world to which everyone goes *up* (10:32). As Jesus's threefold prediction makes clear, he goes up to Jerusalem to die on a cross at the instigation of political and religious authorities inimical to God's righteous rule. Far from escaping Caesarean-Herodian rule (inscribed in city names of Bethsaida Julius and Caesarea Philippi) and their Jewish priestly and scribal collaborators, Jesus heads right into the teeth of unjust, imperious authority in Jerusalem.

As Jesus hurtles toward his deadly showdown in Jerusalem, he seeks with greater urgency to prepare his disciples for the ordeal—and what comes after his departure. Regrettably, they continue to struggle to meet the demands of these difficult days.

Healing an Anonymous Blind Man (8:22-26)

In their previous boat trip, Jesus's disciples sailed toward Bethsaida but were blown off course by "an adverse wind . . . early in the morning" and eventually landed, after Jesus "walked" into the boat, at Gennesaret (6:45-53). But now, on the group's third voyage across the lake, they finally make it to Bethsaida, where they disembark (8:22).

Bethsaida, originally established as a fishing settlement (its name means "House of Fishing"), evokes the first disciples' former fishing business, which they abandoned to follow Jesus (1:16-20). In Mark's account, Simon (Peter) and Andrew made their home in nearby Capernaum on the lake's northwest shore (1:21, 29). But the Fourth Gospel associates these brothers (and Philip the apostle) with Bethsaida (John 1:43-44), and later tradition also identifies Bethsaida as the hometown of Zebedee's sons, James and John (Rousseau and Arav 1995, 19–22). Whatever the precise residences of these earliest disciples, we may regard Capernaum and Bethsaida—only a few miles apart from each other—as sister fishing villages. Further, we may surmise that returning to their home area prompted the disciples to ponder all the incredible experiences they've had with Jesus and all they've given up to follow him (see Mark 10:28). There's still much they don't understand. Has their sacrifice been worth it? In many respects, they've come a long, winding way back where they started. Will the next days and weeks finally bring clarity or more cloudiness?

First-century Bethsaida was not only known as a fishing center but also as a place promoting Roman-Herodian interests. Although close to the Galilee border ruled by Herod Antipas, Bethsaida was located in Gaulinitis (the Golan Heights today) under the jurisdiction of Antipas's brother, Herod Philip. There was little love lost between the brothers after Antipas took Philip's wife Herodias for himself. It was this illicit union that John the Baptist denounced and that cost him his head (6:17-29). Though Philip's territory was generally more peaceful than Antipas's region, Philip still maintained allegiance to Roman overlords. Upon raising the village of Bethsaida to the rank of a Greek city (*polis*) in 30 CE, Philip renamed it Bethsaida-Julias in honor of Livia-Julia, the mother of Emperor Tiberius (Arav and Rousseau

1995, 20–22). Jesus and company can scarcely evade the shadow of Roman rule, a shadow about to become thicker and darker for them in the ensuing days.

Speaking of darkness, "some people" bring to Jesus a blind man from Bethsaida, whose whole world is shrouded in literal darkness. In turn, Jesus leads him by hand to the outskirts of the village (8:22-23). Jesus's desire for privacy persists; he remains committed to helping the disabled but with as little public commotion as possible and maximal attention on instructing his disciples.

As Jesus applied his saliva to the speech-impaired man's tongue (7:33), so he places his spittle on the blind man's eyes. The saliva element again recalls Vespasian's means of curing a blind man in Alexandria to support his claim to the Roman throne in 69 CE. Although doubtful whether he could perform such a miracle, he was urged on by his campaign staff and managed also to heal a lame man and one with a withered hand—as Mark's Jesus does (2:1-12; 3:1-6). Jesus is not trying to prove anything, not promoting himself, and certainly not following the wishes of his power-hungry disciples (9:33-34, 38; 10:35-37, 41). Remember that he heals the blind man offstage.

But *Mark's purpose* is precisely to convince audiences around the time of the Roman-Jewish War of Jesus's bona fide authority as Son of God and Messiah (1:1). It is during these tumultuous years that Nero commits suicide (68 CE), thus ending the Julio-Claudian dynasty and engendering a succession struggle. In the convulsive "Year of the Four Emperors" (69 CE), Otho, Galba, and Vitellius quickly rose and fell from power. Finally, Vespasian solidified his claim to Caesar's seat and the new Flavian line, boosted not only by miraculous acts but also military feats, not least putting down the pesky Jewish revolt in 70 CE. The Jewish historian Flavius Josephus, aiming to maintain favor with Flavian rulers, would later attribute a virtual messianic status to Vespasian (*J. W.* 6.312-13).

Accordingly, Mark's presentation of Jesus as the promised Davidic Messiah and King (11:9-10; 14:61-62; 15:1-2, 9-18) inevitably challenges the rule of Roman Caesars from Tiberius to Vespasian. Whether Mark specifically "introduced spittle into his story of the Blind Man of Bethsaida," as Eric Eve claims, "to create an allusion to the Vespasian story," Mark's account of the Bethsaida healing reinforces "a wider concern to contrast the messiahship of Jesus with such Roman imperial 'messianism'" (2008, 1; cf. 1–17).

In acknowledging the political allusions underlying the vignette of the blind man's cure, we must not lose sight of the vivid literary scene Mark paints. It briskly tracks two stages of "seeing" (with multiple uses of the *blep-* root) following Jesus's application of saliva and hands on the man's eyes. Each stage features a question or answer by Jesus and a response by the blind man.

Stage #1
- *Jesus asks*: "Can you *see* (*blepeis*) anything?" (8:23)—a natural question after applying a remedy, but not a question Jesus asks any other disabled client; this question suggests a possible tinge of doubt on Jesus's part.
- *The blind man responds*: "And the man *looked up* (*anablepsas*) and said, 'I can *see* (*blepō*) people, but they look like trees walking'" (8:24). The compound form of *blepō* with the *ana*-prefix ("up"/"above") connotes not only a physical lift of the head and eyes but also an anticipation of heavenly blessing, a hopeful sense that "things are looking up," as we say. Moreover, in certain contexts *anablepō* means "to gain sight, whether for the first time or again" (BDAG 2000, 59; cf. Mark 10:51-52; Matt 11:5; 20:34; Luke 7:22; 18:41-43; John 9:11, 15, 18; Acts 9:12, 17-18; 22:13).

But while the blind man in the story anticipates a miraculous recovery of sight, this outcome is not entirely realized. At first "sight," he's only able to see partially, hazily; he knows he sees people, "but they look like trees walking." The image of walking trees may not be as scary as that of a walking ghost on the water, as the disciples first envisioned Jesus during the storm (6:49), but it is unsettling and unsatisfying. For all the wondrous events that happen "immediately" in Mark's story, sometimes Jesus takes things more slowly, guiding supplicants and followers *through* a process of enlightenment.

Stage #2
- *Jesus acts*: "Then Jesus laid his hands on his eyes again" (8:25a). Mark's initial report did not pinpoint where Jesus placed his hands on the blind man's body (8:23); now we learn that Jesus laid his hands on the man's eyes after applying and perhaps rubbing in the saliva (Donahue and Harrington 2002, 256–57). This intimate personal touching mirrors Jesus's dealing with the deaf mute (7:31-37). But the need for a *second touch* (a booster shot) stands out among Jesus's healing incidents—which probably accounts for its omission by the other Gospel writers. Was Jesus somehow running low on curative powers on this occasion or not paying sufficient attention to the case at hand? Surely not! What was Mark thinking by featuring such a choppy story? Stay tuned.
- *The blind man responds*: "He *looked intently* (*dieblepsen*) and his sight was restored, and he *saw* (*eneblepen*) everything clearly" (8:25b). Two additional *blepō* compounds describe the man's intense, penetrating gaze, as if

trying to will his vision into clearer focus. The first verb (*diablepō*) suggests "stare with eyes wide open" (BDAG 200, 226; cf. CEB), and the second certifies gaining full, sharp sight with the adverb "clearly" (*tēlaugōs*) and the direct object "everything" (*hapanta*). The adverb, used only here in the New Testament, hints at long-range sight: "clearly though at a distance," "clearly from afar," "far-shining" connected with *tēle*, meaning "far away" (Moulton and Milligan 1930, 463; Donahue and Harrington 2002, 257). Finally, the man is made whole, able to take in the whole world near and far, with precision and proper perspective.

In a small compass, Mark depicts a remarkably detailed scene from multiple visual angles across two distinct stages. As significant, however, as is the miracle of restoring the blind man's physical eyesight, this is not the incident's primary aim. Adding a cure for blindness to Jesus's repertoire is not the main reason he performs this particular act. After treating the blind man, Jesus promptly dismisses him and wants nothing more to do with him and wants no public knowledge of the event: "Then he sent [the man] away to his home, saying, 'Do not even go into the village'" (8:26).

Jesus's attention zooms in on his disciples, whom he directly leads to another village (8:27) *with this incident emblazoned on their minds*. If they have any perceptual skill, they must "see" that *they* are the principal sight-challenged ones needing to move from fuzzy to full sight, from astigmatic vision to perspicacious insight. At best they still only grasp a sketchy outline of Jesus's identity and mission, as if *he* were a walking tree with trunk and limbs. Step 1 to recovery and growth is admitting that you have a long way to go, much to learn. Jesus keeps prodding his student-disciples to this end.

Predicting Jesus's Death and Resurrection #1 (8:27–9:1)

From Bethsaida-Julias, Jesus takes his disciples further north into Herod Philip's realm "to the villages around Caesarea Philippi" (8:27 NIV) in the district of Paneas. Thereby Jesus travels from a fishing village (Bethsaida) to a cultic center (Caesarea Philippi) dedicated to the nature deity Pan, "god of fields, forests and fountain, flocks and shepherds" (Rousseau and Arav 1995, 34). The worship of Pan in the area began in the Hellenistic period with a shrine erected at the mouth of a cave topped by a towering mountain and opening to an underground spring sourcing the Jordan River. In 20 BCE, Caesar Augustus placed the territory under the jurisdiction of Herod the Great, who built a magnificent marble temple in honor of his imperial patron. After Herod the Great died, the region passed to Herod Philip, who established a Greek-style city near the Augustus temple and Pan shrine. Thus

Caesarea Philippi was born (Josephus, *Ant.* 15.363-64; 18.28; *J. W.* 1.404-406; Kutsko 1992; Rousseau and Arav 1995, 33–35; Hoppe 2006).

"On the way (*hodos*)"—the "way" of life and mission, not simply movement from place to place—Jesus poses an uncharacteristically self-referential question to his disciples: "Who do people say that I am?" (8:27). It sounds like Jesus asks for polling information about his campaign, but a campaign for what? And why does Jesus suddenly care about what people think about him? Presumably he wants to gauge his messianic reputation, but this seems like an odd time to worry about that while he's traveling *away* from Galilee toward a heavily Hellenized city with sparse Jewish representation. As we will see, Jesus's question principally functions as a tool to test his disciples' understanding. But may he not also be genuinely curious, even concerned, about social opinion at this critical juncture in his life?

Jesus seems to head deeper into the comparatively friendly territory of Herod Philip for a final retreat with his "staff" before heading back to Galilee, where he's more well known and closely watched by Herod Antipas, and then on to Jerusalem to face hostile Roman and Jewish authorities. As usual, a throng trails after Jesus, but they do not press themselves upon him at Caesarea Philippi. Here Jesus "called the crowd with his disciples" (8:34) after speaking privately to the disciples (8:27-31). Throughout this scene, Jesus appears intensely reflective and revelatory about his destiny.

By asking about people's opinion of him, Jesus is not suffering some deep-seated "identity crisis" (Who am I?), but he may be undertaking an identity check, clarifying and confirming his mission. As social creatures, human beings take formative cues from one another. We cannot help being socially constructed to some degree, however self-determining and ruggedly individualistic we claim to be. Such group dynamics especially shape more intentional community-centered, collectively-oriented, cultures, like that pervading the eastern Mediterranean world (Malina and Rohrbaugh 1992, 341–43; Malina 2001a, 58–80). Although keenly attuned to God's will for his life, the Son of Humankind is also deeply affected by others' perceptions of and interactions with him.

The disciples report Jesus's popular association with John the Baptist, Elijah, and other prophets (8:28-29). All of these make good sense in light of Jesus's identification with John's Elijah-styled mission and Jesus's working of Elijah-like miracles and preaching with prophetic authority (Brown 1971). Recall that even Herod Antipas wondered (fearfully) if the beheaded John had reincarnated in Jesus (6:14-16). But as important as these prophetic models are, do they sufficiently capture Jesus's vocation? Isn't there something different and unique about him? What say his closest followers, who should know if anyone does but who have only shown limited perceptive skills thus far? We do not hold out great hope when Peter proceeds to answer Jesus's question.

But surprisingly Peter aces this exam! In crisp, emphatic terms, he announces, "You [indeed, *You*] are the Messiah/Christ" (*Su ei ho Christos*) (8:29). Recall that Mark's opening verse introduced the "good news of Jesus Messiah/Christ." After a long hiatus, we now hear a disciple's first confession of faith in *Christ* Jesus, marking a watershed moment in the heart of Mark's narrative. Yet this moment is even more crucial than Peter and the other disciples realize. Where we might anticipate some commendation or encouragement from Jesus, he replies with a "stern order . . . not to tell anyone about him" (8:30). Just as he had muzzled obstreperous demons and enthusiastic witnesses of his healing power (1:25-26, 34, 44-45; 3:11-12; 5:43; 7:36; 8:26), Jesus now issues a strong non-disclosure command to his closest followers—at the point where they seem to be making progress!

The problem soon becomes evident as Jesus "began to teach" the disciples "quite openly" about the full scope of his messianic mission (8:31-32). The disciples have the right title—Jesus is indeed God's Anointed One, Israel's Messiah—but only a limited understanding of how he fills out (fulfills) that role. Jesus starts unfolding a new dimension of his vocation sure to shock his confidants; and until they accept this dimension, he does not want them to spread "fake news." Jesus strives to be crystal clear: no parables or metaphors now, just ordinary "plain" speech (8:32 NIV, CEB); no sighing or other wordless gestures to signal release from narrow mindsets, just straightforward, "open" declaration (Owens 2013, 259).

Jesus might have warned his disciples to brace themselves before disclosing that the Son of Humankind—Jesus's principal self-designation stressing solidarity with the whole human condition—"must undergo great suffering . . . be killed [at the instigation of Jewish authorities], and after three days rise again" (8:31). Although we don't know exactly what the disciples expected of this Messiah for whom they left everything, we can be sure they did not anticipate his brutal execution. They might have thought he would execute some who blocked his way, but surely he would not suffer execution himself. A dead Messiah is a failed Messiah. Even a dead Messiah who rises to new life after three days raises more questions than it answers. Peter, James, and John had witnessed Jesus's resuscitating Jairus's deceased daughter *from her deathbed*, not long after she'd passed away (5:37-42). No burial, no three-day limbo for her. But that's what will happen to Jesus? How do we make sense of that?

As abruptly as Peter confessed Jesus as the Messiah, he now takes Jesus aside and takes him to task for his gloomy announcement. Peter "rebukes" Jesus, as if to say like an overwrought campaign manager, "This is not what we signed up for in casting our lot with you as Messiah. And this will not play well with the public. Nobody wants a dead Messiah!" In turn, Jesus literally *turned* his back on Peter, *looked* back at the other disciples (wanting the whole group to see and hear his reaction), and *"rebuked* Peter . . . 'Get behind me, Satan! For you are setting your mind not on divine things but on human things'" (8:32-33). The emotional pitch could hardly be hotter, swirling around a triadic sequence of the intensive verb *epitimaō*, "express[ing] strong disapproval . . . censure" (BDAG 2000, 384; cf. L&N 1988, 33) and a tense conflict among three realms. The three reprimands tumble out in short order, with Peter's rebuke of Jesus squeezed between two rebukes Jesus issues to the disciples.

- Jesus "*sternly ordered* (*epetimēsen*) them not to tell anyone about him" (8:30).
- Peter "took [Jesus] aside and began to *rebuke* (*epitiman*) him" (8:32).
- Jesus, "turning and looking at his disciples . . . *rebuked* (*epetimēsen*) Peter" (8:33).

Epitimaō shares a semantic field with *timaō*, focusing on *evaluation* or *appraisal* in social and economic contexts. *Timaō* (and the noun form *timē*) connotes positive ascriptions of honor to worthy persons, such as God and parents (7:6, 10; 10:19) or to worthy causes, or professional assessments of commercial value, such as the price of property (Acts 4:34; 7:16). The compound form *epitimaō*, however, registers a *negative* appraisal, a judgment of *shame* and blatant *disapproval*—with a strong emotional punch. Aristotelian and many modern emotion theorists stress that emotions function as primary appraisers of people and situations, integrating evaluative feelings and thoughts (Lazarus 1991, 144–52; Nussbaum 2001; Solomon 2004; Moors 2014; Spencer 2017a, 22–24; 2021, 11–12, 46–47). It's not surprising at this life-and-death crossroads for Jesus and his followers that emotions boil. It's because the stakes are so high that Jesus and Peter trade such sharp rebukes, with each side virtually branding the other as a "son of dishonor"—the antithesis of *Bar-timaios* (Bartimaeus), "Son-of honor," whose story of restored sight concludes this unit (10:46-52).

Although Peter misevaluates the situation from Jesus's authoritative viewpoint, it's not simply that Peter is thickheaded or hotheaded. He's also warmhearted and wholehearted. He cares deeply about Jesus and what will happen to him, and not only for selfish reasons affecting Peter's life but also for the sake of God's kingdom, for which Peter and fellow disciples have forsaken everything. And despite the "Satan" label he slaps on Peter, Jesus cares as deeply as ever for this beloved fisherman and first recruit.

Even so, turning his back on Peter, rebranding the "Rock" as "Satan," and ordering him to stay behind are shocking moves on Jesus's part, indicative of the serious point he stresses. He stages a gripping mini-drama, a gob-smacking political ad, with Peter as the principal prop in order to depict the tense three-ring universe in which Jesus and his disciples operate. The three rings or realms—the divine, the human, the satanic—intersect and interfere. Although "the concerns"/"things of God" (*ta tou theou*) ultimately override all other "concerns"/"things" (8:33 NIV), God does not autocratically rule the world but rather *works within and through the world* with all its bent toward evil, freely instigated by demonic powers and human schemes. And although humanity created in God's image is not demonic—and indeed perfectly unites in Jesus, the embodied Son of God—it can be complicit with and controlled by evil forces. So the battle to realize God's righteous realm rages on.

And the chief weapon of this battle wielded against Jesus Messiah and his followers is the *cross* (*stauros*), as Mark's Jesus now discloses for the first time (8:34). As familiar as Christians have become with Jesus's death by crucifixion, we must not mitigate the impact of the disciples' initial hearing about the cross from Jesus himself. If the prospect of a dead Messiah was distressing, the prospect of a *crucified* Messiah was devastating. Although there was scriptural precedent for servants of God suffering for righteousness's sake, nothing suggested that the Messiah would suffer brutal, humiliating execution by crucifixion. As Paul candidly admits, "Christ crucified . . . is a scandal (*skandalon*) to the Jews and foolishness (*mōrian*) to the Greeks" (1 Cor 1:23 CEB).

But there's more. If the disciples are crushed by the prospects of Jesus's crucifixion, it's hard to know how they can possibly bear the weight of Jesus's cross-*sharing* proposition: "If any want to become my followers, let them deny themselves and *take up their cross* and follow me" (8:34). Here Jesus lays down a stunning requirement for discipleship. He presents it as a voluntary decision, not a forced imposition, but that only makes it harder to consider. Who in their right mind would choose to carry a cross on which to die, which is the cross's only purpose? This seems, if I may put it so, utterly at *cross purposes* with Jesus's indomitable will to life.

The mind and will of Christ, however, has its own transcendent, life-saving, and life-flourishing logic, rooted in (at least) three principles:

- *Ecological principle*—how interconnected life-and-death systems work in balance and continuity, including the cycle of wintry death, thawing, and sprouting new life (cf. John 12:24-25). Just so, in Jesus's terms, saving one's life comes through losing it, through giving it away "for [Christ's] sake" and "for the sake of the gospel," which is to say, for the *good of others* (Mark 8:35-37). This is not to endorse self-abuse (masochism) or vain self-glory (martyrdom), and it certainly does not excuse violent killing of innocent victims (murder) by dominant powers. The cross remains the quintessential Christian symbol of *injustice* and *insurrection* against God's commitment to life. But for all its evil intent, the cross—yes, *even the cross* (Phil 2:8)—bridges to restored life in Christian hope and faith, to *resurrection*, even after three days in the grave (Mark 8:31).

- *Ecclesiological principle*—how God's people join in community called together by God (*ekklēsia*) to love and care for one another in a challenging world, to bear one another's burdens (Gal 5:14-15; 6:1-2, 9-10), to help *carry each other's crosses*. To be sure, Jesus speaks to individuals, to *anyone* (*tis*) who would follow him. To quote Paul again, "all must carry their own loads" (Gal 6:4). But that means that no one gets a free pass; there are no free riders on the way of the cross, including no privileged riders on the backs of lowly servants. Because Jesus himself leads the cross-bearing way (he demands nothing of others he does not first take on, full bore) and demands that everyone undertake the same cross-bearing way (he speaks now to the *crowd*, including disciples [8:34], making no distinctions in rank or responsibility), he makes the way of the cross a communal way of material support and mutual encouragement (see Hays 1996, 73–92; 196–97; Reid 2007).

- *Eschatological principle*—how the eternal life of God ultimately overwhelms death at "last," at the "end" (*eschatos*) of the day—the final Day!—when "the Son of Man . . . comes in the glory of his Father with the holy angels" (8:38). Implicit in this climactic event is God's raising to new life those who have given their lives freely and fully to God and others, as Jesus does, in no way "ashamed" of his faithful commitment to God's righteous realm, even to death on a cross. But such is not only a future aspiration but also a present actuality, as Christ has already brought God's kingdom "near" (1:15) in his righteous life and restorative ministry. Indeed, he boldly announces that, even among this "sinful generation," "there are some standing here who will not taste death until they see the kingdom of God has come with power" (8:38–9:1). While this extraordinary statement likely reflects sincere expectation of the Son of Humankind's historical return within the next "generation or two," it also cues a more immediate narrative fulfillment for Jesus's three closest disciples in the next scene.

Interacting with Moses, Elijah, and a Distressed Father (9:2-29)

Mark notes a dramatic temporal and spatial shift: the action springs ahead "six days later" to a "high mountain apart" (9:2). Except for specifying Jesus's forty-day testing period in the wilderness (1:13), Mark had marked time in general spans of "those days," "some days," "that day," and "night and days" (1:9; 2:1, 20; 4:27, 35; 5:5). In chapter 8, however, he began to provide more specific time signatures: "three days" the four thousand stayed in the desert without eating (8:2); and "three days" after Jesus's death when he will rise again (8:31). Now Mark notes a six-day interval after Jesus's ominous forecast of his impending death. As Jesus nears the end of his life, time becomes more precious.

More correctly, the text sets the events in Mark 9:2-29 "*after (meta) six days*" (NIV, NASB, NAB, KJV), which suggests at the dawning of the *seventh* day, evoking the *Sabbath* rest after six days of work. Such scheduling would fit Jesus's moving "apart" from the crowd with a small inner circle of disciples (9:2). It also recalls God's summoning Moses to the "mountain of God" (Sinai), engulfing the mountain in a fiery cloud "for six days," calling Moses out of the cloud "on the seventh day," and etching the commandments on stone tablets for God's people (Exod 24:12, 15-16; Boring 2006, 261). Prominent among these commandments was the duty to keep the Sabbath sacred every seventh day, after six days of toil (Exod 20:8-11; 34:21; 35:1-2). Moses's sudden appearance *with Jesus* on the cloud-shrouded mountain, as we soon see (Mark 9:4-7), reinforces the Sabbath connection.

Jesus is nowhere near Mount Sinai, and Mark and the other evangelists do not name the mountain Jesus ascends here. But the symbolism of a lofty peak as an optimal place for encountering the divine applies. Although tradition has identified Mount Tabor in Galilee as the "Mount of Transfiguration," the majestic snow-capped Mount Hermon in Paneas represents a more likely location, given its proximity to Caesarea Philippi and biblical association with divine blessing (Pss 42:6; 89:12; 133:3) (Arav 1992, 158–59; Rousseau and Arav 1995, 208–10; Green 2013, 967). Previously, Mark's Jesus ascended (unspecified) mountains to select his twelve apostles (Mark 3:3) and to pray alone before walking on the sea to the disciples (6:46). We are thus primed for another significant mountain-related experience for Jesus and his associates.

Mark narrates a sequence of three key experiences: starting *on* the mountain, then heading *down*, and finally confronting a boisterous scene *below*. While Jesus provides critical instruction for his disciples at each stage, other characters also play important roles: God the Father, Moses, Elijah, and a father of a terribly ill boy.

On the mountain: transfiguration (9:2-8)

Mark accentuates the exclusive and reclusive nature of the mountain excursion: "Jesus took with him Peter and James and John . . . up a high mountain apart, by themselves (*kat' idian monous*)" (9:2). Jesus only invites the select disciple-trio of Peter, James, and John (cf. 5:37; 14:33) to a secluded place, apart and alone (Matt 17:1 eliminates Mark's redundant *monous* ["apart"/"alone"], and Luke 9:28 omits the entire "apart, by themselves" phrase). Such a stark, isolated picture, however, is suddenly flooded with dazzling light and inhabited by surprising visitors. Mark crafts the story for maximum shock value.

The blazing spotlight trains on Jesus and "transfigures" him—changes his appearance, causes a metamorphosis (*metemorphōthē*, Mark 9:2). Where does this transforming light come from? The passive verb ("he was transfigured") implies what scholars dub the "divine passive": in the absence of a specified agent, we presume, if the context fits, the work of *God*. How does this transfiguration of Jesus manifest? Notably, while Matthew and Luke focus first on Jesus's shining *face* and secondarily on his shimmering clothes (Matt 17:2//Luke 9:29), Mark focuses exclusively on the *clothes* that "became dazzling white, such as no one on earth could bleach them" (Mark 9:3). The unearthly quality of the whitening effect suggests a heavenly wardrobe like that donned by the enthroned "Ancient One" ("his clothing was white as snow," Dan 7:9), other heavenly beings (Rev 4:4; 7:9; 19:14), and human beings who remain faithful to God and Christ unto death (Rev 3:4-5, 18; 6:11; 7:13) (Heil 1992, 186; 2000, 156). Jesus radiates the very light of God in heavenly splendor or "sunshine," as the old gospel song says.

But however heavenly and otherworldly this scene appears, it remains grounded *on earth*. However elevated and awe-full on snow-crested Hermon or another peak, this site remains rooted in terra firma. Jesus does not receive a new celestial robe; rather, his modest everyday clothes become momentarily sparkling white before resuming their normal shade and fabric. However suffused with divine glory on this occasion, Jesus continues to be a human being, the Son of Humankind, soon to descend the mountain and become embroiled again in ordinary human affairs on his way to the cross.

The transfiguration marks not an escapist extraction from earthly, human reality but the sanctification of this reality through the intimate intersection of heavenly and earthly realms in the incarnate Christ. As God's dovelike Spirit flew through an open heaven and rested on Jesus at his baptism (1:9-10), God's dazzling light shines on Jesus at his transfiguration. As baptism inaugurated Jesus's earthly ministry with divine authority, the transfiguration reaffirms his God-anointed mission at a critical point of impending crucifixion and foreshadows his ensuing resurrection—certified by a figure "dressed in a white robe" at Jesus's empty tomb (16:5)—and eventual return to earth "in clouds" (13:26; cf. Dan 7:13; Rev 1:7). From John the Baptist's camel-hair cloak and leather belt (1:6) to the final white-robed figure (16:5), Mark has a special interest in clothing, not as a covering but as a means of *discovering* the "fabric" of God's realm, the interweaving of "material" and "spiritual" elements in Christ's mission (5:15, 27-30; 6:56; 10:50; 14:51-52, 63; 15:20-24; 16:5).

The mystical aura of this scene is projected not only by Jesus's glistening garments but also by his surprise engagement with two otherworldly figures—two human figures, to be more precise, from a long-gone world, centuries past. These are venerable heroes from Israel's biblical history: "*Elijah* with *Moses*" (9:4). Mark places Elijah first, out of chronological sequence (Matt 17:3//Luke 9:30 reverse the order). Although unexpected and extraordinary, their presence with the transfigured Jesus makes good sense. Both Elijah and Moses were mountain men of God who had special encounters with God on Mount Sinai/Horeb (Exod 24:12-18; 34:2-35; 1 Kgs 19:8-18). Both were miracle-working prophets who aimed to liberate God's people from oppression. Both appeared to transcend space and time.

Elijah was whisked by God's Spirit from place to place (1 Kgs 18:12), booster-charged by God to outrun a royal chariot (18:46), and finally transported to heaven in a chariot of fire and updraft of wind (2 Kgs 2:11-12; Sir 48:9; 1 Macc 2:58). He seems to have been granted a special exemption from normal mortal experience, bodily and brilliantly transferred (transfigured, translated) from earth to heaven without dying. Such a transcendent experience helps account for the prophetic tradition that Elijah would reappear to herald the consummative "day of the Lord" and messianic era (Mal 3:1-2; 4:5). Remember, some had thought that Jesus was Elijah (Mark 6:14-15; 8:27-28).

Likewise, Moses's death and burial on Mount Nebo in Moab overlooking the promised land remains shrouded in divine mystery: "Then Moses, the LORD's servant, died—right there in the land of Moab, according to the LORD's command. The LORD buried him in a valley in Moabite country across from Beth-peor. Even now, *no one knows where Moses' grave is*" (Deut 34:5-6). God's peculiar ordering of Moses' death and burying him in an undisclosed location gave rise to later Jewish traditions of Moses' direct "assumption" into heaven. Philo, for example, speaks of Moses' "pilgrimage from earth to heaven . . . when he was already being exalted and stood at the very barrier, ready at [God's] signal to direct his upward flight to heaven" (Philo, *Moses* 2.288-91; Heil 2000, 111). Elijah and Moses thus provide ideal conversation partners for the transfigured Jesus, reflecting the lighted ladder between earth and heaven.

While scholars and thoughtful readers can take time to contemplate the significance of Jesus's luminous clothes and eminent companions, his three disciples are thunderstruck. Little wonder that Peter, speaking for the equally "terrified" James and John, does "not know what to say" (9:5-6). Yet that doesn't keep Peter from blurting out the first thing that pops into his head: "Rabbi, it is good for us to be here; let us make three dwellings, one for you, one for Moses, and one for Elijah" (9:5).

The Hebrew term "Rabbi" designates a respected "Teacher," similar to the Greek *Didaskale*, used multiple times to address Jesus by both disciples (4:38; 9:38; 10:35; 13:1) and outsiders (5:35; 9:17; 10:17, 20; 12:14, 19, 32). Perhaps Mark uses "Rabbi" here to suggest Peter's sense of this monumental scene's echoes with the Hebrew Bible. At the same time, however, Rabbi/Teacher marks a prosaic perception of Jesus's identity, respectful but unremarkable, and well short of what the transfiguration demands (France 2002, 353–54; Matthew 17:4 reads "Lord," *kyrie*; Luke 9:33 has "Master," *epistata*). Likewise, Peter's banal comment, "it's good to be here," applicable to myriad settings, seems particularly vapid on this extraordinary occasion.

Peter's proposal of a construction project reinforces his offbeat reaction to this heaven-directed drama. The "dwellings" he wants to build for Jesus, Moses, and Elijah are makeshift *tents* (*skēnas*), probably on the order of the branch-and-leaf canopies that Jews erect during the Feast of Tabernacles (*Sukkoth*) in remembrance of Israel's wanderings (France 2002, 354). At least Peter picks up on the Moses connection. Otherwise, his motives are unclear: perhaps he thinks the three dignitaries would be more comfortable, shaded from the sun and other elements (though Jesus's clothes would still be shining); perhaps he wishes to prolong the event and stay on the mountain (though tents are temporary shelters); perhaps he wants to leave some sort of shrine, fragile though it be, to visit later; or perhaps he doesn't know what he desires any more than he knows what to say.

In any event, what Peter wants and what Peter says are widely off base, as becomes obvious when a heavenly cloud envelops the group and a commanding voice emits from it, proclaiming, "This is my Son, the Beloved, listen to him!" (9:7). The voice is patently that of God the Father, echoing the announcement at Jesus's baptism, with a change of audience. At the baptism, God speaks to Jesus himself ("*You* are my Son . . . ," 1:11); at the transfiguration, God speaks to the three disciples about Jesus, exhorting them to "listen to him." The theme continues: the disciples must *hear*—thoughtfully, faithfully, completely—before they speak about Jesus Messiah.

At this "Hear him!" (*akouete autou*) order (9:7 KJV), the curtain abruptly closes on this glorious scene and reopens where it started—with "only (*monon*) Jesus" and the three apostles (9:8; cf. 9:2). While Jesus follows in the footsteps of the prominent prophets Moses and Elijah, he also surpasses them as the filial heir and chief agent of God's kingdom on earth, to say nothing of his imminent greater resurrection *out of death* and ascension to his Father's right hand (16:19), prefigured by the transfiguration (Harris 2019). In the scintillating spotlight of Jesus's transfiguration, Elijah and Moses are effectively "reduced to silent extras" (Grindheim 2018, 133). *Only* Jesus, Jesus *alone*, is the Messiah, the cross-bearing Messiah, a path he will increasingly tread *alone* (14:50; 15:34).

Down the mountain: explanation (9:9-13)

If Peter had desired to camp out on this monumental mountain for an extended heavenly seminar, he is sorely disappointed as Jesus heads down the slope and speaks his first words to the disciples in this episode (only Peter and God speak during the transfiguration). And those words—uttered after God thunders, "Listen to him!"—issue another gag order, forbidding his friends to tell anyone "about what they had seen, until the Son of Man had risen from the dead" (9:9). Sigh. They seem to have made little progress in understanding Jesus beyond what they knew before ascending the mountain (cf. 8:30-33). However, whereas earlier Peter and company particularly stumbled over Jesus's prediction of his crucifixion, now they stew over his befuddling forecast of resurrection: "What's this 'rising from the dead'" mean? (9:10 CEB; cf. 8:31). A reasonable question, since only a few late biblical sources clearly reference the hope of individual resurrection (Dan 12:2-3; 2 Macc 7:10-11, 22-23; though see Levenson 2006; Madigan and Levenson 2008).

But rather than asking Jesus directly about this resurrection issue, they come at the matter sideways by querying what the *scribes* say about *Elijah*, to which Jesus responds by invoking what the *Scriptures* say about the *Son of Humankind* and Elijah. Given Elijah's recent appearance, it's understandable that the three disciples have him on their minds; and given Jesus's tense history with the scribes, the trio may bring them into the discussion to take some heat off themselves (let Jesus argue with the scribes, not us!). But it's not clear what scribal tradition they have in mind. We've noted that some sources associate Elijah's return with end-time judgment, restoration, and preparation for the Lord's coming (Mal 3:1-6; 4:5-6; Sir 48:10). And Rabbi Pinchas ben Yair specifically claimed that "the resurrection of the dead comes from Elijah, blessed be his memory" (m. Soṭah 9.15), a datum that correlates with the disciples' immediate concern over Jesus's talk about "rising from the dead" (Mark 9:9-10). But the precise relationship between the comings of Elijah, the Messiah, and the Son of Humankind remain unclear, specifically whether Elijah must come "first" (Faeirstein 1981; Allison 1984; Fitzmyer 1985b; Miller 2007; Grindheim 2018).

In response to his disciples' question, Jesus affirms that "Elijah is indeed coming first to restore all things" (9:12a); "Elijah *has come*" already! (9:13a). No doubt Mark's Jesus intends to identify Elijah with *John the Baptist* (clothed like Elijah in 1:6, cf. 2 Kgs 1:8). The parallel text in Matthew 17:13 states that "the disciples understood that [Jesus] was speaking to them about John the Baptist." No such understanding by Mark's disciples, however. Moreover, rather than soothing Peter, James, and John with comforting words, Mark's Jesus pushes them to think harder about the paradox of hopes for restoration and resurrection with the harsh reality of Elijah's (John's) death—"they did to him whatever they pleased," that is, "they" arrested and beheaded him!—and of the Son of Humankind's expected "many sufferings" (*polla pathē*) at the hands of contemptuous authorities (Mark 9:13b). Again, it's not clear what "written" Scripture references Jesus has in mind (9:12-13), but Herod's execution of John and the Son of Humankind's predicted "great suffering" have been "quite openly" published in this Gospel (6:14-29; 8:31-32). Still, that doesn't mean this process of suffering and dying "first" before rising to new life is easy to accept—for Jesus or the disciples.

Below the mountain: confrontation (9:14-29)
Whatever Sabbath-type rest and spiritual high Jesus and his three confidants enjoyed on the mountaintop is rudely interrupted by a bustling scene they encounter below. They find the other (nine) disciples arguing with a group of scribes amid a "great crowd" that "immediately" turned, became "awe"-struck upon seeing Jesus, and "ran forward (*prostrechontes*) to greet him" (9:14-15). Jesus's inspiring the people's awe may owe to a residual glow about him, like that which shone from Moses' face after meeting with God on Mount Sinai (Exod 34:29-35; cf. 2 Cor 3:7, 13; Marcus 2009, 657–58). In any event, Jesus is not interested in the crowd's attention or in talking about his transfiguration: he wants to know what the commotion is all about, specifically, "What are you [all] arguing about with them?", that is, "What are you *scribes* disputing with my *disciples*?" (Mark 9:16). The tension between Jesus and the scribes continues, with the disciples caught in the middle. Peter, James, and John had just discussed with Jesus the scribes' written tradition concerning Elijah's coming (9:11); now the other disciples are caught up in an oral argument with present scribes about some matter.

Neither the disciples nor the scribes answer Jesus's question. So absorbed in their flap, it's as if they don't see Jesus or hear his query. As it happens, "someone from the crowd" pipes up to apprise Jesus of the situation. It's a local *father* deeply distressed over his debilitated son seized by a violent spirit. Turns out that he had brought his son *to Jesus*—or at least aimed to— but in Jesus's absence (on the mountain), the father had to settle for Jesus's associates, who did not prove up to the demand of helping his afflicted boy (9:17-18). We might infer, then, that the scribes and disciples were arguing about how to deal with this dire spiritual and medical case; in the meantime, the boy remained just as ill and the father just as desperate.

As we expect, Jesus delivers the father's son from his ailment (9:25-27). But this salutary outcome does not occur before fervent dialogue and dramatic activity ensue; and afterwards the inept disciples receive Jesus's post-operative review. Except for the Gerasene demoniac incident (5:1-20), this is the longest, most detailed healing/exorcism reported in Mark. We may track the story in three stages from the perspectives of (1) the father, (2) Jesus, and (3) the disciples, all in relation to the spirit-seized boy (Spencer 2010a).

Desperate father. Reminiscent of distraught parents who sought Jesus's aid for their infirm "little" daughters (5:22-23; 7:25-26), this father comes to Jesus beside himself with worry over his son's terrible condition that has afflicted him "from childhood" (9:21, 24). Unlike Jairus's and the Syrophoenician woman's bedridden little girls, this boy is beset by a vicious, violent seizure disorder that periodically "dashes him down" to the ground, hurls him into fiery and watery hazards, and causes him to writhe, "roll about," foam at the mouth, gnash his teeth, and be "unable to speak" (*alalon*) and hear (cf. 7:31-37), until he knocks out in a "rigid," comatose state (9:18, 20, 25-26). These are all classic symptoms of grand mal epileptic episodes, which modern science attributes to neurological malfunction; but it's easy to imagine how ancient societies believed that such "fits" were triggered by malign spirits that *seized* their victims (it's less easy to envision a lunar source, being "moonstruck" [*selēniazomai*], as "epilepsy" was commonly diagnosed; see Matt 4:24; 17:15; Kelley 2011). The sheer *strength* of this controlling power is further implied by the father's lament that Jesus's disciples "could not" or "were not strong enough to" (*ouk ischysan*) defuse it (9:18), reminiscent of the Gerasene demoniac whom "no one had the strength (*oudeis ischyen*) to subdue" (5:4).

The father divulges all this terrifying, tumultuous behavior of his son to "Teacher" Jesus as prelude to pleading, "If you are able to do anything, have pity/compassion on us (*splanchnistheis*) and help us" (9:22). Out of heartfelt concern for his son, the father appeals to Jesus's gut-level compassion for the needy, as demonstrated in the two feeding accounts (6:34; 8:2). But after Jesus surprisingly rebuffs the father's plea for not believing (*pisteouonti*) sufficiently (9:23), the father "immediately" bellows (in a burst of tears, according to some later manuscripts), "I believe (*pisteuō*); help my unbelief (*apistia*)" (9:24). Any parent can resonate with this father's gut-wrenching cry on behalf of his tormented child. Why then does Jesus not seem to be much moved by this tragic case? Is this another example of compassion fatigue, like that Jesus possibly felt in dealing with the Syrophoenican mother?

Jesus. His bedside manner with the epileptic boy and his father leaves something to be desired. Perhaps it's because there is no bedside. This is a very public scene with his disciples, the scribes, and a big crowd watching Jesus closely. He has a larger point to make here than simply healing the boy. And it's not a particularly calm or congenial point. Jesus roils with his own emotion, which he doesn't repress. His gruff response, however, is no mere griping or grumbling; its emotional punch is packed with purpose, particularly focused on critical matters of *faith/trust* (*pistis*), itself an important emotional attitude (Spencer 2017b).

Jesus's reaction unfolds in two parts. First, while he accedes to the father's wishes to treat the epileptic boy, Jesus says, "Bring [the child] to me" only after he vents his spleen against "you faithless (*apistos*) generation" (9:19). Jesus thus delivers a sweeping judgment against a swath of people, including the father, scribes, disciples, and present crowd, but also extending to the entire "generation" (*genea*). The "amazement/surprise" he experienced over his hometown's "unbelief" (*apistian*) in his ministry of wisdom and power to advance God's kingdom (6:2-6) has now morphed into frustration and weariness over an epidemic of faithless, trustless spurning of his messianic mission. Jesus expresses personal lament as much as social judgment, doubly bemoaning "how long" (*heōs pote*) he must "be among/put up with" this unreceptive generation (9:19).

Certainly Jesus exaggerates here. He has encountered faith*ful* respondents, even those exhibiting remarkable faith (2:5; 5:34). But as the weight of the cross-way presses harder and harder on his shoulders and as resistance and misguided self-reliance persists and progresses—especially from religious teachers (scribes) and his own disciples, who should know better—the burden becomes too much for Jesus to bear. No guttural sigh will suffice now (cf. 7:34; 8:12); his frustration must be verbalized, put into sharp words. But only briefly. Jesus launches no extended tirade: just a couple of querulous questions before attending to the matter at hand of the sick boy. Still, Jesus's natural sense of emotional exhaustion should not be glossed over. It happens to the best of ministers, even those most intimate with God. It happened to Jesus right after the mountaintop transfiguration! The tension between heaven and earth can be overwhelming sometimes (Spencer 2021, 197–203).

As Jesus kicks into pastoral mode, he shifts from his personal concern with "how long" he must endure his difficult ministry to asking "how long" the poor boy has suffered his malady. This question cues the father to elaborate on his son's fraught medical history and to directly solicit Jesus's compassionate aid (9:21-22). Prefacing his request, however, with the conditional clause, "If you are able" (*ei ti dynē*)—or "If [indeed] (*ei*) you have the power (*dynē*) to do anything (*ti*)" (Zerwick 1993, 16)—triggers Jesus's second stunning retort: "If you are able (*to ei dynē*)! All things can be done (*dynata*) for the one who believes (*pisteuonti*)" (9:23). The article (*to*) signals a specific reaction (objection) to the father's "if you are able" conditional statement (Wallace 1996, 238; Donahue and Harrington 2002, 278).

The father means no disrespect. He has already been disappointed by Jesus's disciples, and the scribes just want to argue the case. No doubt the father had also sought out many healers and teachers through the years, to no avail. He hopes Jesus is a different kind of "teacher" (9:17), but he's not absolutely certain and doesn't want to presume on Jesus's ability or press him beyond his sphere of influence. The father's faith is shaky and immature, which would seem to merit patience and sympathy considering all he has been through with his son and his lack of the scribes' training and the disciples' personal experience with Jesus.

But Jesus cannot abide—in this still very public setting—a slight against his curative power or insufficient trust in him as a healer and teacher. This has nothing to do with Jesus's sensitive ego and everything to do with his passionate concern for the liberation and restoration of this bound and broken "generation." Recall that Mark's Jesus became angry at the skin-diseased man for hedging his healing plea with an "*If* you choose" proviso, to which Jesus vehemently retorted, "I do choose!" (1:40-41). Jesus's *will* to restore flourishing life is unassailable and nonnegotiable. Recall too, however, that though the man queried Jesus's will, he had no qualms about Jesus's restorative *power*—"You *can* (*dynasai*) make me clean" (1:40)—*unlike* the father in the present case. In any case, Jesus has little tolerance for "ifs." His present snapback to the father again bristles with frustration: how dare anyone *not trust* Jesus to give every ounce of willpower and ability he has to help the afflicted?

Yet at the same time, Jesus's sharp-edged rejoinder also sounds a fervent note of invitation to greater faith, to greater willingness to *entrust* one's precious life and the lives of beloved children to Jesus's dynamic (*dynamai*) care. And the father is not deterred by Jesus's rebuke; he humbly and honestly pushes back with all the good faith he can muster. His cry—"I believe; help my unbelief!" (9:24)—could well be considered the banner confession of faith in Mark's Gospel: boldly confessing faith/trust in Christ while also acknowledging the need to grow in that faith/trust. This latter component of humility contrasts with the obstinate myopia that accompanied Peter's Christ-confession at Caesarea Philippi (8:29-33).

Now Jesus is ready to act, all the more so as he sees "a crowd . . . running together (*episyntrechei*)," that is, "running from various points and coming together" (Danker and Krug 2009, 146) around him. Apparently, more people are wanting in on the action than the initial crowd that had already dashed toward Jesus (9:15; France 2002, 368). The swelling throng of frenetic spectators ratchets up the scene's intensity against Jesus's preference to create as little spectacle as possible. But the drama only increases when Jesus "rebuked the unclean spirit" (cf. exchange of "rebukes" between Peter and Jesus in 8:32-33), sparking the spirit's shrieking out of the boy, seizing him one last time with violent convulsions, and leaving him in such a comatose state that most witnesses presume he is dead (9:25-26). Perhaps he is, but only momentarily, as Jesus "took his hand" (as with Jairus's deceased daughter, 5:41), "lifted him up, and he arose (*egeiren*)" (9:27 CEB)—another tantalizing sign of resurrection (cf. 8:31; 9:9-10).

Effectively, Jesus's deliverance of the spirit-seized boy is another *two-stage* operation, like the healing of the blind man in Mark 8:22-26, omitted in Matthew and Luke. Regarding the present miracle, these other Gospels significantly pare down Mark's account, and Matthew eliminates Jesus's extra step of lifting up the corpse-like boy, cutting to the chase: "Jesus rebuked the demon, and it came out of him, and the boy was cured instantly" (Matt 17:18; cf. Luke 9:42). Mark's version of this poignant incident brims with emotive volatility and operative difficulty for all the main characters, Jesus included. It thus merits special review and evaluation with the disciples.

Disconcerted disciples. Following the dramatic exorcism, the disciples, to their credit, "asked [Jesus] privately" in a house, "Why could we not cast [the convulsive spirit] out?" (9:28). Embarrassed publicly by their ineptitude and called to task by censorious scribes, the disciples now seem genuinely open to learning how to improve their ministry. In return, Jesus offers minimal yet notable instruction: "This kind can only come out through prayer" (9:29). Although many early witnesses add "fasting," two significant fourth-century manuscripts (א, B) only mention "prayer." Overall, given the common conjunction of "prayer and fasting" in early Christian practice, it seems less likely that a copyist would delete "fasting" than add it (though France 2002, 361, supports "fasting" in the original text). At any rate, Jesus at least doesn't rebuke the disciples here and acknowledges that some cases are harder than others—for him, too.

The solution is not finding a better formula, potion, or technique, but seeking deeper communion with God. Jesus does not envision prayer (with or without fasting) as a set litany of words or time-frame (e.g., it takes five hours of hard praying to knock out an epileptic demon). Throughout this extended exorcism story, Mark never reports that Jesus prays or recounts any particular prayer. But coming off the mountain of transfiguration, Jesus's intimate fellowship with his heavenly Father is undeniable.

Predicting Jesus's Death and Resurrection #2 (9:30-50)

Jesus's trek to Jerusalem proceeds through Galilee and brings him back to Capernaum (9:30, 33), where he recruited his first followers and performed his first miracles (1:16-32; 2:1-14). During this journey he continues "teaching his disciples" both along "the way/road" and in a house where he visits (9:31, 33), possibly the house of Peter and Andrew (cf. 1:21, 29). Road and home, *hodos* and *oikos*, remain important sites of instruction in the "way" of discipleship. Jesus continues to assess the educative progress of "the twelve" (9:35), especially their understanding of his impending death and resurrection (8:31-32) and his demonstrated care for vulnerable children (*paidia*, 5:39-41; 7:28, 30; 9:24; cf. 10:13-15). Jesus now repeats the forecast of his fate (9:31-32) and trains his disciples' attention on their treatment of a "little child" (*paidion*) and "little ones" (*mikroi*, 9:36-37, 42), building on their encounter with the epileptic "child" (*paidiou*, 9:24).

The way of the cross: not promoting grandiose ambitions (9:30-37)

While Jesus repeats the ominous prediction that the Son of Humankind will be killed and rise again after three days, he shifts responsibility for his looming demise from "the elders, chief priests, and the scribes" who spurn him (8:31) to unspecified parties who will *betray* (*paradidōmi*) him "into human hands" (9:31). When listing the twelve apostles, Mark left Judas Iscariot for last, with the eerie addendum, "who betrayed (*paredōken*) him" (3:19a). Since then Judas has not been mentioned, and Jesus does not name him now. But we readers go on high alert, waiting for Judas to make his move and wondering how the other disciples will react. We are also reminded of Jesus's embodied entanglement in fragile human life with fractious human beings. The Son of God is also Son of Humankind (*Anthrōpou*) destined to be handed over to "human hands" (*cheiras anthrōpōn*). He who has repeatedly laid his *healing hands* on afflicted humans (1:31, 41; 5:23, 41; 6:2, 5; 7:32; 8:23, 25; 9:27) will suffer terrible ill-treatment from hostile hands.

Sadly, even when Jesus raises the specter of betrayal within his own circle of disciples, they react with stunning oblivion to his warning. First, they again fail to understand Jesus's solemn prediction, a problem they compound by being "afraid to ask him" for clarification, even though they just asked him for insight (which he gave!) concerning the spirit-seized boy (9:28-29). They seem throttled both by Jesus's "secret" mission (again we're told "he did not want anyone to know" his whereabouts [9:30]) and by his previous harsh rebuke of Peter (8:33). But this is no excuse for how they respond among themselves—arguing over "who was the greatest" apostle! They're smart enough not to advertise this sophomoric debate to Jesus, but he perceives it all the same and presses them to confess when they arrive at the Capernaum house: "What were you arguing about on the way (*hodō*)?" They clam up in silence once more, no doubt out of fear again but also because of shame over what had preoccupied them "on the way (*hodō*)" (the phrase occurs twice for emphasis in 9:33-34). The *way* of following Christ to his death, carrying their own crosses behind and beside him (8:34), could scarcely be more out of step with petty jockeying for "greatest" apostolic status.

This time Jesus does not lash out with a piercing look and stinging barb, like "Get behind me, Satan!" (8:33). Now he simply "sat down, called the twelve," and tried to teach them again about his messianic mission (9:35). Although sitting was a common teaching posture (cf. 4:1-2), we sense that Jesus might also sit in this scene out of weariness from dealing with his clueless disciples (we almost hear him sigh as he sits). In short order he then delivers a striking lesson in three parts:

- *Exhortation*: "Whoever wants to be first must be last of all and servant of all" (9:35)
- *Demonstration*: places a "little child (*paidion*) . . . among them," or more literally, "in the middle (*en mesō*) of them" and "embraced him" (CEB) (or "her"—the child's gender is unspecified) (9:36)
- *Explanation*: equates "welcom[ing] one such child in my name" with welcoming Jesus himself and his divine Father ("the one who sent me") (9:37)

Jesus is all for the disciples' ambition, for wanting to be great or "first" (*prōtos*)—but only in terms of God's realm that turns the typical worldly ranking system on its head. First places in God's domain go to those commonly regarded as "last" or least, to "servants of all," not to rulers, to "one such" as the little one Jesus takes up in his arms, an ordinary child in the household presently hosting Jesus and his followers (Betsworth 2010, 66).

In terms of status, this child is a "powerless tyke with nothing to offer who might not even live into adulthood" (Spencer 2019, 252; child mortality was high in antiquity). Although loved and nurtured by Jewish parents and extended family as precious gifts from God (Strange 1996, 9–18, 46–50), in the wider social and political economy, children (excepting imperial scions) represented "nobodies and nuisances" unworthy of "great" men's attention (Crossan 1991, 266–68; 1994, 54–64; Caputo 2006 30–38, 45–47, 60, 107). What could little children possibly teach adult (though not so mature!) apostles (Francis 1996, 73)? And children would certainly bog down men on the move up the social ladder in pursuit of a high-level mission, as the Twelve perceived themselves.

But Jesus Messiah—in urgent pursuit of the very way of God—stops his students in their ambitious tracks with a major reordering of priorities. It's not simply that Jesus encourages the disciples to give a little more attention to helping the littlest and the least: Jesus *identifies* personally with them. To embrace a little child is to embrace *him*—and, stunningly, his Father as well who sent him (9:37). He effectively envisions an intimate "trinity" of God-Jesus-child as the "greatest" bond of love in God's kingdom (Spencer 2019, 252).

The way of the cross: not opposing maverick ministers (9:38-41)
Yet again, however, Jesus's teaching falls on deaf ears. This time it is John who speaks for the group, not Peter. It's as if John didn't register a word Jesus was saying but just resumed the train of thought about self-centered greatness. Now the concern is not with internal rankings but with the apostles' collective status vis-à-vis outsiders who dare to minister in Jesus's name. John raises the case of "someone" outside the Twelve, someone "not following us," who was "casting out demons in your name"—apparently with success. In order to protect their privileged position as Jesus's chosen emissaries, they "tried to stop" this maverick exorcist's activity (9:38). The verb for "stop" (*kōlyō*) means "hinder, prevent, forbid" (BDAG 2000, 580), a blocking move the disciples will soon try again on *little children* (*paidia*) brought to Jesus for his blessing (10:13-16; *kōlyō* in v. 14).

The apostles remain remarkably obtuse about Jesus's open, inclusive mission of liberation worthy of his "name," which functions as a symbol of his identity and vocation. Far from welcoming this independent exorcist in Jesus's name, they ward him off as if *he* were a harmful demon (recall the scribes' calumnious claim that Jesus himself was a demon-driven exorcist [3:22]). The apostles are more interested in protecting their name (reputation) than in promoting Jesus's name for others' salvation.

Jesus will have none of this puerile cliquishness. He flatly forbids his disciples' aim to forbid maverick ministers outside their circle (9:39). While he doesn't advocate indiscriminate use of his name as a magical formula (see Acts 19:13-16 for a terribly bungled exorcism in Jesus's name), sincere use of his name by anyone to effect a true redemptive "deed of power" is all to the good (Mark 9:39). And if the act is not some splashy miracle but rather a simple gesture, say, giving a cup of water, that's just as good. In a brilliant twist, Jesus puts John and company who "bear the name of Christ" in the position of *receiving* ministry from "*whoever* gives *you* a cup of water" (9:40). Little children, infants and toddlers, depend on others to give them water, but itinerant disciples and their crucified Lord must also be given drink (see 15:23, 36). In order to be faithful "servant[s] of all" (9:35), Jesus's followers must get off their high horses and learn what it means to *be served*—in their weakness, not their strength—even by strangers.

The way of the cross: not obstructing little ones (9:42-48)

Jesus is not through with his instruction about "little ones," though he changes terminology. Whereas his disciples are preoccupied with "great" *mega*-matters (9:34), Jesus insists that they prioritize "little" *micro*-matters—more specifically, little *persons* (*mikroi*), not just children of little stature but anyone of little status: the poor, the infirm, the marginalized, and those of *little faith*, the "little ones who believe (*pisteuontōn*) in me" (9:42). Ever mindful of their own struggles to mature in faith (4:35), the apostles must deal humbly, sympathetically, and sensitively with fledgling followers of Christ. They are in no position to lord their faith over anyone or to block anyone's spiritual progress. Just as Jesus insisted that the Twelve *not stop* the freelance exorcist operating in Jesus's name, he warns them *not to* "*put a stumbling block* (*skandalisē*) before one of these little ones who believe in me" (9:42). Jesus knew how it felt to be both the subject and object of such blockades, to be both falsely accused by his hometown folk of offensive, "scandalous" activity (6:3) and hindered from performing many "deed[s] of power" because of the Nazarenes' "unbelief" (6:5-6).

At this point Jesus ramps up his rhetoric of rebuke. Though not denouncing his disciples' prospective behavior of "scandalizing" little ones as satanic (cf. 8:33), he does decry it as abysmal and hellish: meriting punishment of being hurled into the sea (abyss) with a "great millstone" noose (lit., "donkey-millstone," *mylos onikos*, i.e., a "millstone so large it can only be turned by donkey power" [Friberg, Friberg, and Miller 2000]) or having body parts (hand, foot, eye) that had been instrumental in causing stumbling blocks chopped off or gouged out, lest one's entire body "be thrown into hell" (9:42-47). The word for "hell"—"Gehenna" (*geenna*)—evokes the valley of Hinnom at the southwest rim of Jerusalem where, at some of the lowest points in Israel's religious history, children were sacrificed to the Canaanite fire god, Moloch (2 Kgs 16:1-4; 23:10; 2 Chr 28:1-4; Jer 7:30-31; 19:1-5); the site eventually became associated with the infernal pit of eternal punishment for the wicked, which Jesus reinforces by describing Gehenna as the place "where their worm never dies, and the fire is never quenched (Mark 9:48; cf. Jer 7:32-8:3; 19:6-9; 4 Ezra 7:36; Matt 5:22, 29-30; 18:9; 23:15, 33; Jas 3:6). Although we may safely assume that Jesus uses hyperbolic figurative language—he's not advocating actual drowning, burning, or mutilating offenders and opponents, as happened to political resistors of Roman-Herodian rule (Derrett 1973, 367)—his shocking rhetoric conveys how seriously Jesus takes this issue. Care for little ones is top priority business in God's kingdom.

The way of the cross: not losing its salty worth (9:49-50)
Jesus abruptly and awkwardly throws "salt" into the mix at the end of this teaching section. Accordingly, these two verses have given rise to multiple textual variants and even more scholarly interpretations, including those that view the verses as random addenda independent of the foregoing context (Frayer-Griggs 2009, 254–66). Throughout Mark 9:30-50, however, Jesus has used a number of catchwords to guide his stream of thought, including "child/little one," "name," and "stumbling." Now the mention of "fire" in 9:48 sparks another "fire" reference in the next verse associated with "salt" and yet more "salt" talk after that (von Wahlde 1985).

- *Fire*: ". . . and the fire (*pyr*) is never quenched" (9:48)
- *Fire → salt*: "For everyone will be salted with fire (*pyri halisthēsetai*)" (9:49)
- *Salt → salt*: "Salt (*halas*) is good; but if salt (*halas*) has lost its saltiness, how can you season it?" (9:50a)
- *Salt → salt*: "Have salt (*hala*) in yourselves, and be at peace with one another" (9:50b)

Beyond the stylistic feature of word-links is their possible semantic function: what *thought*-links do the fire-and-salt elements suggest in Jesus's current argument? The simplest reading carries over the judgment aspect of "hellfire" from 9:47-48, especially in light of the connective particle "for" (*gar*) at the beginning of 9:49. Jesus now applies the stern warnings he issued to "you" disciples regarding maltreatment of "little ones" (9:42-48) to "everyone" (*pas*)

(9:49). *All* who cause little ones to stumble will be subject to final, salty-fiery sifting of their entire bodies, presumably, not just the odd treacherous hand, foot, or eye. Since the verb for "salt" (*halizō*) can also mean "collect, gather," Robert Doran has proposed the reading "for everyone will be *gathered* by fire" for the ultimate fire-test of one's work, similar to that which Paul envisions in 1 Corinthians 3:13-15 (2020, 361, 366–74).

Both salt and fire are "highly polyvalent images" in the Bible (Frayer-Griggs, 2009, 266), ranging from symbols of pain and punishment on the negative side (remember the fate of Sodom and Lot's wife [cf. Luke 17:29-32]) to purification and preservation on the positive end. From tilting toward the negative pole in Mark 9:49, Jesus quickly swings to the positive pole in the next statements, beginning with the crisp affirmation, "Salt is good" (9:50). But its value only lasts as long as it retains its salty essence. If it goes flat, it's no spicier than white sand.

This observation about the good value of good salt (of salty salt) leads to Jesus's final exhortation, now directed back to the disciples: "Have salt in yourselves" or, better reflecting the context and the present tense imperative, "Keep having (*echete*) salt. Don't let it go stale in yourselves." We might say that Jesus urges his followers to be "worth their salt"—but to what end? He adds a key parallel phrase that effectively defines what "having salt" means:

Have salt in yourselves (*echete en heautois hala*)
+ and (*kai*) =
Be at peace with one another (*eirēneuete en allēlois*)

The ministry of salt is preserving and enhancing peace—peacekeeping and peacemaking (Matt 5:9, 13). It is the ministry of reconciliation (2 Cor 5:17-21). It is the holy offering of one's entire embodied self (hand, feet, eyes, and everything else) in covenantal communion with God and people (little ones, outsiders, and everyone else), as the Torah's principle of "salt" stipulates: "And every gift of your sacrifice shall be salted with salt (*hali halisthēsetai*). You shall not omit from your sacrifices *the salt of the Lord's covenant* (*hala diathēkēs*); on each gift of yours you shall offer salt (*halas*) to the Lord your God" (Lev 2:13 NETS; cf. Rom 12:1-8; Donahue and Harrington 2002, 289).

Interacting with Pharisees, Little Children, and a Rich Man (10:1-31)

Jesus's southward journey takes him into "the region of Judea" around the Jordan River (10:1a). This marks his first return to the area since his baptism by John (see 1:5, 9-11). On the one hand, it's business as usual: "crowds again gathered around him; and, as was his custom, he again taught them" (10:1b), with special asides and admonitions to the disciples (10:10-12, 13-15, 23-30). Moreover, "some Pharisees" confront Jesus with another test (10:2-4); Moses makes another appearance, in scriptural rather than visual form (10:3-4); and more "little children" receive Jesus's blessing (10:13-16). On the other hand, the Pharisees set off a debate with Jesus about a new controversial issue: biblical law regarding marriage and divorce (10:2-9); and a new character, a man with "many possessions," engages Jesus and prompts his most challenging teaching about economics in this Gospel (10:21-31).

In the shadow of the cross, lurking nearer and nearer after Jesus's first and second death notices (8:31; 9:31) and just before his third (10:33-34), we might not think that familial and financial matters would be uppermost in Jesus's mind. He evinces no particular concern with getting his own familial and financial affairs in order before his death or at any other time in his career. As a single, poor, itinerant prophet and teacher, he lives free of marital and monetary encumbrances. Yet while his teaching in this current section is not about his own life and livelihood, it serves as a vehicle for conveying his *authority* in God's kingdom—a matter he *does* assert in his last days on earth—not for his own glorification but for his followers' edification as they prepare to carry on his mission after his departure.

The two larger teaching segments, responding to some Pharisees and a rich man, respectively, focus on God's Torah commandments (*entolai*) commanded (*entellomai*) through Moses (10:3-5, 19). By affirming and interpreting these orders, Jesus assumes his position as commander-in-chief of God's realm, which includes his right to determine who can and cannot enter God's kingdom (10:15, 23, 24, 25; cf. 9:42) and to lay down the rules for participating in it.

Such bold claims of authority, however, are not authoritarian, as if Jesus finally sheds his milder-mannered image of the humble servant to bust out as the super-strongman Messiah. He commandingly promotes God's ethical order established in Scripture in order to protect the most vulnerable people in his society: women (10:3-9), children (10:13-16), and the poor (10:21). Jesus's last statement in this section vividly encapsulates the social dynamics of God's realm: "But many who are first will be last, and the last will be first" (10:31; cf. 9:35).

Husbands and wives (10:1-12)
As some Pharisees previously questioned Jesus's position on Sabbath law (2:23–3:6), others now probe his perspective on family law, specifically, "Is

it lawful for a man to divorce his wife?" (10:2). Again Jesus responds by referencing the Jewish scriptures, the moral code he shares with the Pharisees but doesn't always read in the same way. In the Sabbath case, Jesus appealed to David's practice in 1 Samuel 21; now he focuses on Moses' teaching in Deuteronomy 24 in light of Genesis 1–2. In both instances, Jesus speaks directly to the legal experts: "Have *you* never read what David did?" (Mark 2:25); "What did Moses command *you*?" (10:3). These issues are deeply personal and practical. And they do not fit into neat ideological boxes of "conservative" and "liberal" that often demarcate today's legal and moral viewpoints. Whereas Jesus's wider view of Sabbath rest/restoration in Mark 2:23–3:6 might be considered more "liberal" than some Pharisees' stricter position, his stance on divorce in the present passage may fairly be described as hard-line "conservative" (Spencer 2010b).

The Pharisees give a correct response to Jesus's query about Moses' teaching, summarizing the proviso in Deuteronomy 24:1-4: "Moses allowed a man to write a certificate of dismissal to divorce her" (Mark 10:3). Notice that while Jesus asks what Moses *commanded*, the Pharisees answer, properly, in terms of what Moses *allowed*. They are not anti-marriage or pro-divorce by any means. But they do try to ensnare Jesus in some "family values" trap regarding an issue as complicated and controversial then as it is now in religious circles. The full text of Deuteronomy 24:1-4 entwines a number of elements. First, marriage and divorce are deemed a man's prerogative: *he* "enters into marriage with a woman"; *he* "writes her a certificate of divorce . . . and sends her out of *his* house." Second, the grounds for divorce are stipulated in maddeningly loose terms: "Suppose . . . she doesn't please him because he finds *something objectionable* about her" (24:1)—or "something indecent" (NIV, NAB)/"obnoxious" (NJPS)/"inappropriate" (CEB) "about her" or "something shameful in her" (NETS). Third, *if* a man divorces his wife, he *must* provide her a "certificate of divorce," thus allowing her marriage to another man. Fourth, if the woman is divorced or widowed by a second husband, the first husband cannot remarry her. The woman receives some protection in this male-dominated system: she is not simply cast out as damaged goods that no other man would want (the "certificate" legitimates her to some extent); and she is spared the indignity and possible injury of returning to a man who kicked her out in the first place.

The notion of "objectionable" behavior creates a loophole big enough to drive a chariot through. The former Pharisee Josephus divorced his wife (after she had borne him three children) for some unspecified displeasure she had caused him and married a woman of supposedly impeccable character (*Life* 426–27). As strict constructionists, the rabbinic House of Shammai simply reasserted the "objectionable/unseemly" language of Deuteronomy 24:1 without elaboration. The House of Hillel, however, allowed a husband to divorce his wife for burning his dinner (apparently even one time), while Rabbi Akiva allowed a man to trade his wife in for a more beautiful model (m. Giṭṭin 9.10). Though these are likely outlandish cases presented tongue-in-cheek, they still make a point. Checking tendencies to divorce based on a husband's whims, Philo called for judges to examine divorce claims made by loveless, abusive husbands who trumped up *false accusations* of sexual infidelity against their wives (*Spec. Laws* 3.79–82). Addressing the same issue from the other side, Matthew's Jesus prohibited divorce, *except* in the singular case of the wife's "unchastity" (Matt 5:31-32; 19:8-9). This brief sample of different views on divorce supports the conclusion of Phillip Sigal: "The halakhah [practical laws/ways] of divorce practiced by the diverse communities of a many-faceted Judaism was in no way monolithic. There was no orthodoxy and no orthopraxy" (2007, 142).

Mark's Jesus does not wade into these choppy legal waters because he flatly concedes *no grounds* for divorce in this debate with the Pharisees. What then does he do with Moses' commandment in Deuteronomy 24? In an adroit interpretive move, Jesus both *contextualizes* the Deuteronomy text and *subordinates* it to a foundational principle in Genesis 1–2. Deuteronomy 24, he contends, represents a provisional concession to "your hardness of heart" (Mark 10:5), like that displayed by the ancient Israelites in the wilderness. Apparently, their struggle to maintain loyal, loving covenant with God (remember the golden calf) spilled over into lax commitments and infidelities to marital covenants.

Jesus strives to restore ideal first principles rather than merely to accept and compensate for moral erosion. Hence, he goes back to "the beginning of creation" when "God made them male and female" (Gen 1:27) and a man was called to "be joined to his wife, and the two shall become one flesh" (Gen 2:24; Mark 10:6-8). As Jesus affirmed the basic creational principle of Sabbath wholeness over particular regulations of prohibited behavior, he prioritizes the creational ideal of *marital oneness*, in which a man "joins" (*proskollaomai*) his wife in the closest, tightest of unions ("one flesh")—clinging and sticking to her like glue (*kolla*; Danker and Krug 2009, 204, 304; BDAG 2000, 555–56, 881–82). The couple *is joined* (passive verb) by a higher authority, the Creator God; and as Jesus enjoins, "Therefore what God has joined together, let no one separate"—period, no exceptions (10:9).

In another private debriefing in a house, the disciples ask Jesus to clarify "this matter" (10:10). His answer implies their sexist stance on adultery, their presumed view that a wife's sexual unfaithfulness to her husband breaks the marital bond and legitimates divorce proceedings against her, as Matthew 5:31-32 and 19:8-9 permit. But Mark's Jesus grants no such exception. He defines an adulterer or adulteress strictly as one who divorces his/her spouse and remarries another (10:11-12). Though according agency to the wife to initiate divorce, Jesus only does so to indicate that the divorced person (female or male) who remarries commits adultery. Technically speaking, we might say that Jesus allows either spouse to separate but not to sever the original marriage bond and forge another union.

Such technicalities, however, are scarcely the point of Jesus's teaching about marriage and divorce. Here he draws a hard, "conservative," covenantal line, along the line of the postexilic prophet Malachi:

> The LORD was a witness between you and the wife of your youth . . . she is your companion and your wife by covenant. Did not one God make her? . . . And what does the one God desire? Godly offspring. So look to yourselves, and do not let anyone be faithless to the wife of his youth. For *I hate divorce*, says the LORD, the God of Israel. (Mal 3:14-16)

Only a few extended families in our culture—including church families—have not been touched by divorce, thereby implicating us in behavior that God *hates*. So where is the love, the compassion, the forgiveness we expect from Jesus for those who *suffer* divorce (whatever freedom might be gained in divorce comes at a steep, painful price)? And what about the many wives who suffer terrible abuse from their husbands? Labeling a woman an adulteress if she leaves her husband and remarries provides cold comfort. But Mark's Jesus is not writing a family policy manual or pastoral counseling guide. He's in a legal-scriptural debate with disputatious Pharisees. Moreover, the upshot of his argument reinforces the sanctity of marriage and rescinds all grounds men might cavalierly claim to divorce their wives. To be sure, Jesus does not address abusive marriages or what to do about marriages that have already been dissolved. But nothing in Jesus's principled discussion with the Pharisees abrogates his commitment to forgiveness and restoration of "sinners" and other broken people. Indeed, his emphasis on creational oneness goes hand in glove with creational wholeness.

Little children (again) (10:13-16)

The "family values" fracas moves from marriage and divorce to childcare, and Jesus's disputants shift from some Pharisees to his disciples. Although Jesus called his apostles away from their families (which no doubt included wives and children as well as father Zebedee [see 1:16–20]) and has a fraught relationship with his family of origin (3:21, 31-35; 6:1-6) and no wife or children of his own, he ministers to needy women and children as opportunity allows.

The present vignette depicts caretakers bringing "little children" (*paidia*) to Jesus for his healing "touch," as in previous pediatric cases (5:41-42; 9:26-27), or more general blessing (10:16). The fact that Mark does not specify any particular ailment or need signals Jesus's embracive ministry to "all boys and girls" (Betsworth 2010, 68). The scene soon becomes quite emotional but not out of tender compassion for these little ones as we might expect. To be sure, Jesus takes the children in his arms and blesses them, but not before his disciples erupt with a rude rebuke that ignites Jesus's "indignant" counter-response.

The disciples "spoke sternly" (*epetimēsan*) to those who presented the little children to Jesus (10:13), rebuffing them with the same vehement resistance (*epitimaō*) that Jesus directed against the Satan-motivated Peter (8:32) and the vicious spirit that seized the convulsive boy (9:25). Evidently still preoccupied with worldly standards of greatness (9:34-41), the disciples think that these little ones are not worth Jesus's or *their* time and distract Jesus from his messianic campaign as it benefits *them*. Children can be such bothers, yes; but in Jesus's view, they are precisely what the realm of God and Jesus is most bothered about!

Jesus is hot and bothered (negatively) with his disciples for not bothering (positively) about what (who) matters most. Remember that emotions reveal one's deepest, gut-level concerns. Jesus becomes *indignant* (*ēganaktēsen*), an anger-related emotion that means to "'be upset about someth[ing] that violates one's sense of propriety', be vexed, be distressed, be annoyed" (Danker and Krug 2009, 2). Far from an irascible, knee-jerk reaction, however, Jesus is moved here with resolute *righteous indignation*, according to the just, merciful, right-making standards of God's kingdom. Reprising language from recent lessons that the disciples have not yet grasped, Jesus identifies "such" (*toioutōn*) "little children" (*paidia*) as honored members of God's family whom no one must "stop" (*kōlyō*) from full entry into (*eiserchomai*) God's realm (10:14; cf. 9:36-39, 42, 47). Indeed, the kingdom of God may be rightly called the kingdom *of* such as these (*tōn toioutōn*) little ones, understood either in a possessive or participative sense, or both: *to* such the kingdom *belongs* and/or *of* such the kingdom *consists* (10:14; Betsworth 2010, 68–69; cf. Wallace 1996, 78–83, 91–94).

Jesus also adds a new twist to his previous "welcome/receive" policy in relation to little children and God's sphere. Whereas before the child was the *object* of action—"whoever welcomes (*dexētai*) one such child . . . welcomes me . . . [and] the one who sent me" (9:37)—now the child is the *subject*: "whoever does not receive (*dexētai*) the kingdom of God *as a little child* will never enter it" (10:16). But the action of the little "subjects" in the present scene is *passive*: they are *brought to* Jesus, and he *takes them up* in his arms. They can only "receive" God's kingdom as a *gift* and "enter" as a *guest*: no striving for admission, no fighting for advancement. Their only qualification is their need (Gundry-Volf 2008, 152–53). They are inherently "great" in God's book: "The reign of God [is defined] *as a children's world*, where children are the measure . . . where the small are great and the great must become small" (Gundry-Volf 2000, 480 [emphasis original]).

The picture in Mark 9:37 and 10:16 of Jesus embracing (*enanchalizomai*) little children evokes a vivid gesture of "fling[ing] the arms around and hug[ging] to oneself" (Derrett 1983, 10). It also presents a tender portrait of a maternal nurturer ("They drank milk from the same fountains. From such embraces [*enanchalismatōn*] brotherly-loving souls are nourished," 4 Macc 13:21), dramatically counterpoising Jesus's indignant indictment of his disciples and repeating role as a spiritual warrior battling the forces of evil and injustice. Moreover, combining this embracive image with laying hands of blessing on the children—recalling Jacob's deathbed bequest to his grandsons Ephraim and Manasseh (Gen 48:8-20)—effectively establishes the little ones brought to Jesus as "his relations and co-heirs," thoroughly vested by and with Christ in God's kingdom (Derrett 1983, 10, 14–16).

Rich and poor (10:17-31)

The inheriting component of participating in God's kingdom—inheriting as God's children to whom God's bounty "belongs"—becomes explicit as an anonymous man asks Jesus, "as he was setting out on a journey/way (*hodon*), 'Good Teacher, what must I do to inherit (*kleronomēsō*) eternal life?'" (10:17; Derrett 1983, 4).

This man has gotten a bad rap in many sermons and lessons about him as a greedy rich person in love with his money and power; however, Mark waits several verses before mentioning the man's wealthy financial status (10:22) and never identifies him as a person of authority (he's only called a "ruler" in Luke 18:18). Before the man's wealth becomes an issue, he has a lively, mostly positive exchange with Jesus. He *runs* to catch Jesus (cf. the enthusiastic running crowd in Mark 9:15, 25), *kneels* before him, and respectfully *addresses* him as "Good Teacher" (10:17). Although not rising to the level of "Lord" or "Christ," this address is a notch above the generic "Teacher." And the man sincerely believes that Jesus knows the path to obtaining eternal life, which he is anxious to follow: "What *must I do*?" This questioner is *not* seeking to trap or test Jesus; he is seeking the way of eternal life, the very life of God.

Initially, however, we're taken aback by Jesus's brusque first response, objecting to being labeled "good." If anyone seems testy in this exchange, it's Jesus! Is he detecting insincerity, even mockery, in the man's calling him "Good"? Not at all. Before addressing the man's concern, Jesus remarkably asserts his own humility in relation to the sole priority of the One God: "Why do you call me good? No one is good but God alone" (10:18). From the start Jesus confesses his commitment to the fundamental tenet of Jewish faith, known as the *Shema*: "Hear (*shema*), O Israel: the LORD is our God, the LORD alone" (Deut 6:4). This One God alone grants "lawful" access to the "riches" of eternal life through faithfulness to God's Torah—God's *life-giving* Law. So anyone who wants to know what they *must do* to inherit God's life must keep "the commandments," which Jesus assumes his interlocutor "knows" (10:19a). The Torah is the sacred common ground the man and Jesus share.

Notably, however, as Jesus proceeds to recite the fundamental Ten Commandments, he only mentions the second group focusing on loving actions toward other people (10:19b; cf. Exod 20:12-17; Deut 5:16-21), glossing over the first four laws commanding exclusive loyalty to God. Jesus apparently assumes the man's sincere devotion to God's singularity, invisibility, name identity, and Sabbath sanctity (Exod 20:1-11; Deut 5:6-15).

In listing the second cluster of commandments, Mark's Jesus both omits the prohibition against coveting and uniquely *adds*, "You shall not defraud," which reinforces "You shall not steal" others' fortunes and possessions (Mark 10:19b). Jesus may accentuate these financial laws in light of the man's "many possessions" which will not be reported until 10:22 but are no doubt obvious to Jesus and his disciples from the man's attire and mien. But note well: when the man contends, "Teacher [not "*Good* Teacher" this time!], I have kept all these since my youth" (10:20), Jesus offers no rebuttal. By all accounts, Jesus grants that this inquirer is a morally upright man. He's not claiming to be sinless; he's not trying to preen and impress Jesus; he's no hypocrite. He just answers Jesus's question as honestly as can: he has long taken all these commandments with utmost seriousness.

But Jesus does not leave the matter there. The Law—as good as it is and as faithfully as this man has followed it—is necessary but not sufficient for his interlocutor's flourishing life in God's kingdom. Significantly, Jesus informs this "one" man (*heis*, 10:17) of the "one thing (*hen*)" he lacks, while "looking at him" (10:21), while seeing him as an individual, not as a stereotype for all wealthy persons or a mere object lesson for his disciples, though they will learn a lot in this scene. Seeing is perceiving in this incident; and seeing is also keenly *feeling* the demands of discipleship. Perception and emotion tightly intertwine (see Brady 2013, 45–117; Price 2015, 81–104). Notice four poignant "looks" leading into key statements (three by Jesus, one by Peter) that structure the rest of this story (Spencer 2021, 210).

1. Jesus, *looking at* (*emblepsas*) him, loved (*ēgapēsen*) him and said, "You lack one thing; go, sell what you own, and give the money to the poor" (10:21).

The first verb, an intensified form of *blepō* ("look/see"), depicts Jesus's "look[ing] straight at/directly at" (L&N 1988, 278) the man or "look[ing] carefully at him" (CEB) with rapt concentration and concern. But more than that, Mark reports that Jesus looked at and *loved* the man; as it happens, among Matthew, Mark, and Luke—known as the Synoptic Gospels because of their shared viewpoints—this marks the *only* time Jesus is explicitly said to love (*agapaō*) an individual. The rigorous challenge Jesus is about to issue proceeds from love. Jesus genuinely cares for this man, even likes him, we might assume. By exposing what this good man lacks, Jesus is not gleefully making a "gotcha" move. He knows full well how *hard* (10:23-24) it will be for this man to meet Jesus's demanding standard of discipleship.

The "one thing" Jesus requires is totalizing, but not totalitarian, since Jesus does not *force* this man or any other follower to comply. If the man wants to follow Jesus's way—which Jesus invites him to do ("come, follow me")—he must sell his possessions and give the proceeds to the poor (10:21). It's at this crucial point in the story that we learn that the man has "many possessions," which he is unwilling to leave behind for the poor in order to take up Jesus's poor way of life (6:8; 8:34-37), to take a vow of poverty.

Jesus is not demanding more of this man because he is wealthy or because Jesus would like to knock him off his high horse. Remember that Jesus *loves* this man. But Jesus cuts him no slack either. He asks no more and no less of him than he does any covenant partner in God's realm compliant with God's Law. As clearly as Deuteronomy enjoins loving the One God with all one's heart, soul, and might (6:4-5), it mandates loving the poor by generously sharing one's resources: "If there is among you anyone in need . . . do not be hard-hearted or tight-fisted toward your needy neighbor. You should rather open your hand, willingly lending enough to meet the need. . . . Give liberally and be ungrudging when you do so. . . . Since there will never cease to be some in need on the earth, I therefore command you, 'Open your hand to the poor and needy neighbor in the land'" (15:7-11).

Again, there is no reason to assume that this rich man has not given aid to the poor, even generous aid. But Jesus has upped the ante by effectively calling him to leave behind all his resources for the poor's sake in order to follow Jesus's self-emptying way. This sweeping injunction triggers an emotional crisis: "When [the rich man] heard this, he was shocked and went away grieving" (10:22). The term for "shocked" or "appalled" (*stygnazō*) may carry tinges of anger or hatred (see Dan 2:12 LXX; Rom 12:9) and "perhaps suggests physical appearance which betrays emotion" (France 2002, 403), reflected in the observation that "the man's face/countenance fell" (Mark 10:22 NIV, RSV, NAB, NASB; cf. Isa 57:17; Ezek 27:35 LXX). Yet however upset or "dismayed" (CEB) the man might have been, he doesn't storm out of Jesus's presence in a huff but rather goes "away *grieving* (*lypoumenos*)" in painful sorrow. The rich man appears both mad and sad, aggrieved and bereaved (cf. Jesus's similar mixed emotions in Mark 3:5) at Jesus's audacious demand and at his reluctance to meet that demand. The rich man's lack of commitment and loss of opportunity hits him hard.

This emotional crisis has an intriguing parallel in Isaiah 57:17, involving common elements of greed, anger, grief, face movement, and turning away or going one's own way. The Hebrew and Greek texts may be rendered, respectively:

> For their sinful greed I was angry; I struck them and turned away in My wrath. Though stubborn, they follow the way of their hearts (NJPS).

> Because of sin I grieved (*elypēsa*) him a little while; I struck him and turned my face away from him, and he was grieved (*elypēthē*) and went on sullen (*stygnos*) in his ways (*hodois*) (NETS).

This text speaks of *God's* anger and anguish over Israel's recalcitrance and the consequent turning of *God's* face away from Israel—sparking the people's shock and grief as they go their own ways. But this dour message immediately gives way to promises of hope and healing, peace and comfort: "I have seen his ways, and I healed him and comforted him, yes, gave him true comfort—peace upon peace to those that are far and to those that are near" (Isa 57:18-19; cf. 57:16). Hope springs eternal for the wealthy seeker of eternal life who comes to Jesus. His sorrowful turning away from Jesus now does not preclude his welcome return later.

2. Jesus *looked around* (*periblepsamenas*) and said to his disciples, "How hard it will be for those who have wealth to enter the kingdom of God!" (10:23).

Though Jesus had given his full, considered attention to the rich man and did not simply use him as a lesson prop, he was certainly aware of his disciples' witness to the scene. After the man's departure, Jesus surveys his confidants and stresses to them *how hard* it is for people of great means to embrace the humble way of God's realm. The wealthy are not little children (note that Jesus addresses his followers as "children" [*tekna*] when repeating his point in 10:24). Rich men can take care of themselves—and others too, if they are generous—but not if they give up everything and become like poor children. Where is the sense in that?

Jesus agrees: it does *not* make sense in normal economics, in business as usual. It makes no more sense than trying to squeeze a gangly, lumpy camel through the eye of a needle (10:24)! The image is intentionally ridiculous, even absurd, ratcheting the effect from hard to *impossible*. Popular sermon illustrations, based on dubious evidence, about camels shedding all baggage they carry and scooting through some supposed "Needle's Gate" on their knobby knees miss the point entirely (Boring 2006, 292). Rich persons, who might own a fleet of camels to carry their possessions, *cannot* and *will not* participate in God's kingdom *on their own merits*.

Already "perplexed" at Jesus's first pronouncement (10:24), the disciples now become "greatly astounded" when he repeats it and adds the camel comedy. While they might let out a nervous chuckle, they can scarcely hide their emotional upheaval, reflected in their muttering to one another, "Who then can be saved?" (10:26). Everybody has some possessions, if only the shirts on their backs or just their naked backs and bodies. Where exactly is the line between rich and poor? And no one, nobody, whatever their social status, is getting through the miniscule aperture of a needle any easier than a camel.

3. Jesus *looked at* (*emblepsas*) them and said, "For mortals it is impossible (*adynaton*), but not for God; for God all things are possible (*dynata*)" (10:27).

In the disciples' emotional turmoil, Jesus now trains his focus directly on (*emblepō*) them, just as he had done with the rich man, to deliver his crucial point. The futility of human salvation is not final because what is impossible for mortals is possible *for God*; indeed, with respect to saving (forgiving, freeing, redeeming, healing, restoring), it is purposeful: God wills to save all people, rich and poor.

A power glitch is never terminal in God's realm. Recall that Jesus experienced occasional irregular power (*dynamis*) surges (5:30) and shortages: he "could do (*edynato*) no deed of power (*dynamin*)" on his last visit to Nazareth (6:6). But he has performed many powerful acts since then in difficult environments as he has remained in intimate fellowship with the God of infinite possibilities (6:41; 7:34; 8:6; 9:2-8, 29). Again, there is every possibility that

God can yet lift the rich man's grieving spirit, change his hesitant heart, and bring him into the fullness of God's household.

4. Peter began to say to [Jesus], "*Look (idou)*, we have left everything and followed you" (10:28).

Peter urges Jesus to take another look at him and his fellow disciples and acknowledge that they have left everything—their businesses, families, and possessions (1:16-20; 6:8-10)—to follow him. In the disciples' present state of perplexity and astonishment over Jesus's "hard" demands (10:24, 26), compounded by his recent rebukes of their attitudes (8:32; 9:19, 35-50; 10:14-16), Peter seems less to be asserting a point of pride than seeking assurance of the Twelve's place in God's Christ-led kingdom. And this time, Jesus offers abundant assurance—one hundredfold!

Mark's Jesus spells out the benefits of wholehearted, costly commitment to him and the gospel in material, communal, and eternal terms. Anyone who forsakes "house or brothers or sisters or mother or father or children (*tekna*) or fields" (notice the jarring "children" reference) for the sake of God's kingdom receives the same one hundred times over (10:29). Although including material houses and fields, these are not private holdings; they remain wholly embedded in communal-familial fellowship (households and home fields). This is no "prosperity gospel": Jesus promises no one—not the rich man, not the disciples—a hundredfold return on their investment. What they get is a "social gospel," rightly conceived (Rauschenbusch 1997 [1917]; Evans 2017; Spencer 2019, 691–706; Malina 2001b), a mutually supporting community of love and grace.

And they get it on earth as it is in heaven, "now in this age . . . and in the age to come, eternal life" (10:30). The story has come full circle, from the rich man's query about inheriting eternal life (10:17) to Jesus's final statement about eternal life granted to many "last" (*eschatoi*) ranking persons (in worldly eyes) in the last days (*eschaton*) (10:30-31). Again, however, the first fruits of God's love-rooted life may be enjoyed now, on earth—but with a key codicil. In itemizing the benefits of life in God's realm—houses, brothers and sisters, and so on—Mark's Jesus appends "with persecutions" (*meta diōgmōn*, 10:30; cf. 4:17; 13:9-13). Jesus continues to mark the hard way of the cross as the way to true life and salvation, as the ensuing scene further drives home to the disciples.

Predicting Jesus's Death and Resurrection #3 (10:32-45)

Jesus and his travel party get back "on the road (*hodō*)," which, let's not forget, marks not only a mode of travel but a *way of life*, a purposeful, God-directed way that Mark now explicitly tracks en route "to Jerusalem," the climactic destination of Jesus Messiah in the center of Jewish religion and politics (10:32). While "going up" to Jerusalem, Jesus is "walking ahead" (*proagōn*) of the group, aptly leading the way. The narrator now sorts the entourage in Jesus's train into "three concentric circles . . . : the Twelve, 'those following,' and a more loosely defined set of sympathizers" (cf. 3:13-14; 4:10; 8:34; 11:8; Marcus 2009, 742). And the emotions of the company are pulsing with amazement and fear over the uncertain events that lie ahead (8:32).

For a third time, Jesus takes the Twelve aside and tries to let them know exactly what will happen to him in Jerusalem (8:32b). In reannouncing his impending execution and resurrection three days later, he adds details about the events leading to his death. Jesus makes clear that Jewish authorities (chief priests and scribes) will "hand him over to the Gentiles," that is, to the Roman governor and soldiers who will "mock . . . spit on . . . flog, and kill" him (10:33-34). This sharp staccato of one-syllable English terms—mock-spit-flog-kill—though accurate translations, blunt the drawn-out, torturous effect of the harsh-sounding multisyllabic Greek terms: *empaixousin-emptysousin-mastigōsousin-apoktenousin*. In this final prediction of his fate, Jesus amps up the anticipated political charge and physical pain.

Such a forecast would seem to offer little relief for the disciples' fear and anxiety. But James and John have tuned to a whole other wavelength. Completely ignoring Jesus's dire statement about his death, the brothers Zebedee remain preoccupied with their aspirations to greatness, which they voice in a most audacious way: "Teacher, we want (*thelomen*) you to do for us whatever we ask you" (10:35). "Oh, is that all you want? And what pray tell might that be?" (I paraphrase Jesus's response, with a dash of sarcasm that I "hear" in his voice; see 10:36.) "All" they want is to flank Jesus's throne when he comes into his "glory" (10:37)! At least they're honest in their stunning oblivion. They never left the Mount of Transfiguration, it seems. They want to rank up there with Moses and Elijah. They're stuck on the glory, blithely skipping the suffering, serving, cross-bearing, and dying parts of Jesus's messianic mission that he has so passionately expressed, embodied, and *willed/wanted/desired* (*thelō*)—the indomitable *will to life* out of death. Jesus doesn't care about power and status markers; who sits next to him in God's kingdom is none of his business or concern (10:40). At this critical point in Jesus's life, two of his closest associates are woefully out of sync with Jesus's will.

But whatever James and John want, they will not be able to sidestep the way of suffering and service that Jesus treads—the way that Jesus now depicts in liquid imagery as the *cup* he drinks and the *baptism* he undergoes—the cup/baptism the sons of Zebedee and all disciples will *share* with

Jesus (10:38-39). Recently Jesus commended to John and his fellow cliquish disciples the simple gesture of giving a cup of water, especially to outsiders, as a model act of service in his name (9:38-41). Now he focuses not on a cup he and his followers will dispense to others but on a cup they will drink themselves.

The "cup" was a familiar biblical image for one's God-given lot in life that must be "drunk." Ideally, it would be a cup of "overflowing" blessing and "goodness" amid an otherwise hostile environment (Ps 23:5-6), a "pleasant" and "goodly" fellowship with "the LORD" who personally "is my chosen portion . . . my cup . . . my lot" (Ps 16:5-6). More often, however, the image goes sour, representing a bitter cup of sorrow, pain, and punishment that God pours out on perpetrators of injustice and idolatry, precipitating their "staggering" and stumbling to their doom (Pss 11:6; 75:8; Isa 51:17, 22; Jer 25:15-28; 49:12; 51:7; Lam 4:21; Ezek 23:31-34; Hab 2:15-16). In the present setting where Jesus has just predicted his violent demise, this harsh picture of the cup predominates (Spencer 2003, 115–16, 127).

Jesus will not be draining the dregs of *God's* judgment *against him*, but he will be drinking the poison cup of anguished suffering and death administered by malevolent authorities. At his last supper, a Passover meal, Jesus and his disciples will drink from an actual cup, a common cup of wine, commemorating Israel's historic release from Egyptian enslavement *and* signifying Jesus's imminent outpouring of his lifeblood "for many" (Mark 14:23-24). Although James, John, and the other disciples will not die with Jesus on the cross, they will drink in various ways from this same cruciform cup, this crucible of suffering, this blood-filled cruse. At this point, Jesus does not raise a victory cup in paradise or toast James and John's promotions!

The brothers Zebedee and all who seek Christ's right-hand power and glory—without accompanying service and humility—might well ponder the provocative prophetic word of Habakkuk. Addressing those who maliciously manipulate others for their own gain, "who make your neighbors drunk, pouring out your wrath [or poison] . . . in order to gaze on their nakedness," Habakkuk throws their drink and cup back in their faces: "You will be sated with contempt instead of glory. Drink, you yourself and stagger! *The cup in the LORD's right hand* will come around to you and shame will come upon your glory!" (Hab 2:16). Warning: the *right (and left) hand* of honor and power that James and John covet in God's kingdom might slap them down with shame and humiliation if their ambitions do not align with the ministerial-diaconal (Mark 10:43) mission of God's Messiah, epitomized in giving cups of water to the thirsty and sharing cups of wine with this death-fated Messiah.

Likewise, Jesus announces the "baptism" he will undergo—together with James, John, and fellow disciples. Not only does baptizing have a liquid link with drinking; baptism also joins with Communion (Lord's Supper, Eucharist) as two fundamental ordinances or sacraments of the early church. But hasn't Jesus already been baptized by John the Baptizer (1:9-11)? In the present context, Mark's Jesus likely draws on the symbolism of baptism as a dramatic enactment of death, burial, and resurrection, as Paul depicts in Romans 6:3-4. (If Mark wrote from Rome 65–75 CE [see Introduction], he would doubtless be familiar with Paul's letter to the Romans, written a decade or so earlier.)

Baptism represents an ongoing way of life as much as a onetime ritual, the way of suffering-dying-rising with Christ, the path to "newness of life" *through* dying to the "old" life of self-obsession and ambition—the mode of life in which James and John remain mired. Their flippant response to Jesus's question concerning whether they are able to drink Jesus's "cup" and dip into his baptism—"We are able" (the single Greek word *dynometha*)—is too overconfident and under-informed by half. We could easily append the same indictment lodged against Peter's outburst at the transfiguration: they "did not know what to say" (9:6).

The other ten disciples are no happier with the Zebedee brothers than Jesus is; they become "angry" (10:41) or "indignant" (NIV, NASB, NAB) with the pair, precisely the same reaction (*aganakteō*) Jesus had to the whole group when they tried to block little children's access (10:14). It is doubtful now, however, that the ten have righteous motives in their indignation against James and John. The entire circle of apostles has been caught up in rivalry and self-promotion (9:33-35); the ten are just mad that James and John lobbied Jesus directly for top executive positions. The whole company still distorts the true nature of Jesus's mission. So he tries again to teach them.

Whereas Jesus previously countered the disciples' illusions of grandeur with the positive image of a little child (9:36-37), now he invokes the negative model of *lordly tyrants*, of worldly rulers, self-styled "great ones" (*megaloi*) who lord their sovereignty over (*katakyrieuousin*) and press their authority upon (*katexousiazousin*) the people, regarded as underlings. In no way is that the way of Jesus in God's realm, the way of manifest Lordship (*kyrios*, 1:3; 2:28; 5:19; 7:28) and authority (*exousia*, 1:22, 27, 2:10), to be sure, but exercised as a *servant* (*diakonos*) and *slave* (*doulos*) in solidarity with and charity toward the least, littlest, and lowliest. Hereby Jesus dramatically flips the "dominant script" of authoritarian, strongman rule (Scott 1990; Thiessen 2016, 462–63).

As the Son of Humankind, Mark's Jesus identifies, as we have seen, with the viceroy of God's realm heralded by Daniel, sent from heaven to deliver God's people from foreign oppressors (Dan 7:13-14, 23-27). But Jesus makes clear that his way of liberation is not through domination, not through overpowering the powers that be and re-subjugating the people to him, not through out-tyrannizing the tyrants. Rather, "The Son of Man came not to be served but to serve, and to give his life a ransom for many" (10:45). The redemptive way of Jesus is the way of *his* service and sacrifice "for many."

This view diametrically differs from imperial ideology that regarded the sovereign as the inviolable head of state to be protected at all costs (Thiessen 2016; Winn 2014). For the good of the nation, the people must be ready and able to lay down *their lives* for the emperor. For example, in a treatise written to and about Nero Caesar in the mid-50s CE, Seneca declares that "*he* [Caesar] is the bond that holds the commonwealth together, *he* is the living breath drawn by the many, many thousands who would themselves be nothing but a dead weight, prey for the taking, absent the central authority's great intellect" (Seneca, *Clem.* 1.4.1; translation and emphasis by Kaster 2010, 150). So Caesar embodies the entire populace (the body politic) and therefore must use his power and glory for the common good. He must be "for them [the people] as much as he is above them," attendant to their daily anxiety "for their well-being, individually and collectively" (1.3.3).

Good enough—except for the fact that the emperor's life is presumed to be of inestimably higher value than that of his subjects. Their value depends on him; without him they are nothing. Accordingly, in Seneca's view, "for that man's sake, people are utterly prepared . . . to lay down their lives" for him; "if his path to safety must be paved with their corpses," then so be it (*Clem.* 1.3.3). Nero's way makes his own security paramount. Everyone else is expendable. If need be, everyone else—certainly all his servants and slaves—must be ransomed *for his life*. Lord Jesus flatly turns this headship on its head as *he* assumes the position of servant-slave who will ransom many with *his* lifeblood (Thiessen 2016, 456–59).

The Greek term for "ransom" (*lytron*) denotes the "price of release" or redemption; similarly, the verb form (*lytroō*) means "to free by paying a ransom, redeem" (cf. 1 Pet 1:18) or "to liberate from an oppressive situation, set free, rescue, redeem" (BDAG 2000, 606). In Luke 24:21, the pair of Emmaus-road travelers voice their hope that Jesus Messiah would emancipate the whole Jewish nation from imperial rule: "We had hoped that he was the one to redeem (*lytrousthai*) Israel" (cf. Luke 1:68). Evidence from papyri and inscriptions also supports ransom language in reference to releasing slaves and remitting sins (BDAG 2000, 605; Moulton and Milligan 1930,

382; Deissman 1978 [1927], 327–30). Mark's Jesus remarkably lays down his life in the form of a servant-slave in order to free enslaved persons (cf. Phil 2:7-8) and to forgive sinners (cf. Isa 53:3-6, 11; 4 Macc 17:21-22; Johnson 2018, 148-50).

While Mark 10:45 supports the belief that "Jesus paid it all," as the popular hymn states—that is, paid the ransom price to liberate us from the bondage of sin—it's important to understand the concept as a *metaphor*, a rich and dynamic metaphor to be sure but not a literal payment or transaction. Further, the metaphor is general and suggestive, not specific and definitive. For example, though it includes Jesus's death in the redemptive picture, it does not limit the "payment" to Jesus's "precious blood" (1 Pet 2:18-19). As the theologian Elizabeth Johnson puts it, "This saying [Mark 10:45] sweeps the whole course of Jesus's life into the purse that wins freedom" (2018, 128). Moreover, the New Testament never insinuates that Jesus paid the ransom price of his blood *to God* (or any other "payee"), as if God demanded a human blood-price for humanity's salvation or that God must receive "satisfaction" or payment rendered for the service of atonement. The emphasis of Jesus's ransom work falls not on its economic accounting process but on its *cathartic liberating purpose* "for many" from all walks of life with whom Jesus identifies, in whose fragile and broken lives he becomes wholly immersed (baptized).

Healing a Blind Man Named Bartimaeus (10:46-52)

Jesus continues to forge the redemptive way of the servant Messiah in the next scene involving a blind beggar "sitting by the roadside/wayside (*hodon*)" outside of Jericho (10:46); after the man's sight is restored, he "followed [Jesus] on the way (*hodō*)" into Jerusalem (10:52). He thus embodies the way of seeing/perceiving/understanding that Mark's Jesus has been advancing in this unit. Compared with the anonymous, passive blind man whom Jesus healed privately outside the village (8:22-26), this man stands out as a named, proactive model of faith in the presence of Jesus's "disciples and a large crowd" (10:46-52).

Before being identified as a "blind beggar," the man is introduced by name and parentage as "Bartimaeus, the son of Timaeus" (10:46). This represents the only healing case in Mark where the beneficiary is named (omitted in Matt 20:29-34//Luke 18:35-43). Naming accords the man special respect, enhanced by the particular name's meaning related to *timē/ timaō*, "honor, respect, worth." Bar-Timaeus designates "son of Honor" or "son of Worthy One." The terminology has economic as well as social connotations concerning the *price* or *value* of goods and services (Matt 27:6, 9; Acts

4:32; 5:2-3; 7:16; 19:19; 1 Cor 6:20; 7:23; 1 Pet 2:7). Then as now, one's social honor was related to one's financial wealth, though not as tightly as in modern capitalist societies.

Having a name like Bartimaeus (Richie Rich) does not guarantee that you will have high standing or great prosperity. In worldly terms, as a blind beggar Bartimaeus sits on the lowest rung of the socioeconomic ladder— the very antithesis of his name. Although some Greco-Roman traditions attributed special gifts of revelatory insight to certain blind persons (Beavis 1998, 25–27, 36–38), these were exceptions; generally the blind were lumped with the poorest and lowliest (Luke 4:18; 7:21-22; 14:12-13; Just 1997). In the present scene, the crowds show their disdain for Bartimaeus by shouting him down when he cries out for aid from the passing Jesus: "Many sternly ordered (*epetimōn*) him to be quiet" (10:48). We've heard Jesus "sternly order" silence from obstreperous demons and obstinate disciples (Mark 1:25; 3:12; 8:30, 33; 9:25); and recently Peter and the disciples levied a "rebuke" or "stern order" against Jesus himself (8:32) and against little children being brought to Jesus (10:13). Directed at Bartimaeus, however, a telling wordplay amplifies the shout-down. The "sternly order" verb, *epitimaō*, is a compound of *timaō* from which Bartimaeus's name derives. Thus, in aiming to dismiss Bartimaeus's plea for help, the people effectively *dishonor* him and everything he represents as *not worth* their or Jesus's attention. Silence is the *price* he must pay for his disgusting condition.

But remember, it is precisely despised, destitute, "last" ones, like Bartimaeus, who rank highest in Jesus's book (9:35; 10:30), whom the poor "slave" Jesus has come to serve at the cost—the *ransom price!*—of his whole life even unto death (10:44-45). Honor and wealth assessments in God's realm run counter to the scales of earthly kingdoms: an esteemed rich seeker may be turned away (though not forever) (10:17-22), while a debased blind beggar is welcomed to join the way of Jesus Messiah (10:52).

For his part, Bartimaeus refuses to accept a marginal social role and to miss the opportunity for merciful aid that he believes Jesus can provide. He thus aligns with the paralytic's four friends (2:3-5) and with the bleeding woman (5:25-34) as people of determined, proactive faith in the face of an obstructive crowd. Jesus commends such dynamic faith: as with the bleeding woman who touched his clothing, Jesus emphasizes to blind Bartimaeus, "Your faith has made you well" (5:34; 10:52; Spencer 2017b). (We should add to this faith-in-action group the demon-possessed girl's mother, though her "faith" is not explicitly highlighted [7:24-30], and the epileptic boy's father, though his faith is a tad shaky [9:17-24].)

As one scholar notes, Bartimaeus's "many actions appear as a manifestation of a single reality, his faith" (Ossandón 2012, 391). These actions briskly unfold in four stages focused on shouting out, throwing off, springing up, and asking for.

Shouting out to Jesus (10:46-49)
Bartimaeus twice shouts to the passing "Jesus of Nazareth . . . 'Jesus, Son of David, have mercy on me!'"—the second time "even more loudly" over the crowd's attempts to silence him (10:47-48). He will not be shushed. And he makes the first identification of Jesus as "Son of David" in this Gospel—a connection that is by no means obvious, since David had no historical link with Nazareth and Jesus himself has said nothing about his Davidic roots.

If we were reading *Luke's* story, we might imagine the blind man had heard of Jesus's birth in Bethlehem, the city of David, from Judean shepherds who bore witness to the event (Luke 2:8-20; 18:35-39); but Mark has no nativity account. We are thus left to surmise that blind Bartimaeus has been given special revelation or insight into Jesus's identity—and acts on it with boldness (Beavis 1998, 36–38; Spencer 2017b, 235–36). While Jesus's messianic mission will be further associated with Davidic rule in the next two chapters (11:9-10; 12:35-37), this first instance grounds Jesus's kingship in merciful service to the needy, consistent with David's early attraction of "everyone who was in distress" (1 Sam 22:1-2), not David's later exploitations of royal power (2 Samuel 11–12, 24) and certainly not Caesar's pompous, tyrannical rule (Thiessen 2016, 463–65).

The shouting prompts Jesus to stop and order the dismissive crowd to call Bartimaeus to encounter Jesus directly (Mark 10:49). The same "call" (*phoneō*) verb described Jesus's summoning (*ephōnēsen*) his ambitious twelve disciples to reinforce his ranking system: "Whoever wants to be first must be last of all and servant of all" (9:35). As Jesus then embraced a little child as a living lesson of this principle (9:36-37), he now engages a blind man for the same purpose.

Throwing off his cloak (10:50a)
Whereas the bleeding woman pressed through a crowd to touch Jesus's cloak or outer garment (*himation*, 5:27), the blind man sheds his own cloak (*himation*, 10:50) to respond to Jesus's call, letting nothing hold him down or impede his progress. This shirt on his back is one of the few things he owns; but in true disciple form, he leaves everything behind to follow Jesus (cf. 1:18-20; 10:28).

The term for "throw off" (*apoballō*) also appears, interestingly enough, in the Hellenistic-Jewish book of Tobit, describing a medicinal remedy for the main character's blindness, making "the white films shrink and *peel off* (*apobalei*) from his eyes" so that he "will regain his sight (*anablepsei*)" (Tob 11:8). Bartimaeus peels off his cloak and leaves it behind in anticipation of shedding his blinders and regaining his vision.

Springing up to Jesus (10:50b)

Free of his outer garment, the sitting and begging Bartimaeus springs up and bounds toward Jesus. Such action (*anapēdaō*) is typically motivated by strong emotion, like "fierce anger" (1 Sam 20:34 NETS), tearful joy (Tob 7:6), or, as we may assume in Bartimaeus's case, effervescent hope. We should not miss the fact that Bartimaeus is still blind at this point. No one guides him to Jesus; he leaps up and scrambles to Jesus on his own, sensing where Jesus is as he sensed who Jesus was.

Asking for renewed sight (10:51-52)

Jesus now poses the same question to Bartimaeus that he did to James and John: "What do you want me to do for you?" (10:51; see 10:36). We sense that Jesus asks this more for his disciples' benefit than for Bartimaeus's, as if to say, "All right, men, you want high kingdom status above everything else: listen well to what *this man wants* from me." What he wants is simply to "see again," which is precisely what James, John, and company *should* be asking for: "Give us spiritual (in)sight again (and again and again). Let us see clearly to follow you on your true way" (cf. 8:17-25).

Bartimaeus also represents a model disciple by addressing Jesus as *Rabbouni* ("My teacher," 10:51), an intensified Aramaic form of *Rabbi* designating a venerable "teacher of the Jewish Scriptures, implying an important personal relationship—'my teacher'" (L&N 1988, 416). The only other Gospel use of *Rabbouni* comes from Mary Magdalene when she finally recognizes her beloved risen Lord Jesus in the garden area around his tomb (John 20:16). By contrast, James and John addressed Jesus with the less personal, blander title "Teacher," the basic Greek term *Didaskale*, not the more intimate *Rabbouni* (10:35; cf. 4:38; 9:38; 13:1).

Question Marks about Jesus's Wisdom and Authority

Mark 11:1–12:44

From Jericho (10:46), Jesus and his travel party—now including the re-sighted Bartimaeus (10:52)—continue southwest toward Jerusalem via the villages of Bethphage and Bethany, located around the Mount of Olives, one to two miles east of the temple. Jesus enters the holy city from here and returns to camp at night over the next several days (11:1-2, 11-12; 13:3; 14:3, 26, 32). Along with being known for olive production and processing, the area was also hospitable to fig trees. The Aramaic name Bethphage means "house of green/early figs," representing a "type of fig that never appears to be ripe" (Moreland 2006, 445; cf. Carroll 1992, 715; Rousseau and Arav 1995, 18). Fig trees figure prominently in Jesus's final teachings (11:12-14, 20-24; 13:28-31).

Within Jerusalem, Jesus spends most of his time in the temple compound, the house of God (11:17), the Jewish worship center. But this will not be a joyful or restful time for Jesus, as he publicly challenges temple authorities and other leaders and in turn is interrogated by them. Mark variously designates these Jerusalem officials, singly or together, as "chief priests, scribes, and elders" (8:31; 10:33; 11:18, 27; 12:35, 38-40; 14:10, 43, 53; 15:1, 10-11, 31). The Pharisees also make one final appearance, again associated with the Herodians (12:13; cf. 3:6; 8:15); and another group, the Sadducees—the party of the priestly elites—makes its first appearance (12:18-23).

Jesus's disciples continue to attend him and receive some private instruction (11:1-7, 11-14, 20-25; 12:43-44). But throughout most of this unit, his closest followers join the crowds who witness his clashes with the temple hierarchs.

In these heated debates, Jesus uses various means to drive home his points. He delivers one final *parable* (12:1-12) and continues to appeal to the common ground of *sacred Scripture*: "Is it not written?" (11:17); "Have you not read this scripture?" (12:10-11); "Is not this the reason you are wrong, that you know neither the scriptures nor the power of God?"

(12:24; cf. 11:9-10; 12:29-31, 35-37). Jesus also punctuates his arguments with dramatic *symbolic actions* after the fashion of Old Testament kings and prophets (11:1-25).

With the buildup of Jesus's triple forecast of his death in the preceding chapters, tensions are running high. The specter of his demise looms large and heavy. Before tracking his entry into Jerusalem and the conflict he both instigates and confronts, we might reasonably ask, "Why does Jesus march full steam ahead into the lion's den? Knowing that he would be killed there, why does he not retreat, regroup, and reconsider his options? Does he harbor some kind of strange death wish? A martyr complex?"

Some scholars regard Jesus's three predictions of his death as Mark's scheme constructed for the benefit of his distressed community in the period around the Roman-Jewish War. Presumably, believers in Jesus Messiah— whom the Roman authorities had crucified as an insurrectionist—would come under special scrutiny and pressure during this time of Jewish revolt. By portraying the earthly Jesus as knowingly and faithfully pursuing the way of the cross, Mark assures his audience of Jesus's knowing and faithful solidarity with them in their current crisis (cf. Carr 2014, 225–38). Granting, however, the narrative design of Jesus's threefold death forecast as a means of providing pastoral support care for Mark's traumatized community does not preclude that Jesus anticipated his ominous fate in Jerusalem and accepted it, though not easily, as part of his God-charted way. Mark's story of Jesus deftly weaves together both historical and interpretive threads: the way it *was* and what that way *means* for Jesus's followers now.

Moreover, granting that Jesus came to Jerusalem to die in some purposeful sense does not mean that he had some death or martyr drive or that Mark casts Jesus's "long anticipated . . . death on a cross," as David Carr suggests, as "no traumatic ending of a life. It was a voluntary death suffered by a divinely empowered hero" (2014, 230). As will become most evident in Jesus's fervent prayer before his arrest, he does "not go gentle into that good night" (Thomas 2003, 239) but rather struggles mightily with his Father's will that he drink the lethal cup (14:32-39). He's no classic Socratic hero (see Bond 2019, 427–39). Carr is closer to the mark when he later adds that Mark's abrupt "ending only faintly anticipated the resurrection, still preserving some of the sting of the traumatic loss of Jesus" (2014, 231).

Jerusalem Demonstrations (11:1-25)

Jesus knows how to make an entrance into the holy city and the temple— dramatic entrances that command rapt attention. But while demonstrating eminent kingly and priestly authority, he does so in unconventional ways.

Jesus does not enter the city like chief rulers Caesar or Herod or the temple like high priests Annas or Caiaphas. Jesus culminates his earthly mission as the unique Messiah/Christ and Son of God (Mark 1:1), the consummate agent of God's realm (1:14-15).

Jesus enters the city as Davidic king (11:1-11)
Coming into eastern Jerusalem from the Mount of Olives likely indicates a strategic, symbolic move on Jesus's part. The postexilic prophet Zechariah envisioned the Mount of Olives as the base of operations for the Lord's climactic (apocalyptic) liberation of Jerusalem from foreign enemies and exaltation as rightful ruler of Israel and the world: "On that day his feet shall stand on the Mount of Olives. . . . And the LORD will become king over all the earth; on that day the LORD will be one and his name one" (Zech 14:4, 9; cf. 14:1-11). But Zechariah pictured this divine deliverance via a mighty military battle in "which the LORD will strike all the peoples that wage war against Jerusalem" (14:12; cf. 14:3, 12-15). No doubt tapping into this prophecy, a popular mid-first-century CE messianic figure known as "the Egyptian" marshaled a large fighting mob at the Mount of Olives with the aim of storming Jerusalem's walls and freeing the city from imperial control. The Roman Governor Felix, however, brutally squashed this rebellion (Josephus, *Ant.* 20.169–72; *J.W.* 2.261–63; Acts 21:38; Novenson 2017, 140; Gray 1993, 116–18; Horsley and Hanson 1985, 168–72).

Jesus's procession into Jerusalem from the apocalyptically charged Mount of Olives both feeds and defies popular expectations. On the one hand, he makes a kind of royal entrance and accepts the crowd's hailing him as God's royal emissary (Mark 10:9-10). But on the other hand, he makes no pretense of coming as a conquering warrior, either celebrating past victories or launching a new campaign to liberate Jerusalem from Roman domination. He comes with no arms or army, no battle strategy, no militant banners, no publicity agents. Despite what this event has been commonly labeled, Jesus makes *no* "Triumphal Entry."

His main entry plans, which Mark describes at some length (11:2-7), concern his transport into the city—not on a noble steed, mighty warhorse, military chariot, or royal carriage but on an ordinary "colt that has never been ridden" (11:2). Yet Jesus takes some pains to ensure that such an animal is procured in a certain way, an odd way. He dispatches two disciples into a nearby village where, he tells them, they will "immediately" find a tethered, never-ridden colt, which they should untie and bring to him. We're not told whether this colt's availability owes to some prearranged human scheme or to divine intervention. In any case, Jesus anticipates that someone might object to his disciples' walking up and taking (stealing!) the animal. If that occurs, Jesus instructs his representatives to say, "The Lord needs it and will send it back here immediately" (11:3) As it happens, the scene plays out just this way, and the villagers allow the pair of disciples to borrow the colt for Jesus's use (11:4-6).

Four points follow from this peculiar scene:

- We're reminded again of how lightly Jesus travels; he has no animal of his own to ride and no money to buy or lease one. Except for the times he sails across the lake by boat (likely belonging to one of the disciples), he travels by foot (even across the water one time!) (Spencer 2003, 148–51).

- This is the only time Mark's Jesus uses his authority for his own personal benefit. As the Lord and ruler of all creation, he exercises the right to commandeer someone else's colt. This imperious action through authorized agents resembles Caesar's use of soldiers to press people and their animals into carrier service (see 15:21; Matt 5:41; 27:32; Chapman and Schnabel 2015, 276–82; Leander 2010, 324–25; Wink 1992, 202–204). However, Jesus tempers this authority by promising (through his messengers) to return the colt as soon as he is finished riding it into town (11:3; the other Gospels omit this key point).

- Jesus's authority is furthered moderated by his *humility*. A "colt" (*pōlos*) could refer to a young horse, donkey, or another equine. Matthew and John specify a donkey (*onos*) in fulfillment of Zechariah's prophecy: "Rejoice greatly, O daughter Zion! Shout aloud, O daughter Jerusalem! Lo, your king comes to you; triumphant and victorious is he, humble and riding on a donkey, on a colt, the foal of donkey" (Zech 9:9; see Matt 21:2-5; John 12:14-15). Whether or not Mark knew the Zechariah text, he likely presumes the tradition that Jesus rode a donkey, a common beast of burden, in stark contrast to the typical conveyance of a "triumphant and victorious" conqueror. Unlike Zechariah's expected king, however, Mark's Jesus is no military hero, although he has waged winning battles against Satan and demons. Rather, he participates in "carefully choreographed political street theater . . . designed to repudiate Messianic triumphalism" (Myers et al. 2003, 145).

Jesus's striking humility is evidenced not merely by choosing a lowly donkey but by stressing that "the Lord *needs* it." Although such language may again smack of imperial demand ("Lord Caesar requires it"), in Jesus's case, as an itinerant preacher with meager possessions, he has *real* material needs (Leander 2010, 323–26; Derrett 1971, 246–47). *This Lord* is not self-sufficient but interdependent. As he graciously gives of himself and his spiritual power, he humbly receives help from others. As he has *necessarily* relied on others' hospitality throughout his journeys, he now *needs* to borrow a donkey and is not ashamed to admit it. This is how a servant-king functions in the interest of God's servant-oriented realm, which ranks the littlest and least as the highest and greatest.

• Along with alluding to Zechariah's prophecy, the figure of the colt may also evoke other royal and priestly associations. In establishing his successor, the aged king David arranged for his son Solomon to ride to the spring of Gihon (near Jerusalem) on David's *mule* (half-donkey) and be anointed by the prophet Nathan and the priest Zadok (1 Kgs 1:32-46). Further, Jesus's choice of a *young, never-ridden* (never-worked, unyoked) animal may recall similar consecrated animals used in various priestly rites, like the two cows yoked for the first time to pull the cart carrying the ark of the covenant (1 Sam 6:7; cf. Num 19:2; Deut 21:3). Though not a priestly official, Jesus will soon display some priest-like authority in the temple (Mark 11:15-19).

While Jesus comes into Jerusalem on a young donkey with no preplanned fanfare, a spontaneous celebration breaks out with a kind of rolling-out-the-red-carpet and striking up a hail-to-the-king chorus. As the two disciples "threw their cloaks" on the donkey's back as a saddle for Jesus, "many people" spread their cloaks "on the road (*hodon*)" while others added "leafy branches that they had cut in the fields" to the makeshift runway (11:7-8).

The cloak-throwing (*epiballō*) matches Bartimaeus's action as he sprang to meet Jesus on the road out of Jericho (10:50). It also recalls the impromptu response of Jehu's officers upon learning of his sudden anointing by the prophet Elisha to overthrow and replace the wicked dynasty of Omri and Ahab: "Then hurriedly they all took their cloaks and spread them for him on the bare steps; and they blew the trumpet, and proclaimed, 'Jehu is king'" (2 Kgs 9:13). But that was a rogue, rebel operation. Jehu would not officially rule Israel until he had slaughtered Ahab's descendants and many worshipers of Baal who supported the house of Ahab and Jezebel (2 Kings 9–10). Many of those who lay down their cloaks for King Jesus probably expect him to launch a violent coup against Rome. But this is not Jesus's way: he will shed his own blood, no one else's, to save his people.

The leaf-strewing represents further spontaneous action by the crowd. Only Mark mentions that the people "cut" the branches "in the fields," thus offering Jesus their manual labor as well as giving him the shirts from their backs (11:8). These cuttings (*stibadas*) would have been "a litter of reeds or rushes" (Moulton and Milligan 1930, 589), "'a spray of plant with leaves', leafy pieces, non-specific, with the idea of providing a leaf-covered path"

(Danker and Krug 2009, 328). Only the Gospel of John specifies *palm* fronds (John 12:13), which may be implied in Mark's general picture of flora.

The Maccabeans celebrated their successful revolt from the Greek-Syrian tyrant Antiochus IV with parades festooned with branches. When Judas Maccabeus liberated Jerusalem and purified the temple, the people launched an eight-day festival, "carrying ivy-wreathed wands and beautiful branches and also fronds of palm" and singing "hymns of thanksgiving to [the Lord] who had given success to the purifying of his own holy place" (2 Macc 10:7). Such displays evoked the Festival of Tabernacles/Booths (*Sukkoth*), which commemorated Israel's post-exodus way through the wilderness, "wandering in the mountains and caves like wild animals" and sheltering in portable tents made from branches and other desert debris (2 Macc 10:6). Jesus's journey to Jerusalem in Mark has followed a similar rough, "new exodus" way (Watts 2001) and will soon lead to his own peculiar "purification" of the temple (Mark 11:15-17).

A few decades later, Judas's brother, Simon, reclaimed and consecrated the citadel ("elevated fortress," 1 Macc 13:49 CEB) at Jerusalem, which the Jews jubilantly entered "with praise and palm branches, and with harps and cymbals and stringed instruments, and with hymns and songs, because a great enemy had been crushed and removed from Israel" (13:51). Again, Jesus's procession into Jerusalem culminates a mission of resistance to evil forces oppressing God's people, but unlike the Maccabeans, he engages in *nonviolent* resistance, militant but not military, liberating but not destructive.

As the Maccabean parades joined branch-waving with hymn-singing, the crowd attending Jesus's entry into the holy city breaks out in song, specifically a stanza adapted from Psalm 118:25-26:

> LORD, save us!
>   LORD, grant us success!
> Blessed is he who comes in the name of the LORD.
>   From the house of the LORD we bless you. (Ps 118:25-26 NIV)

Although not quoted in Mark, the next verse in this psalm alludes to a festival with branches (the Festival of Tabernacles involved reciting Ps 118:1, 25 along with waving the *lulav* or palm branch; see m. Sukkah 3:9; 4:5).

> The LORD is God,
>   and he has given us light.
> Bind the festal procession with branches
>   up to the horns of the altar. (Ps 118:27 NRSV)

> The LORD is God,
>   and he has made his light shine on us.
> With boughs in hand, join in the festal procession
>   up to the horns of the altar. (Ps 118:27 NIV)

"Hosanna" in Mark's quotation transliterates the Hebrew term meaning "Save now!" (a slight change from the psalm's "Save us"). The people make this impassioned cry their own out of their pressing sense of need for salvation and refuge. However, after the initial benediction—"Blessed is he who comes in the name of the LORD" (Ps 118:26a NIV)—they modify the second benediction, "From the house of the LORD we bless you" (Ps 118:26b NIV), to announce "Blessed is the coming kingdom of our father David" (Mark 11:10 NIV). The reference to the advent of the Davidic kingdom is striking. Throughout its extended paean to the Lord as Israel's strong loving and saving refuge, Psalm 118 makes no explicit reference to a royal figure in general or a Davidic ruler in particular (only Aaron is named among Israel's past leaders [118:3]). But references to "cutting off" enemy nations and breaking out in "glad songs of victory" (118:10-16) have a royal military tone appropriate for exalting a conquering king like David (Watts 2007, 207–208). Clearly the throng hailing Mark's Jesus believes that he enters the city as the Davidic Messiah, following on the heels of Bartimaeus's full-throated plea to Jesus as the merciful Son of David (10:47-48). Exactly how the people expect Jesus to save them is not specified but likely involves some overthrow of corrupt and oppressive overlords. At any rate, they certainly do not anticipate his death on a Roman cross by week's end. In this respect, Jesus does *not* fit the psalmist's prototype: "I shall not die, but I shall live. . . . The LORD has punished me severely, but he did not give me over to death" (Ps 118:17-18).

The importance of Psalm 118 for understanding Mark's Passion/Holy Week narrative (cf. Mark 12:10-11) also relates to its grouping with the Praise/Hallel songs in Psalms 113–118 that became part of annual Passover (as well as Tabernacles) festivities, remembering ancient Israel's exodus from Egyptian enslavement (see Ps 114:1-5; m. Pesaḥ 10:6; Watts 2007, 207). Mark later discloses that Jesus comes to Jerusalem precisely to celebrate "Passover and the festival of Unleavened Bread" (14:1, 12-26), with all its redemptive Exodus associations, to share one last supper—the Passover meal!—with his disciples (Horsley 2001, 109–10; 2011, 169–70). Following Passover custom, Jesus and company conclude the meal by singing "the hymn" (14:26), most likely from Psalm 118 or one of its Hallel companions.

In the Greco-Roman world, royal parades into major cities typically culminated in the local temple with priestly ceremonies blessing the august, divinely authorized figure (Duff 1992, 58–64; Leander 2010, 318–20). After entering Jerusalem, Jesus heads straight to the temple—but not for some glorious finale (Leander 2010, 319–20, calls it an "anticlimax"). The narrative gives the impression that Jesus pays scant attention to the adoring crowds, scoots right past them, and proceeds to the temple where he intently surveys the environment, casing the place, as it were: "he looked around (*periblepsamenos*) at everything" (Mark 11:11). Jesus has previously "looked around" at various audiences, sizing them up before issuing some critical statement or question (3:5, 34; 5:32; 10:23). His provocative temple message, however, will have to wait until the next day, since the hour "was already late." Mark thus creates narrative suspense for the reader. In the meantime, Jesus exits the city "with the twelve" to spend the night in nearby Bethany (11:11).

Jesus enters the temple as priest-like prophet (11:12-25)

Jesus reenters Jerusalem the next day in a very different disposition. Far from riding an ambling donkey and remaining calm amid shouts of praise, Jesus now strides, even stomps, into the city, we imagine, with vehement words and actions directed, first, against a fig tree and, second, at temple furniture and functionaries. By any reckoning these are weird moves—and not very wise moves, since they provoke urgent plots from temple officials "to kill him" (11:18). Jesus pushes the envelope, virtually daring the authorities to seize and execute him.

Again the issue arises of Jesus's *intent*. Sensing that deathly forces are poised against him, he stokes their hostility, all but inviting the authorities to get on with their lethal business. But precipitating death is not Jesus's prime purpose. There is strategic method to his madness, premeditated motivation behind his emotion. Although not described as "angry" in these scenes, Jesus's vehement words and actions of protest signal a heated emotional state (Spencer 2021, 62–65; Lawrence 2016, 95–104). But while far from calm and cool, he remains "collected," that is, in control of his behavior. He does not impulsively fly off the handle in bursts of pique. He has no "fig fit" or "temple tantrum" (Fredriksen 2000, xxi).

Rather, Jesus deliberately stages *destructive public demonstrations* unlike anything he's done before—no restorative healing, deliverance, or calming on this day—to drive home *critical prophetic challenges* after the fashion of the great Hebrew prophets he quotes, Isaiah and Jeremiah (Mark 11:17; Isa 56:7; Jer 7:11). For example, to punctuate their messages that Jerusalem and the kingdom of Judah faced foreign conquest (if they did not change their idolatrous and unjust ways), Isaiah walked naked around Jerusalem, role-playing a shamed, stripped slave (Isaiah 20); and Jeremiah smashed an earthenware pot in the Hinnom Valley below the city, enacting a broken, shattered people (Jeremiah 19).

Mark reprises the "sandwich" technique to tightly intertwine the fig tree and temple incidents—focused on two emotionally "evocative . . . national symbols," one rural-agricultural, one urban-architectural (Lawrence 2016, 99)—with the temple demonstration at the center.

Sandwich #4
A Cursing the Fig Tree (Barren) (11:12-14)
B Clearing the Temple House (11:15-19)
A Cursing the Fig Tree (Withered) (11:20-25)

The barren fig tree (11:12-14). Curiously, Mark notes that Jesus reenters Jerusalem in a *hungry* state (11:12), not exactly what we expect to hear about a royal messianic figure—how he satisfies others' hunger, yes; his own growling stomach, not so much. Again, Mark matter-of-factly acknowledges Jesus's basic human *needs*. In this case, Mark may be drawing another suggestive parallel between Jesus and David. Remember in the Sabbath debate over eating restrictions, Jesus appealed to what "David did when he and his companions were *hungry and in need of food*," namely, enter the "house of God" and consume the priestly consecrated bread (Mark 2:25-26; 1 Sam 21:1-6). Thus Jesus affirmed that he is "lord even of the sabbath" (Mark 2:27). The Davidic episode occurred before he was formally installed as king, while he was on the run from the current ruler, the jealous and maniacal Saul. Similarly, a hungry Jesus enters the temple as "Lord" of God's house in the midst of opposition from current authorities who "kept looking for a way to kill him" (11:18).

But first, Jesus has a fig tree to deal with—a leaf-laden tree that he hopes, it seems, will have some juicy figs to satisfy his hunger. But no such luck—"for it was not the season for figs" (11:13). Only Mark adds this odd "season" comment, odd in part because it was well known that ripe figs were available in early summer, not spring (Passover season). The scene becomes odder, bordering on the "irrational" (Donahue and Harrington 2002, 331), as Jesus proceeds to curse the tree permanently: "May no one ever eat fruit from you again" (11:12). Why punish this poor tree for failing to follow its natural course? The final note that Jesus's "disciples heard" his malediction hints that he intends to teach his followers an important lesson. But what lesson?

Consider two points. First, a *symbolic* element: the fig tree (along with a grapevine) was a common biblical-prophetic image for the people of Israel, whom God planted in the land and from whom God expected fruitfulness in return, that is, fruitful love for God and one another (Jer 8:13-15; Hos 9:10; Mic 7:1-6; cf. Isa 5:1-7; Ezek 15:1-8). Yet prophets challenged the leaders (especially) and people for failing to live up to this calling, for failing to produce the desired fruits of faithfulness and righteousness. A lament from the ancient Judahite prophet Micah closely relates to Mark's fig story (Donahue and Harrington 2002, 327).

> Woe is me! For I have become like one who,
>   after the summer fruit has been gathered,
>   after the vintage has been gleaned,
> finds no cluster to eat;
>   There is no first-ripe fig for which I hunger.
>   The faithful have disappeared from the land,
> and there is no one left who is upright. (Mic 7:1-2a)

Like his prophetic forebear, Mark's Jesus hungers for figs, only to be woefully disappointed. This is not about Jesus's (or Micah's) food craving, however, but rather about his deep longing for Israel's faithful following of God's way—a longing love that largely remains unrequited, particularly by the leaders. But Jesus also no doubt senses how quickly the adoring crowd that ushered him into Jerusalem can become fickle and turn against him (see Mark 15:8-15).

As much as Mark's Jesus seems to resonate with Micah, a glaring point of difference emerges. Micah's woe regarding the fig tree's barrenness is set "after the summer fruit has been gathered," while Jesus, remember, seeks figs in the spring (out of season). But both scenarios reflect a timing problem: the "first-ripe fig" Micah desires is no more available *after* the spring harvest than *before* fig season, as Jesus desires. The situation is asynchronous.

It doesn't add up chronologically—or theologically—which leads to a second point: a *lexical* matter. The "season" term in Mark 11:13—*kairos*—connotes eventful, momentous time (it's time to eat!) more than momentary clock, calendar, or *chronos* time (it's noon time). Accordingly, Werner Kelber interprets Mark's use of *kairos* here "not [as] a botanical term indicating the season for figs" but rather as a "loaded religious term" indicating the "'right time' of the kingdom of God," the significant gospel "time (*kairos*) [that is being] fulfilled" in Jesus's entire ministry," as Mark's story established from the beginning (1:14-15) (Kelber 1979, 59–60; Moloney 2002, 221–22). As Jesus's messianic time on earth approaches its climactic end, it runs diametrically counter (clockwise) to ungodly, ill-timed (for ill) schemes and schedules.

The dysfunctional house of God (11:15-19). From a key agricultural symbol of God's people in the holy land, Jesus moves to the main architectural symbol of God's holy presence with the people—the temple in Jerusalem. And he continues to be primed for disruptive action, now exhibited in three moves: (1) expelling sellers and buyers in the temple compound; (2) upending tables and chairs of money changers and dove merchants; and (3) obstructing conveyances through the area (11:15-16). From the start, we should expose some common misconceptions.

• Jesus does *not* perform a ritual "cleansing" or purification of the temple, like the Maccabeans did after driving Antiochus's Syrian-Greek forces from Jerusalem. Although briefly taking high-priest-like charge of the temple and antagonizing the official chief priests (11:18), Jesus has no priestly pedigree and is not angling to become high priest (the Maccabean rulers assumed royal and priestly authority). He dons no special vestments and offers no atoning sacrifices. The priests Jesus most resembles are the *prophet*-priests Jeremiah, Ezekiel, and Zechariah, who sharply critiqued Israel's leaders and institutions.

• Jesus does *not* launch a revolutionary coup against the current religious-political authorities. Although throwing out some temple functionaries and throwing over their furniture, Jesus does not seek to take over the temple institution. After staging his demonstration, teaching the "spellbound" crowd, and angering the chief priests and scribes, he leaves the temple area and goes back to his campsite outside the city (11:17-19).

• Jesus does *not* curse the temple (as he did the fig tree) or utterly reject it. He is not anti-temple. His dramatic actions and words reflect a passionate concern for the temple's proper place as God's house for all people (11:17a; Isa 56:7).

• Jesus does *not* enact a symbolic destruction of the temple. He will later predict that every stone in the "great buildings" of the temple complex "will be thrown down" (Mark 13:2), precisely what Roman armies accomplish in 70 CE (only the Western Wall [Kotel] remained). But Jesus's act of toppling a few tables and chairs is a far cry from dismantling all temple structures. Jesus does not declare war on the temple. His demonstration marks a disruption in temple operation, not its destruction. It carries an implicit warning of further judgment against the temple establishment does not repent and accept the gospel of God's kingdom in Christ (1:14–15)—but no pronouncement of final doom.

Jesus speaks and acts as reformer and idealist, not as rebel and iconoclast. He seeks to clear out a disorderly house (Kirk 2012, 510, calls it the "temple-clearing incident") or to "'clean house,' with a view to recovering a fully operational sacred space" (Perrin 2018, 184, describing a parallel perspective in the Psalms of Solomon)—but *not* to cleanse the temple in some antiviral sense of wiping it out, as a tyrant might target a hated group for "ethnic cleansing." To be sure, Jesus's words and actions have political overtones. You don't go in and disturb the peace of Herod the Great's magnificently renovated temple (a marvel throughout the empire)—where daily prayers were offered for Caesar by priestly hierarchs who maintained their power by not ruffling Roman feathers—without creating some political stir (Leander 2010, 328). But Jesus's demonstration is comparatively controlled. It's a one-man act with his bare hands: Mark puts no whips in Jesus's hands (as in John 2:15), and Jesus makes no move to whip up the crowd into a rampaging mob. While he makes his point with vehemence, he does not aim to provoke violence.

So what is his principal point? He targets the commercial business of the temple: buying and selling animals for sacrifice, including doves for the poor with tight budgets (see Lev 12:8; Luke 2:22-24), and exchanging everyday currency into the Tyrian coinage required for such transactions. Again, as a faithful Jew, Jesus is not opposed to such temple business or even to the merchants and money changers he disrupts (he also obstructs workers who carry any "merchandise" [NIV], "goods" [NASB], or "vessels" [*skeuos*, 11:16] containing oil, salt, and other elements used in offerings; Myers et al. 2003, 147). These functionaries are simply doing their jobs. Some may have been overcharging the people, but Jesus's concern stretches beyond a financial audit of these sellers and tellers. He temporarily disturbs basic temple operations because he is greatly disturbed by the whole present temple system's way of doing business—both religious and economic business, which were tightly enmeshed (the temple treasury was the central Jewish "bank"; see Sanders 1992, 85–92; Wright 1996, 406–28; Hanson and Oakman 1998, 135–46).

Most responsible for the current deplorable state of affairs would be the temple CEOs, the chief priests, to whom all supporting staff answered. And these leaders should know, if anyone should, what Isaiah and Jeremiah said in their day about honorable service in God's house. Whether or not they saw Jesus's upsetting actions in the temple, they "heard" his challenging quotations from Isaiah and Jeremiah and did not like what he was insinuating through these prophets (11:17-18).

From Isaiah, Jesus reiterates the temple's positive purpose: "My house shall be called a house of prayer for all the nations" (Isa 56:7), that is, a place to worship God and welcome all peoples in God's name who honor God. Or, to anticipate Jesus's affirmation of the two greatest commandments (Mark 12:28-34), which are "much more important than all whole burnt offerings and sacrifices" (12:33), we may gloss Isaiah to characterize the temple's core mission as promoting *love for God* and *love for neighbor* with all of one's being. All temple personnel, from highest to lowest, serve in God's house at God's pleasure for God's purposes.

The current temple establishment, however, has fallen woefully short of this mission in Jesus's view, as he makes clear by reprising Jeremiah's negative point: "But you have made it a den of robbers" (Jer 7:11)—a "hideout for crooks" (CEB), a "cave of thugs" (Chilton 2000, 213, 230) or "bandits" (*lēstōn*). Ironically, as K. C. Hanson (2002, 293) notes, "Herod the Great—who had renovated and expanded the Jerusalem temple—had made his initial reputation by rooting out a band of Galilean bandits from their caves" (Josephus, *J.W.* 1.304–13; *Ant.* 14.420–31).

Jeremiah's larger sermon in 7:1-15, delivered "in the gate of the LORD's house" (7:2), illuminates Jesus's message. The temple's dysfunctional system in both Jeremiah's and Jesus's days tolerated idolatry by cozying up to foreign powers and practiced injustice by "oppress[ing] the alien, the orphan, and the widow . . . shed[ding] innocent blood in this place" (7:5-6). Mark's Jesus will soon directly denounce the scribes' unscrupulous practice of "devour[ing] widows' houses" (Mark 12:40; cf. 12:38-44). Temple administrators and agents have effectively set up the holy sanctuary as a safe house or hideout for those who exploit the poor, thus mocking and morally polluting God's house. In Jeremiah's fuller prosecution of God's case,

> Here you are, trusting in deceptive words to no avail. Will you steal, murder, commit adultery, swear falsely . . . and go after other gods that you have not known, and then come and stand before in this house, which is called by my name, and say, "We are safe!"—only to go on doing all these abominations? (Jer 7:10)

Be warned, Jesus communicates, in his own implicit jeremiad: "The temple, as marvelous as it is, cannot ultimately keep you safe, cannot save you." Only God can save, and only faithfulness to the holy and just God—in moral action, not simply ritual observance—forges the way of salvation.

To Jeremiah's priestly-prophetic warning that Jesus echoes, we may add the implicit background of Malachi's judgment:

> The Lord whom you seek will suddenly come *to his temple*. . . . he will sit as a refiner and purifier. . . . Then I [the LORD] will draw near to you for

judgment; I will be swift to bear witness against . . . those who oppress the hired workers in their wages, the widow and the orphan, against those who thrust aside the alien. . . . You are cursed with a curse, for *you are robbing me*—the whole nation of you! (Mal 3:1-2, 5, 9; Myers et al. 2003, 149)

Malachi particularly indicts the priests (3:3) of his day for robbing God of the "tithes and offerings" due God and God's house (3:8-10). Jesus is less concerned with filling temple coffers, but he shares Malachi's social-justice advocacy for disadvantaged people being "robbed" by temple elites; also, Malachi's interest in a full treasury is "so that there may be food in [God's] house" (3:10)—for the poor, not only the priests.

The withered fig tree (11:20-25). The next morning, en route back to Jerusalem from Bethany, Jesus gives his disciples a lesson in faith, with the events of cursing the fig tree and disrupting the temple still raw in their minds. Coming upon the same tree, Peter notices that it is not merely fruitless but has become lifeless, "withered away to its roots" (11:20-21). Jesus thus cursed it *to death*, an extraordinary though not unique move in Mark's narrative. This killing of the fig tree recalls the destroying of the pig herd (5:11-13), though in that case the demonic Legion that Jesus dispatched into the herd bears some, if not most, of the blame. In neither instance does Jesus snuff out *human* life, but figs and pigs are still part of God's good creation inextricably connected to human life. Nature is sustained by cycles of dying and rising, consuming and replenishing. Humans expend sweat and labor tending to crops and animals for food (though kosher Jews and vegetarians avoid pig flesh). But no one benefits from a dried-up fig tree or drowned pig herd. These seem like pure waste.

Fortunately, these are exceptional, not standard, acts Jesus undertakes. At least he incorporates the fig tree into his prophetic challenge to his wayward people at this critical "season/time" (*kairos*). He wants the people to repent, to rededicate themselves to being fruitful, faithful members of God's field and God's house (cf. 1 Cor 3:9, 16). But *annihilating* the tree, rather than only incapacitating its fruit bearing (or temporarily inconveniencing temple business), seems hopeless and vindictive. What purpose does that serve?

Without denying the distressing shock of Jesus's tree-withering curse, which Peter voices, we should also consider two mitigating factors: one simmering in the "withering" language used by Mark; the other contained in the lesson about faith, prayer, and forgiveness that Jesus draws from the fig tree drama.

The passive form of the verb *xērainō*, meaning "become withered" or "dried up" ("cause a dry non-functioning condition," Danker and Krug 2009,

245), used twice regarding the fig tree (11:20-21), appears four previous times in Mark. The parable of the soils provides the most direct link: Jesus spoke of the crop being "withered away (*exēranthē*)" due to its shallow roots in rocky ground (4:6). But in that seminal parable about relative degrees of responsiveness to God's proclaimed (sown) word, Jesus also held out hope for abundant fruitfulness and great harvest in God's kingdom (4:8, 20; cf. 4:26-32).

The other three "withered" cases shift from the agricultural to the medical sphere and from parable to healing incident:

- Jesus restored the full functionality of a man's "withered (*exērammenēn*) hand" (3:1-5).
- Upon touching the back of Jesus's cloak, a woman's chronic, debilitating flow of blood "stopped" or "dried up (*exēranthē*)" (5:29 NAB, NASB).
- Jesus revived a boy after he had a seizure that rendered him comatose and corpse-like—typical of other convulsive episodes the boy's father described as dashing his son to the ground and causing him to foam at the mouth, gnash his teeth, and "become rigid (*xērainetai*)" or "stiffen[ed] up" (9:18 CEB).

These withering cases evince a basic problem of *drying up* or *draining* essential life forces as vital fluids: field crops drained of water, fruit trees drained of sap, bodies in part or whole drained of blood or energy. But as in Ezekiel's valley of dry bones (Ezek 37:1-14), in Mark's narrative environment of desiccated horticultural and human bodies, *withering is not a terminal condition*. Rehydration, rejuvenation, and restoration to fruitful life remain possible, indeed promised, in God's flourishing realm.

The encounter between the hemorrhaging woman and Jesus demonstrates the point in reverse. Rather than replenishing depleted life fluids, the faith-filled woman triggered Jesus's flow of (dis)charged energy into her body that *dried up* (*xērainō*) her flow of draining blood. Thus, in God's living, dynamic realm channeled through Mark's Jesus, withering can even be a therapeutic operation, stanching life-threatening seepages and eruptions.

All of this is well and good—until we come to the withered fig tree that *stays withered* in the story. Is Jesus's hope for restoring a beleaguered, broken people and world also withering as the end of his earthly life draws near? Or can the personal resurrection he anticipates (8:31; 9:31; 10:34) yet extend to his beloved people and even to all nations (11:17)? To adapt God's question to Ezekiel, "Can this withered fig tree live again?" In turn, we might appropriate Ezekiel's wistful answer in responding to Mark's Jesus: "O Lord GOD, only You know" (Ezek 37:3 NJPS; cf. CEB).

As it happens, Jesus redirects Peter's and other disciples' attention from the withered fig tree *to God* and to possibilities that "faith in God" might open up—faith that Jesus commands them to "have" (*echete* [plural imperative], Mark 11:22). Most translations and interpreters assume that that "God" (*theou*) is the *object* of "faith" (*pistin*)—hence: "Have faith *in/toward* God (*pistin theou*)." A trustful relationship with God keeps hope alive, since "for God all things are possible" (10:27; cf. 9:23; 14:36). But Jesus may also point to God as faith-full *subject*, meaning that he exhorts his associates to "hold to the faithfulness *of* God"—that is, count on the steadfast love of God for God's fickle people to never let them go, to always draw them back and lift them up.

As if he hasn't jolted his followers enough, Jesus hits them with a staggering example of faith in action that *they* can effect if they wholeheartedly "believe" (*pisteuē*): "If you say to this mountain, 'Be taken up and thrown into the sea' . . . it will be done for you" (11:23). By any reckoning, this is an odd proposition. Rome's corps of engineers moved great mounds of earth to construct highways and buildings (Henderson 2018, 1852) yet would not normally dump the dirt into a river or sea. More to the point, why on earth would the disciples (or anyone) want to catapult a mountain into the sea? Even if one had supernatural power to remove a mountain obstacle from one's path, why not smash it flat in place instead of send it careening into the sea, wreaking havoc on the environment? This devastation would far outstrip the withering of a single fig tree. It seems safe to assume that Jesus continues to operate in dramatic-symbolic mode (he's not in the earth-moving business), but what is he getting at in this wild image?

Isaiah again provides a key clue, picturing the restoration of God's scattered people as a construction project of smoothing and straightening the rough desert highway to the promised land by leveling the mountains, lifting the valleys, and untwisting the crooked paths. Thus "all flesh," not only Israel, "will see the salvation of God (*sōtērion tou theou*)," the restorative way that God personally leads and prepares (Isa 40:3-5 NETS). Luke quotes this Isaiah text and applies it to John the Baptist's proclamation of God's saving path blazed by Jesus Messiah (Luke 3:3-6, 15-17). So what appears as imagery of geological removal and ecological upheaval might signify a salutary re-creating or reordering of the world. But imagery can only be stretched so far. We still have to deal with Jesus's particular topographical references to "this mountain" and the sea, the latter of which has no counterpart in Isaiah 40.

En route from Bethany near the Mount of Olives to the temple site associated with Mount Zion, Jesus could be thinking of either of these or any other mountains in the Judean hill country. He doesn't identify "this mountain" by name. Following his disruptive demonstration in the temple the previous day, Jesus may particularly have in view the temple mount "as a figure for the unbelieving temple system" (Marshall 1989, 169) destined for dismantlement, even destruction (Ortlund 2018). But even if Mark's Jesus has a prescient eye to the temple's demolition by Rome, this will be entirely a land siege (no naval battles, no sinking anything in the sea), and, more to the point, Jesus's disciples will have nothing to do with it. He is talking emphatically and directly to them: "Truly I tell *you* (*hymin*), if *you* say to this mountain . . ." (11:23). Even if they could, why would they want to drown the temple mount or obliterate it by any other means?

Suggesting that Jesus and/or Mark intend to *replace* or *supplant* the temple institution with the faith community of disciples (Marshall 1989, 159–69) doesn't hold historically or ideologically. The book of Acts depicts the commitment of Jesus's earliest followers to daily worship, prayer, and fellowship *in the temple* as well as in their homes (Acts 2:46; 3:1; 5:42). To be sure, after the devastation of 70 CE, various Jewish groups (not only Christ-believers) had to reassess the place of the temple in Jewish life and reconfigure worship patterns and practices. But faith in God and faithfulness to God persisted after Rome's razing of Jerusalem and the temple as it did after Babylon's conquest in the sixth century BCE. Ultimately the God of the universe "does not live in shrines made by human hands" (Acts 17:24), including the magnificent temple in Jerusalem (1 Kgs 8:27; Isa 57:15; 66:1-2; Mark 14:58; Acts 7:48-50). Even so, the high value of this temple—when rightly managed—as the focal center of Israel's covenantal relationship with God should not be depreciated. In Jewish thought, the temple is no disposable object or replaceable part. Precisely because of the temple's glorious history and purpose, its leaders merit rebuke when they betray its God-centered mission, and it remains worth rebuilding when it crumbles. Later, priestly leaders claim that Jesus himself spoke of rebuilding the temple in some form (Mark 14:58; 15:29), though the reliability of their secondhand testimony is suspect.

In any case, rather than presuming a strict temple replacement agenda beyond Mark's story (the temple still stands at the end, albeit with a torn curtain [15:38]), we look within the narrative for interpretive clues to Jesus's teaching about faith connected with images of throwing (*ballō*) objects into the sea.

- Jesus drove the herd of Legion-infested pigs into the sea (5:13), symbolizing, as a political drama, the drowning of Roman troops, not of the Jewish temple, whose demolition will be carried out *by* Roman armies! Further, this episode signaled Jesus's non-military, spiritual resistance movement against death-dealing evil forces. Whatever the current temple system's failings, it is not demonic or imperialistic.
- The father of the convulsive boy reported that an evil spirit had often seized his son and "cast/threw (*ebalen*) him into the water, to destroy him" (9:22). In turn Jesus expelled the demon, but not before rebuking the "*faithless* (*apistos*) generation" who had proven unable to help the child (9:19). As discussed above, Jesus cast a wide net in indicting those with deficient faith, including the scribes, the boy's father, the crowd—and his own faith-challenged disciples, who tried and *failed* to cast out the tormenting spirit.
- Unfortunately, however, the disciples proved to be not only limited in operative faith on behalf of an afflicted boy but also oblivious to the "greatest" work of serving little children (9:33-37) and obstructive to "little ones who believe/trust (*pisteuontōn*)" (9:42), including infants brought to Jesus for blessing (10:13-16. Recall Jesus's "indignant" rebuke of his disciples (10:14-15) and stern warning to them for blocking little ones' access to him and to God's nurturing kingdom (10:14-15): "If any of you put a stumbling block before one these little ones who believe in me, it would be better for you if a great millstone were hung around your neck and *you were thrown into the sea (beblētai eis tēn thalassan)*" (9:42).

All three cases—demonized pigs driven into the sea, a demon throwing a boy into the water, disciples thrown into the sea with a millstone noose—present frightening pictures of destruction. The last case is the most relevant to Jesus's present image of a mountain being "thrown into the sea" (*blēthēti eis tēn thalassan*) (11:23) because of almost identical language, common use of metaphor (millstone/mountain; the two demon cases are "real" events), and shared focus on disciples—*except* with a notable shift from what Jesus proposes as judgment *for* his disciples to what he suggests as action taken *by* them. On the one hand, if they block believing little ones' path, *the disciples themselves* deserve to plunge to the depths of the sea; on the other hand, if they trust in God wholeheartedly, they have the power to hurl mountain-sized obstacles out of their and others' ways into the sea.

The colossal millstone necklace and flying mountain images are fantastically figurative—but instructionally forceful all the same. Mark's Jesus cares passionately about breaking down barriers that block free and open access to God's restorative and flourishing realm. And he doesn't care whom he challenges as obstructers of this way, if the shoe (or millstone!) fits their character and conduct: demonic spirits, imperial forces, temple leaders and workers, his own apostles and followers—anyone who fails to serve God's mission of justice, love, and mercy. By the same token, Jesus persists in proclaiming good news of repentance and faith to anyone or any group, allowing them, if they will, to change their hearts, minds, and ways in harmony with God's realm (1:14-15). He does not engage in partisan politics, even on behalf of his own "Messiah Party," as his ambitious disciples might call it. Jesus serves God and seeks to bring God's right-making rule to all people. If he favors any "special interests," it would be those of the broken and beaten down; if he shows partiality, it would be to the poor and peripheral.

So how can Jesus's disciples bolster their faithful response to God's faithful love in order to remove barriers—not least their own—to God's highway of salvation? Answer: through *prayer* (11:24). Just as the disciples could only cast out the sinister spirit that seized the boy "through prayer" (9:28-29) and just as the temple managers can only put God's sacred house in order by recommitting themselves to uphold the temple's chief purpose as a "house of prayer" (11:17), so again Jesus's disciples can only advance God's way in a rocky and crooked world as a prayerful community seeking God's guidance regarding the right paths to follow and the right means to make it through "mountain"-like obstacles.

And, Jesus hastens to add, such prayer must coordinate with *forgiveness* toward all: "Whenever you stand praying, forgive, if you have anything against anyone" (11:25). The ultimate goal of prayer is restoration and reconciliation, not retribution and annihilation. Although the Bible has a strain of imprecatory (curse) prayers against oppressors (Pss 7:6-16; 10:12-16; 17:13-14; 59:4-13; 69:22-28; 83:1-18; 94:1-23), it also trumpets compassion and forgiveness at the core of God's divine nature (Exod 34:6-7; Num 14:18-19; Neh 9:16-17; Pss 86:14-15; 103:8-14; 145:8-9; Joel 2:12-14; Jonah 4:1-2). In the present Markan scene, Jesus tempers his destructive tree-cursing and mountain-drowning images with a final call for prayerful forgiveness. Nicholas Perrin thus misses the mark in proposing that Jesus "is issuing a warrant to pray against the Mount-Zion-based temple elite who would . . . soon be hounding his followers for decades to come" (2018, 186). Jesus does not urge his disciples to pray *against* anyone but rather to pray *for* forgiveness for anything they might have "*against* anyone, so that your Father in heaven may also forgive you your trespasses" (Mark 11:25). At the end of his article, however, Perrin hits the bull's-eye, nicely summarizing Jesus's urgent challenge to his followers "to double down in maintaining their faith, persisting in prayer, and forgiving 'anyone' (11:25), even their fiercest enemies" (2018, 187).

Temple Debates (11:27–12:44)

When Jesus next enters the temple arena, we can imagine, on the one hand, the authorities not drawing an easy breath and, on the other hand, the crowds waiting with bated breath. Will he launch another disruptive demonstration? Will he continue to mesmerize the people with his teaching and strike fear into the temple officials' hearts, threatening their leadership on their turf (11:18; cf. 11:32; 12:12)? As it happens, except for one instance where Jesus calls out the scribes to the "delight" of the "large crowd" (12:37), various groups initiate debate with him while "he was walking" (11:27) or "teaching in the temple" (12:35)—but not making any big dramatic moves. Again, with one notable exception (12:28-34), various interrogators seek "to trap" (12:13) Jesus into voicing some incendiary or traitorous opinion. They effectively stage a pre-trial in the temple in hopes of provoking a decisive capital trial before Jewish and Roman judges.

At every point Jesus responds calmly, cleverly, and courageously, often posing critical counter questions before delivering potent punch lines that set his interlocutors back on their heels. This section features five debate sessions, charted below, intermitted by Jesus's final parable in Mark (12:1-12) and capped off by his critique of scribes and wealthy temple supporters (12:38-44) (see pg. 207).

Jesus, John the Baptist, and authority (11:27-33)

The opening salvo comes from the cadre of chief priests, scribes, and elders concerned about the source of Jesus's authoritative activity: "By what authority are you doing these things?" (11:28)—with particular reference no doubt to the boisterous "things" Jesus did in the temple the day before. From the outset of his ministry, Mark's Jesus has demonstrated remarkable authority (*exousia*) to teach, to expel demons, and to forgive sins beyond the authority exercised by the scribes (1:21-28; 2:5-11). Such authoritative displays raised the eyebrows of certain groups, including scribes who aligned Jesus with Beelzebul/Satan (3:22-27) and his own hometown folk who "took offense" at his high-powered ways (6:2-4).

By now in Mark's story, it should be obvious that Jesus's authority comes directly from God. If people still resist that authority, it is unlikely that they will be convinced by further arguments. And the fact is, Jesus does not try to argue the point directly but rather turns the tables on his questioners by demanding that they first answer his question, which surprisingly turns the

	Debate #1, 11:27-33	Debate #2, 12:13-17	Debate #3, 12:18-27	Debate #4, 12:28-34	Debate #5, 12:35-37
Main Issue	Authority	Taxes	Resurrection	Commandments	Messiah
Debate Opponents	Chief priests, scribes, and elders *v.* Jesus	Pharisees and Herodians *v.* Jesus	Sadducees *v.* Jesus	***One sympathetic scribe *with* Jesus	Jesus *v.* Scribes
Key Question	By what authority are you [Jesus] doing these things?	Is it lawful to pay taxes to the emperor, or not?	Whose wife will she be? For the seven [men] had married her.	Which commandment is the first of all?	David himself calls him Lord; so how can he be his son?
Key Figure	John the Baptist	Caesar	Moses	The Lord our God	David
Jesus's Punch Line	Neither will I tell you by what authority I am doing these things.	Give to the emperor the things that are the emperor's, and to God the things that are God's.	He is God not of the dead, but of the living; you are quite wrong.	The first is: "You shall love the Lord your God." The second is this: "You shall love you neighbor as yourself."	***Jesus initiates the debate here: his question is the punch line.

focus from his authority to John the Baptist's: "Did the baptism of John come from heaven, or was it of human origin?" (11:29-30). Other than pushing his opponents off balance, why does Jesus bring John back into the picture now, after John's beheading by Herod in chapter 6?

Consider these possibilities. First, recall that John's "baptism" was fundamentally "a baptism of *repentance*" (1:4), stressing the need for God's people—not least their leaders—to change their hearts, minds, and wills to walk in God's true way blazed by Jesus Messiah. Unfortunately, the present leadership remains entrenched in their opposition to Jesus, with little openness to reform, unlike Jesus himself who has not only continued to proclaim John's message of repentance (1:14-15) but also demonstrated a willingness to change and expand his own horizons (7:24-30).

Second, John's popularity with the common people as a true prophet authorized by God threatened the status of insecure authorities. As Herod "feared John" (6:19) but still arrested him and conceded to having him killed

(6:17-28), so the chief priests and cohorts challenged by Jesus "were afraid of the crowd, for all regarded John as truly a prophet" (11:32)—as they now regard Jesus who was baptized and heralded by John!

Third, by posing to the temple leaders a clear-cut choice of heavenly *versus* human origin for John's authority—which they refuse to make (if they answer "from heaven," they indict themselves for not supporting John; if they say "of human origin," the crowd will erupt [11:31-32])—Jesus undercuts this choice. God's realm intersects, not dissects, heaven-and-earth, divine-and-human. John the Baptist sought to bring God to the people and the people to God in renewed communion. And he prepared the way for the "more powerful" one (1:7) to come, "Jesus Christ, the Son of God" (1:1)—stronger in Spirit-power (1:8), God's power in-Spirited within Jesus: the very incarnation, not segregation, of heavenly-and-human being.

While these perspectives may underlie Jesus's counter-question concerning John's authority, the direct point he makes is a non-point. He refuses to reveal "by what authority I am doing these things" (11:33), as if authority is beside the point, particularly establishment authority that the leaders seem so intent on protecting. As theologian Paul Tillich stresses in his incisive sermon on Luke's parallel scene,

> There is something in the Christian message which is opposed to established authority. . . . That which makes an answer [to the question in Luke 20:2//Mark 11:28] impossible is the nature of an authority which derives from God and not man. The place where God gives authority to a man [human being] cannot be circumscribed. (Tillich 2005 [1955], 88)

Authority is God's business. All creation, not least all humanity, is called to serve the one God who graciously exercises divine authority with perfect love. Sadly, when human beings push their authority, it tends to serve their own selfish interests at others' expense. Too often, as Jesus highlights in the next scene, authoritarians use violent means to promote and protect their interests.

Parable interlude: violent tenants and the beloved son (12:1-12)

Although the parable Jesus now spins breaks the intense question-and-answer mode of debate, it is not designed to lighten the mood. Jesus continues to press the issue of authority by presenting a horror tale depicting the violent misuse of authority by greedy managers.

The story features a landowner who "planted a vineyard" and made every effort to secure its commercial success, protecting it from predators with a surrounding fence and towering watch post and providing an onsite winepress for processing the grapes (12:1). So far so good—until everything turns sour when the vineyard owner leases out his estate to tenant managers while he is out of the country (a common business model in the ancient world). In the landlord's absence, the tenants in charge of the vineyard take advantage of their delegated authority to pad their own pockets. When a slave-agent comes at harvest time to collect the owner's profit, per the arranged contract, the tenants beat the agent and "sent him away empty-handed" (12:3). Patient and optimistic to a fault, the landlord sends two more agents. Again the tenants respond with violence, physically assaulting and verbally deriding the first agent and killing the second one (12:4-5)! Finally, the vineyard owner sends "a beloved son," thinking that he would surely command the tenants' "respect." But they see this as their golden opportunity to take over the estate by killing the heir (12:6-8). The death of his beloved son is the last straw for the owner, pushing him to "destroy the tenants and give the vineyard to others" (12:9).

Again Jesus draws on familiar horticultural images of God's relationship with Israel, now focused on grapevines rather than fig trees. God's "love song" for "my beloved" people symbolized as a vineyard in Isaiah 5:1-7 most closely parallels Jesus's parable (Weren 1998; Evans 2003; Snodgrass 2008, 287–95). Along with the "beloved" reference, Isaiah's Song of the Vineyard matches Jesus's story in terms of the owner's (God's) planting the vineyard, digging around it, "buil[ding] a watchtower in the midst of it," and "hew[ing] out a wine vat"—all to a futile end provoking the landlord's retribution (Isa 5:1-2). But there is also a critical difference. In Isaiah's poem, the *people*—as the beloved vineyard—yield only "wild grapes" of injustice and "bloodshed" and thus face disastrous judgment, including the demolition of "its wall" of protection (Isa 5:2-7). In Jesus's parable, however, the *tenant managers* of the vineyard—which itself produces good grapes—incur the owners' wrath for their violent, rapacious conduct, culminating in the murder of the "beloved son."

These tenant managers represent Israel's leaders who are failing miserably, in Jesus's view, in their mission to nurture God's people. That much is obvious: even the officials themselves "realized that [Jesus] had told this parable *against them*" (12:12). But the way that Jesus denounces the authorities in this case—via a parabolic narrative drama with multiple characters—suggests several more subtle points that Jesus aims to score.

Tenant managers. Comparing the Jerusalem hierarchs to vineyard laborers is both instructive and insulting. On the one hand, it reinforces their vocation as stewards of God's house, land, and people. They are not proprietors but ministers entrusted with caring for God's saving realm in accord with God's sacred will. On the other hand, while chief priests and other high-level temple authorities might give lip service to being God's servants, they would bristle at being imaged as tenant workers, not only because Jesus depicts them as *wicked* tenants but also because of their aristocratic status as wealthy estate owners who had tenant farmers and other servants working for them (see Hanson and Oakman 1998, 117–19)!

Stone builders. Although Jesus mainly paints an agricultural picture in this parable, he also uses landscape and architectural elements, such as the landowner's digging a pit for the winepress and building a watchtower for his vineyard (12:1) or, more accurately, contracting to have this work done. In Jesus's commentary on the parable, he refers to construction workers themselves, specifically stubborn "builders" who refuse to use the best stone materials. He quotes Psalm 118:22-23, which casts these builders as obstructers (anti-constructors) of access into God's saving sanctuary (cf. 118:19-21). This text comes just before the people's plea for salvation ("Hosanna!") and blessing of "the one who comes in the name of the LORD" to God's house (118:25-26)—which the crowd recently sang in honor of King Jesus's entry into Jerusalem en route to scoping out the temple area (Mark 11:9-11). Jesus thus seems to reinforce his critique of the current temple leaders, imaging them as both exploitative tenants of God's people and obstructive builders of God's house (renowned for its magnificent stonework [see 13:1]). Further, the reference to a singular rejected stone suggests an allusion to Israel's chosen king in Psalm 118 and to Jesus Messiah, God's "beloved son" in the parable (Mark 12:6), whom the temple establishment spurned.

We must not miss, however, the dominant hopeful theme sounded in Psalm 118:22-23 echoed by Jesus and overriding his polemical tone. The good news, "amazing in our eyes," is that God has worked ("this is the Lord's doing") to make the rejected stone the *cornerstone*—either the capstone or foundation stone (Eaton 2005, 405)—of the entire structure. Despite the bullheadedness and blockade of some leaders, God's rule through God's Messiah will ultimately survive and thrive.

Beloved son. Although Jesus does not typically cast himself as a character in his parables, the "beloved son" in this story (Mark 12:6) clearly represents Jesus, previously affirmed by God's own voice at his baptism and transfiguration as "my Son, the Beloved" (1:11; 9:7). The killing of the parable's beloved son by self-aggrandizing vineyard tenants corresponds with Jesus's prediction that he will be "handed over to chief priests and scribes, and they will condemn him to death" (10:33).

The tenants' acknowledgment (though not acceptance) of the son as the rightful heir of the father's estate (12:7) hints at Jesus's role as the messianic heir of God's realm, a royal "son of God," to invoke another psalm, destined to rule first on "Zion, my holy hill" and from there all the "nations . . . and the ends of the earth" (Ps 2:6-8). The son's premature death in the parable means that he won't inherit or rule anything, but that is not the whole story for God's Son, whose rejection by religious and political authorities will give way to *resurrection* as Lord of life (10:34) and to *reconstruction* as the cornerstone of God's kingdom (12:10-11).

Nevertheless, within the bounds of the parable, the future of the vineyard remains ambiguous. The dead son cannot inherit the estate, and the father's eventual judgment against the wicked tenant managers eliminates the workforce. The parable simply ends by stating that the landowner will "give the vineyard to others (*allois*)" (12:9). But who are they?

The "others." Perhaps these "others" don't matter. Jesus primarily warns the present Jerusalem leaders that *they* don't matter as much as they think they do. They are not exempt from faithful adherence to God's law. They are not indispensable or irreplaceable ministers of God if they fail to live up to their high calling. "Others," any "others," can carry on the work.

Nonetheless, if we venture to identify the "others" more specifically, Jesus may have in mind two broad groups: first, all those who accept (not reject) Jesus as God's Son and Messiah; second, *Gentile* believers in Christ more particularly (Iverson 2012). The first option corresponds with a Pauline view of inheritance in which all believers enjoy the full benefits of God's household as adopted children, "heirs of God and joint heirs with Christ" (Rom 8:16-17; cf. Gal 3:26-29). The second option aligns with the multinational scope of Israel's mission envisioned in the Isaiah text proclaimed by Jesus in the temple—"My house shall be called a house of prayer for all peoples/nations" (Isa 56:7; Mark 11:17)—and in Jesus's ultimate missionary agenda: "And the good news must first be proclaimed to all nations" (13:10).

Jesus, Caesar, and taxes (12:13-17)

Fuming and frustrated about Jesus's showing them up before the temple crowd, the priestly officials slink away (12:12) and shift their tactics to undermine Jesus's authority and popularity. They now send a team of Pharisee and Herodian allies (12:13; cf. 3:6; 8:15) to entrap Jesus into making some gaffe about tax payments to Caesar, a controversial issue guaranteed to offend some party among the Roman authorities or Jewish people or both. But before posing their loaded tax question, they use a common rhetorical technique known as "benevolent capture" (*captatio benevolentiae*) or "cordial hypocrisy" (Solomon and Flores 2001, 4, 13, 36, 58–59, 113, 121), designed to disarm opponents with false flattery before challenging them. In the present case, Jesus's interrogators lay it on thick: "Teacher, we know that you are sincere, and show deference to no one; for you do not regard people with partiality, but teach the way of God in accordance with truth" (12:14). Ironically, though they are anything but "sincere" in their flattery of Jesus, they speak the "truth" about Jesus's open and honest instruction about the "way of God."

The simple yes-no tax question—"Is it lawful to pay taxes to the emperor [Caesar, *Kaisari*], or not? Should we pay them, or should we not?" (12:14-15)—belies the complexity of the issue and seeks to elicit a sound bite to use against Jesus. If he says "Yes," he risks riling the people crushed under heavy taxation; if he says "No," he risks criminal charges for tax evasion under Roman law (Leander 2016, 273–75). "Knowing their hypocrisy" and sinister aims, Jesus refuses to take his questioners' bait but rather involves them in his response, which in turn "utterly amazed" (*exethaumazon*) them (12:17; cf. 12:11—"it is amazing [*thaumastē*] in our eyes"). Notice the quick-fire exchange and exhibition that Jesus controls from start to finish (12:15-17).

Jesus's Counter-Question and Command
"Why are you putting me to the test? Bring me a denarius and let me see it."
↓
Pharisees'/Herodians' Compliance
"And they brought it."
↓
Jesus's Leading Question
"Whose head is this, and whose title?"
↓
Pharisees'/Herodians' Answer
"The emperor's."
↓
Jesus's Punch Line
"Give to the emperor the things that are the emperor's, and to God the things that are God's."
↓
Pharisees'/Herodians' Awe
"And they were utterly amazed at him."

Jesus's order, "Bring me a denarius and let me see it," is a brilliant strategic move on several levels. A denarius—the common coin of the Roman realm with which subjects paid both annual head taxes and regular sales taxes on goods and services—is more than a simple prop for Jesus to show. The fact that he evidently has no coin of his own (cf. 6:8) and orders his questioners to "bring/offer" (*pherete*) him a denarius at once sets him apart from the oppressive Roman economic system represented by the coin, implicates his opponents in that system, and affords him the opportunity to disclose how he *sees* through the system ("let me see it" in 12:15 is not a throwaway phrase, though omitted in Matt 22:19//Luke 20:24). Moreover, delicious irony obtains in the Pharisees'/Herodians' offering Roman money *to Jesus*, as if he were king!

But Jesus repudiates this coin and everything it stands for, though he does so more subtly than a fellow first-century Galilean named Judas did. This Judas organized a tax resistance movement against Roman overlords on the grounds that such foreign imposts effectively enslaved God's people and blasphemed against the one true God. Predictably, Rome squashed this movement (Josephus, *Ant.* 18.3–9, 23–25; *J.W.* 2.118; Horsley and Hanson 1985, 190–92). Jesus shrewdly pushes his disputants to acknowledge the unjust and sacrilegious nature of Roman taxation by asking them—"Whose head [image, icon, *eikōn*] is this [on the coin], and whose title [inscription, *epigraphē*]?"—to which they tersely answer, "The emperor's [Caesar's, *Kaisaros*]" (12:16).

A typical denarius in Jesus's day featured the engraved head-image of Caesar ringed by the inscription "Tiberius Caesar Augustus, son of the Divine Augustus." This is the only place in Mark's story where Caesar directly shows his face (Leander 2013, 273–75, 283); but while a denarius may seem to offer only a cold, lifeless metal face, it represents the corporate face of the imperial economic juggernaut: the supreme, "August" Econ-Icon. The denarius effectively functioned as the bestselling mini-idol to Caesar and as the top-trending meme throughout the empire. Not only every tax payment but also every transaction spat out the text message "Hail, Caesar"— a message diametrically opposed to the chief commands in sacred Scripture (inspired "Inscription") to worship the Lord God above all other so-called gods *without means of any graven images* (Exod 20:4; Deut 5:8). But here we are with some Pharisees supposedly devoted to Jewish law carrying and "offering" this oppressive, profane image *in the temple*, in *God's house*, which forbade the use of Roman currency in its operations. We might expect the wealthy Herodian politicians to play both sides of the coin, but not the Pharisees and scribes. As we will see, one scribe sympathizes wholeheartedly with

Jesus's viewpoint (12:28-34). But in the current case, these Pharisees incriminate themselves.

The terminology that the Pharisees and Herodians use for "paying taxes"—literally, "giving/paying a census" (*dounai kēnson*) (12:14)—is awkward. The Latin "census" became a loanword passing into Hebrew/Aramaic (*q-n-s*), Greek (*kēnsos*), and English (census). Roman emperors regularly ordered censuses to register individuals for tax assessments. But one paid *taxes*, not censuses; paying a census makes no sense. Greek lexicons gloss Mark's usage with definitions for *kēnsos* like "[Lat. census] 'the poll or head tax determined by the census'" (Danker and Krug 2009, 200); but technically Mark uses the wrong word, as Luke recognizes and changes to *phoros*, a standard word for "tribute, tax" paid to Rome (Luke 20:22).

Yet Mark's supposed linguistic error may intentionally signal a bigger point about the scope of Rome's domination—reaching not only into every subject's pocket but into the whole fabric of their lives. As Hans Leander astutely comments,

> Since the information that was gathered far exceeded what was necessary for the levying of taxes, the *census* was more than a financial endeavor; it communicated Rome's ultimate ownership of the land and property. A *census* therefore involved a more penetrating enterprise than the perpetual collecting of money and/or goods. . . . the *census* encroached upon social life in a way that was both greater and more enduring than simple physical interference. (2013, 279–280 [emphasis original])

So what does Jesus have to say, not simply about tax matters but about Caesar's entire rule and realm? Enter one of Jesus's most memorable and oft-quoted statements: "Give to the emperor the things that are the emperor's, and to God the things that are God's" (Mark 12:17). Or more succinctly, reflecting Greek word order, "Give Caesar Caesar's things and God God's things." Although commonly interpreted as endorsing civic duty and governmental support, proving that it doesn't contravene primary devotion to God, this statement packs more potential punch. From Jesus'—and the Pharisees'!—Jewish perspective, *all things* belong to God, the Creator of heaven and earth (also implied in the parable of the tenants). That leaves Caesar and everyone else irrespective of their place in society with *nothing* except what God has given them in sacred trust. And what has Caesar done except usurp God's authority and violate God's trust? To contemporize his scheme, he has recast coinage in his name and image, replacing "In God We Trust" with "In Caesar We Trust."

What should Caesar get then? What is due him, what he deserves, his just deserts—which open up a world of protest options without specifying the means of protest, though we should again stress that Jesus never advocates violent reprisals. Still, Jesus by no means lets Caesar off the hook. Pay Caesar his due. Pay him back according to his deeds and edicts in accord with God's sovereign will and your calling to be God's faithful people.

Jesus, Moses, and resurrection (12:18-27)
As if in a tag-team match, the Pharisees and Herodians give way to "some Sadducees" who step into the temple ring to fuel a fresh line of debate with Jesus. The hot topic shifts from the financial and political arena of taxation to the familial and theological sphere of marriage and resurrection. We might invoke Benjamin Franklin's famous quip that "in this world nothing can be said to be certain but death and taxes" as a truism in first-century Roman Judea as much as in colonial America—and in our world today. Concerning mortality, the inexorable reality of death continues to spark endless interest in the afterlife, including details of heavenly life.

What does the Bible have to say about such matters? Alas, not as much as we might like or what is often presumed in popular thought (see Wright 2008). But the Scripture remains foundational for instruction about life and death and provides common ground for discussion between Jesus and fellow Jews. We meet the Sadducees for the first and only time in Mark. The limited evidence we have on this group suggests members "were drawn from the governing class and aristocrats in Jerusalem" (Saldarini 2001, 304). Their name possibly derived from Zadok, the high priest during the reigns of David and Solomon, and the book of Acts indicates that the chief temple priests in the first century were Sadducees (Acts 4:1; 5:17). In terms of scriptural authority, the Sadducees focused on the written Torah in Genesis–Deuteronomy (Pentateuch), as did all faithful Jews; but they were less interested, it seems, than the Pharisees in other parts of the Bible (like the Prophets and Psalms) and in codifying oral traditions. Also unlike the Pharisees, the Sadducees did not believe in unseen spirits (angels, demons), divine providence, or the general resurrection of dead bodies—this last issue is front and center in the present debate with Jesus (see Acts 23:6-10; Josephus, *Ant.* 13.293, 297–98; 18:16–17; *J.W.* 2.164–65; Saldarini 2001, 107–23, 298–308). They were firmly focused on this world rather than the one to come, this current world in which they enjoyed considerable wealth and status. Still, to maintain their position they had to tread cautiously, careful not to unduly offend Roman overlords or the Pharisees who remained popular with the people (*Ant.* 18.17).

Jesus has also proved to be popular, but he's a Galilean maverick leading an upstart movement that can still be nipped in the bud—or so this Sadducean group thinks. They try to discredit Jesus by exposing the foolishness, as they see it, of his pro-resurrection stance. They propose a hypothetical scenario concerning the heavenly marital status of a serial widow wedded to a succession of seven brothers in her earthly life. Here's the crux: "In the resurrection whose wife will she be?" (Mark 12:23). The situation is not as absurd as it may appear to us. The Torah endorses the custom of levirate remarriage for vulnerable childless widows: the widow's brother-in-law (*levir*) was responsible for marrying her and, if possible, having children by her in her dead husband's name (Deut 25:5-10; cf. Genesis 38; Ruth 4:9-10). The prospect of this happening seven times to one woman may be exceptional, but in a society where men, whose life expectancy averaged around forty, typically married much younger women, it was not uncommon for women to be widowed multiple times.

In any event, Jesus does not quibble about the social propriety of the case on earth but rather about its *scriptural accuracy* and *theological potency* in heaven. He minces no words this time, framing his response with a double denunciation: starting with "you are wrong" (*planasthe*, 12:24) and ending with the extra flourish, "you are *quite* wrong" (*poly planasthe*, 12:27)—dead wrong on many levels (*poly*-wrong). And the Sadducees' wrongness particularly manifests in ignorance: "you know neither the scriptures nor the power of God" (12:24).

To enlighten them, Jesus begins by invalidating the premise of the proposed afterlife scenario, since the community of resurrected persons will not have marital relations but rather be asexual, "like angels in heaven" (12:25). Though this view was not unusual in Jewish thought, it is not explicitly supported by the Torah or any other part of the Hebrew Bible; accordingly, Jesus does not dwell on this matter. He focuses more on the fundamental reality of resurrected life certified by the living God than on particular features of that life. To be sure, the Hebrew Bible also does not say much about a general resurrection to eternal life (though the theme of God's victory over death is prominent; see Levenson 2006; Madigan and Levenson, 2008). The clearest supporting text is Daniel 12:2—"Many of those who sleep in the dust of the earth shall awake, some to everlasting life, and some to shame and everlasting contempt." But being outside the Torah, the book of Daniel probably carried less weight with the Sadducees.

So Jesus appeals to a watershed event in the Torah—"the story about the bush," the famous burning bush through which God revealed God's special name and identity to Moses (Mark 12:26; Exod 3:13-15). In that story, God announces, "I am the God of Abraham, the God of Isaac, and the God of Jacob," the God of Israel's founding fathers, all dead and buried by Moses' time. But not irrevocably dead and gone! God must have raised them to new life in God's living presence. Otherwise, why would God use the present tense, "*I am* the God of Abraham"? God's eternal aliveness and dynamic activity as Creator, Redeemer, and Re-Creator constitutes the very essence of God's being, the ever and always "I AM" (Exod 3:14), from first to last the God of life, the God "of the living" (Mark 12:27).

Jesus, God, and the commandments to love (12:28-34)
When Jesus's next questioner is introduced as "one of the scribes [who] came near and heard them disputing," we naturally expect him to continue the oppositional debate with Jesus. Yet this is no stereotypical scribal adversary of Jesus. First, he scores the preceding round as a win for Jesus, judging that Jesus "answered [the Sadducees] *well* (*kalōs*)" (12:28). Then, after posing his non-confrontational question to Jesus, he affirms Jesus's correct answer: "*Well* (*kalōs*) *said*, Teacher; you have *truthfully*" spoken (12:32 CEB). In turn, after this scribe comments further on the issue at hand, Jesus commends him for speaking "wisely" and being "not far from the kingdom of God" (12:34).

In this section dominated by conflict and mistrust, this congenial exchange seems too good to be true. That appears to be Matthew's view as he changes Mark's scribe (*grammateus*) into a Pharisee "lawyer" (*nomikos*) who comes to "test" Jesus and finally gives no response, yea or nay, to Jesus's answer (Matt 22:34-40). But Mark's positive portrayal of this scribe should not be dismissed as naïve or misguided. Mark has no illusions about Jesus winning over the religious-political establishment and avoiding arrest and death. But in the midst of tension and suspicion, Mark holds out *hope* of change based on commitment to the bedrock commandments of *love* for God and neighbor mutually affirmed by the scribe and Jesus.

In response to the scribe's sincere question, "Which commandment is the first of all?" (12:28)—a question designed to override side issues (like marital arrangements in heaven) by attending to the most important matters—Jesus responds by reaffirming God's oneness, as he did with the rich seeker (10:18), and the Torah's mandate to "love the Lord your God with all your heart (*kardias*), and with all your soul (*psychēs*), and with all your mind (*dianoias*), and with all your strength (*ischyos*)" (12:29-30; cf. Deut 6:4-5). Mark's version of this top-priority command calls for a holistic bond of love with God "with all" (*ex holēs*) of one's integrated emotional-volitional-mental-physical being, a view of the unitary, interpersonal self supported by contemporary biological and social-science research (Siegel 2017; Green 2008; Palmer 2011, 49–57).

The "strength" (*ischys*) component (omitted in Matt 22:37) of love is particularly telling, coming from Jesus the "Stronger One" (*ischyroteros*, Mark 1:7) who liberates those bound in the clutches of the Satanic "strong man" and his evil cohorts (3:26-27). Love is the strongest force in the universe, rivaled only by death (Song 8:6). Only God's love and love for God can redeem mortal beings from the life-sapping power of death and death-dealing "strong men."

But love's saving strength flows not only from and to God but also through God's people to one another. God's strong men and women show their strength above all through love, especially to those most weak and vulnerable. Without being asked to provide another great commandment, Jesus nonetheless adds a second: "You shall love your neighbor as yourself" (Mark 12:31). This is not a separate mandate but an extension of the first, the other side of the love coin. Loving God and neighbor go hand in hand; you can't honestly do one without the other (see 1 John 3:11-21; 4:7-20; 5:2). These two—together—constitute the greatest commandment (Mark 12:31).

Such prioritizing of the dual love commandment is embracive, not reductive. Love for God and love for people encompass all Ten Commandments and all other Torah stipulations; love is the motivational (emotive) force driving all just legal systems (Nussbaum 2013; Marshall 2012; Wolterstorff 2011). By stressing the primacy of love, Jesus by no means seeks to reduce, still less to replace, Jewish law. Rather, in terms echoed by other Jewish teachers of the time, Jesus pinpoints holistic love—as intention, emotion, ideation, and action—as the main way to fulfill the entire law. The scribe currently engaging Jesus couldn't agree more as he repeats Jesus's answer virtually verbatim with a reinforcing addendum: "this [dual love commandment] is much more important than all whole burnt offerings and sacrifices," that is, temple rituals for their own sake (12:33; cf. Hos 6:6; Mic 6:6-8).

In turn, Jesus concludes this exchange with an encouraging word for this "wise" scribe: "You are not far from the kingdom of God" (12:34). But why commend the scribe in a way that seems to leave him short, though not by much, of full participation in God's realm? Is this another case like that of the good rich man who comes close to God's loving way but *lacks one thing* that will bring him all the way (10:21-22)? So we wait for Jesus to drop the other shoe with the scribe. But this time Jesus has nothing further to say. Being "not far" from God's kingdom coincides with the dynamic, developing dimension of God's work in Christ—already operative but "not yet" culminated, "near"

(1:15; 13:28-29) but not fully realized. Mark's Jesus thus effectively calls this scribe to the way of discipleship, the way of continuing growth, increasing insight, and persisting faithfulness in the things of God. Like Jesus himself, his followers must press on (go *far*ther) in the face of resistance from worldly authorities to realize the fullness of God's loving rule.

With Jesus's constructive discussion about the greatest commandment, the temple debates seem concluded in Jesus's favor: "After that no one dared to ask him any questions" (12:34). Love has the last word. Amen.

Jesus, David, and the Messiah (12:35-37)

Yet Jesus is not finished "teaching in the temple" or challenging the scribes as a problematic group (12:35, 38-40). He now initiates the questioning, though not directly. In a move designed to "delight" the common people naturally wary of scribal elites, Jesus asks *about* the scribes before a "large crowd," posing a tantalizing interpretive riddle or "word game" (Novenson 2017, 16, cf. 85–86): "How can the scribes say that the Messiah is the son of David," since the Spirit-inspired "David himself calls [the Messiah] Lord?" (12:35-37). Simply put, how can the Messiah be both David's *son* and *Lord*? The father has lordly authority over the son, not vice versa.

The issue turns on interpreting the Psalms, traditionally attributed to David as the Pentateuch was to Moses (cf. 12:19, 26). We've already heard the crowd singing from Psalm 118, praising the saving Messiah who "comes in the name of the Lord" to establish "the kingdom of our ancestor David" (Mark 11:9-10; Ps 118:25-26). The idea that the Messiah would be heir to David's throne was normative in early Jewish thought. The more particular relation of *sonship*, however, focused on the messianic king as *God's* son, epitomized in David himself. As Psalm 2 announces concerning "the LORD and his anointed . . . 'I have set my king on Zion.' . . . The LORD . . . said to me, 'You are my son; today I have begotten you'" (Ps 2:2, 6-7). In biblical royal theology, God is Israel's true and only King. David and his dynastic successors operate as anointed sons and servants to God the Father-King, not as independent ruling lords and sires of successive kings.

So back to Jesus's question: Why would David ever call his son *Lord*? Only God is Lord—the one Lord God worthy of loving devotion, as Jesus and the scribe just affirmed (Mark 12:30). To support his riddle, Jesus brings in yet another psalm—not Psalm 2 or 118 but 110—where "David . . . declared, 'The LORD says to my Lord, "Sit at my right hand"'" (Ps 110:1; Mark 12:36). As it happens, Psalm 110 says nothing about a *son*—God's or David's—or about an anointed messiah figure. Further, Joseph Fitzmyer notes, "There is simply no evidence of the Davidic messianic interpretation of Psalm 110 in pre-Christian Palestinian Judaism" (1985a, 1311; cf. Rowe 2009, 172). The writer of Hebrews uses this psalm to buttress belief in Jesus as the promised Messiah, but not through the royal Davidic line. Instead, Hebrews portrays Jesus as a *priestly* (and kingly) Messiah in the line of the mysterious figure *Melchizedek* by interpreting both Psalm 2:7 and 110:1 in light of 110:4, "You are a priest forever according the order of Melchizedek" (Heb 1:5, 13; 5:5-6; 7:17, 21-22; cf. 11Q13 in the Dead Sea Scrolls). Mark's Jesus, however, says nothing about Melchizedek.

If all this acrobatic maneuvering among the Psalms seems disorienting, that might just be the point of Jesus's son-lord riddle! How does one sort out these poetic portraits of God's anointed one? Scribes are supposed to be experts in unraveling such scriptural tangles, but good luck to them in sorting out the thorny question Jesus poses. Apart from his having a little "delightful" fun at the scribes' expense (12:37), Jesus seems to reinforce his earlier exposure of the temple leaders' ignorance of "the scriptures and the power of God" (12:24). Life-giving biblical interpretation, not least regarding God's liberating Messiah, is not some word game, textual puzzle, or secret code for clever experts to decipher. It is a dynamic process embodied in the person of Jesus Messiah, Son of God and Son of Humankind, and worked out in a confused and conflicted world by the incomparable wisdom and power of God.

Warning epilogue: exploitative scribes and exemplary widow (12:38-44)

Despite Jesus's congenial exchange with a singular scribe (12:28-34) and his somewhat playful riddling about the scribes (12:35-37), he concludes this teaching unit with an exposé of scribal malfeasance that the people should "beware" (12:38). Jesus warns that the scribes often act purely "for the sake of appearance"—for show, for showing off (12:40). Instead of loving and serving God and neighbor, they love and serve themselves, strutting about in elegant robes and craving public honor and prime places in marketplaces, synagogues, and banquet halls. Such pretentious, exhibitionist social behavior is bad enough in itself, but it becomes worse as it masks predatory financial schemes.

It's safe to say that such scribes would not give a poor person the robe off their backs (or travel without spare robes in their valises [cf. 6:8]). But Jesus particularly lambasts them for "devour[ing] widows' houses" (12:40). He also used the term for "devour" or "eat up" (*katesthiō*) in the parable of the soils to describe the birds' consumption of seeds scattered on the path—they "ate it up" (*katephagen*, 4:4)—typifying Satan's extraction of God's word from hardhearted hearers (4:15). As literate experts in law and finance, the scribes were in a unique position to help or harm vulnerable widows in managing their financial affairs, which their (now deceased) husbands had likely controlled. While many first-century widows were poor, some could have wealthy inheritances. In either case, then as now, settling an estate was a complex legal affair. Enter the unscrupulous scribal lawyers whom Jesus decries for taking advantage of widows and bilking them from their means of support (Spencer 1994; 2012, 266–93).

It doesn't get much worse than this in God's book: "The LORD your God . . . mighty and awesome . . . executes justice for . . . the widow" (Deut 10:18); God is "protector of widows" (Ps 68:5); "The LORD watches over the strangers; he upholds the orphan and the widow, but the way of the wicked he brings to ruin" (Ps 146:9). Reprehensibly, the widow-devouring scribes of Jesus's day align with the God-opposing "wicked." Jesus's "greater condemnation" of these scribes who should know better (Mark 12:40) continues in the train of Jeremiah's excoriating the overseers of God's house for "robbing" widows and other vulnerable people (Jer 7:5-6, 11; Mark 11:17).

Isaiah's designation of the temple as God's "house of prayer," which Jesus recently quoted alongside the "den of robbers" statement (Isa 56:7; Mark 11:17), also links with his upbraiding the scribes for their pretentious "long prayers" as a cover-up for insidiously shortchanging widows (12:40). The term for "long" (*makra*) can be temporal (long time), as here in characterizing the scribes' long-winded praying, or spatial (long distance), as when Jesus positioned the one perceptive scribe "not far (*makran*)" from God's realm (12:34). Ironically and shamefully, the long prayers of the widow-exploiting scribes signal their long way *from* God's just and merciful rule.

The next scene continues the concern for widows' financial status, as Jesus calls his disciples' attention to one particular widow putting a contribution into the temple "treasury" (*gazophylakion*), more specifically the "offering box" (L&N 1988, 71) or "collection box for the temple treasury" (12:41 CEB). The sanctuary had thirteen money "chests"—designated for different types of offerings—with horn-shaped openings for depositing coins (m. Šeqalim 6.5; BDAG 2000, 186). Tellingly, Jesus observes this woman among a stream of pilgrims making their donations, while he "sat down *opposite* the treasury" (12:41; cf. 13:3), perhaps signifying his opposition to the motives of some wealthy contributors. Now he juxtaposes the poor widow with "many rich people" (not just the scribes) who "were throwing in lots of money" (12:41 CEB). The more coins thrown into the offering "horn," the bigger clatter they make, trumpeting the generosity of the wealthy contributors for all to hear.

By contrast, the widow's offering of "two small copper coins (*lepta*)" would only make the tiniest tinkle. And it would scarcely register on the temple ledger. A *leptos* was the thinnest and smallest coin in circulation worth a "fraction of a cent" (Friberg, Friberg, and Miller 2000), 1/128 of a *denarius*, the daily wage for an ordinary laborer (BDAG 2000, 592; Black and Collins 2006, 1749). So this widow's "two cents' worth" is not even worth a single "penny" in monetary value.

But in Jesus's book, the poor widow's gift is worth *more* than all the offerings of the wealthy donors because she has given her *all*, literally: "Out of her poverty [she] has put in *everything* she had, *all* she had to live on" (12:43-44). This last phrase could be rendered, "She threw in her whole life" or "whole livelihood" (*holon bion*). She succeeds, we might say, where the basically good rich man failed in 10:22: this destitute woman gives all her financial resources to God's house for the benefit of poor people like her!

But is this a success story? Not entirely. While one side of the story lauds the widow's wholehearted devotion to God and trust in God's tender care, another side laments the failure of the priestly custodians and scribal accountants of God's treasury to use these resources to aid the needy, like this poor widow. In effect, this currently corrupt financial system potentially "robs" her of her last pennies (Wright 1982). Then what will become of her "life"? How can she sustain her "livelihood"? Mark freezes the widow's story at this telling moment at the temple's collection box. But we can imaginatively hope that the wider Jewish community, including Jesus's self-giving followers, would readily receive and care for her (see 10:28-31).

Mark My Words: Jesus's Prophecy

Mark 13:1-37

Once more Jesus exits the temple compound (13:1) and heads to his campsite at the Mount of Olives (13:3). But he will not visit the temple again or debate the religious-political leaders anymore. Jesus's position vis-à-vis the present temple institution becomes more oppositional, signified by his sitting down on the Mount of Olives directly "*opposite* (*katenanti*) the temple." He now concentrates on instructing his disciples "privately" (13:3; cf. 4:10, 34; 9:28-32).

The temporal focus of this teaching unit, compared with the previous two (4:1-34; 7:1-23), falls more on the future ("When will this be?" 13:4), although this lesson still has profound implications for the disciples' present attitudes and actions. Jesus casts his prophetic eye to the climactic "end" (*telos*, 13:3, 9) of the present age but with greater attention to current events leading up to the end than on the end itself ("What will be the sign that all these things are *about to be* accomplished?" 13:4). His tone modulates between ominous and optimistic, between warning and assuring. The warning signal reverberates in seven cautionary imperatives, including Jesus's very last word in this lengthy speech: "Keep awake (*grēgoreite*)" (13:37).

- *Beware* (*blepete*) that no one leads you astray (13:5).
- As for *yourselves* [*you*] *beware* (*blepete hymeis*), for they will hand you over (13:9).
- But [*you yourselves*] *be alert* (*hymeis blepete*); I have already told you everything (13:23).
- *Beware* (*blepete*) (13:33).
- *Keep alert* (*agrypneite*), for you do not know when the time will come (13:33).
- Therefore, *keep awake* (*grēgoreite*)—for you do not know when the master of the house will come (13:35).
- And what I say to you I say to all: *Keep awake* (*grēgoreite*) (13:37).

Jesus uses three similar verbs, all conveying an urgent sense of open-eyed alertness in the face of impending disaster and "great suffering" (13:19). But his ultimate purpose is to inspire saving hope and endurance, not fear and despair (13:13; Lawrence 2016, 95–97). To be forewarned is to be forearmed and "not alarmed" (13:6). We know that Jesus is keenly aware of his own imminent suffering, death, and resurrection after three days! But we also know how slow the disciples have been to grasp this destiny (8:31-33; 9:31-34; 10:32-37). Jesus now presses his associates further in order to prepare *them* for the trouble *they* can expect after Jesus's death. In two of the seven imperatives listed above, Jesus adds the emphatic second person plural pronoun: "You *yourselves* (*hymeis*) beware/be alert" (13:9, 23; Fowler 1991, 85). But at the same time he calls them to stay alert, he also compels them to rest assured in God's saving purpose realized through the guiding wisdom of the indwelling Holy Spirit (13:11) and the glorious power of the returning Son of Humankind (13:26-27).

Still, however, tension remains. In this revelatory teaching about end-time matters, not all is revealed. Some things remain unknown—even for Jesus, God's Son (13:32)—especially matters of timing, the "when" questions that have preoccupied Jesus's disciples (13:4) and countless other believers in Christ for over two millennia now. "About that day or hour"—the precise timetable of consummating God's messianic work—"no one knows . . . only the Father" (13:32; cf. Acts 1:6-7).

Another temporal tension concerns audiences. Throughout Mark's narrative, we negotiate two interwoven literary and historical levels of hearers/readers: (1) Jesus's audience of disciples and other characters within the time of the story and (2) Mark's audience of hearers/readers at the time of writing. A gap of some forty years (a generation) spans Level 1 (circa 30 CE) and Level 2 (circa 70 CE). Mark 13 makes this dual level explicit in a narrative aside to the reader ("let the reader understand," 13:14) and in Jesus's concluding universal application of his teaching: "What I say to you [disciples] I say to *all* (*pasin*)" (13:37). The "private" lesson to Jesus's closest followers (13:3) becomes public in Mark's written account.

A number of scholars regard the prophetic-apocalyptic discourse in Mark 13 as particularly shaped and targeted to Mark's first readers/hearers during the tumultuous period surrounding the Jewish revolt against Rome in 66–70 CE, culminating in Rome's destruction of Jerusalem and its temple (Collins 1996). Though it remains uncertain which revolutionary persons and events Mark may have in mind, the Jewish-Roman War provides the most probable context for interpreting Mark 13.

Stay Alert to Destructive Times (13:1-4)

This extended instruction to Jesus's disciples focuses on the "emotionally saturated space" of the temple (Lawrence 2016, 103), where Jesus has spent two intense days demonstrating against and debating with the authorities. As he exits the temple area, an unspecified disciple calls his attention ("Look, Teacher") to the spectacular one-of-a-kind "stones" and "buildings" that make up the entire temple complex (13:1). Jesus acknowledges these magnificent materials, even as he turns the issue back to the disciple: "Do you see these great buildings?" (13:2), that is, "Do you *perceive* their significance? Do you *understand* what they mean and what will happen to them?" (13:2; cf. 8:17-26).

Part of Herod the Great's temple renewal project, these "stones" included massive square limestone boulders weighing up to eighty tons, quarried, shaped, and fit together in an incredible feat of engineering (Ritmeyer 1989, 46–48; Josephus, *Ant.* 13.392–425). This temple thus stood as a seemingly impregnable monument to Herod's greatness and also, beyond Herod's self-glorifying aims, to the majesty and might of Israel's God. Yet Jesus dares to announce, following in the train of Jeremiah and other prophets, that these colossal stones will be dismantled and demolished. They will not stand forever; they will not protect the city or the people. However impressive, temple stone-blocks are inanimate objects—symbols of God's strong, abiding presence but *not* repositories of the living God. God is not encased in stone, not confined to temples "made with [human] hands" (cf. 14:58; Isa 66:1-2; Acts 7:48-50; 17:24-25). The true strength of an institution dedicated to serving God lies not in its physical structure but in the moral integrity of its leaders and members. Jesus's recent critiques of priestly and scribal officials have exposed the shaky ground on which the current temple institution rests. Now for the first time Jesus plainly forecasts the temple's total destruction!

The reference to dislodged temple stones evokes the psalmist's image of "the stone that the builders rejected," which Jesus evoked following the parable of the wicked tenants to reinforce his censure of temple leaders and to hint at his role as the "cornerstone" of God's work (Mark 12:10; Ps 118:25). But presently and elsewhere, Jesus never mentions his own involvement in the temple's destruction or reconstruction, as his accusers later falsely claim (Mark 14:57-59). The historical context suggests an ominous sensing of Rome's razing of Jerusalem and the temple, which occurred in 70 CE but was already on Jesus's (and others') radar and on the more immediate horizon of Mark's audience.

Naturally Jesus's prediction of the temple's destruction piqued his disciples' interest. Beyond the unidentified disciple who triggered Jesus's shocking comment, the first four disciples Jesus called—the fishermen Peter, James, John, and Andrew (1:16-20)—prove particularly curious about Jesus's ominous forecast (13:3). Specifically, they want a set schedule of events culminating in the temple's fall: "When will this be, and what will be the sign?" (13:4). Asking Jesus for a sign is risky, given his previous resistance to some Pharisees' request for a special "sign from heaven" (8:11-12). But here the four disciples are more interested in knowing the *earthly* signs pointing toward the temple's doom. Still, they ask Jesus "privately" (13:3), perhaps anticipating his rebuke of their question or trying to avoid distressing the entire group unduly. In any event, discussing the temple's devastation is dangerous political talk fraught with emotional angst.

Stay Alert to Deceptive Times (13:5-8)

As it happens, Jesus is willing to unveil various signs of troubling times to come, though notably, "Nothing in the ensuing prophecies of Mark 13 . . . has anything to do with the *destruction* of Jerusalem or the Temple" (Horsley 2001, 136 [emphasis added]). Jesus pulls back from his stark announcement of final collapse to more immediate and intermediate crises before "the end." Moreover, framing his comment that "the end is still to come" (13:7) are references to *beginnings*:

- "Then Jesus *began* (*ērxato*) to say to them" (13:5)—a signal in Mark that Jesus is about to disclose critical information to his followers (see 8:31; 10:32; Collins 1996, 13–14)
- "This is but the *beginning* (*archē*) of the birth pangs" (13:8)—honestly admitting the onset of painful times but also hopefully affirming these "pangs" as prelude to the *birth of new life* (see Mic 4:9-10; John 16:20-24; 1 Thess 5:3-5; Rohr 2021, 54–55)

Jesus offers both summary *descriptions* of the looming turbulent events and typical *reactions* to these disasters. The descriptions focus on military-political, geological, and agricultural upheavals: "wars and rumors of wars" between nations and kingdoms, "earthquakes in various places," and "famines" (13:7-8). Although no era of human history has been free of warfare and natural calamities, the reign of Gaius Caesar (also known as Caligula) in 37–41 CE, not long after Jesus's death, proved particularly precarious for Jews in Jerusalem and throughout the eastern Mediterranean world (Horsley 2001, 132–33; Josephus, *Ant.* 18.256–309; *J.W.* 2.184–203; Philo, *Embassy* 197–307).

Megalomaniacal and volatile, Gaius claimed he was a god meriting worship throughout the empire. To boost his supposed divine status, he ordered statues of himself erected in various Jewish sacred places—including the Jerusalem temple! Since making any material image of God was anathema to the Jews (Exod 20:4, 23; 34:17; Lev 19:4; 26:1; Deut 4:15-20; 5:8), the notion of placing a shrine to a foreign god, especially in the form of a foreign human ruler who thinks he is divine, was blasphemous in the extreme. The threat of Gaius's planned statues was enough to set off "rumors of war" against Rome among Jews in various "nations." Besides mobilizing for battle, some Jews protested by launching a farming labor strike (Josephus, *Ant.* 18.273–74; *J.W.* 2.199–201), which in turn contributed to famine conditions that were exacerbated in the late 40s by a severe drought in Roman Judea (*Ant.* 3.320–21; Acts 11:27-30).

Such dire conditions provide fertile ground not only for paralyzing emotions of despair and futility—for helpless inaction—but also for opportunistic *reactions* by would-be heroes promising to save the day. Soon Jesus will warn about the machinations of "false messiahs and false prophets" (13:20-21), but for now he targets those who tout themselves as the great "I am" (*egō eimi*, 13:6). Such an egocentric claim may be taken in the broad sense of "I'm the one!" (CEB), that is, "I'm the only one who can save you!" Or Jesus may intend a more specific allusion to the God of Israel, the "I AM" revealed to Moses at the burning bush, the "I AM" who, through Moses, delivered God's people from bitter affliction (Exod 3:13-17). In counteroffensive missions against oppressive, self-deifying foreign rulers like Pharaoh in Egypt or Gaius in Rome, "many" others, Jesus portends, will use his name to claim divine identity or authorization for themselves (Mark 13:6).

In Mark's view, only Jesus qualifies as the true Messiah and Son of God (1:1). But what are his followers to do in his absence, after his death, especially during the hard times that will persist? The temptation may be strong to seek another redeemer or fall prey to some charismatic figure pretending to be Jesus *redivivus*—Jesus returned from the dead (cf. 6:14-16)! But to thwart such tendencies, Jesus issues two injunctions: don't be *led astray* and don't be *alarmed* (13:5, 7). Or stated more positively: stay careful and calm. Tough times will surely ensue, "but the end is still to come" (13:7)—not the disintegrative end into oblivion but the restorative "end" (*telos*) or completion of God's saving purpose for the world, the "beginning" of rebirth (13:8).

Stay Alert to Defensive Times (13:9-13)

In the turbulent interim before the consummative "end" (*telos*) or goal of salvation, Jesus urges his disciples not only to be attitudinally careful and calm but actively to "endure to the end" (13:13). Such perseverance demands a strong defensive position in the face of physical assault and judicial prosecution from Jewish and Roman authorities—and even from one's close family members—at times on pain of death (13:9, 11-12a). Jesus doesn't sugarcoat the trials his disciples will soon face "because of me" (13:9), "because of my name" (13:13), because of their allegiance to him.

Yet neither does he leave them to fend for themselves in his absence but rather promises that the Holy Spirit will "speak" through them and empower them to bear courageous "testimony" before their prosecutors (13:9-11). The promise is not that the Spirit will deliver them or defend them personally: "The Spirit is not an escape clause or a defense attorney" (Levison 2020, 122). The Spirit is a dynamic force of witness or testimony (*martyrion*) in defense of the truth about Christ, which may result in the witness's *martyrdom* (13:12). Jesus assures his followers that the same divine Spirit who came upon him at his baptism and propelled him into and through his initial testing (1:9-10, 11-12; cf. 1:8) would enable them to persevere through their trials—even unto death, if need be (as it will for Jesus)—but ultimately, in "the end," ensuring they will "be saved" (13:13).

Complementing the disciples' defense of the gospel (not themselves) before prosecutors is a counteroffensive broadcasting the "good news" of God's saving realm (13:10). Significantly, Jesus splices this positive forecast of a wider gospel mission (13:10) between ominous predictions of persecution (13:9, 11), thus stressing that "the Gospel will be proclaimed not by the popular, but by the persecuted, not by the wise but by the wretched" (Levison 2020, 121). Again, the disciples' work aligns with Jesus's from the outset of his public ministry (1:14-15; see 8:35; 10:29; 14:9)—but with a new emphasis. They will proclaim the gospel "*to all nations* (*ethnē*)," to all ethnic groups in all parts of the world, promoting an extensive global mission that Jesus began, but just barely, during his earthly life (5:1-20; 7:24–8:10).

This universal, multinational scope of God's saving realm is firmly rooted in Jesus's Jewish scriptural faith, as he recently underscored in channeling Isaiah's message that the temple "shall be called [God's] house of prayer for *all the nations*" (11:17; Isa 56:7). Further echoes of Isaiah resound in Jesus's current evangelistic vision, echoes of Israel's vocation as a "light to the *nations*" (Isa 42:6; 49:6), a "messenger who announces peace, who brings *good news*, who announces [God's] salvation . . . [for] his people . . . and before the eyes of *all the nations* [such that] all the ends of the earth shall see the salvation of our God" (52:7-10). Isaiah's accent on spreading the gospel of *peace* to the ends of the earth (52:7) provides a salutary challenge to the irrepressible threats of war-making and war-mongering among the nations. Moreover, saving outreach to the nations runs counter to the messianic vision in the Psalms of Solomon (first century BCE) that the coming "king, the son of David" will "purge Jerusalem from gentiles who trample her to destruction . . . [and] destroy the unlawful nations with the word of his mouth" (17:21-24; cf. 17:28-29; cf. Perrin 2018; Strauss 2018).

Stay Alert to Desolate Times (13:14-23)

The prospects of betrayal, arrest, trial, and possible death are certainly ominous for Jesus's disciples. But they will also be embroiled in a larger struggle, a "progressive" crisis (Black 1991, 75). Jesus's forecast now expands the scope of sufferers to include "those in Judea" (Mark 13:14) and escalates the degree of suffering to an unprecedented wartime level "such as has not been" before in human history (13:19; cf. Dan 12:1). Like other prophets and seers, Jesus expects the world to get immeasurably worse before it gets better.

How bad will it get? Bad enough to beat a hasty retreat to the hills. There will be no use fighting back and no time to waste. If they find themselves on their flat rooftops (sites of drying food and clothes, sleeping, praying, and other activities in the ancient world; Josh 2:6, 8; 1 Sam 9:25-26; Acts 10:9-10) when trouble strikes, they should leave right away—perhaps jumping across adjacent rooftops (Josephus, *Ant*. 13.140; Gundry 2004 [1993], 776; cf. France 2002, 526)—without grabbing any provisions. Likewise they should immediately cease working in their fields and leave (Mark 13:14-15). Unfortunately, travel conditions will be especially dire for refugees fleeing during the rainy winter season (13:18; Keener 2014, 163), not least for pregnant and nursing women (13:17). The hope of birthing and nurturing new life out of the "pangs" (13:8) of battle will become dimmer before it is realized.

Who is to blame for this tragic situation? Jesus pinpoints a prime *instigator* of the anticipated troubles along with "false" *resistors* that complicate the crisis. Jesus calls the precipitant sign of trouble "the desolating sacrilege set up where it ought not be" (13:14). The awkward grammatical construction links a material object with a personal figure: literally, "the desolating sacrilege [neuter noun] set up where *he* [masculine participle] ought not be." This hybrid picture fits the scheme of Gaius Caesar, noted above, to erect a statue of *himself* in the Jerusalem temple, where it/he should absolutely not stand. Historically, Gaius died before his image was placed in this most holy place, but he did manage to ensconce his self-monuments in other sites in the Jewish homeland.

Whatever first-century CE abhorrent image Mark's Jesus has in view, the language of "desolating sacrilege" echoes past scriptural language and events. The "sacrilege" term (*bdelygma*) appears across the Greek Bible to denote any "loathsome, detestable thing" in God's sight (BDAG 2000, 172), variously associated with impurity, idolatry, and immorality. The "desolating" modifier (*erēmōseōs*), related to the common word for "desert/wilderness" (*erēmos*), suggests that the sacrilegious icon renders the transgressed sacred space desolate, barren, haunted, and void. As a unit, however, the "desolating sacrilege" or "abomination that desolates" matches what the writers of Daniel and 1 Maccabees called the polluted altar dedicated to Zeus Olympios set up in the Jerusalem temple by the Greco-Syrian tyrant Antiochus IV in the second century BCE as part of his campaign to eradicate the Jewish faith (Dan 9:26-27; 11:31; 12:11; 1 Macc 1:54; cf. 1:41-59).

Jesus, Mark, and Matthew (24:15) envision a similar desolating and desecrating crisis in their first-century context, with Roman rulers like Gaius reprising the role of Antiochus IV. The match is not perfect, however, as Gaius never succeeded in transforming (deforming) the Jerusalem temple into his own shrine, and the Romans generally allowed the Jews to worship as they pleased as long as they did not revolt against the empire. Speaking of revolution, this is where the parallel in Jewish history between the second century BCE and the first century CE breaks down the most. Whereas the Maccabean freedom fighters successfully drove Antiochus IV out of Jerusalem, cleansed the temple of its defiled altar and vessels, and rededicated the temple to proper worship (1 Macc 4:36-58), Jewish rebels against Rome were repeatedly defeated, culminating in General Titus's demolition of the holy city and temple in 70 CE.

In both the prospective view of Mark's Jesus and the retrospective view of the historian Josephus, the insurgent resistors of Roman overlords (and their elite Jewish collaborators) were misguided, driven by base motives, and doomed to fail—unlike the noble Maccabean revolutionary heroes. Jesus cautions his disciples to beware the wave of "false messiahs and false prophets" who will arise, sporting outwardly impressive but effectively impotent "signs and wonders" (13:22 NIV). Josephus recounts the rise and fall of numerous "bandits, prophets, and messiahs" (Horsley and Hanson 1985) in the turbulent times surrounding the First Roman-Jewish War.

In discussing Mark 11:1-11, we contrasted Jesus's peaceful entry into Jerusalem from the Mount of Olives with the ill-fated militant plan of an

Egyptian-Jewish "false prophet" (*pseudoprophētēs*), as Josephus calls him, who expected the Roman-protected walls of Jerusalem to fall at his command, à la Jericho of old (Josh 6:1-21). But the Egyptian was no Joshua. When Governor Felix got wind of the plot, it was the only thing that fell apart. As Felix's Roman forces attacked, the Egyptian skulked away never to be heard from again, while hundreds of his followers were killed (*Ant.* 20.167–72; *J.W.* 2.258–63).

As an example of a first-century "false messiah," consider the pretentious "bandit-king" named Simon, the son of Gioras (Novenson 2017, 142–45; Horsley and Hanson 1985, 118–27). This Simon led a ragtag band of guerilla fighters against Roman armies in areas north of Jerusalem. His power and popularity swelled as he marshaled thousands of additional troops and increasing acclamations of his kingly authority. Josephus brands Simon a tyrant who used brutal means against his own people as well as the enemy in order to seize control (*J.W.* 2.652–53). Pushed back by advancing Roman troops, Simon made his last stand in Jerusalem where Jewish Zealot forces had already occupied the temple compound—and polluted it, according to priestly officials. In the vortex of competing rebel and ruffian gangs, Simon emerged as the commander-in-chief of the Jews' fight against Rome. But whatever hopes he and the people had that he would reign as a victorious messiah were shattered by the Roman army's destruction of the holy city and temple. Donning a purple cape draped around white undergarments, Simon surrendered to his conquerors on the grounds where the temple had stood; he was brought to Caesar for judgment and incarcerated in Caesarea (*J.W.* 7.29–36). So much for this "false messiah."

It's not just vulgar, irreligious folk, however, who fall under the spell of charlatan, charismatic strong men during times of crises. Jesus warns that even "the elect" (*eklektoi*) risk being deluded if they're not careful (Mark 13:22). This term designates the people "whom [God] chose (*exelexato*)" (13:20), not as a select, privileged group within Israel but as representative of a whole community "elected" by God's grace for covenantal partnership with God. Such a gracious, loving choice on God's part demands in return the people's steadfast faithfulness to God as king and to the ways of God's kingdom embodied in God's anointed (messianic) agents—especially and ultimately Jesus the Christ. No substitutes, however attractive for the moment, whatever promises they make in desperate times, should be accepted.

But the question of survival remains: how will Jesus's disciples make it through the tough times he discloses (13:23)? In addition to promising the Holy Spirit's inspiration (13:11), Jesus paints a panoramic historical vision "from the beginning of the creation that God created until now" and even further into "those days" of future tribulation (13:19-20). Since the beginning, human history has been fraught with terrible turmoil. Yet through it all, God's good purpose for all creation has persisted and sustained God's beleaguered people. Therefore, in the cataclysms to come, Jesus's "chosen" followers may be assured that the Lord will "cut short those days" in time for them to "be saved" (13:20).

Although evil events have been set in motion by evil forces, they do not and will not have final control. Jesus's and "Mark's God is like that of Daniel, the Creator who can change times and seasons (Dan 2:21)" (Boring 2006, 369). And while Jesus says that he has "already told [the disciples] everything" (13:23), he has one more big event to announce concerning "those days" to come (13:24), a climactic change in the entire world order for the glory of God and the good of the world.

Stay Alert to Deliverance Times (13:24-27)

"After that suffering" that will afflict earth in "those days" (13:19, 24), God's people can expect explosive responses in the heavenly realm—mobilizing both celestial bodies (sun, moon, and stars) and personal agents (Son of Humankind and angels) to rescue the sufferers and renew the entire universe, heaven and earth together.

Cosmic shake-up (13:24-25)

The great celestial bodies will cease their normal light-giving operations as part of a total cosmic revolution in which "stars will be falling from heaven, and the powers in the heavens will be shaken" (13:24-25). Such dramatic doomsday images signaling the "end" of a wicked and woeful world were the stock-in-trade of prophetic and apocalyptic visionaries (Isa 13:10; 34:4; Ezek 32:7-8; Joel 2:10, 30-31; Amos 8:9; 2 Esdr 5:4-5; Acts 2:19-20; 2 Pet 3:12; Rev 6:12-14). But for all the gloom and doom these images project, they do not portend the *literal end* or annihilation of the world but rather a *new beginning*, a rejuvenation, a re-creation of the world order encompassing both heaven and earth: a "passing away" of the present heaven and earth (Mark 13:31) giving way to a "new heaven and a new earth" (Isa 65:17; 66:22; 2 Pet 3:12-13; Rev 21:1). As the great theologian of hope, Jürgen Moltmann, titled one of his books *In the End—the Beginning* (2004, especially 33–52).

Although Mark's Jesus does not explicitly announce the renewal of heaven and earth, his language leaves open the possibility. "Shaking" is not shattering, demolishing, obliterating but rather signifies reordering, reorienting, rearranging. Further, in the Markan Jesus's view of God's redemptive realm, "blinding/darkening" gives way to seeing/enlightening (8:22-25; 10:46-52) and "falling" (*piptō*) leads to rising—like "falling" seeds sprouting into crops (4:4-5, 7-8) or a "falling" boy suffering a violent seizure being lifted up (9:20, 27). And though not using "falling" language to reference his impending death as the Son of Humankind, Jesus assures his followers that he will "rise again" (8:31; 9:31; 10:34). Yet more than that, Jesus now promises that the Son of Humankind will *return* "with great power and glory" (13:26) as God's right-hand man (Human) "to set the world right" (Pennington 2018, 215).

Coming Son of Humankind (13:26-27)
In the midst of the celestial gloom, darkness, and power(s) disruption, God's beleaguered people "will *see* 'the Son of Man coming in clouds' with great power and glory" (13:26). Not simply one "*like* a human being [son of man] coming with the clouds of heaven" (Dan 7:13; cf. Rev 1:7, 13), but *the* definitive Son of Humankind coming in "glory" (*doxa*), reflecting radiant bright light (cf. Acts 22:11; Friberg, Friberg, and Miller 2000). The Son of Humankind will break through the ominous cloudy skies riding on glorious clouds suffused with renewing power and light. By now we know that Mark's Jesus refers to *himself* as this Son of Humankind—God's embodied agent on earth who forgives sins, makes disabled bodies whole (Mark 2:10, 28), and is destined to die and rise again (8:31; 9:31; 10:32). And he has already alluded to his return to earth in a judicial capacity (8:38).

Presently, however, Jesus does not stress a final judgment-seat reckoning or a battlefield routing of enemies and evildoers, as in other "Son of Man" scenarios (Dan 7:9-12, 23-26; 1 En 46:1-6; 48:2-3, 8-10; 62:7-12). Rather, he focuses exclusively here on saving his beloved people. Instead of delivering "to the angels for punishment" those who have brutally oppressed his people (1 En 62:11; Nickelsburg and VanderKam 2004, 81), the Son of Humankind will dispatch his angelic aides to "gather his elect . . . from the ends of the earth to the ends of heaven" (Mark 13:27; cf. Isa 11:11-12). Notice again the cosmic scope stretching across and up and down the "ends" or "extreme limit[s]" of earth and heaven, tip to tip (*akron*) (L&N 1988, 707).

Stay Alert to Delayed Times (13:28-37)

Thus far Jesus has not directly addressed the disciples' original temporal question about the temple's fate: "*When* will this be?"—this prediction you just made about the temple's destruction (13:4). He has said nothing more about the temple institution or structure per se, focusing instead on "those days" of suffering awaiting the disciples, the people of Judea, and the wider world leading up to the "end" that is "still to come" (13:6). While generally warning about menacing events and misleading figures within the broad horizon of the disciples' lifetimes (up to the time of Mark's writing), Jesus sets *no specific dates and times*. No doubt this vagueness frustrates these first disciples, as it has frustrated many curious time-charters since.

A big part of this frustration has to do with the problem of God's *delay* in alleviating suffering and overcoming evil. Applied to Christ's climactic return to earth as God's chief agent of redemption, the problem is often dubbed by scholars as the *delay of the parousia* (the "appearing"). How long, O Lord? When will it all "end"? "Cutting short those days" of tribulation is nice, but how short is "short"? Even one day of excruciating pain can seem like an eternity.

Mark's Jesus addresses this issue of "delay" but not to the complete satisfaction of his hearers then or now. He reinforces the basic temporal pattern sketched thus far: culminating events are "near" (13:28-29), generally speaking, but *unknown* concerning precisely when they will occur, *even for Jesus*. While Jesus anticipates and paints "those days" in broad strokes, "*that day or hour no one knows*, neither the angels in heaven, *nor the Son*, but only [God] the Father" (13:32; cf. Acts 1:6-7)—a fact that should put an end to all scheduling schemes about the end!

Jesus's persisting vagueness about time reinforces his call to vigilance: stay alert at all times so as not to get caught unprepared. His medium for this message is parabolic (*parabolē*, "lesson," 13:28), leaving two short stories ringing in the ears of "all" (*pasin*) his followers, present and future (13:37).

The fig tree (13:28-31)

Jesus offers another lesson using a fig tree but without withering an actual tree this time for having fig-less leaves—out of season (11:12-14, 20-24)! Now he evokes a more natural image of the seasonal cycle: when a fig tree re-sprouts "its leaves, you know that summer is near," when the good fruit forms and ripens (13:28). The promising "summer" reference contrasts with Jesus's previous "winter" warning of a dismal and dangerous time to flee from escalating trouble (13:18). Now the hope of a more "fruitful" period tempers the wintry desolation. The budding fig leaves function as a dual sign: on the one side, overlapping "these [troubling] things taking place" that Jesus has just predicted but, on the other side, signaling the "new leaf" about to be turned over by the coming Son of Humankind "before this generation . . . pass[es] away" (13:28-30).

Jesus adds another image, that of a "gate" or "door" (*thyra*) at the threshold between heaven and earth where "he," the Son of Humankind, will stand close by—"at the very gates"—pressing to break through the "thin" portal between heavenly and earthly sectors of God's universal realm (Borg

2003, 155–63; Newell 2016, 46, 59). Present configurations of "heaven and earth will pass away," but Christ's dynamic "words" (13:31)—evidenced in his commanding miracles of healing and sea-calming (1:25-27; 2:9-12; 4:39-41; 7:29-30, 34-35; 9:25-27)—"will not pass away" (13:31), implying a restored, recreated cosmos, a new heaven and a new earth flourishing under God's gracious rule.

The estate "lord" (13:32-37)

Counterpointing the fig tree parable's sign of Jesus's coming back to earth in the *near* future, the story of a traveling householder or "master/lord (*kyrios*) of the house" (13:35) underscores the *unknown* time of the Son of God-and-Humankind's return. The "lord" leaves home "on a journey" (business trip), placing his "slaves in charge, each with his work" of managing the estate's enterprise. The householder singles out a particular worker—the door/gatekeeper (*thyrōros*)—with the pointed command to be extra alert "on the watch" (13:34). Balancing the Son of Humankind figure "near, at the very gates" looking *in*, awaiting (re)entry to the newly blossoming earth (13:29), this "gatekeeper" represents a dedicated servant looking *out* for both raiding menaces and his returning master.

This situation stays on the highest alert level because all the servants—estate workers and gatekeepers—"*do not know* when the master of the house will come" back (13:35). It could be a longer time, shorter time—really, any time—although it seems to be a matter of proximate *days and hours*, not extended years and eras (13:32). But again, it could be any day, any hour of the day—or night! It is especially critical to stay awake throughout the night when enemies are most prone to attack, pressures to sleep are heaviest, and the master might return after a long day of conducting outside business. Roman time divided the hours of darkness into four blocks or "watches" (cf. 6:48), and Jesus's story urges diligent vigilance during each one of these (13:35).

- Evening: 6:00–9:00 p.m.
- Midnight: 9:00 p.m.–12:00 a.m.
- Cockcrow: 12:00–3:00 a.m.
- Dawn: 3:00–6:00 a.m.

The application to Jesus and his disciples is obvious: Jesus is the *Master/Lord* who will soon leave his followers after his death and resurrection with assurance of his return at some *unspecified time*. In the interim period, Jesus charges the disciples to carry on his messianic mission as faithful *servants* and to operate as watchful *gatekeepers* on guard against fraudulent messiahs, prophets, and other self-promoters (13:6, 14, 21-22; Collins 1996, 34–35) and on alert to welcome the true Lord and Christ whenever he arrives.

But the call to acute alertness applies not only to the period after Jesus's death. It also has immediate relevance *now* in Jesus's final days of earthly life. The pace of Mark's storytelling, almost breakneck to this point, slows down considerably in chapters 14–16, disproportionate to the time of the story's events. Mark lingers long over Jesus's last days and hours, frequently marking times across day and night, including the ominous hours of *cockcrowing* first mentioned in 13:37 (cf. 14:30, 68, 72). Every moment now is fraught with significance meriting keen attention from characters within the story and hearers/readers of the story. This is no time to drop one's guard or droop one's head in sleep, as Jesus's disciples soon learn the hard way (14:26-72). The watchword is *Watch!*

Making His Final Mark: Jesus's Death and Resurrection

Mark 14:1–16:20

"The hour has come. . . . See, my betrayer is at hand" (14:41-42). Mark's story of Jesus Messiah has reached its ominous, climactic end after a long but fast-paced buildup. Now Mark retards the narrative tempo to give close attention to Jesus's last days and hours. Jesus's story ends with a simmering plot, not a sudden bang. Every moment counts.

"Plot" works in two ways, as a detailed *narrative plot* of Jesus's last days by Mark and a dark *political plot* against Jesus's life hatched by his opponents. The following table delineates the rich array of temporal, spatial, and social elements of what is commonly called Jesus's "Passion Narrative," the story of his final suffering (*paschō*) experienced with intense pathos or "passion" culminating in crucifixion. I list these elements in order of appearance in the story. Note well: the presence of Jesus the protagonist is assumed throughout this unit (see pg. 238).

While each element contributes to the rich texture of Mark's Passion account, major strands feature (1) the *time* of the Passover festival, (2) the *places* of Gethsemane, Golgotha, and Jesus's tomb, and (3) the *characters* of Judas the betrayer and Peter the denier among Jesus's disciples and the Jewish high priest and Roman governor Pilate as Jesus's judges.

Betrayal and Arrest (14:1-52)

By Jesus's time, "Passover and the festival of Unleavened Bread" (14:1) were combined into one annual weeklong celebration in the spring (Nisan 14–21 [March–April]; Twelftree 2013, 273). It drew scores of pilgrims from the Jewish homeland and Diaspora to commemorate ancient Israel's glorious liberation from Egyptian enslavement. During times of continuing domination by a foreign power—as in the first century under Roman rule—this freedom festival became a tinderbox for political protest and mob unrest. But overall, it remained a joyous period of feasting, singing, and fellowship in

Times	Places	People
Two days before Passover and festival of Unleavened Bread	House in Bethany	Chief priests, scribes, and elders
First day of Unleavened Bread	Upstairs room in Jerusalem	The people/crowd
Evening	Mount of Olives	Simon the "leper"
Night cock-crowing "watch"	Gethsemane	Anonymous anointing woman
One hour	Galilee	Judas Iscariot
The hour	High priest's courtyard	Peter, James, and John
Morning	Pilate's tribunal	"Young man"
9:00 AM	Pilate's headquarters/ Praetorium	High priest
Noon	Golgatha/Place of the Skull	High priest's slave
3:00 PM	Temple	High priest's servant-girl
Day of preparation	Rock tomb	Guards at high priest's residence
Sabbath		Pilate
Very early on the first day of the week		Barabbas
		Roman soldiers
		Simon of Cyrene
		Two crucified bandits
		Centurion
		Mary Magdalene and other women
		Joseph of Arimathea

Jerusalem—a welcome break from hard times and an infusion of fresh hope for better things to come.

Although Jesus and his disciples celebrate the Passover feast with careful meal preparation (14:12-16) and joyful hymn singing (14:26), the prevailing mood is somber and foreboding. At a pre-Passover dinner party in Bethany, Jesus interprets a woman's lavish anointing of his head—typically a refreshing experience—as a pre-anointing for his *burial* (14:8). At the same time the scent of fragrant perfume fills the house, a sour trace of *betrayal* fouls the air (14:1-2, 10-11). Jesus then puts a damper on the Passover meal by plainly telling his followers, while they "were eating," that "one of you will betray me" (14:18). Before the evening passes, Jesus is arrested by the authorities while all his disciples *desert* him (14:50). A swirl of negative emotions surrounds these events: anger (14:4), distress (14:19, 33), vehemence (14:31), agitation (14:33), and grief (14:34). Even the one pleasant emotion has a malicious motivation: the chief priests "were greatly pleased" or "delighted" (CEB) (*echarēsan*, "rejoiced") that Judas had come forward to betray Jesus into their hands (14:11)!

The narrative flow of ominous events in this section is facilitated not only by a flood of emotions but also by multiple actions related to liquids:

- A woman pouring out perfume (14:3)
- A man carrying water (14:13)
- Jesus and the disciples dipping bread into a sauce bowl (14:20)
- Jesus and the disciples drinking wine from a common cup (14:23)
- Jesus correlating the wine with "my blood of the covenant . . . poured out for many" (14:24)
- Jesus praying for "this cup" to be removed (14:36)

Jesus's final struggles thus play out in the context of tense occasions of table fellowship or mealtime communion threatening to split fellowship and break communion.

Perfuming at the house of Simon the Leper in Bethany and being betrayed (14:1-11)

Two days before the official start of the Passover festival, Jesus dines in the Bethany home of one Simon the *lepros*, that is, a man who had "leprosy" (14:3). While it is possible that he had been recently cured from his disease (maybe by Jesus), Mark says nothing to this effect (Shinall 2018, 932); in any case, Simon is distinguished from the anonymous *lepros* whom Jesus healed at the outset of his ministry (1:40-45). The Gospel traditions are mixed regarding the host of the dinner party and the anointing woman. While Matthew agrees with Mark (Matt 26:6-7), Luke places the event earlier in the home of Simon *the Pharisee* (no mention of his medical condition) who criticizes Jesus's welcome of a "sinful" woman's anointing (Luke 7:36-44); and John stages the scene "six days before the Passover . . . [in] the home of *Lazarus*, whom he had raised from the dead," where Lazarus's sister *Mary* anoints Jesus's feet (John 12:1-3). Mark's version, featuring a former "leper" and an anonymous woman, accentuates Jesus's continuing fellowship with people who have experienced suffering and subordination.

The literary placement of this poignant story is also significant, centered in another "sandwich" and framed by short but shocking notes of the plot against Jesus's life.

Sandwich #5
A Plotting Jesus's Death: Chief Priests and Scribes (14:1-2)
  B Preparing for Jesus's Death: Anonymous Woman (14:3-9)
A Plotting Jesus's Death: Chief Priests and Judas (14:10-11)

This section presents a stark *contrast* between central and flanking components, similar to Sandwich #3 (6:6b-44), except that here the central story features an admirable woman pre-anointing Jesus for his burial (14:3-9), unlike the Herodian (including Herodias and daughter) beheading of John the Baptist (6:14-29) at the heart of the other "sandwich." Both centerpieces are set at dinner parties that become laced with the scent of death around a "head" figure. But the overall effects couldn't be more opposite: "King" Herod's serving up John the Baptist's putrid severed head on a platter versus an anonymous woman's perfuming Jesus's head as an act of loving devotion, doing "what she could" for Jesus (14:8) on the cusp of his execution and burial.

We may taste the clashing flavors of the current "sandwich" in relation to four ingredients: characters, objectives, means, and e/motives.

Characters. Jesus previously predicted that the chief priests and scribes would play a leading role in his arrest and execution (8:31; 10:33). More recently this cadre had taken great offense at Jesus's temple "housecleaning" theatrics (11:18) and tried to trip him up with politically charged questions (11:27-28; 12:13-15). In turn Jesus exposed the flimsy basis of their interrogations (11:27-33; 12:13-37) and told a stinging parable "against them" (12:12; cf. 12:1-11). The fuse has been lit, the stage has been set for the chief priests and scribes to launch their nefarious plot against Jesus (14:1;

cf. 11:18; 12:12)—especially since a traitor among Jesus's disciples, *Judas Iscariot*, places himself at their service (14:10; cf. 3:19).

Counterpointed with these religious-political leaders and a member of Jesus's circle of twelve chosen male apostles are the lepros Simon and the unnamed woman, who stand apart from the hostile of Jesus as hospitable ministers to Jesus, with Simon hosting Jesus at a meal and the woman anointing his head.

Objectives. The framing snippets and the central story both focus on the imminent death of Jesus—but to very different ends. Whereas the priestly and scribal officials, together with Judas, seek to precipitate Jesus's death, the anointing woman aims to mitigate his suffering. Thereby the two parties send contrary messages about Jesus's life and death. On the one pole, Jesus is bad news and must die. On the other end, Jesus is worthy of loving service up to his moment of death and beyond, including his burial and continuing mission through his followers who proclaim the "good news" of his saving life, death, and resurrection "in the whole world" (14:8).

Jesus himself makes this last point with a remarkable statement about the woman's legacy: "She has anointed my body beforehand for its burial. . . . What she has done will be told in remembrance of her," told, that is, as part and parcel of the global witness to the gospel (14:8-9). Such a memorable act must carry more significance than basic burial service to mask (temporarily) the smell of a rotting corpse—a service routinely performed by women at gravesites. What this woman "has done" for Jesus is done *before* his death presciently, prophetically. Thus many scholars view her deed as a "prophetic sign-action" (Schüssler Fiorenza 1994, xlvi) of anointing Jesus as the royal Anointed One (Messiah/Christ), similar to the prophet Samuel's (pre)anointing of young David with oil in his family's home (1 Sam 16:6-13)—but with a key distinction.

This unnamed "woman [prophet] anointing Jesus clearly recognizes that Jesus's messiahship means suffering and death" (Schüssler Fiorenza 1994, xliv; cf. Malbon 2012, 490). This woman's "grooming of the Messiah," to borrow Marianne Sawicki's evocative phrase (2001, 136), is grooming him for death! In marked contrast to Peter and the other male disciples—who fail to embrace Jesus's mission as the suffering servant-Messiah who gives his life in solidarity with and as a "ransom" for the oppressed and the enslaved (8:31-33; 9:30-35; 10:32-44)—this woman represents a "true disciple" (Schüssler Fiorenza 1994, xliv) and a faithful witness-in-action to the gospel grounded in Jesus's life, death, burial, and resurrection (cf. 1 Cor 15:1-4).

Moreover, her very act of outpouring precious oil on Jesus prefigures Jesus's outpouring his precious lifeblood (see Mark 14:23-24). She thus assumes an honored place in Mark's Gospel with two other women previewers of Jesus's self-emptying ministry: the chronic bleeding woman who drew out Jesus's "flow" of healing energy (5:25-29) and the poor widow who gave her last "penny" and whole "life/livelihood" (*bios*) to God (12:42-44).

As admirable, however, as these three women's actions are in relation to Jesus, they are not accompanied by any direct women's speech. Although we may rightly claim that their actions speak for themselves, we should not minimize the power of voice that has too often been denied women in the history of the church (Spencer 2010c, 295–300). Concerning the anointing woman in particular, Jesus insists ("Truly I tell you," 14:9) that all future gospel preachers should speak about her, tell her story, give her voice where she originally had none—an assignment that many male evangelists and churchmen have failed to carry out. We properly "proclaim the Lord's death" as we eat and drink with him "in remembrance of me," as he commanded (1 Cor 11:24-26; cf. Luke 22:19). But we still have a ways to go in embracing and embodying the gospel mission "in remembrance of *her*," the anointing woman of Bethany (Mark 14:9).

Means. How do the characters carry out their objectives in relation to Jesus? Briefly put, those who aim to arrest Jesus operate secretly and strategically, while the woman who anoints Jesus does so openly and profusely. And money factors prominently into both parties' actions.

The chief priests/scribes seek to seize and kill Jesus "by stealth (*dolō*)" (14:1), "cunning" tactics (CEB), or "treachery" (BDAG 2000, 256), effectively bringing a biblical curse on their heads: "Cursed be he who strikes down a neighbor with treachery (*dolō*)" (Deut 27:24 NETS; cf. Exod 21:14). They launch a secret operation against Jesus—a sinister twist on Mark's secrecy theme regarding Jesus's mission—lest they provoke the people to riot "during the festival" (14:1-2). As high-spirited events celebrated by throngs of pilgrims, the Jerusalem festivals—not least Passover—were prime times for "sedition . . . to break out" (Josephus, *J.W.* 1.88; on Passover uprisings, cf. 2.4–13, 224–27, 280–83; 4.398–409; 6.420–29; Carter 2019, 302). Jesus's surging popularity poses a real challenge to the established authorities. The chief priests and scribes should be worried! To protect their turf and keep the peace, they have to do something to stop Jesus; but if they come out too loud and strong, they will only rile up Jesus's fans and make matters worse (cf. 11:18; 12:12). Hence the covert plot.

How better to pull off this clandestine operation than with an inside informant and traitor—one who comes to the chief priests and offers his perfidious services (14:10) . . . for a price, it seems. Mark makes no mention of the infamous thirty pieces of silver (Matt 26:15; 27:3-6) but does indicate that the priestly leaders "promised to give him [Judas] money" for betraying Jesus into their hands (Mark 14:11).

In stark contrast to these officials' secret plot to take Jesus down, the anointing woman makes a public scene in Simon's house, "perform[ing] a good service" for Jesus (14:6). It's not clear whether she's an invited guest or gate-crasher to Simon's dinner's party (cf. Luke 7:36-39), but in any case, she draws criticism from other guests for her extravagant action (Mark 14:4-5). She (and Jesus) couldn't care less, however, about what others think. She couldn't be more open about her love for Jesus as she "broke open (*syntripsasa*)" an alabaster vase of perfume, that is, "shattered [it] in pieces" (no delicate snapping off the tip or removing a stopper) (14:3). The verb appears elsewhere in Mark to describe the Gerasene demoniac's violent ripping off his restraints—"the shackles he broke in pieces (*syntetriphthai*)" (5:4)—and in Revelation to characterize conquering rulers who wield their authority "with an iron rod, as when clay pots are shattered (*syntribetai*)" (Rev 2:27; cf. Ps 2:9 LXX). The verb does not suit soothing, genteel action. Picture—see and hear—the woman shattering her perfume pot and showering Jesus's head with the liquid that splashes out on his hair and face, streams down his clothes, and pools at his feet. This "pouring" of perfume is more like a thunderous downpour on Jesus, certainly no prim dabbing on his forehead or behind his ears.

The eccentricity and extravagance of the woman's action are intensified by the expensiveness of the ointment: "very costly" nard (spikenard) priced at more than 300 denarii, close to a worker's wages for a whole year. The only other New Testament uses of the term for "very costly" (*polytelēs*) appear in contexts that counsel women to adorn themselves modestly, eschewing luxury garments and jewelry (1 Tim 2:9; 1 Pet 3:3-4). There's nothing modest about the conduct of Mark's anointing woman.

Yet she does not use her valuable oil to flaunt her wealth or enhance her allure. She pours it all out *for* Jesus as a prophetic sign, if we accept the interpretation offered above, and also as an *erotic act* (the two are not mutually exclusive). I use "erotic" in the broad sense of sensual, passionate bodily treatment connected with "show[ing] kindness" (*eu poiēsai*, Mark 14:7) or "doing good" (BDAG 2000, 401) and carrying out a "beautiful work" (*kalon ergon*, 14:6; "good service" in the NRSV is too clinical; Carter 2019, 383, 386). The woman's perfuming gesture powerfully evokes senses of smell, sight, hearing, and touch (and possibly taste, if the oil streams down to Jesus's lips). It also recalls the intimate love language between the young woman and man in the Song of Songs, including references to "ointment/perfume" (*myron*) in general and "nard" (*nardos*) in particular (Mark 14:3-5; Collins 2007, 642).

- Woman → Man: For . . . the fragrance of your anointing oils (*myrōn*) [is] beyond any spice. Your name is perfume (*myron*) poured out. . . . We shall run after you into the fragrance of your anointing oils (*myrōn*). (Song 1:3-4 NETS)
- Man → Woman: Your scents are an orchard of pomegranates with fruit of fruit-trees, henna with nard (*nardōn*), nard (*nardos*) and saffron . . . with all chief perfumes (*myrōn*) (Song 4:13-14 NETS).

Another characteristic of the nard the woman pours out on Jesus is its "pure" state, as most English versions render *pistikēs* (Mark 14:3). But this rare biblical term, used only here and in the John 12:3 parallel, has various possible nuances.

E/motives. The link between "emotive" and "motive" is not a linguistic accident. As emotion researchers stress, emotions play an integral role in motivating human behavior, in moving us to do or not do something, in affecting our wills and desires. Emotions signal motives (Lazarus 1991, 92–112; Lazarus and Lazarus 1994, 39–51; Goldstein 2018). The common translation of *pistikēs* as "pure" may not only attest to the natural high quality of the woman's offering (BDAG 2000, 818) but also signify her motivational sincerity, her "pure" motives: she presents a free-flowing gift of love to Jesus, not a transactional payment to secure her own interests like the chief priests arranged with Judas.

But in light of its possible connection with *pistis*, a favorite term in Mark usually rendered "faith" or "belief," *pistikēs* might also carry notions of being "faithful," "loyal," or "persuasive"—worthy of believing and trusting (Sawicki 2001, 147–49, 167–68). This meaning scarcely applies to an inanimate substance like nard. But it may color the woman's *use* of the perfume: anointing Jesus with precious perfume may signify *her* faithfulness to Jesus *because* of his willingness to pour out his life for others. (The feminine adjective *pistikēs* modifying the feminine noun *nardou* makes for a happy connection with a woman's action revealing *her* character.) Moreover, since in various contexts *pistis* and related terms may include *emotional-relational* strains of *trust*—feeling a deep trustful bond with friends or lovers (Spencer 2017b; Morgan 2015, 6–7, 20–23, 28–30, 444–72; BDAG 2000, 816–18)—the woman's anointing of Jesus appears to be motivated by her close sympathetic relationship with Jesus. She wants to show him and make him sense (feel) her undying devotion to him on the brink of his death and burial. Whereas all the male disciples soon desert him in his direst hour (14:50), succumbing to their own selfish interests spurred by "impure" motives, the anointing woman remains wholeheartedly faithful to Jesus.

Marianne Sawicki further suggests that the woman engages in a dramatic act of *persuasion*. She regards "persuasive" as the primary meaning of *pistikēs*, "a variant spelling of πειστικός [*peistikos*] . . . from the verb πείθω [*peithō*] (active: 'persuade'; middle: 'comply, obey, trust in') which also gives us πίστις [*pistis*], the New Testament term for faith" (2001, 147). Therefore, through her emotive demonstration the anointing woman aims to persuade (e/motivate) both Jesus himself and the witnessing audience to respond faithfully to his pending death and burial. In Jesus's case, she seeks to bolster his commitment to follow through with his cross-bearing mission; as for the audience, she tries to convince them "that Jesus dies obediently, faithfully, divinely and freely" as the true Messiah (Anointed One) (Sawicki 2001, 167–68). With respect to Jesus, Christian readers who may not be accustomed to thinking he needed any encouragement or persuasion to make his final way to the cross should suspend their judgment until absorbing his wrenching emotional struggle later in the chapter prior to his arrest (14:32-42).

As it happens, the woman's emotional outburst—not vocally but demonstratively through her outpouring of perfume—meets with strong emotional resistance from some guests in Simon's house. After buzzing to another "in anger" about the supposed waste of a valuable commodity, they directly "scolded" the woman (14:4-5).

The "anger" term (*aganakteō*) used here has occurred twice before in Mark's story: first, as Jesus became "indignant" (*ēganagtēsen*) at his disciples' obstruction of those trying to bring little children to him (10:14); second, as ten disciples "began to be angry (*aganaktein*)" with James and John for lobbying Jesus for special advancement (10:41). They feel resentful, shortchanged, and upstaged by James and John, much like some dinner guests feel about the spotlighted anointing woman.

The "scolding" term (*embrimaomai*), connoting "snorting in anger," appeared once before in Jesus's emotionally charged encounter with the skin-diseased man. Having been "moved with anger" at the way the man with "leprosy" requests healing (1:41), Jesus proceeds to "sternly warn" (*embrimēsamenos*) the man after he heals him to head straight to the priest for certification without reporting to anyone along the way (1:43). In commenting on this incident, I argued that Jesus was upset with the man's supposed challenge of Jesus's indomitable will to heal, along with the unwelcome publicity Jesus would receive when the man broadcast his miraculous cure.

Now, however, at the end of his ministry, Jesus happily receives a local woman's lavish public attention as prototypical of publishing the good news of his life-giving death throughout the "whole world" (14:9). Rather than squelching her exuberant action, he encourages it, telling her critics to "leave her alone" and take keen notice of her "beautiful work" of love and devotion (14:6). Although Jesus doesn't come back at these obstructers in anger, as he did with the disciples who impeded little children's access to him, he does insist that the critical guests "let (*aphete*) [the anointing woman] alone" to attend to Jesus's body (14:6), just as he ordered the disciples to "let (*aphete*) the little children come to me" so that he may take up their little bodies in his arms (10:14-16). The realm of God is open, welcoming, and attendant to the well-being of all embodied persons regardless of age, gender, or social status.

But what about the charge of wasting precious resources? Isn't there a point to calculating how 300 denarii worth of perfume might be put to better use if cashed out and "given to the poor" (14:5)? Didn't Jesus tell the rich man to sell everything he owned and "give the money to the poor" (10:21)? If you're hungry enough, you might eat crumbs that fall from a well-stocked table (recalling the Syrophoenician woman's trenchant image [7:28]), but you can't get any nourishment from licking up spilt perfume. Powerful leaders and strong men commonly grant themselves privileged services they deny to others. Is the normally austere Jesus going soft as death looms? Yet isn't a condemned man entitled to one last good meal and one special salon treatment? Such questions are fair game, given Jesus's core mission of suffering with and for the poor and afflicted.

Nevertheless, they don't stand up to close examination. Jesus does not ask for this woman's "service" or luxuriate in it. He simply accepts it for what it is—a follower who has "done what she could" for him while she can (14:7-8)—and interprets it in light of broader gospel interests (14:9). While the sumptuous anointing is appropriate for appointing a king, Jesus does not bask in the glory of his coronation or flex his messianic ego. And he certainly does not set himself apart from the many poor people who will always be around. He himself will soon die *as a poor man*, naked and alone. The statement, "You always have the poor with you," is not an excuse to do nothing to alleviate poverty, still less a cause for blaming the poor for their condition. It's a statement of fact, of reality. This side of the consummation of God's right-making rule, Jesus entertains no utopian illusions: there will always be people in need who must be ministered to with intentional acts of "kindness"—"*doing* good [deeds]" (*eu poiēsai*, 14:7), not merely offering perfunctory thoughts and prayers. And such ministry is best motivated and sustained by a dynamic, passionate relationship with Christ who incarnates love for God and all persons (cf. 12:30-31).

So-called "social service" to the needy is demanding, exhaustive work, ripe for burnout. Ministers of the gospel—the "social gospel" intrinsically committed to social justice—are not exempt from becoming depleted and discouraged. Accordingly, they must regularly renew their emotional, motivational energy in good, "beautiful" (*kalon*) intimacy with the sympathizing, suffering Jesus. By showing her overflowing love for Jesus, the anointing woman taps into his flow of love and power (as the bleeding woman literally does in 5:29-30), inspiring her and others' gospel ministry to the poor in Jesus's stead and for Jesus's sake after his death.

One more emotion remains to be considered: the *pleasure* the chief priests felt when Judas offered to betray Jesus into their hands. The verb translated "greatly pleased" in the NRSV (14:11) is the standard term for "rejoice" (*chairō*) or "have joy (*charan*)". The New Testament often uses *chara* language to connote spiritual joy "in the Lord" (Phil 4:4, 10), a choice "fruit of the Spirit" (Gal 5:22). But here the ruling priests' joy has no virtue; it reflects a sadistic glee over the anticipated downfall of this upstart Galilean prophet who is threatening their authority. They experience *Schadenfreude* (harm-related joy) before the fact of Jesus's arrest and execution. As it happens, Mark's only other "joy" reference also appears in a negative context, describing "rocky" respondents to God's word whose initial "joy" response proves to be a mere burst of shallow enthusiasm with no solid root structure. As a result, they "fall away" from God's way (4:16-17)—precisely what Judas now does after first following with hopeful enthusiasm. Mark does not, however, disclose Judas's motivation for betraying Jesus, except for hinting that it contained an element of greed. Luke (but not Mark) attributes Judas's treachery to satanic possession (Luke 22:3). We may also imagine traces of affective disillusionment and cognitive dissonance with the apparent downward direction of Jesus's messianic movement, but again, Mark doesn't clarify Judas's motives.

Preparing and consuming the Passover meal in an upstairs room in Jerusalem (14:12-25)

The story continues in a supper setting, though shifted now to a new venue with new character roles. Jesus arranges to celebrate the Passover meal in a "large upstairs room" in Jerusalem (14:15); rather than being the honored guest receiving others' ministrations, he now acts as both *host* and *servant*. The dinner table—a U-shaped structure around which guests reclined on couches—remains a focal point for vital insight into Jesus's identity and mission in his final hours.

Table fellowship signals close friendship, which is why Jesus's dining with "tax collectors and sinners" triggered sharp criticism from some scribes and Pharisees (2:15-16). Presently, however, Jesus eats in private with his twelve closest confidants. Yet all is far from bliss around the holiday supper table, as Jesus's *betrayal* (14:17-21)—by one of the Twelve!—and *death* (14:22-25) become the main topics of conversation. The true community of Jesus's followers in God's kingdom (14:25) is being refined and redefined in the crucible of suffering.

This meal features three actions involving potable substances in various containers: carrying water in a jar (*keramion*, 14:13); dipping bread into a sauce bowl (*tryblion*, 14:20); and drinking wine from a common cup (*potērion*, 14:23). I will consider the significance of these actions as they occur, but for now I simply note Mark's mixing of ordinary material elements with profound spiritual experiences, consistent with a sacramental view of the world—a sacred-material perspective that resists body/spirit, secular/spiritual, everyday/eternal divisions in favor of an interconnected, holistic vision.

Jesus complements and interprets these signs with his authoritative *word*, twice introduced with the solemn announcement, "Truly I tell you" (14:18, 25). Moreover, the two disciples Jesus sends into Jerusalem to check on Passover arrangements "found everything [just] *as he had told them*" (14:16). Jesus's word is reliable and prescient in matters small and large—the word of a true prophet. Unfortunately, while his followers readily acknowledge his prophetic authority in this case, they struggle to accept what he tells them regarding his death and resurrection (14:19, 29, 37-42; 16:7).

Arranging the event (14:12-16). The banner events of the Passover festival involved each household's bringing an unblemished, year-old male "Passover lamb (*pascha*)" for slaughter in the temple precincts; the animal would then be roasted and eaten for supper with unleavened bread and bitter herbs in the family's dwelling. At the inaugural Passover centuries before, the blood of the sacrificed lamb was smeared on the doorframes of every Israelite residence in Egypt, marking it as a safe house while the Lord "passed over" the land, struck down the firstborn in every Egyptian household, and enabled the Israelites' escape (exodus) from slavery (Exod 12:1-28). Mark explicitly mentions the sacrificed lamb only in 14:12 and not at all during the meal itself. But the flesh and blood of the Passover lamb and all it symbolized hover over the entire Passion narrative.

Jesus pays special attention to securing a place in Jerusalem and preparing the feast. Such attention may seem misplaced or diversionary amid the pressing threat against Jesus's life. But the idea of making "preparations" (*hetoimazō*) and getting everything "ready" (*hetoimon*)—stressed four times in this passage (14:12, 15 [twice], 16)—is not trivial or negligible. It marks the concern to "prepare (*hetoimasate*) the way of the Lord" from beginning (1:3) to end. But what is the importance of having everything laid out just so, neatly "furnished" or "spread" (*strōnnyō*, BDAG 2000, 949) on and around the table? It's hard to imagine that Jesus has a sudden compulsion for dining etiquette.

The salient point does not concern the arrangements themselves but *how* Jesus makes them. Similar to the way he *pre*arranged to secure a colt for his first Jerusalem entrance (11:1-6), here Jesus sends "two of his disciples" into the city to locate an *already* furnished room and prepared meal (14:13-15). The exact process of recruiting a homeowner and a caterer is irrelevant; what matters is that Jesus knows the setup and tells the disciples how to find it— which they do, precisely "as he told them" (14:16). As his deadly pursuers close in, Jesus maintains a measure of control and keeps his trustworthy word to the end. His disciples will not prove to be so steady or reliable, but this memory of Jesus's integrity and authority will help sustain them after his crucifixion.

Prearranging a "meet" with a mysterious "man carrying a jar of water" seems like the stuff of spy novels. But, as suggested above, I don't think there's much mystery here. It's the very *ordinariness*, the *everydayness* of the event that stands out, what Latina/Mujerista biblical scholars call *lo cotidiano* (the "quotidian," Isasi-Diaz 2004; 2006, 92–106). What could be more ordinary than a man toting a jar of water—except perhaps a woman carrying it (cf. John 4:7, 28)? No alabaster vial of oil, no chalice of wine—just a plain earthenware jug of water. But Jesus enlists this ordinary water-carrier in his final mission on earth as Teacher (14:12), Lord, and Messiah. Soon another random man, "a passer-by," will be summoned to help Jesus carry his cross. Mark gives us this man's name and place of origin (15:21). But God's saving work through Christ Jesus involves all creation, all people named and not, small and great, last and first, temporary and permanent "employees."

Exposing the traitor (14:17-21). While the two disciples were no doubt pleased to find the large upstairs room nicely laid out, as Jesus had said, what he first tells and shows them in the evening when all twelve gather with him for the meal causes them "to be distressed" (*lypeisthai*, "pained/anguished"): "Truly I tell you, one of you will betray me, one who is eating with me" (14:18-19). Notice the personal and poignant punch of Jesus's remark: "One of *you*"—whom I chose to be *with me* from the start (3:14)—"one . . . eating *with me* now," will betray me! What a shocking accusation with an appalling implication: at this most sacred meal marking deep communion with Israel's ancestors and between Jesus and chosen followers, one participates falsely as a shameless undercover agent plotting to undermine Jesus and blow apart his redemptive mission!

Jesus punctuates his verbal bombshell with an arresting visual aid, calling attention to his betrayer dipping into the bowl of sauce "with me" (14:20). The Greek neither provides a direct object of the dipping nor identifies the sauce, but we might assume that Jesus and his betrayer dip their hands holding unleavened bread into the same bowl of sauce seasoned with bitter herbs, as custom required (Exod 12:8). The elements of this scene reinforce the travesty of betrayal. Instead of representing shared elements of a common loaf (as in Mark 14:22), here the broken bread pieces betoken broken communion between Jesus and his associates. Likewise, mingling hands in the common bowl exposes the underhanded scheme of Jesus's betrayer rather than signals the binding "hand of fellowship" (cf. Gal 2:9). And the act of dipping (*embaptō*) or "baptizing" becomes a sign of treachery and death-dealing instead of renewal and shared suffering (cf. 1:4-11; 10:38-39). The betrayer thus makes a mockery of both baptism and communion, two vital practices of the developing Christ-centered community. On a more personal level, he betrays Jesus's trust, the hallmark of friendship. As the psalmist lamented, "Even my bosom friend in whom I trusted, who ate of my bread, has lifted the heel against me" (NRSV)—or "kicked me with his heel—a betrayer!" (Ps 42:9 CEB; cf. 55:12-15; Donahue and Harrington 2002, 394).

The sauce mixture with bitter herbs may subtly portend Jesus's harsh experience of betrayal and abandonment in Gethsemane (meaning "oil press") on the Mount of Olives (Mark 14:32-52). And as the bitter herbs of the Passover meal evoked memory of ancient Israelites' "lives [made] bitter with hard service in mortar and brick and in every kind of field labor" in Egypt (Exod 1:4), so Jesus is about to suffer like an enslaved person (Mark 10:44-45), even to the point of brutal death. What makes it all the bitterer for him is that he will suffer not only at the violent hands of imperial soldiers but also at the devious and cowardly hands of his own disciples.

So how do they respond to Jesus's announcement of a traitor in their midst? He deliberately does not expose Judas by name and evidently dips his hand in the bowl multiple times with other disciples. Such a strategy allows Judas to carry out his plan unimpeded. (At this moment Jesus is resigned to his fate, though he resists it later in the evening [14:34-35].) And it also allows Jesus to test the commitment of all twelve apostles.

Tellingly, they each become defensive and individualistic: "Surely, not I?" (14:19), rendering a short two-word question in Greek (*mēti egō*) with an expected negative answer. Hence, "Surely, not I?" (NRSV). "Surely you don't mean me?" (NIV). "Don't look at me! I would never betray you for any reason!" (14:29-31; see Zerwick 1993, 155; BDAG 2000, 649). Forget what betrayal means for Jesus and the group; forget how they might ferret out the traitor and forestall his treachery. "Just keep *me* out of this; *I* don't want any part of it!" But does each one perhaps protest too much out of some underlying anxiety about his own level of commitment to Jesus? The CEB translation opens up this possibility: "It's not me, is it?"—to which we might add an internal "No, of course not! It can't be me! (*Or can it?*)." Before the night ends, it *will be* all of them, to some degree, not just Judas: "You will all become deserters," Jesus says (14:27); and sure enough, "All of them deserted and fled" (14:50).

Although Jesus's destiny as the suffering Son of Humankind must be fulfilled ("as it is written") and although all the disciples fail to support Jesus one way or another, Judas still bears the greater guilt—so much so that Jesus admits "it would have been better for that one [Judas] not to have been born" (14:21). Other New Testament accounts indicate that after Jesus's death Judas became so guilt-ridden that he hanged himself (Matt 27:3-5) or otherwise suffered a gruesome death (Acts 1:18-19). For his part, Jesus's "woe" regarding his betrayer seems less a pronouncement of judgment than a statement of reality, with a possible tinge of sympathy for the tragic role Judas plays in this messianic drama.

Renewing the covenant (14:22-25). After disrupting the Passover supper with his stunning disclosure about a betrayer, Jesus proceeds as the dutiful host with serving the normal bread and wine courses. But he scarcely lets the disciples catch their breath before he makes another shocking revelation. Along with commemorating Israel's past liberation from slavery, the elements of bread and wine, Jesus claims, represent *his own body and blood*—"This *is* my body. . . . This *is* my blood" (14:22-24)—now, in the next pressing hours, and beyond "until that day" of full and final realization of God's rule (14:25).

As unique, however, as this self-identification with the Passover elements is, Jesus does not thereby set himself apart from others but rather gives his bread/body and wine/blood "to them" to take into their bodies (14:22-23) and pours out his life in redemptive love "for many" (14:24; cf. 10:45). At this Last Supper on the eve of Jesus's abandonment by his disciples and separation from them in death, he enacts a dramatic reconciliation and intimate communion with them. As he broke a piece of bread to dip into the bowl with his betrayer, Jesus breaks other pieces—pieces of his body, as he dares call them—for all twelve disciples (including Judas!) to *share together* with him (unlike in John 13:21-30, where Judas exits after the bread-dipping scene, here Judas stays for the full meal). And from the same cup, "*all of them* drank" (Mark 14:23). Beyond exchanging hands of fellowship, Jesus invites his associates to take into themselves, to ingest, as it were, his nurturing body and lifeblood, to re-incarnate Jesus in their flesh-and-blood lives. Jesus the host and server of this supper becomes the *meal!*

There's no denying a mysterious, mystical, metaphorical dimension to Jesus's Last Supper drama. But to insist that this act is "just" a metaphor or "mere" symbol, as has been common in many Baptist and other Protestant traditions, dilutes and undervalues its significance (for more welcoming Baptist "sacramentalist" views, see Fowler 2002; Cross and Thompson, eds., 2003; Freeman 2014, 311–38; Spencer 2019, 674–90). Metaphors convey powerful truths about material reality (Lakoff and Johnson 2003). Enacted religious metaphors—whether we call them signs, symbols, or sacraments—reveal vital truths about God and God's world in all its holistic, sacred-material beauty and profundity. Such truths merit deep poetic reflection more than cool scientific analysis. Neither Mark nor any other New Testament writer engages in metaphysical theories about what "actually" happens to the "substance" of the elements in the Lord's Supper. The focus falls on *thankful communion* with and in the body of Christ, captured in other common names for this ritual: Eucharist, from the Greek *eucharisteō*, "give thanks" (14:23), and Holy Communion. The Lord's Supper is meant to be experienced more than examined (though see 1 Cor 12:28), celebrated more than calibrated.

Although Jesus offers little commentary beyond the straightforward "This is my body/blood" declaration, he does provide one significant clarification: his blood will be poured out to certify the *covenant* (some later copyists read "*new* covenant" in Mark 14:24; Omanson 2006, 96). Covenant represents a core biblical concept defining the relationship between God and God's people from the foundational times of Noah (Gen 9:9-17), Abraham (Gen 15:18; 17:1-22), and Moses (Exod 6:4-5; 19:5; 24:8; 34:10-15, 27-28) (Brueggemann 1997, 407–91; Levenson 1985, 15–86; 2016, 1–58; Block 2021). Adapted from the world of international politics, where victorious kings dictated treaties (covenants) with conquered peoples, the God of Israel in Moses' era renews the covenant with the people whom God rescues from an oppressive tyrant (Pharaoh). A political pact of power takes on more personal dimensions of a paternal bond of love for God's "firstborn son," Israel (Exod 4:22-23; cf. Jer 31:9; Hos 11:1; Levenson 1993, 36–42). And it becomes codified in the Torah, the "book of the covenant" (Exod 24:7), etched by God's "finger" (Exod 31:18; Deut 9:10) and sealed with a blood ritual (Exod 24:1-8).

But codification is not calcification. God's word is living word, always remaining in force but also being revised, revitalized, renegotiated, and renewed over the course of changing history. In the chaotic days of Babylonian conquest, the prophet Jeremiah envisioned God's making a "new covenant" with God's estranged and exiled people, rooted yet more deeply in their hearts than the older Mosaic covenant. Hopefully, then, as this renewed covenant reinforced God's gracious commitment to forgiveness and restoration, it also prompted the people's greater faithfulness to God (Jer 31:31-33; cf. Exod 34:6-7).

Jesus's dramatic covenant renewal act further personalizes and internalizes God's love bond with God's children. God, Israel, and all humanity join together faithfully in the embodied person of Christ, Son of God, and Son of Humankind. Jesus seals this divine-human union with *his own blood* as a sign of freedom from enslavement and forgiveness of sins (cf. Matt 26:28) to be taken *into* one's body as a life-giving infusion.

As in Israel's terrible time of suffering under Egyptian taskmasters and Babylonian conquerors, during the turbulent first century of oppressive Roman rule, so vividly sketched in Mark 13, the hope of endurance and ultimate salvation remains alive. Now on the brink of his death, Jesus fires his disciples' hope with the promise of one day sharing again the bracing "fruit of the vine" with them, "drink[ing] it *new* in the kingdom of God" (14:25). God the King never breaks covenant with God's people.

Praying and being abandoned at Gethsemane on the Mount of Olives (14:26-52)

Despite Jesus's solemn talk about his betrayal and death, the Passover meal concludes with singing the customary "hymn" (14:26), probably one of the Hallel psalms (Psalms 113–118). After ending on this jubilant high note, Jesus and company return to the Mount of Olives (Olivet). But soon the mood turns even gloomier than before.

This section is framed by haunting reports of the disciples' *deserting* Jesus in his direst hours.

- *Mark's Jesus predicts*: You will all become deserters (*skandalisthēsesthe*) (14:27)
- *Mark's narrator reports*: All of them deserted (*aphentes*) him and fled (*ephygon*) (14:50)

Here the NRSV uses "desert" language for different Greek terms. Although closely related in meaning, these words carry distinct nuances. The "scandalize" (*skandalizō*) term in 14:27 suggests "taking offense at" or "stumbling over" (cf. 4:17; 6:3; 9:42-43, 45, 47; 14:29). The CEB aptly captures the word-picture: "You will all *falter in your faithfulness* (*skandalisthēsesthe*) to me." The second statement uses a common term for "leave" (*aphiēmi*) punctuated by "fleeing" (*pheugō*) like a fugitive or refugee (14:50, 52). Sadly, the disciples will not simply "stumble" in their futile attempts to support Jesus; they will turn on their heels and run away as fast as they can to save their necks.

While Jesus knows and accepts that his followers will forsake him, he does not do so with complete stoical resignation and equanimity. Spliced between these desertion announcements is the poignant scene at "a place called Gethsemane" on Olivet, where Jesus pours out his heart in agonizing distress over his impending death and pleads with his divine Father for a way out, "if it were possible" (14:32-35). It's not possible, as it happens, and Jesus readily submits to his terminal fate. But he does "not go gentle into that good night" (Thomas 2003, 239). As a lover of life as well as a giver of life (the two are connected), Jesus resists death as much as possible.

Peter's predicted denial (14:26-31). Jesus elaborates his forecast of the disciples' desertion with pastoral imagery from the prophet Zechariah: "For it is written, 'I will strike the shepherd, and the sheep will be scattered'" (14:27; Zech 13:7). Mark has previously featured Jesus's role as a faithful, compassionate shepherd for God's wandering people in "a deserted place," an isolated wilderness locale representing their vulnerable state of being *deserted* by callous leaders. The crowds came to Jesus "like sheep without a shepherd" (Mark 6:34)—until they found the true guiding and feeding shepherd in him (6:33-44). Now, via Zechariah, Mark's Jesus turns the pastoral simile on its head. His followers will again be like shepherd-less sheep because *he* is about to be struck down; and they will scatter because they have *deserted him*, their shepherd, in his hour of desperate need.

The larger pastoral picture in Zechariah juxtaposes a faithful, nurturing "shepherd of the flock" with neglectful, uncaring shepherds led by a "worthless shepherd" (Zech 10:3; 11:4-5, 15-17). The true, good shepherd, perhaps an image of the prophet himself, is "doomed for slaughter" at the hands of the false, evil shepherds, likely representing feckless leaders who were "annulling the covenant that [God] had made with all the peoples" (11:4, 7-11). In particular the chief "worthless shepherd . . . *deserts* the flock!" (11:17). Applied to Jesus's ominous prediction in Mark 14:27, he becomes the shepherd led to the slaughter (Acts 8:32, quoting Isa 53:7, links Jesus with the "*sheep/lamb* led to the slaughter"), while his disciples assume the role of feckless under-shepherds who *desert him* and thus strain the *covenant* he has just renewed with them (Mark 14:24) to the breaking point.

But death, desertion, and dispersion do not have the last word in Zechariah or Mark. Although the Lord's "shepherd . . . my associate" in Zechariah will be struck dead as the sheep abandon the shepherd and scatter abroad, the Lord will not abandon them. They will emerge from the experience "refined/tested" as precious "silver/gold," and "they will call on my name, and I will answer them. I will say, 'They are my people'; and they will say, 'The LORD is our God'" (Zech 13:7-9). And Mark's Jesus hastens to follow his ominous forecast with a promise of resurrection and reconciliation: "But after I am raised up, I will go before you into Galilee" (Mark 14:28)—implying that he will meet and welcome them there (see 16:7).

But as before, Peter and his cohorts seem not to register Jesus's promise of resurrection. They miss the big picture, buck against it, and fixate on the negative. Again Peter speaks first, blurting out, "Even though all become deserters, I will not," or more literally, "But not I" (*all' ouk egō*, 14:29). Jesus then doubles down on his prediction, pinpointing that Peter will not just desert Jesus but will "*deny* me three times" in the middle of the night, "this very night," "before the cock crows twice" (14:30; cf. 13:35). How dare Jesus think so badly of Peter, who bites back "vehemently" with even more bravado—"Even though I must die with you, I will not deny you"—prompting similar pledges from the other disciples, though doubtless in more muted tones.

If an actor read aloud and performed Peter's part (Shiner 2003), we would imagine him booming out Peter's protest with piercing voice, jutted jaw, jabbing finger, and puffed chest. But we think that Peter definitely protests too much! The word translated "vehemently" (*ekperissōs*) more literally means "excessively" or "too much." Peter's mention of dying with Jesus suggests that he thinks he's ready to take up his cross and follow Jesus (see 8:34). But unfortunately, that's all bluster and pretense at this stage. Neither Peter nor any fellow-apostle follows through on their oath to Jesus.

Jesus's agonized demurral (14:32-36). Popular Christian perceptions of Gethsemane conjure up a pleasant *garden* area on the side of the Mount of Olives, though "Garden of Gethsemane" appears nowhere in the New Testament. Only the Gospel of John paints a garden picture, with no mention of "Gethsemane" (John 18:1, 26; cf. 19:41; 20:15). Mark's *Gethsēmani* (also Matt 26:36) transliterates the Hebrew term meaning "oil press," an appropriate name for a place with olive groves and presses where Mark stages Jesus's mounting sense of pressure and depression over his imminent death (Powery 2007; Rousseau and Arav 1995, 111–12, Thorsen 1992). No more enjoyment of fragrant oil, no savoring of garden delights. This scene more readily evokes David's beleaguered "ascent of the Mount of Olives, weeping as he goes, with his head covered and walking barefoot," after his son Absalom had usurped the kingdom with the aid of David's traitorous counselor, Ahitophel (2 Sam 15:30-31; Powery 2007, 562).

Three strong emotion terms in Mark 14:33-34 characterize Jesus's struggle (Spencer 2021, 97-98):

- "Distressed" (*ekthambeomai*), a term used only by Mark in the New Testament, denotes being "moved to a relatively intense emotional state because of something causing great surprise or perplexity" (BDAG 2000, 302). Other cases reflect others' reactions *to* the exalted Jesus, either with "awe" after his transfiguration (9:15) or "alarm" after his resurrection (16:5-6). But here Jesus himself becomes overwhelmed at the prospect of crucifixion. His earlier matter-of-fact predictions of his death (8:31; 9:31; 10:33-34) give way to emotion-charged upheaval as the crucial "hour" looms.

- "Agitated" (*adēmoneō*), no mere irritation but rather "intense inner agitation" (Danker and Krug 2009, 7), appears outside Mark 14:33//Matthew 26:37 only in the imprisoned Paul's impassioned reflection on his beloved friend Epaphroditus's recovery from a life-threatening illness. Epaphroditus himself had been deeply "distressed/agitated" (*adēmonōn*) about how news of his illness affected his home congregation in Philippi (Phil 2:26). For Paul's part, he expresses gratitude to God for healing Epaphroditus, whose death would have caused Paul extreme "sorrow" (*lypē*) (2:27; cf. Jesus's *perilypos* in Mark 14:34). Is it possible that, like Epaphroditus, Jesus is agitated about *his disciples'* distress over his impending death? Perhaps, but such sympathy does not discount his own struggle with the terrible fate awaiting him.

- "Deeply grieved" (*perilypos*) is how Jesus describes his emotional state, more fully, "I am deeply grieved, even unto death" (14:34). The "I" here renders "my soul/life" (*psychē mou*), not as a separate soul-part of Jesus but as a descriptor of his whole "psychic" being or "self." "Even unto death" specifies his preoccupation with the pressing reality of dying and suggests the dire valence of his emotion, as if to say, "I am so sorrowful as to almost die" (Friberg, Friberg, and Miller 2000). The *perilypos* term, an intensified form of *lypē* ("grief," "pain") appears only one other time in Mark, ironically characterizing Herod Antipas's "deep grieving" over Herodias's wish for John the Baptist's decapitation (6:26)! Herod doesn't grieve enough to refuse his wife's request, which he had sworn to grant; so as not to lose face before his cronies, despite his qualms, Herod orders John's immediate beheading (6:22-28). Herod cares more about vain honor than about human life, in stark contrast to Jesus's passionate love of life, including his own. Jesus's selfless love for others is paradoxically but authentically fueled by healthy self-love (see 12:31).

Making His Final Mark: Jesus's Death and Resurrection

But the tension of this paradox is almost more than Jesus can bear, as his actual death, even death on a cross, closes in. In this greatest crisis of his life, Jesus naturally turns to prayer. He unashamedly asks Peter, James, and John to support him by staying nearby and keeping alert. Needing to wrestle one on one with his Father, he moves "a little farther" from his followers and hits the ground in fervent supplication (14:34-35a). This is no time for extended prayer and contemplation. Jesus's request is personal and to the point, reinforced in the narrative by both indirect speech and direct plea (Spencer 2021, 99–101).

- *Indirect Speech*: Jesus "prayed that, if it were possible, the hour might pass from him" (14:35).
- *Direct Plea*: "Abba, Father, for you all things are possible; remove this cup from me" (14:36).

Two images reflect Jesus's explicit desire that his Father rescue him from death: passing by (*parerchomai*) the hour of death and carrying away (*parapherō*) the cup of death. "Passing by" recalls the death angel's "pass over" the Israelites' homes and their "pass through" the Red Sea out of enslavement to freedom (the same verb [*parerchomai*] Jesus uses in prayer characterizes both "passing" events in Exod 12:23; 15:16 LXX). And Jesus's "cup" reference pleads for a stunning rescission of the new covenantal "cup" he just drank at the Last Supper/Passover (14:23-24).

But doesn't he quickly qualify his bold request with the conditional "if it were possible" and the compliant "yet, not what I want, but you want" (14:35-36)? Based on Jesus's prayer, many Christians today tag "if it be thy will" to all their supplications to God. Certainly, desiring that "God's will be done" is central to faithful prayer (Matt 6:10). But Jesus's affirmation of his Father's will does not blunt the force of his own will to life. The type of conditional request Jesus makes comes close to meaning "*since* it *is* possible" (Mark 14:35; see Wallace 1996, 690–94), paralleling his straightforward assertion, "Father, for you all things *are* possible" (14:36). Moreover, the "possible" term (*dynatos*) in both clauses connotes dynamic "power": Jesus knows that his Father, the source of life, has the *power* to stop the deadly forces arrayed against Jesus. God *can* remove the lethal cup if God wants to. And Jesus fervently wants God ("what I want") to do just that.

There is no getting around a clash of wills between Father and Son at this critical moment. Although Jesus ultimately submits to his Father's will, he makes his preference clear: Jesus *wants to live*. But in turn, let us be clear about the respective wills of Jesus and the Father. Jesus's will to life does not stem from some craven fear of death or unwillingness to suffer, sacrifice, and serve on others' behalf. Indeed, he lives to love others and to lead them to flourishing life. Can his "ransom" death, even followed by resurrection (10:34, 45), do as much for broken humanity as his continuing liberating life would do? From Christianity's larger historical and theological perspective, we would answer "Yes." But in the heat of the moment with *his life on the line*, Jesus makes a request as reasonable as it is emotional.

As for God's part, we must not twist God's choice not to intervene in the dire events about to overtake Jesus as some perverse lust for child sacrifice or sadistic desire to pour out wrath on Jesus for all the wickedness in the world. If no decent human father could imagine treating his son like that, how much less the divine Father (Matt 7:9-11//Luke 11:11-13)? Again, we take much heart in God's faithful working out good from evil throughout history (see Gen 50:20; Rom 8:28-30), not least the horrific unjust crucifixion of the Son of God. But a great theological gulf separates God's supposed willing and bringing about (executing!) Jesus's death from God's determined working in and through this ungodly event to bring about—in spite of its unspeakable evil—healing, salvation, redemption, restoration, re-creation.

Peter, James, and John's lapsed vigilance (14:37-42). By now we're not surprised when the disciples let Jesus down. This current lapse, however, both seems particularly tragic, coming as it does at Jesus's direst "hour," and moves us to more sympathy than usual with the disciples' struggles. Notice three poignant contrasts between Jesus and his three companions.

- *Contrasting spans of attention.* Jesus is on high alert in the middle of the night, wrestling with his imminent death; he couldn't sleep if he wanted to. By contrast, despite Jesus's pleas for them to "keep awake" (14:34, 38; cf. 13:32-37), the three apostles succumb to sleep—after all *three times* Jesus interrupts his prayer to wake them (14:37-41; cf. Peter's three denials, 14:30, 66-72)! The current scene flips the script on the storm incident in 4:35-41, where Jesus sleeps confidently through the tempest while the disciples panic at the prospect of drowning to death. Now Jesus grapples with his own death—which he cannot stop like he stilled the storm—while the soporific disciples refuse to deal with Jesus's death, to be "with him" (cf. 3:14) in his desperate hour. What drives their drowsiness: denial of death, fear for their own lives, unbearable grief (cf. Luke 22:45)? Likely some mix of these attitudes and emotions as they try to absorb the deadly fate that awaits their Lord. It's all more than they can consciously take in.

- *Contrasting senses of the moment.* As Jesus faces "*the* hour" (Mark 14:35, 41), the last moments of his life, he can scarcely believe that his three confidants fail to keep vigil for even "*one* hour" (14:37). They think they have time for a nap when there's no time to waste to be with their Lord. A tragic irony may be detected in Peter's/"Rock's" (*Petros*) sleeping like a rock, dead to the world as his world is about to crumble.

• *Contrasting spurs to action.* Although not pleased with Peter and company's lack of vigilance, Jesus appears sympathetic to their tugs-of-war between a *willing spirit* and *weak flesh* (14:38). "Willing" (*prothymos*) combines volitional, emotional, and behavioral elements, connoting "filled with zeal for rendering service" (Danker and Krug 2009, 300). Emotions play a vital role in stimulating "action readiness" (Frijda 1986, 69–93, 231–41; 1988, 351). But this e/motivational potency necessarily operates in and through the body, flesh and all, with all of the body's wonderful potentialities and irksome limitations. Mark's Jesus does not set up a dichotomy between pure spirit and polluted flesh, between good will (intentions) and evil deed (actions): tension, yes, in certain contexts, like the crisis facing Jesus and his companions—but not division. We are unitary, living beings—spirited bodies/embodied spirits imbued with the breath (*pneuma*) of life (Gen 2:7). In the face of life's disruptive challenges and conflicts, our "operating systems" seek to restore optimal flow and balance ("homeostasis," see Damasio 2018, 3–68; 2003, 30–40, 269–72) as soon as possible. Jesus gets there much sooner than his associates. After lodging his clear objection to the Father, he resolves to accept his fatal destiny. No more pleading—with God or with Peter, James, and John. The die is cast. "Enough! The hour has come . . . Get up, let us be going. See, my betrayer is at hand" (Mark 14:42).

The announcement that Jesus's betrayal is "at hand (*ēngiken*)" eerily evokes Jesus's foundational message that "the kingdom of God is at hand (*ēngiken*)" (1:15 NASB, NAB). Bookending Mark's Gospel is this jarring juxtaposition of the "beginning of the good news of Jesus Christ, the Son of God" (1:1) who embodies the "good news" (*euangelion*) of God's just and peaceful rule (1:14) on the one hand, and the betraying of this "evangelical" mission by delivering Jesus to ungodly, murderous powers on the other hand. Does this mean that the promise of God's kingdom has been thwarted, that evil has gained the upper hand? For the moment it seems so, as Luke's Jesus puts it to his arrestors: "This is your hour, the power of darkness" (Luke 22:53).

But it is not the final hour. Death will not have the last word in the gospel story. The dynamic realm of God works through darkness and death to bring light and life. God does not, however, vaporize into oblivion the forces set against Christ. They are allowed to play their hand, and Jesus—in solidarity with all suffering humanity—is allowed to experience both the agony of God's seeming hands-off approach (Mark 15:34) and the assurance that God's hand persistently operates in and through bad events to good, life-flourishing ends.

Judas's enacted betrayal (14:43-49). The pace of the story picks up: for the first time in a while (since 11:2-3), Mark uses his favorite word, *euthys*, twice to describe Judas's swift, interruptive action: "*Immediately* (*euthys*), while [Jesus] was still speaking, Judas . . . arrived. . . . when [Judas] came, he went up to [Jesus] *at once* (*euthys*) and said, 'Rabbi!' and kissed him" (14:43-44). If Judas has any second thoughts about betraying Jesus (as he shows post facto in Matt 27:3-5), he takes no time to entertain them now. He has brought with him a "large" armed posse under the authority of the temple officials (14:47), as if Jesus and his eleven apostles might try to resist arrest militarily (though Jesus has never called his followers to arms) or miraculously (though Jesus has never used his power to benefit himself).

Perhaps the most invidious aspect of Judas's behavior is the "sign" he gives to the temple guards identifying Jesus—the sign of a *kiss* on Jesus's cheek or neck (14:44-45). Though not a cosmic or cataclysmic sign (*sēmeion*, 8:11-12; 13:4, 22), this simple signal (*syssēmon*) reveals the tragic truth of a world gone awry: a mark of beloved fellowship becomes a blotch of cruel treachery; a holy kiss becomes a heinous means of pinpointing the kill target.

Jesus, however, does not respond to Judas personally, to the unidentified disciple who hacks off the ear of a servant of the high priest (14:47), or to the injured servant himself. Whereas Luke's Jesus heals the man's severed ear (Luke 22:50-51) and the Fourth Gospel identifies the swordsman as Simon Peter and the servant as Malchus (John 18:10), Mark's Jesus only addresses the arrest party as a unit, particularly challenging their treating him like a "bandit." Otherwise, he offers no impassioned legal defense, only a simple query and comment wondering why they hadn't nabbed him sooner if they thought he was such a bad guy (14:48-49). Jesus makes no attempt to resist arrest: he accepts his fate, after communing with his Father, and again views his betrayal and death as previewed in "the scriptures" (14:49; cf. 14:21). He cites no specific authors or verses but likely senses his affinity with God's righteous servants in the Psalms and book of Isaiah who suffer at the hands of unjust attackers (e.g., Psalm 22; Isaiah 53).

But amid this generally compliant response, Jesus deems it important to distance himself from bandits. The "bandit" term (*lēstēs*) designates "one who engages in violent activity against established social order" (Danker and Krug 2009, 215), in distinction from a petty pilferer or "thief" (*kleptēs*, Friberg, Friberg, and Miller 2000). Common tactics of bandits (rebels, vigilantes) included armed robbery, severe beating, and even murder of wealthy ruling elites (Hanson 2002; Shaw 2004; Horsley and Hanson 1985, 48–87). Jesus certainly challenged abusive establishments such as the present temple system, which he dared to compare (with Jeremiah) to a "den of *robbers/bandits* (*lēstois*)" (11:17)! But Jesus robbed no one of anything and launched no physical attack against any human being. His expelling temple clerks and overturning their counting tables was boisterous but not bloody. This disruptive action made its sharp point *without violence*. After a little housekeeping, the temple business would hum along just as before.

Whatever you do, Jesus indicates to the armed arrest party, "Don't take me as a violent bandit!" Implied in his retort is another ironic table turning: "You and your priestly bosses are the real bandits who use the holy temple as your hideout—in plain sight of everyone!" Under the guise of rooting out alleged violent resistors of the dominant political order, the establishment itself self-righteously resorts to violent reprisals. The ends of retaining power justify bandit-style means (Hanson 2002, 293–95; cf. Malina 1994). Make no mistake: Jesus is the victim and opponent of violence (nonviolently), not its agent and proponent.

The disciples' "naked" desertion (14:50-52). As Jesus predicted en route to the Mount of Olives that his disciples would be "scandalized" (*skandalisthēsesthe*) by him and "scattered" from him (14:27), "all of them deserted/left (*aphentes*) him," now leaving him behind as they once left everything *for him* (1:18-20; 10:28-29). This move is no casual drifting away but a concerted running away like fugitives, even for the one impetuous sword-wielder. No more fight from him or anyone else: it's all flight and fleeing (*ephygon*, 14:50).

And it's not just the eleven disciples who flee their former colleague Judas and the arrest party he brings with him. A surprise figure who "was following [along with] (*synēkolouthei*)" Jesus enters the picture. He is strangely identified as "a certain young man (*neaniskos*)" skimpily clad in "nothing but a linen cloth (*sindōn*)" (14:51), a "light piece of clothing" (BDAG 2000, 924) suitable for sleeping (nightshirt) or covering a corpse (burial cloth) (Friberg, Friberg, and Miller 2000). Where does this youth come from in this garb? Has he just hopped out of bed for a stroll in Gethsemane where he gets caught up in this police scene? Does his attire somehow foreshadow the "linen cloth" (*sindōn*) that will soon enwrap Jesus's dead body (15:46)? The situation gets stranger when the guards try to seize him, only to be left holding his single garment while the young man streaks away "naked"! He "ran off/fled" (*ephygen*) like the other disciples, except for waiting a little longer and leaving more behind than they did (14:50-52).

This is one of the few unparalleled scenes in Mark. It's not hard to see why the other Gospels writers omitted it, but why, pray tell, did Mark include it? The popular interpretation that this Gospel's author, "Mark" himself, throws in this clip as a personal cameo is purely speculative and makes little sense, given its unflattering portrait. More likely, the young man with his wardrobe malfunction plays a symbolic role. We have previously noted the motif of clothing in Mark's narrative, and the final scenes will provide other examples (14:63; 15:17-20, 24). Here the stripped, streaking young man may represent a figure of shame and shunning. On the shame side, losing his nightshirt exposes his naked shame, as Adam and Eve's donning the fig leaf revealed their loss of innocence, their dawning sense of shame (originally, they were "naked and *not ashamed*," Gen 2:25), resulting in their expulsion from Eden, albeit no longer naked or wearing a withering leaf-cloth but covered with durable animal hides provided by God (Gen 3:7, 10-11, 21-24). The fleeing young man in Mark has no redeeming cover (at the moment, but see Mark 16:5), and there is no freedom or glory in running naked (*gymnos*, 14:52), as the Greeks celebrated in their "gyms" (*gymnasia*) or centers for "naked" recreation (Greenblatt 2017, 141–44).

In terms of shunning, the young man turns his bare back on Jesus, wanting nothing more to do with him, utterly abandoning him in his greatest hour of need, as do all the disciples. This youth represents the potential fickleness of Jesus's followers, particularly among the next (younger) generations that constitute Mark's original audience. "Let the reader/hearer understand" (Mark 13:14): "How will *you* respond *now* to Christ in times of hardship? Will *you* keep faithfully following or flee in fear?" (cf. 16:8a).

It's also possible that the mysterious young man represents an angelic figure. It's not unusual for the Bible to identify an angel as a "man" or "young man"; a "young man" (*neaniskos*) will appear at Jesus's empty tomb (16:5; cf. Dan 8:15-16; 9:21; 2 Macc 3:26, 33-34). But these angelic "men" are invariably strong, powerful agents, "guardian angels," as we often say, not those who flit away from trouble and abandon their posts. This, however, is a strange, apocalyptic "hour" in Mark's story. Nothing is normal; the world is falling apart. Perhaps the young man is one of Jesus's ministering angels (Mark 1:13), staying around a bit longer than the eleven disciples, only to dash away at the last minute. Perhaps Mark provides an eerie hint of the unthinkable abandonment of Jesus at one horrible moment on the cross by the *Father himself* (15:34).

Jewish and Roman Trials (14:53–15:15)

Following his arrest, Jesus is granted a speedy trial—two, to be accurate—before Jewish and Roman magistrates, respectively—which may seem preferable to a long period of languishing in prison before trial. But these prove to be shotgun trials with little concern for justice. Lacking Roman citizenship, Jesus is not entitled to due process under Roman law, and the temple officials have already made up their minds about him. In the current political environment, the Jewish high court in Jerusalem needed to tread carefully in capital cases, seeking if possible Roman approval and apparatus (the cross) for executing dangerous criminals.

The high priest (Caiaphas at this time) and Jewish council thus had to make some show of trying Jesus before bringing to Pilate their charges and capital verdict against Jesus; they also whipped up a mob to pressure Pilate (14:64; 15:1, 11-13). But a sham trial featuring a string of "false" witnesses is all Mark's Jesus gets before the Jewish high court (14:55-65). As for Pilate's part, he first plays it closer to the legal book by appearing to judge the evidence on its merits, which he claims to find wanting: "What evil has [Jesus] done?" (15:14). But the truth of the case promptly gives way to political expedience. No need to alienate the Judean leaders and the crowd to spare one Galilean royal pretender, however harmless he seems to be.

No one is committed to defending Jesus—including his leading deputy, Peter, who after fleeing the scene at Gethsemane follows the arrest party to the high priest's residence, though at a distance (14:54). It's possible that Peter looks for some opportunity to intervene on Jesus's behalf. But when the spotlight falls on Peter between the two trial scenes (14:66-72), he buckles in fear and thrice denies he even knows Jesus, just as Jesus predicted he would earlier that evening (14:30).

Mark thus sets a bleak stage for Jesus's execution as a gross miscarriage of justice—a veritable lynching (Cone 2011)—by the authorities and a callous case of abandonment by his associates. He will die a torturous death as an innocent and forsaken man.

Sham trial by the high priest and Jewish council (14:53-65)

Jesus had predicted his followers would be hauled before various local Jewish "councils" in the difficult times to come (13:9). Now he is brought before the "whole council" in Jerusalem, the Jewish Supreme Court ("Sanhedrin," *synedrion*) composed of "all the chief priests, the [leading] elders, and the scribes" (14:53, 55). The high priest or Chief Justice convenes the high court in his residence in the middle of the night—not a move designed to showcase transparency.

Honesty and integrity also go by the boards in Mark's account of the trial, as "many gave false testimony" against Jesus without any great concern that these witnesses present consistent reports: "their testimony did not agree" (14:56; cf. 14:55-59). Some prevaricators claim that they "heard [Jesus] say" that he planned to "destroy this temple" and personally replace it "in three days" with a spiritual temple, "not made with hands" (14:57). But Mark's Jesus has said no such thing. Following in the train of Israel's prophets, Jesus challenges the corrupt temple institution of his day and forecasts the destruction of its buildings in the next generation (13:1-2), but he never claims that *he himself* will raze or reconstruct it.

As often happens when unscrupulous authorities sense their power being threatened, they try to turn their critics' words against them and paint them as the real "enemy of the people" (Ben-Ghiat 2020, 1–15, 247–61). In Jesus's case, the Jerusalem council recruits shady witnesses who make Jesus out to be a marauding royal pretender intent on committing further "desolating sacrilege" against the temple (cf. 13:14) and then refashioning it in his image for his glory, much like Antiochus IV Epiphanes and Gaius Caesar aimed to do and Herod the Great succeeded in doing, though he was a renovator, not an iconoclast (see discussion on 13:1-8, 14-23).

After misrepresenting Jesus's past words, the hostile court tries to get him to incriminate himself on the spot, as the high priest now shoots a loaded, point-blank question at Jesus: "Are you the Messiah, the Son of the Blessed One?" (14:61). The *Messiah* question seems designed to ensnare Jesus in a political trap. Jewish law did not prohibit anyone from making a messianic claim. But given the expected Messiah's association with "anointed" Davidic kingship, Rome would be highly suspicious of any royal claimant, and the Jewish council needed to appease Rome in order to maintain its authority.

The *Son of the Blessed One* question, with "Blessed One" standing in for God's sacred name, reflects a theological concern of idolatry. Has Jesus dared to make himself equal with God as God's unique "Son," not simply one of God's children? More particularly, has he dared to identify himself by the divine name for which "the Blessed One" stands? Such claims would indict Jesus as a blasphemer in the extreme. Early in his ministry, some scribes privately accused Jesus of blasphemy for assuming divine authority to forgive sins (2:7). But appropriating the divine *name* is the ultimate sacrilegious act, demanding the death penalty. Leviticus 24:16 lays down the law in no uncertain terms: "One who blasphemes the name of the LORD shall be put to death; the whole congregation shall stone the blasphemer. Aliens, as well as citizens, when they blaspheme the Name, shall be put to death." Josephus meshes this punishment with Deuteronomy 21:22-23: "He that blasphemes God, let him be stoned; and let him hang upon a tree all that day; and then let him be buried in an ignominious and obscure manner" (*Ant.* 4.202; in the New Testament, "tree" can represent the *cross* [Acts 5:30; 10:39; 13:29; Gal 3:13]). And early rabbinic literature specifies, "'The blasphemer' is not culpable unless he pronounces the Name itself" (m. Sanhedrin 7.5; Danby 1933, 392; Collins 2004, 381).

Although Mark titles his narrative, "The beginning of the good news of *Jesus Christ/Messiah, the Son of God*" (1:1), within the story Jesus has studiously avoided promoting these titles *for himself* and tried to prohibit others, including demons and disciples, from publicizing these roles for him. Jesus has advanced the gospel and kingdom of God (1:14-15), not himself, though he holds rightful claim to being God's beloved Son and the chief agent of God's realm. Now, however, as his story nears its end, after initially offering no riposte to the false witnesses (14:60-61), Jesus openly answers the high priest's queries concerning his messianic and divine identity: "I am" (14:62). No grandstanding, no chest-thumping, but no waffling either: a straightforward, emphatic "I [myself] am" (*Egō eimi*). If the high priest within the scene or any hearers/readers of Mark's narrative associate this statement with the holy "I AM" Name of God revealed to Moses (Exod 3:14), so be it. Technically, Jesus skirts a clear-cut violation of blaspheming God's name. But effectively he accepts the charge leveled against him—not as blasphemy, however, but as the truth of *who he is* (cf. 4:41).

And as it happens, Jesus has more to say than his crisp "I am" affirmation of his divine Sonship and Messiahship. He adds a somewhat lengthier statement, shifting to his future (continuing) role as *Son of Humankind*, which he contends "You [all] will see" and be compelled to confirm. He again appeals to Scripture, blending texts from Psalm 110:1-3 and Daniel 7:13-14 to support his authority as God's co-regent of both heaven and earth: "'You will see the Son of Man seated at the right hand of the Power (*dynameōs*),' and 'coming with the clouds of heaven'" (14:62). The "Power" is another way, like the "Blessed One," of referring to God without saying the sacred Name. The Greek version of the Psalm text reads, "Sit on my right [hand].... A rod of your *power* (*dynameōs*) the Lord will send out from Sion.... With you is rule on a day of your *power* (*dynameōs*) among the splendors of the holy ones" (Ps 109[110]:1-3 NETS).

While some Jewish traditions allowed for special beings to share the heavenly ruling platform with God (1 Enoch 51:3; 55:4; 61:8; 62:1-9), other traditions were more protective of God's exclusive, supreme sovereignty

(Bock 2018, 232–34). The high priest in Mark takes the latter view. Jesus's personal claim to be God's "right-hand Man" is the last straw for the priestly judge, causing him to rip his clothes in protest, declare Jesus guilty of blasphemy, and lead the council to demand the death penalty. He further condones the court's abusive treatment of Jesus: spitting on him and striking him blindfolded, with taunts of "Prophesy!"—that is, "Tell us who hit you!" (14:63-65). The high priest's horror over Jesus's alleged sharing of God's throne exceeds the shock over anything Jesus might say or do concerning God's temple. As Darrell Bock writes, Jesus's latest "claim was worse than someone saying, 'I will go and live in the holy of holies in the temple,' because Jesus has in mind God's very presence above, not the sacred locale where that presence was represented on earth" (Bock 2018, 235). This is as blasphemous as it gets from the council's myopic perspective in Mark.

Shameful denial by the apostle Peter (14:66-72)

Meanwhile, back in the high priest's courtyard, while Jesus is under fire from the interrogating council, Peter is "warming himself at the [literal] fire" with the guards who had arrested Jesus! Having fled the Gethsemane scene, Peter slinks back to follow Jesus but only at a safe "distance" (14:54.) Yet however much he tries to fit in with the guards—"sitting [together] with (*sygkathēmenos*) with them" (14:54)—Peter winds up undergoing an ad hoc trial of his own, prosecuted first by a servant-girl of the high priest and then by unspecified bystanders. Desperate to keep his cover and save his neck, he blatantly disavows any knowledge of Jesus three times (as Jesus forecast in 14:30), the last time punctuated with vehement cursing (14:66-71). We may chart Peter's ignominious swan song in Mark's story as below.

Notice that Mark carefully tracks Peter's locations and movements in, down, and out: he "followed" (*ēkolouthēsen*) Jesus, as a disciple should, "*into* (*esō eis*) [→] the courtyard" but only after Jesus had been led through it into the high priest's residence; Peter has modulated from a deserted disciple to a *distant* one. He stays "*below/down* (*katō*) [↓] in the courtyard" warming himself and denying he knows Jesus, who is being questioned in an upper floor "or at least a raised part" of the palace (Donahue and Harrington 2002, 425). After a servant-girl (not a guard or officer) makes the first query about his identity, Peter edges back "*out into* (*exō eis*) [←] the forecourt" near the villa's gates. He's back to deserting mode. And when he disavows Jesus two more times with a final profane flourish and hears the cock crow, Peter—now left alone in the dark with nothing but his disloyal guilt—"*broke down* [↓] and wept." The breakdown term (*epibalōn*), literally "throwing down/upon," "prob[ably] intends the reader to understand a wild gesture connected with lamentation" (BDAG 2000, 368). Salient parallels in Mark include forceful waves "breaking over" (*epeballen*) a storm-tossed boat (4:37 NAB, NASB; "waves beat into the boat," NRSV) and the police squad who "laid hands on (*epebalon*) [Jesus] and arrested him" (14:46) or "took him down," we might say. Peter is overthrown by waves of regretful emotion, overtaken by metaphorical cardiac arrest as a consequence of his fragile flesh and weak will.

Peter exits the stage in terrible shame—distanced from Jesus, spiraling downward, emotionally devastated. Other Gospels and the book of Acts rehabilitate Peter with assurances from Jesus, post-resurrection appearances by Jesus, and Peter's Spirit-filled leadership in the Jerusalem congregation (Matt 28:16-20; Luke 22:31-32; 24:12, 34, 36-53; John 20:1-10, 19-30; 21:1-23; Acts 1:15-26; 2:14-36; 3:1-5:11). But not Mark, except for a glimmer of hope in the next-to-last verse, in which the women at the empty tomb are instructed, "Go, tell his disciples *and Peter* that [the risen Jesus] is going ahead of you into Galilee" (Mark 16:7). The longer ending in Mark

Text	Location	Company	Actions/Words
14:54	Followed Jesus "at a distance" into the high priest's courtyard (*aulē*)	"Sitting with the guards" who had arrested Jesus	"Warming himself at the fire" Still "warming himself"
14:66-68a	"Below in the courtyard" (*kata en tē aulē*)	Guards (presumably) and "one of the servant-girls of the high priest"	Denial #1 to servant-girl: "I do not know or understand what you are talking about"
14:68b-70a	"He went out into the forecourt" (*proaulion*) of the high priest's courtyard	Servant-girl and "bystanders"	Denial #2 to servant-girl (reported, no direct speech)
14:70b-71	No change	"Bystanders" (no further mention of servant-girl)	Denial #3 to bystanders: "I do not know this man you are talking about"—punctuated with cursing
14:72	No change	No change—though spotlight falls on Peter alone	Peter "broke down and wept"

16:8b mentions Peter again, but most scholars regard this as later, added material (see below on 16:8b-20).

Shrewd trial by the Roman governor Pilate (15:1-15)

At morning's first light, following their nocturnal kangaroo court, the "whole council" of Jewish leaders in Jerusalem "formed a plan" (15:1 CEB), bound by "common purpose" (*symboulion* [my translation]), to deliver Jesus to the Roman governor Pilate for official sentencing and execution of Jesus. Moreover, "the chief priests," in particular, "stirred up the crowd" to pressure Pilate even more (15:11). We should not regard this "crowd" (cf. 15:8, 15), however, as representing the whole or even majority of Passover pilgrims and local Jerusalem residents, "many" of whom welcomed Jesus into the city as the coming Davidic king (11:9-10). Although some may now turn against Jesus, it's unlikely the entire company would suddenly clamor for his crucifixion. This "crowd" constitutes a hastily assembled mob looking for trouble, seeking a violent spectacle. Who knows what they even know about Jesus beyond rumors?

Pilate has to tread carefully at the Passover festival, with its influx of visitors celebrating ancient Israel's freedom from imperial rule. He can't afford simply to slough off the demands of the Roman-appointed Jewish leaders and their rabble-rousing recruits. But neither can he appear to cede too readily to their wishes. Pilate is Caesar's man in Judea and must keep the peace, if possible, but never at the expense of Roman rule and law. At his tribunal, he sits as chief judge and interrogator with an ostensible aim of fairly assessing the charges brought against Jesus.

Pilate poses five questions—two to Jesus, three to the gathered crowd—intermitted with their responses. Leaving aside Jewish religious accusations of blasphemy against Jesus, Pilate focuses on Roman political concerns of treachery. Bottom line: Is Jesus an enemy of the Roman state? Does he claim to be "King of the Jews" (15:2, 9, 12), thus displacing Caesar?

Pilate questions Jesus (15:1-5)

Pilate: Are you the king of the Jews?
Jesus: You say so.
Pilate: Have you no answer? See how many charges they bring against you.
Jesus: [Made no further reply]

Pilate questions the crowd (15:6-15)
Pilate: Do you want me to release for you the King of the Jews?
Crowd: [Chief priests stirred up the crowd to have him release Barabbas]
Pilate: Then what do you wish me to do with the man you call the King of the Jews?
Crowd: Crucify him!
Pilate: Why, what evil has he done?
Crowd: Crucify him!

If Jesus is a rebel, rival king, then he must be crucified: that's what Rome does to insurrectionists to keep the vaunted Roman "peace" of its own iron-fisted dominion. But Pilate is not so sure that Jesus fits the bill of a dangerous political revolutionary, or at least he wants the Jewish prosecutors to think he's not convinced. Again, Pilate has to play it coolly, shrewdly, lest the Jewish leaders presume that he will automatically do their bidding. He ultimately consents to have Jesus crucified, despite his doubts of Jesus's guilt (15.14), but only after pressing the leaders and their supporters and exposing their violent intentions that he is compelled to appease. Pilate is no profile in courage or justice here. He operates on sheer expedience: no wringing of hands (or mock washing of hands, as in Matt 27:24), no losing sleep over Jesus's fate (as Pilate's wife does in Matt 27:19). What does he care about another Jew nailed to a cross? Anything to keep the "peace."

Pilate Questions Jesus (15:1-5). Whatever grudging respect Pilate needs to show toward the Jewish council and public opinion, he's not obliged to give much consideration to the beaten and "bound" Galilean commoner Jesus brought to him for judgment (14:65; 15:1). Since sadistic mockery pervades the Jewish and Roman authorities' treatment of Jesus in Mark (14:63-65; 15:16-32), we may assume "the sarcastic tone of Pilate's initial question" concerning Jesus's royal pretentions (Marcus 2009, 1033). When he asks Jesus, "Are you the King of the Jews?" (15:2a), Pilate is not expecting an answer as much as expressing acerbic incredulity: "Seriously, *You* [*Su*] are supposed to be a king? What a joke!" (Schwiebert 2017, 946).

"King of the Jews (*Ioudaiōn*)" may also be rendered "King of the Judeans," focused on ruling the province of Judea and city of Jerusalem (Horsley 2001, 99–100, 167; cf. Barclay 2018)—the territory that Pilate governed by imperial appointment. Pilate thus mocks Jesus as a pathetic rival to his authority, as if to point out the obvious: "Who's appearing before whom here? Who's obviously in charge here, Jesus? Where's your imperial imprimatur, your army, your tribunal? Are you crazy?" Pilate more likely judges Jesus to be an insane nuisance than a serious insurrectionist.

Although Pilate may not seek or expect an answer to his question, Jesus gives one anyway—a brief two-word response that carries more bite than it might appear. Jesus throws Pilate's emphatic "You" (*Su*) right back at him: "You (*Su*) [yourself] say (*legeis*)" (15:2b). This reply may be grammatically and rhetorically read/heard as a statement—"*You* say so"; "So *you* say"; or as a counter question—"What do *you* say?" (I'm tempted to embellish, "What do *you* say, your Honor? It's *your* court.") "Do I look like a king to *you*?" (Schwiebert 2017, 946). Either way, Jesus "cheekily shifts" the announcement and assessment of "Jesus's kingship onto Pilate himself" (Marcus 2006, 87; 2009, 1034). Jesus makes Pilate fully own these proceedings and the final death verdict. Whatever supporting parts Jewish antagonists play in no way exonerates Pontius Pilate. The imperial buck stops with him.

For his part, Jesus refuses to own the title of "King of the Jews/Judeans" or any other realm, here or anywhere else in Mark (Horsley 2001, 46; Marcus 2006, 73–74). Mark's Jesus wholeheartedly serves the kingdom of *God*; God alone is the rightful ruler of all (1:14-15). That attitude in itself undercuts Caesarean supremacy, as Jesus more than hinted when pressed about paying taxes to the emperor (12:13-17). But Jesus never explicitly claims to be king himself, especially not in the strongman mold of Caesar and his client-rulers. To be sure, he answered the high priest's question about whether he was God's Messiah and Son in the affirmative ("I am," 14:61-62), cognizant no doubt of popular hopes that the Messiah would restore the throne of David. But while acting as a merciful, restorative son of David (10:46-52), Mark's Jesus never assumes the David-Solomon mantle as militant king and megabuilder, taking on instead the role of a suffering servant giving his lifeblood to liberate others (10:45). When it comes to Rome's dominating models of ruling, however, no modifications are suitable. Caesar and Pilate's totalitarian, strongman conception of kingly/lordly rule is irredeemable (10:42-44). Jesus advances no mere "alternative kingdom" but rather an entirely renewed "rule" of life rooted in the foundations of the world—the rule of the Creator God.

Sensing Jesus's evasive as well as "derisive rejoinder" (Marcus 2006, 87), the chief priests interject "many" other accusations (15:3), hoping to pad their case and push Pilate to authorize Jesus's execution. As Jesus remains silent (he's already said his piece to the high priest), Pilate tries to egg Jesus on with another query: "Have you no answer" to the "many charges" lodged against you? (15:4). But Jesus has nothing more to say on the matter. He only has only one more speaking line in Mark—in his last moments on the cross (15:34). Between now and then, all the noise comes from others.

Jesus's silence elicits a rare emotional reaction from Pilate: he becomes "amazed" (*thaumazein*, 15:5). While the term can mean "extraordinarily impressed" (Danker and Krug 2009, 167) in a positive way, that connotation seems unlikely in this setting. Pilate is not easily impressed by any subordinate, certainly not a ragtag nobody from Galilee. More likely, Pilate is surprised, bemused perhaps, at Jesus's reticence, particularly after Jesus's tart little response to the first question. Is that all you've got, Jesus? No more smart remarks? From Jesus's point of view, it's not worth hammering back further at Pilate or the Jewish council. He will not deign to play their corrupt political games. His defense, such as it is, rests.

Pilate questions the crowd (15:6-15). Having gotten an earful from the priestly rulers about Jesus's alleged criminality and getting all he's going to get from Jesus himself, Pilate's attention turns to the crowd clamoring for him to fulfill the Passover festival custom of "releas[ing] a prisoner for them, anyone for whom they asked" (15:6, 8). We should acknowledge that no independent evidence outside the Gospels has corroborated this practice in Roman Judea (see Merritt 1985; Wilkins 1992; Bond 2011, 59–60). Be that as it may, our interest is in the function of this scenario in Mark's narrative.

It never hurts to throw a bone (or piece of bread or a circus) now and then to appease the masses and keep them otherwise docile and subordinate to state authority. The act of freeing "*one (hena) prisoner*" (15:6 CEB), though scarcely representing a national liberation movement, still marks a shrewd move during the festival that specifically celebrates ancient Israel's freedom from enslavement. Give them a little taste of that freedom once a year so they'll keep swallowing their normal diet of crumbs from Rome's imperial table.

Pilate hopes to kill two birds with one stone, using the trial of Jesus to satisfy his obligation to set a prisoner free. To suit his political purposes, he stacks the deal he offers the people. Here's the choice: one, "a man called Barabbas," a convicted *murderer* and *insurrectionist* (15:7); two, this man Jesus put forward by some as "King of the Jews" (15:9). Pilate trusts they will make the obvious choice. Far from being a killer and violent insurgent like Barabbas, Jesus had a reputation for healing and raising the dead, issued no call to arms, and instigated no plot to overthrow the government. His own "kingdom" talk and others' hailing him as king make him a figure worth watching. But his good works blunt accusations that he is an "evil" man (15:14) worthy of death. In Pilate's view, Jesus has thus far proven to be relatively harmless, with the exception of toppling some furniture and disrupting some temple business. But Pilate has no problem overriding the temple establishment to keep them in line, especially since he assumes that their prime motivation in opposing Jesus is "jealousy" or "envy" (*phthonos*, 15:10) of Jesus's popularity rather than concern for national or imperial security. The priestly officials calculated Jesus's gain of honor as diminishing their status (Hagedorn and Neyrey 1998). Again Pilate schemes to gain his own political advantage on multiple fronts. He cares for Jesus only to the extent he can use him.

So Jesus or Barabbas? Two men distinct but not altogether different from one another. Barabbas's name is remarkably generic, meaning in Aramaic, "son of a father/abba." "Bar-abbas" thus applies to every male, including Jesus. (In some texts of Matthew 27:16, he's called "*Jesus* Barsabbas," pairing him more closely with Jesus of Nazareth.) But in Mark only Jesus addresses *God* as his "Abba," the divine Father who alone can release Jesus from death (14:36). Neither Pilate nor the Jewish council nor the crowd ultimately holds Jesus's destiny in their hands. But human schemes must play themselves out, as Pilate polls the crowd before making his final decision.

Apart from the savvy political move of gauging public opinion, it can be a prudent strategy to "crowdsource," as we say, to consider the "wisdom of the crowd," which studies have shown to be more reliable in settling certain issues than individual judgments, provided that the "crowd" is reasonably large and diverse (Surowiecki 2005). Local mobs whipped up by agitators, however, reflect more biased "groupthink" than objectivity and generate more clattering "noise" than clarity (Kahneman, Sibony, and Sunstein 2021, 83–85 94–99). We don't know the size of the crowd at Jesus's trial, but it hardly represents an informed cross-section of the people. The group is hastily "stirred up" by the chief priests (15:11). Who knows what they know about Jesus? Their repeated cries of "Crucify him!" (15:13-14) betray a rabid desire for spectacle more than a sober call for justice.

So it happens that Pilate isn't so shrewd after all in reading the crowd. But he is quick to adjust. He doesn't need a riot in his court. Jesus's life is not worth the hassle. Therefore, Pilate mollifies the mob by freeing Barabbas, flogging Jesus, and fating him "to be crucified" (15:15). That's Pilate's last act in Mark. And make no mistake: it is *Pilate's* act. Again, the buck stops with him.

This all turns out well for Barabbas, though the story is not about him. This scene is all we know about him. Yet his brief appearance as "son of a father," an "everyman" type who gains a new lease on life at the expense of Jesus's death, presents a suggestive image of salvation. Jesus literally dies in place of Barabbas, gives his life to "ransom" Barabbas. Jesus dies as "Son of Abba," his divine Father, and as Son of Humankind in solidarity with all human sons and daughters in order to release all sons and daughters of fathers and mothers—which is to say, all people, even imprisoned murderers and insurrectionists!—from death, affording them a new chance on life, even life eternal (10:17). Jesus's resurrection is the ultimate insurrection—the overcoming of all forces of death. Such theologizing, more reminiscent of Paul's thought (e.g., 1 Cor 15:3-4, 12-28, 54-57), goes beyond the text of Mark's narrative. But perhaps we can be forgiven for reading a little Paul between the lines of Mark (see Dunn 1990).

Torture and Crucifixion (15:16-41)

We have come to the climactic events of Good Friday, as it is commonly called in Christian tradition. But there's nothing *good* about it in Mark's account, as Jesus is subjected to horrible abuse and abandonment in his final hours. Being mocked, beaten, and crucified by the Jerusalem authorities is bad enough. But Jesus also feels utterly forsaken by his divine Father. The only words Mark's Jesus speaks during this ordeal (his last words) are his gut-wrenching cry from the cross, "My God, my God, why have you forsaken me?" (15:34). Mark forces us to hear/read these words in both Jesus's native Aramaic tongue and Mark's Greek translation. The larger theological vision of Jesus's redemptive death, which we alluded to in the Barabbas incident, should not blunt the stark reality of Jesus's unjust, unspeakable mistreatment at the hands of callous authorities and their accomplices.

Yet while Jesus's opponents have their day in the sun—a cosmic *dark* day, as Mark casts it, from noon to three o'clock (15:33)—not everyone piles on Jesus. Even though his male disciples continue to desert him, his female followers stay on the scene, albeit at a distance (15:40-41, 47); and a surprising set of new characters steps up to help him: one Simon of Cyrene (15:21), Joseph of Arimathea (15:42-46), and possibly even a Roman centurion (15:39). We may chart the various opposing and supporting characters as below.

We also note further development of two motifs related to *cups* and *clothes*, to basic human needs of *drinking* and *dressing*. Through these motifs, we also see traces of both enmity and charity toward Jesus.

Drink
• Soldiers offer Jesus perfumed wine, either mocking his kingship or perhaps extending the kindness of a last refreshing drink (15:23) (Black and Collins 2006, 1756).
• A bystander gives Jesus a sponge soaked with sour wine, placed on a long stick to reach Jesus's mouth as he hangs from the cross; the drink-bearer aims to revive Jesus enough to see if he will call Elijah to rescue him (15:36).

Dress
- Roman soldiers undertake a cruel mock investiture of "King" Jesus, placing a crown of thorns on his head, stripping his clothes and replacing them with a purple robe, and then reversing the process (15:17, 20).
- Roman soldiers gamble for Jesus's clothes at Golgotha, the place of execution; Jesus is thus crucified naked.
- Joseph of Arimathea buys a linen cloth and wraps it around Jesus's dead body for burial (15:46)—a caring act according dignity to Jesus.

	Name/Group	Words/Actions
Opponents	Roman soldiers	Mock, beat, strip Jesus; lead Jesus to Golgotha and crucify him; gamble for Jesus's clothes; offer Jesus wine spiced with myrrh
	Roman centurion	"Truly this man was God's Son" (sarcasm)
	Bypassers/bystanders	Deride Jesus: "Look, [Jesus] is calling for Elijah"; give Jesus sour wine
	Chief priests and scribes	Mock Jesus: "He saved others; he cannot save himself. Let the Messiah, the king of Israel, come down from the cross now, so that we may see and believe."
Supporters	Simon of Cyrene	Carries Jesus's cross
	Roman centurion	"Truly this man was God's Son" (confession)
	Mary Magdalene, Mary the mother of Joses, Salome, and other Galilean women	Observe Jesus's crucifixion from a distance; observe Jesus's burial
	Joseph of Arimathea	Asks for Jesus's corpse, wraps it in linen cloth, and places it in a tomb—though the level of support Joseph exhibits toward Jesus is somewhat ambiguous

Mark unfolds Jesus's last hours in three scenes, proceeding from (1) Pilate's courtyard to (2) Skull Hill (Golgotha) to (3) Joseph's tomb.

Beaten in Pilate's courtyard (15:16-20)

Jesus has already been struck and spit on by the Jewish council (14:65a), beaten by council guards (14:65b), and flogged by Pilate's soldiers before "being . . . handed over to be crucified" (15:15). But he is subjected to yet more abuse before the final torture of crucifixion. Jesus's body is no longer his own; it has become an expendable object for powerful men's sport and spoilage. Although brief in length, this first torturous scene is described in vivid detail.

Places and actors (15:16). The first abusive action occurs outside Pilate's tribunal in the "courtyard of the palace" (*aulē*) or "governor's headquarters" (*praitōrion*). As in the case of the high priest's "courtyard," where servants and soldiers (and Peter!) gathered while Jesus was on trial in the judicial palace where the high priest resided (14:54, 66), Pilate's courtyard fits the landscape of an opulent mansion and tribunal occupied by the governor and his security squad. The regnant powers are arrayed in full force against Jesus. Pilate's place was known as the Praetorium, a term applied to a Roman military officer's base of operations in the field or, in Pilate's case, in a provincial capital city. Likely Pilate occupied one of Herod the Great's palaces in Jerusalem (Pixner 1992, 447–48; Riesner 2009, 577; Keener 2014, 171).

"The whole cohort" of Pilate's troops, a unit of about 600 men, assembles in the courtyard. Such a sizeable brigade seems like overkill, although the Passover festival required extra security. In any case, Jesus faces alone an overwhelming array of brute military-police force. Yet the soldiers first taunt and tease Jesus like a plaything, further humiliating him before delivering the final hammer blows on the cross.

Props and gestures (15:17-20). As earlier in the high priest's courtyard, Jesus again is spit on and mocked for his supposed grandiose aspirations. But whereas before he was blindfolded, struck, and goaded as a *prophet* (14:65), now he is garbed, greeted, and mock-worshiped as a *king*, the "King of the Jews" (15:18). His harassers use various props to enhance their cruel charade.

- *Purple robe.* Part of the clothing pattern noted above, this dressing Jesus up in royal apparel subjects him to public indignity, both because it drives home that he has no regal accoutrements of his own and because he is double-stripped in the process: first, of his own clothes before dressing him in the purple robe; then, in removing the robe to "put his own clothes [back] on him" (15:20), Jesus's naked body is exposed twice for all to see.

- *Thorny crown.* A king needs a crown, the more gold and jewels the better; a victor needs a wreath on his head, typically fashioned from laurel branches as the ancient "gold medal" for winning athletes. The soldiers weave the shoots of some variety of thorny, "spiny plant" into a makeshift wreath and "put it on [Jesus]" (Moldenke and Moldenke 1986, 165–66). The verb indicates the action of "placing around" (*perititheasin*) Jesus's head. But it is doubtful this "crown" was put gently into place; thorns piercing Jesus's skull and drawing blood would be an apt prelude to his crucifixion on Skull Hill/ Golgotha.
- *Wispy reed.* A king also needs a scepter, a suitable ruling rod (cf. Gen 49:10; Num 24:17; Collins 2010, 67–90, 103–104, 110, 115, 126–27, 212, 226, 228). A reed hardly fits the bill. Though reeds could be stiff, stick-like stalks (see 15:36), their marshy roots typically made them more bendable and breakable (Matt 11:7; 12:20; Luke 7:24). The image (not the actual object) of a reed could have royal resonance, as with the coins of Herod Antipas's realm centered in his new capital of Tiberias on the shore of the Sea of Galilee: one side of the coin depicted the head of Emperor Tiberius; the other side showed a reed common to the area (Rousseau and Arav 1995, 58; Spencer 2003, 59). The soldiers take an actual reed but do not place it in Jesus's hand to complete the mock investiture. Instead they beat Jesus with it! It may not physically hurt that much, but the public humiliation is palpable.

Crucified on Skull Hill (15:21-41)
The site and times of Jesus's crucifixion are set. The place is *Golgotha*, as Mark again uses an Aramaic term (= Latin *Calvariae* ["Calvary"]), meaning "place of a skull/cranium" (*kranion*) (15:22), here denoting a hill in the rough shape of a skull and/or a site where skeletons of crucified criminals lay strewn about (victims of crucifixion typically did not receive decent burials). A grisly place by any account.

And crucifixion was no model of swift justice. As Rome's preferred and perfected means of execution, it exacted a long torturous toll before finally terminating its victims, typically by asphyxiation (Hengel 1977, 22–38). Jesus's ordeal stretched over six hours, 9:00 AM–3:00 PM (15:25, 33, 37). During the last half, however, starting at high noon, "darkness" engulfs "the whole land/earth ($g\bar{e}n$)" (15:33), putting a damper on the spectacle and diminishing the whole point of this capital penalty: let everyone *see* what happens when you dare defy the Roman state. But what can be seen in the dark? Plenty for readers of Mark, as we see and feel the dark horror of Jesus's death all too poignantly, punctuated by hearing his piercing cry of lament to God (15:34).

But while not glossing over the gruesome effects of Jesus's crucifixion, Mark does not belabor them. The narrative moves apace through the six hours of story time. Yet Mark packs the brisk account with several significant details. We do well to pause and ponder the following ten elements.

Cross (15:21, 30, 32). Three times Mark names the material object of the "cross" (*stauros*) to which Jesus's body is bound (15:21, 30, 32). The Roman cross was a large pole or spike secured vertically into the ground with an attached crossbeam, together forming a crossed "T/t" or *tau* (Greek Τ/τ)-shape (L&N 1988, 56–57). Typically the sentenced criminal was required to carry the crossbar to the execution site, where he would be nailed or tied to it; then this apparatus and victim would be hoisted up and fixed to the upright post (hence the taunts to "come *down*" from the cross [15:30, 32, 36]). The body was virtually embedded into the wood: criminal and cross became one.

Except that Jesus gets a brief reprieve on the way to Golgotha. The soldiers commandeer a "passer-by," one Simon of Cyrene, to "carry [Jesus'] cross[beam]" for him (15:21). No reason is given for this move; perhaps Jesus is already too weak to carry his own cross, or perhaps the soldiers want fresh legs to speed up the process. In any event, it is striking that Jesus does not carry his cross alone (see above on 8:34 regarding the ecclesiological/communal dimension of cross-bearing discipleship). It is also noteworthy that a random stranger, probably a Passover pilgrim "coming in from the country," is enlisted to help Jesus (in the absence of his disciples), a man whom Mark identifies by name, place of origin, and his two sons' names: "Simon of Cyrene, the father of Alexander and Rufus" (15:21). And thus he goes down in Christian history—a stranger no more!

His Cyrenean background roots him in northern Africa, likely as a dark-skinned person. The distinguished African American theologian James Cone wrote in his final book, *The Cross and the Lynching Tree*, that "Black ministers, searching for ways to identify racially with the story of salvation in the scriptures, have since slavery times liked to preach about 'Black Simon' (as they called him) who carried Jesus's cross." However, "although blacks like to think that Simon volunteered to carry Jesus's cross, he did not," as Cone rightly reads Mark's account as a bridge to a more piercing application to African American history: "The Gospel of Mark says that 'they compelled' Simon 'to carry his cross' (15:21), just as some African Americans were compelled to suffer lynching when another could not be found." Fired by such acute "theological imagination," Cone urges our "seeing blacks as crucified like Jesus and forced like Simon to carry the crosses of slavery, segregation, and lynching" (Cone 2011, 46–48). To see "Black Simon" in that blinding light is to plumb the depths of human moral darkness that also overshadowed Jesus (15:33-34).

Cup (15:23). Although "cup" is not used here, the soldiers' offer of wine to the death-fated Jesus recalls the "cup" signifying his outpoured blood at the Last Supper (14:23-24), with the key distinction that he freely *gave* that drink to his disciples whereas now his opponents try to foist it upon him. Their motive is uncertain: either another mocking gesture ("Would your Highness care for an aperitif?") or a customary "last drink" for a condemned man to dull the pain—or maybe a mixture of both, like the drink itself, a cocktail of wine and myrrh. In any case, Jesus "did not take it," perhaps because he wants no palliative—not so much to prove his mettle as a brave martyr as to feel the full brunt of humanity's pain and suffering. Or perhaps he wants nothing to do with these agents of violence and injustice; accepting Simon's help in carrying the crossbeam is one thing; accepting anything from Pilate's henchmen is another.

As the wine recalls the Last Supper, the myrrh evokes the perfume—the "ointment (*myros*) of nard" (14:3-5)—that the woman used to anoint Jesus's head and body "beforehand for his burial," a pure act of "kindness" (14:7-8), unlike the mixed motives at best of the soldiers' drink offer. Further, a stock image of elite behavior in the ancient world accessorizes the perfume with a floral head of garland: "A young man ready for a social outing is stereotypically described as 'perfumed and wreathed' (*myrisamenos kai stephanōsamenos*)" (Sawicki 2001, 147). The contrast with the Romans' preparation of Jesus for his "outing" at Golgotha couldn't be starker: wreathed with a tiara of thorns (15:17) and offered a perfume quaff for his execution!

Clothes (15:24). Jesus has already been stripped twice in the purple robe charade in Pilate's courtyard (15:17, 20). Now the soldiers strip him again of his own clothes, probably including his "sandals" (15:24 CEB), with nothing to replace them. He will die naked (no loincloth as commonly depicted in Christian art), publicly laid bare for all to see (unable to flee like the naked young man in 14:51). Though rarely mentioned in preaching and teaching across the sweep of Christian history, in recent years some scholars have begun to call the executioners' brutal exposure of Jesus for what it is: an act of public sexual abuse. The pastoral theologian and former dean of Duke Divinity School, Elaine Heath, candidly states,

> Jesus was crucified naked. Being stripped publicly . . . was a calculated act of sexual violence. In Jesus's culture, as in Middle Eastern cultures today, to be stripped naked in front of a watching crowd was an act of sexual violation. Witness the dreadful images coming out of Abu Graib prison.

The torture was sadistic, carried out while he was naked in order to maximize his humiliation in front of a voyeuristic crowd. . . . Jesus was pinned down, bound, violated, penetrated, torn. He was displayed as a naked object of contempt, while the blood poured from his broken body. (Heath 2019, 125–26; cf. Tombs 1999)

Yes, *Jesus too* (#MeToo), personally, viscerally (Reaves and Tombs 2020). His solidarity with and sympathy for suffering humanity includes victims of sexual violence.

Standard dress in Jesus's day comprised an outer wrap or cloak (*himation*) and an undergarment or tunic (*chitōn*). The Fourth Gospel specifies that soldiers took both pieces from Jesus (John 19:23), but Mark simply lumps everything under the plural "clothes" (*himatia*). He who traveled so light and advised his followers to do the same (Mark 6:8-9) dies utterly bereft of even the little he possessed.

Adding further insult to injury, the soldiers amuse themselves at Jesus's expense by gambling for pieces of his clothing—a stunning picture of the "banality of evil" (Arendt 2006 [1965]; see Robin 2004, 110–26; Young 2011, 75–93). No telling how many crucifixions they've carried out; it gets boring and tedious over the long hours of waiting for victims to die. Ho-hum: shoot a few craps to while away the hours; get a little souvenir (notch in the belt) to hang on the mantel; maybe even sell a swatch or two. Tragically, however, this is how evil authorities often treat God's righteous servants, as David (by popular attribution) testified in Psalm 22:16-17:

> For dogs are all around me;
> > a company of evildoers encircles me.
> My hands and feet have shriveled;
> I can count all my bones.
> They stare and gloat over me;
> *they divide my clothes among themselves,*
> > *and for my clothing they cast lots.*

Not surprisingly, this psalm weighs on Jesus's mind; he soon screams out the first verse from the cross for all to hear (15:34).

Inscription (15:26). By design, crucifixion was a major media spectacle to thrill the crowds and thwart would-be criminals. Punctuating the grisly sights and sounds was a text message of the capital crime carved into a wooden placard. This mini-billboard would typically hang around the neck of the condemned party as he trudged to the place of crucifixion and then be posted above his head on the vertical cross-pole. The Roman historian Dio

Cassio, for example, describes a slaveholder in 23 BCE parading his treacherous slave "in the midst of the [Roman] Forum with an inscription declaring the reason [or 'lettering the charge' (*grammatōn tēn aitian*)] why he was to be put to death, and afterwards crucified him" (*Hist. rom.*, 54.3.7; Maier 1996, 59–63; cf. Suetonius, *Cal.* 32.2; *Dom.* 10.1; McLaren 2008).

The "inscription of the charge (*epigraphē tēs aitias*) against [Jesus] read [or 'was lettered' (*epigegrammenē*)], 'The King of the Jews/Judeans'" (Mark 15:26). Lampooning Jesus's putative regal status continues. The full charge would be "Falsely and traitorously claiming to be King of the Jews." But posting only the royal title both mocks Jesus's authority (how ridiculous for a "king" to hang dying on a bloody, splintery "throne") and ironically declares his true status for Mark and fellow believers: yes, the true agent of God's kingdom is a suffering slave and Son of Humankind giving his life a "ransom for many" (10:45).

A further irony emerges related to the inscribed "graphic" or "epigraph" presented in "grammatical" form. Both *graphai* and *grammatta* can refer to the Jewish scriptures, including the Mosaic Law (see the former term in 12:10, 24; 14:49; the latter in John 5:46-47; Rom 2:27; 7:6; 2 Cor 3:7; 2 Tim 3:15). From Mark's perspective, these inspired inscriptions of God trump any self-exalting scribbles and scripts in imperial Roman font—whether etched on Roman coins (Mark 12:15-17) or on crosses. Even when Roman power seems ascendant, as when crucifying Jesus as a supposed enemy of the state, God's word, God's script, is paradoxically being "fulfilled" (14:49) for those with eyes to see and ears to hear.

Criminals (15:27-28, 32). The theme of Jesus's abandonment by his followers and dying in abject aloneness takes a new twist. Technically Jesus is not crucified by himself. Sometimes Rome would execute hundreds at one time for maximum effect (Josephus *Life* 420; *Ant.* 17.295; *J.W.* 5.449–51). Mark only mentions two other criminals crucified with Jesus, both referred to as "bandits" or "insurrectionists" (*lēstai*), the same term we have encountered before in 11:17 at the temple ("den of robbers [*lēstōn*]") and 14:28 at Gethsemane ("Have you come . . . to arrest me as though I were a bandit [*lēstēn*]?"). In Luke's famous version of the story, one of these two condemned men defends Jesus and is granted his plea to be remembered in Jesus's kingdom (Luke 23:39-43). Mark, however, states that both "those who were crucified with him also taunted him" (15:32).

Mark also positions the two bandits flanking Jesus, "one on his right and one on his left" (15:27), projecting a stark counterpoise to the disciple-brothers James and John, who earlier coveted these places at Jesus's side and claimed they were ready and "able" to join him in drinking his deadly "cup" and drowning in his lethal "baptism" (10:35-39). But they are nowhere to be found now. They prove unwilling and unable to take up their crosses and follow Jesus (8:34), ceding their cross-bearing duties to the bypassing Simon of Cyrene and two anonymous criminals.

After noting that two men were crucified with Jesus, some copyists added, "And the scripture (*graphē*) was fulfilled that says, 'And he was counted among the lawless'" (15:28). Though not attested in the best manuscripts and probably inserted from Luke 22:37 (Omanson 2006, 101), this statement represents an appropriate scriptural interpretation of the scene, drawn from the suffering servant song in Isaiah 53:12.

Taunts (15:29-32). Whereas Mark gives no direct voice to the two taunting bandits, he puts abusive speech in the mouths of two other character groups—both Jewish and both less concerned about Jesus's threat to Rome as "King of Judea" (15:26) and more focused on his messianic mission as savior, healer, and restorer of God's people as "King of Israel" (15:32).

- Some unnamed *passersby* "derided" ("blasphemed," *eblasphēmoun*) Jesus by the physical act of "shaking their heads" and a verbal dig at his ridiculous temple reform plans and ability to save people: "Aha!"—the similar-sounding Greek interjection *Oua* (two syllables, *Ou-a*!) that introduces an insult (Friberg, Friberg, and Miller 2000)—"You who would destroy the temple and rebuild it in three days, save yourself, and come down from the cross!" (15:29).
- The *chief priests and scribes* deliver their final words in Mark's story, "mocking [Jesus] among themselves—and saying, 'He saved others; he cannot save himself. Let the Messiah, the King of Israel, come down from the cross now, so that we may see and believe'" (15:31-32).

Yet again Jesus's experience echoes Psalm 22 with the exception that the suffering psalmist's mockers put the onus on *God* to save God's beloved servant rather than taunting the sufferer to save himself:

> All who see me mock at me;
>   they make mouths at me, they *shake their heads*;
> "Commit your cause to the Lord; *let him deliver*—
>   *Let him rescue* the one in whom he delights!" (Ps 22:7-8)

Regarding the distinction between the "Let God save him" in Psalm 22 and "Save yourself" in Mark, Amy-Jill Levine and Marc Brettler plausibly suggest, "There may be Marcan irony here: the taunters place Jesus in the role of God" (2020, 348).

At any rate, the rub of Jesus's mockers is clear: If he can't *save himself*, how can he credibly save others? How can a dying Messiah be anything but a fake and a failure? If he can't *come down* from the cross with divine energy, how can he *lift up* anyone who has been laid low or *build up* anything that has been beaten down, such as the temple that he says he will destroy and rebuild? As noted above, Mark's Jesus never says that *he* will bring down the temple—only that it will be destroyed by some means (13:2). But legal correctness has already been thrown by the boards. False witness abounds. Still, the main point stands from the perspective of Jesus's accusers: a crucified Messiah is incapable of saving anyone.

This viewpoint is not without logic, even biblical logic, since while the Jewish scriptures envision a righteous, suffering servant of God, they provide no clear template for a *crucified Messiah*. The beastly imagery in Psalm 22:12-21, for example, is more suitable to a public lion-mauling (v. 20) than to a crucifixion. For all its continuity with the Old Testament, the New Testament dares to embrace a "new" dimension of God's saving work: a mysterious, paradoxical theo-logic that overrides conventional worldly wisdom and power. Mark's story alludes to this expansive "new" (14:24) *cruciform* theological, Christological vision. The apostle Paul asserts it outright: "Christ crucified . . . the power of God and the wisdom of God" (1 Cor 1:23-24; cf. 1:17-25).

Eloi/Elijah (15:33-37). The good news that the saving God works in and through the brutal death of his beloved Son Jesus does not come cheaply or easily to the Father or Son. Jesus's agonizing, futile plea amid the olive trees at Gethsemane that his divine Abba would release him from the "cup" of death (14:33-36) ramps up to a wrenching cry on the cross at Golgotha lamenting God's forsaking him in his direst moment. Jesus's mega-phonic "voice/cry" (*megalē phōnē*) frames the death scene (15:34, 37). The stage "lighting" for this utterance fits the mood: everything—"the whole land/earth (*gēn*)"—goes dark for three hours at the brightest part of the day (15:33), reverting back, as it were, to the dark chaotic void before creation (Gen 1:2). Jesus's world is being shattered—and ours with it. The hope of remaking, renewing, re-creating looms on the horizon, but we should not rush there too quickly, as if this forsaken feeling is a mere hiccup for Jesus. It is, as the great spiritual writers put it, a devastating "dark night of the soul," erupting in what African American poet and cultural critic Stanley Crouch calls "perhaps the greatest blues lines of all time" (Crouch 1995–1996, 82; quoted in Cone 2011, 124; Caputo 2019, 88).

From the depths of his soul Jesus cries "Eloi, Eloi" in Aramaic (though writing in Greek, Mark makes us "hear" Jesus's anguished voice), meaning "My God, My God." The personal, repeated address sets the grave tone for his perplexed query, "Why have You [My God, My God] forsaken me?" (15:34). Not stopping this ordeal, as Jesus requested, is one thing; not supporting Jesus through it, not being there for him, seems unconscionable. How could a father, especially the heavenly Father, do this to his son/Son? Does Jesus perhaps betray this searing sense of paternal abandonment in his use of "My God" rather than "My Father"?

Perhaps, but more likely Jesus simply quotes a well-known prayer in the Jewish lament tradition of honestly expressing one's wonderment at God's apparent absence (*Deus absconditus*) in crisis situations. And not surprisingly, the prayer Jesus appropriates comes again from Psalm 22, the opening verse. The psalmist's and Jesus's "cry of dereliction," as it is commonly called, charges God with dereliction of duty. More accurately this lament calls God to account, calls God to live up to God's commitment to steadfast love. The "charge" arises out of *faithfulness*, not bitterness—out of a faithful, trusting relationship with the faithful, loving God. Not by accident, the last section of Psalm 22 turns from the long run of lament (22:1-18) to more confident supplication and expectation: "But you, O LORD, do not be far away! O my help, come quickly to my aid! Deliver my soul. . . . future generations will be told about the Lord, and proclaim his deliverance . . . saying that he has done it" (22:19-20a, 30b-31). Mark's Jesus (certainly) and readers (probably) know the entire arc of Psalm 22. In his weak, gasping state, Jesus may be forgiven for not quoting all thirty-one verses. Again, however, we should not dismiss the shocking jolt of Jesus's cry of abandonment—which is all that Mark leaves ringing in our ears— and briskly skip over the psalmist's extended lamentation to get to the happy ending. Three hours of darkness on the cross and three days (two nights) in the tomb are not negligible preludes to resurrection. They are part of an event complex—Jesus's crucifixion-burial-resurrection—the scars of which Jesus carries ever after. Although Mark does not report the nail prints in the risen Jesus's feet and hands and the sword wound in his side (John 20:20, 25-27; cf. Luke 24:39-40), the brutality of crucifixion implies unimaginable physical and psychological post-traumatic stress.

So what shall we say about this cry of dereliction? Solemn contemplation —taking in Jesus's haunting lament until we can't take it anymore—seems more apt than analytic commentary. But perhaps a few words can provide some perspective, starting with a negative appraisal. The God of the psalmist, the Father of Jesus, is *not by any means* an abusive father who beats his son and abandons him to die. To say otherwise is blasphemy against God if anything is. The great theologian of hope, Jürgen Moltmann, who has also reflected profoundly on the "crucified God," thinks that we should understand God's "forsaking" of Jesus as part and parcel of *God's pain and suffering*. The Father cannot bear to look on the terrible debility and demise of his Son. It effectively—and affectively—*kills* the Father, as it would any normal father, to see his beloved child being tortured to death. Moltmann suggests, the Father feels *worse* than the Son, since the Father's anguish persists and festers after the Son's death, which ends the Son's pain (Moltmann 2015, 41; cf. 2003, 77–79; 1993a, 242–47).

The classic problem of evil presses in: if God's *love* is so intense, why does God not use God's *power* to rescue the Son, to relieve the Son's suffering and indeed the suffering of all God's children? Because, as noted above, God's power is not raw, brute, "all-mighty" force but rather a weak, vulnerable power subsumed by loving solidarity with the lowliest and least by worldly standards. The "power of God *is* Christ crucified" (1 Cor 1:23-24; cf. 1:18-2:10; Caputo 2015; 2019, 17–26). God lives and works *within* a pained, groaning creation (Rom 8:18-28) deeply felt *within* the heart of God. The intimate communion between Father and Son is precisely what makes the Son's suffering so heart-rending for the Father—a veritable ripping apart of God's self. The Passion of Christ is "the passion of the passionate God" (Moltmann 2003, 74), the passion of the suffering God who knows and feels the piercing pain of injustice firsthand (Spencer 2019, 722–32; 2021, 21–34).

From engaging in reader/hearer-response on a theological level, we return to Mark's text and the response of characters within the story to Jesus's cry. "Some of the bystanders" either mishear or misinterpret Jesus's cry to *Eloi* ("my God") as a call to *Elijah* ("the Lord is my God"). Recall the expectation that Elijah's return to earth would signal the culmination of God's reign on "the great and terrible day of the LORD" (Mal 4:5; cf. 3:1-2; Mark 1:2; 6:14-16; 8:28; 9:4-5, 9-13). One member of the crowd seems anxious to see whether Elijah might answer Jesus's plea and "come to take him down" from the cross. So he "ran" to get some "sour wine" (or "vinegar wine," a cheap drink—no myrrh) delivered to Jesus on a sponge stuck to the end of a long, stiff reed (15:36). We're not told whether Jesus accepts the drink or not. Michael Whitenton argues that the narrative leaves the matter "intentionally vague" in order to invite hearers to "infer" that Jesus does drink the proffered wine as an "ironic foretaste" of God's communal (communion) kingdom (cf. 14:25) (Whitenton 2018, 403).

The wine-server's motives are also left open. At base, he apparently wants to revive the flagging Jesus long enough to give Elijah time to arrive. But what underlies this move? Is he simply curious?—Who knows, maybe this Jesus has Elijah's number? Or is he genuinely hopeful?—Lord knows we need a regime change around here! Or is he just another malign mocker?—Here's a stick and sponge full of wine for you, milord, another scepter and cup suited to your faux kingship; if Elijah has anything to do with you, he would expose your royal charade! In any event, no sooner is the drink offered (and accepted or not) than "Jesus gave [another] loud cry and breathed his last" (15:37). He is only coming down from the cross to be buried.

Curtain (15:38). As the sun in the noonday sky is totally shrouded and the heart of the Father broken in two, the cosmic disruption triggered by Jesus's crucifixion leads to the rending of the temple curtain "from top to bottom" at the moment Jesus expires. This thick curtain or "veil" separated the innermost sanctum known as the holy of holies from the holy place; the holy of holies contained the ark of the covenant and the mercy seat on which the high priest alone would sprinkle blood once a year on the Day of Atonement to restore the people's full fellowship with God (Heb 9:1-7; Exod 26:31-37; 30:6-10). The curtain was carefully woven from specified colored fabrics and threads (Exod 26:31; 36:35). An early Christian legend claimed that the high priest commissioned "the true virgins from the tribe of David" to fashion a new temple curtain—including the young Mary, destined to be the mother of Jesus, who worked with "the true purple and scarlet threads" (*Infancy Gospel of James* 10:1-10; 12:1-2; Hock 1995, 51–53; BDAG 2000, 524).

The dramatic tearing of the temple curtain at the moment of Jesus's death surely represents a significant act, but Mark offers no commentary on it. We might first think that such a rending event symbolizes the temple's destruction, as Jesus forecast (Mark 13:2). By rejecting Jesus Messiah and abetting his death, the chief priests and elders have, so to speak, brought the temple house down on their own heads. But closer consideration of Mark's narrative discloses a more hopeful picture.

The verb for "tear" or "rip" (*schizō*)—"to divide by use of force" (BDAG 2000, 931)—uniquely parallels in Mark the "splitting open" (*schizomenous*) of the heavens through which the Spirit descends on Jesus at his baptism (1:10 CEB). From beginning to end, from his in-spiriting (*pneuma . . . eis*, 1:10) at his baptism to his ex-spiriting at his crucifixion (*exepneusen*, 15:39; Shiner 2000, 20), Jesus carries out his mission on a cosmic battlefield in a broken world—a war-"torn" world that "rips" him and many sufferers apart. But the goal of this messianic campaign is to *mend the world* (the Jewish concept of *tikkun olam*; Sacks 2005, 71–83), to reweave its ripped fabric; to bring together heaven and earth, priest and people, Jew and Gentile; to make all spaces safe and sacred; to open full access to God's holy realm for all creatures, for "all nations" (11:17; Isa 56:7). As the book of Hebrews unveils through the eyes of faith the significance of the torn temple veil, the horrific death of Christ is transformed into a hopeful vision: "a sure and steadfast anchor of the soul, a hope that enters the inner shrine behind the curtain, where Jesus, a forerunner on our behalf, has entered" (Heb 6:19-20; see 9:1-12). Using theater language, we might say that the tearing of the temple curtain represents a "curtain call" of the crucified-resurrected Christ who welcomes the audience and invites them backstage for intimate fellowship with him and the Director God.

Centurion (15:39). A remarkable sign of this hopeful openness breaking through the baneful demise of Jesus may emerge in the stunning confession of the centurion—the Roman officer likely supervising the crucifixion—in response to "the way [Jesus] breathed his last" with a "loud cry" (triggering the rip of the temple curtain) (15:37-38): "Truly this man was God's Son!" Up to this point in Mark's narrative, the Roman troops under Pontius Pilate's command have been thoroughly despicable agents of Jesus's torture and death. The caring, humble, pious centurions of Matthew 8:5-13//Luke 7:1-10 and Acts 10 (Cornelius) are absent in Mark. Suddenly the captain of the crucifixion squad acknowledges Jesus's divine sonship right after Jesus dies, prompted in some fashion by the way Jesus dies.

To this point, under the Gospel heading acclaiming Jesus as the Son of God (1:1), only God (1:11; 9:7), demons (1:24; 5:7), and Jesus himself, belatedly (12:6-8; 14:61), announce Jesus as God's Son. As we have repeatedly seen, Jesus's disciples remain muddled about Jesus's true identity, while the Jerusalem leaders, both Jewish and Roman, stand opposed to exalted claims about and by Jesus. No human being confesses Jesus as Son of God—*until* this centurion, of all people, at the most unexpected place and time: the foot of the cross just after Jesus expires.

Amazing! Almost too good to be true—and it may not be "truly" good, which is to say that the centurion's "Truly" (*alēthōs*) lead-in may not be sincere. We've already observed how Mark has peppered his account of Jesus's final days with an "abundance of irony, parody, and mockery" (Leander 2013, 288). Mark's unique placement of the centurion "facing" (*ex enantias*) Jesus already hints at a slippery meaning. While this may be the best physical vantage point to "see" how Jesus dies, the term *enantios* normally suggests an oppositional *force*, a *faceoff*, not merely an opposite-facing location. It is used of storm winds blowing *against* a seafaring vessel (6:48; Matt 14:24; Acts

27:4), of *contrary* views or actions ("I myself was convinced that I ought to do many things *against* [*enantia*]) the name of Jesus of Nazareth," Acts 26:9; cf. 28:17), and of hostile *opponents* to people (1 Thess 2:15; Titus 2:8). This anti-position to Jesus is what we would expect from the centurion. Accordingly, this opposing stance either bleeds into the centurion's statement about Jesus or it marks an incredible contrast to it, nothing short of a miraculous conversion.

Either way accommodates irony (on this "double irony," see Fowler 1991, 202–209; 2008, 74–79). If, on the one hand, the centurion truly affirms Jesus as God's Son, it is ironic indeed that an agent of Roman military might who superintends the crucifixion affirms the truth about Jesus that everyone else denies or equivocates. What extraordinary power Jesus's crucifixion must have to elicit this response! But if, on the other hand, the centurion indulges in "grim gallows humor" dripping with "scathing sarcasm," effectively mocking the dead Jesus as "Some Son of God!" (Moore 2008, 107), then irony kicks in on the "discourse" level of Mark's overriding meaning (Fowler 1991, 208). Like the bystanders and chief priests who snidely dare Jesus to show his saving ability (15:29-32), the centurion who parodies Jesus's status as God's Son unwittingly preaches the gospel: Jesus *is* the divine Savior and Son, as you say but foolishly fail to realize.

The story level provides scant evidence for determining the centurion's intent, though the normal oppositional nuance of *enantion* tilts toward a negative aim, along with the centurion's insouciant, business-as-usual reporting about Jesus's death to Pilate in 15:44-45 (Leander 2013, 288). Moreover, Jesus's "loud cry" as he expired (15:37), echoing his early scream of abandonment (15:33-34), would typically strike a Roman officer as a weak, unmanly, ignoble way to die, especially for a claimant of divine regal authority (Origen, *Contra Celsum* 2.24; Bowersock 1995, 74–76; Leander 2013, 289). Certainly the Roman army would not endorse deifying a Roman emperor as son of God (*divi filius*) who died in such a pathetic manner. Nevertheless, the lack of explicitly labeling the centurion's response as mockery leaves it ambiguous—perhaps purposefully so (Shiner 2000).

Biblical interpreters alert to postcolonial criticism suggest that Mark's shadowy portrait of the centurion at the cross occupies a "third space," an in-between zone between "mimicry" and "mockery" of Roman imperial power (Bhabha 2004, 53–56, 171–73, 314–19; Leander 2013, 288–91; Peppard 2012, 130–31). Even if the centurion is sincerely moved to acclaim Jesus as God's son, what would he mean by that? He would be most familiar with Roman emperors' claim to divine parentage and sonship, not with the Father God of Israel and Jesus. He would find himself in a strange borderland with much to learn and experience of *Jesus* as Son of God. While Mark's Jesus may appear to resemble emperors like Augustus, Tiberius, and Vespasian, he is "almost the same, *but not quite*" (Peppard 2012, 131; Leander 2013, 288, 291 [emphasis original]). If Mark would let it rip openly instead of hint obliquely, he would insist that Lord, King, and Son of God Jesus is the polar *opposite* of any earthly rulers, Roman or otherwise.

Women (15:40-41). Jesus's "weak" way of ruling particularly diverges from Caesar's "strongman" approach in terms of his supporters. Caesar's "strength" is martial: without his masculine-militant generals, tribunes, centurions, and soldiers, Caesar would be nothing. By contrast, Jesus's power is diaconal: he leads as chief "servant" (*diakonos*) and "slave (*doulos*) of all," even unto death on a cross "for many"—unlike Roman rulers who "lord" themselves as "tyrants" over their subjects (10:43-45). To be sure, Jesus has his deputies, his dozen *men* who fancy themselves as great fighters and powerful figures (9:34; 10:35-39, 41; 14:47). But Jesus never calls them to arms and persistently resists their pretentious patriarchal aspirations, insisting that the truly "first" and "greatest" ones in God's realms are self-giving servants to the littlest, lowliest, and least ones (9:35-37; 10:43-44). Moreover, apart from their reluctance to follow Jesus's servant model, the twelve apostles prove more flaccid than muscular, scarcely living up to their own machismo ideals. They've all betrayed, denied, and deserted Jesus. In military terms they are AWOL.

That's not quite the whole story, however, of Jesus's followers. Only now in Mark do we learn that Mary Magdalene (from Magdala on the west coast of the Sea of Galilee), Mary the mother of James and Joses, Salome, and "many other women" who "used to follow him and provided for [Jesus] when he was in Galilee" have trailed Jesus to Jerusalem and Golgotha to witness his crucifixion (15:40-41). Although hanging back "a distance" (15:40) from the rowdy soldiers and crowds closer to the cross (a prudent decision for the women's safety), at least they haven't abandoned Jesus like the twelve men.

Although the characters within the story—including Jesus—seem unaware of these background women, Mark makes sure readers/hearers of this story notice them. At the end of this Gospel, they are the best examples of discipleship and diaconal mission we have. The verbs rendered "followed" and "provided for" in the NRSV are standard terms for "following like a disciple" (*akoloutheō*) and "serving/ministering" (*diakoneō*). Saying "these [women] *used to* follow" (NRSV) Jesus is slightly misleading because it could suggest a past commitment they no longer have. The imperfect forms of both verbs (*ēkolouthoun, diēkonoun*) signal *continuing* action. Better readings would be that they "began to follow and provide for" or "have been following and providing for" Jesus. "Providing for" properly designates one aspect of *diakon*-work, which encompasses a wide range of material service, including feeding and financing the needy. Feeding or table service—typically the work of women and enslaved persons in the ancient world—seems to be the primary form of service Simon's mother-in-law performs after Jesus relieves her fever (1:31); but it is also appropriate ministry for angels to Jesus (1:13) and for Jesus himself (and reluctant apostles) to the hungry multitudes in desert areas (6:30-44; 8:1-10). Yet, *diakon-* may also connote giving money and goods, as in Luke 8:2-3: "Some women [including Mary Magdalene] . . . and many others . . . provided for (*diēkonoun*) [Jesus and the Twelve] out of their resources [possessions]" (Spencer 2012, 113–24).

We might wish that Mark, like Luke, had noted the presence of these female Galilean ministers along with the twelve apostles (Luke 8:1-3) earlier in Jesus's mission rather than wait until the end of the narrative. But better late than never and better being there for Jesus at the end than fleeing the scene (though see Mark 16:8a). It's also nice to recognize three named women disciples rather than lump them all into a general group, although the second Mary's status is diminished somewhat by defining her in relation to her sons, "James the younger and . . . Joses" (perhaps better well known than she; Bauckham 2002, 206). A further peculiarity relates to the fact that Jesus's brothers—also mothered by Mary—are called James (though not "the younger") and Joses in Mark 6:3 in addition to two more brothers, Judas and Simon, and unspecified sisters. So why does Mark *not* label the Mary at the cross "the mother of *Jesus*"? The matter becomes more puzzling as this Mary is called the "mother of *Joses*" in 15:47 and the "mother of *James*" in 16:1. Though stylistic or random variation may account for these different mentions of James and Joses, the avoidance of characterizing Mary as *Jesus's* mother is striking. Moreover, fairly strong early Christian tradition identified Salome as Jesus's (and James and Joses's) *sister* (Bauckham 2002, 226–34).

Perhaps this implied minimizing of Jesus's bloodlines relates to his mother and siblings' prior perplexity over his mission (3:21, 31-32) and his hometown's "offense" at the aberrant behavior of this "son of Mary" and brother of several siblings (6:3). Jesus's family ties extend to "whoever does the will of God"—such "is my brother and sister and mother" (3:34-35)—not limited to but also not excluding his biological kin. If this maternal Mary at the cross (and tomb, 15:47–16:2) is Jesus's natural mother (as Mark's narrative suggests) and Salome is his sister (possible but more speculative), then Mark intimates that early on they became disciples of their son/brother in Galilee and continued to follow and minister to him to the end of his life (cf. Acts

1:14). Again, we might wish that Mark had clued us in about Mary's (and Salome's) support before now.

Whichever particular female disciples stuck with Jesus to the end, their presence at the cross would have scarcely impressed the Roman authorities, if they even noticed the women at all. With Jesus's male deputies on the run, showing nothing but their backsides in retreat (14:50-52), Jesus is effectively left leading a women's movement, and even these followers keep some distance from him. With his battered, bleeding body and wailing victim voice, Jesus has become feeble, foolish, and effeminate from an imperial perspective. But again, what rates as power and wisdom in "this age" or with "the rulers of this age" (1 Cor 2:6) is turned upside down among the called-out ("churched") community of the crucified Christ, "not many [of whom] were wise by human standards, not many were powerful, not many were of noble birth. But God chose what is foolish in the world to shame the wise; God chose what is weak in the world to shame the strong" (1 Cor 1:26-27). Or back to Mark's Jesus: "Whoever wants to be first must be last of all and servant of all" (Mark 9:34; cf. 10:43-44).

Burial and Resurrection (15:42–16:8a)

Although not mentioned until now, Mary Magdalene and other Galilean female disciples remain on stage to the end of Mark's story. Including the last two verses of the previous unit, we may track these women's movements across three brief scenes, from

1. Their remote observation post of Jesus's death on the cross on Friday afternoon (15:40-41) →
2. Their observation of Jesus's burial in a tomb as Friday evening draws near (15:42-47) →
3. Their visit to Jesus's (empty) tomb early Sunday morning (16:1-8a)

Mary Magdalene and company are minor, supporting characters in the first two scenes depicting Jesus's death and burial. But they become the principal figures in the closing scene at Jesus's tomb where they learn he has been raised from the dead. In all three scenes, the women are juxtaposed with male characters: first, the centurion (15:39); second, a Jewish councilman named Joseph (15:43); and third, a mysterious "young man" (16:5).

Further, this concluding triad of scenes knit together in Mark's final "sandwich":

Sandwich #6
A ***Crucifixion***: Mary Magdalene, Mary the Mother of James and Joses, Salome, and other Women at the Cross (15:40-41)
   B ***Burial***: Joseph of Arimathea and Mary Magdalene and Mary the Mother of Joses at the Tomb (15:42-47)
A ***Resurrection***: Mary Magdalene, Mary the Mother of James, and Salome at the Empty Tomb (16:1-8)

As it happens, four of the five preceding "sandwich" sections also feature female figures (11:12-25 is the only exception): three involve women followers of Jesus or beneficiaries of his ministry (3:19b-35; 5:21-43; 14:1-11), and one depicts the mother-daughter Herodian tandem who orchestrate John's beheading (6:6b-30). Although Mark's Gospel remains a product of patriarchal culture, women play key roles in the story.

And again, it should not be missed that Mary Magdalene, another Mary, and Salome stand alone when the curtain falls as the *only* witnesses to the full complex of Jesus's death-burial-resurrection. Yet we also see these women fleeing offstage (16:8a), and they make no curtain call. Mark maintains suspense to the last moment—and beyond.

Joseph of Arimathea lays Jesus's body in a tomb (15:42-47)

Crucifixion was a brutally long, languishing means of execution designed to maximize its impression on anyone considering bucking the Roman system. And there was no rush to take down the desiccated corpse from the cross. Let the curs and vultures do their work and the mauled body hang for days. When the skeletal scraps were finally removed, there was little concern for a burial, decent or otherwise. Just throw the remains in a pit somewhere for further depredation (cf. 2 Sam 21:9-10; Crossan 1995, 160–88), though Rome might sometimes accommodate Jewish burial scruples in Judea (McCane 2003, 89–108; Evans 2012, 113–40).

Jews indeed had strong commitments to burying the dead, even convicted criminals. Mosaic law stipulated that those condemned to "God's curse" of capital punishment should not be left hanging on a tree through the night but rather buried "that same day" in order not to pollute the sacred land God had given the people (Deut 21:22-23; cf. Josh 8:29; 10:26-27). It was especially vital to leave no defiling corpse unburied before the onset of the Sabbath. Since "evening" had now fallen on "the day before the sabbath" (15:42), it was incumbent that Jesus's body be buried before the next sunset. Accordingly, one Joseph of Arimathea—a city in Judea, perhaps an alternative name for Ramah (Josh 18:25) or Samuel's birthplace, Harmathaim

(1 Sam 1:1 LXX; Carey 2006, 259)—petitions Pilate for Jesus's body in order to dispose of it properly (15:43). It was always risky to ask a favor of the volatile Pilate, but he granted Joseph's request after "summoning the centurion"—presumably the same one who had just declared or denounced Jesus as "God's Son" (15:39)—and confirming that Jesus was dead (15:44-45).

Once Pilate renders his final verdict against Jesus, the governor doesn't involve himself in the messy details of crucifixion or in the mix of a rowdy rabble. He stays behind in his luxury palace. He does, however, seem surprised that Jesus died so quickly by normal crucifixion standards. Though a six-hour ordeal hardly constitutes a swift execution, Jesus's torture is mercifully cut shorter than most other victims. Again, by supercilious Roman measures, Jesus might appear to be a feeble fighter, surrendering too soon, not bravely pressing to the bloody end. Easy perhaps for Pilate to think from his cozy perch but not a fair representation of Jesus's indomitable will to life: for himself and for others.

Pilate's certification of Jesus's death may seem to be a trivial detail, but it serves to reinforce a significant point (further highlighted by its placement in the center of the "sandwich"). Jesus does not drift into an unconscious coma, does not faint dead away (swoon), and certainly does not play dead on the cross to set up some clandestine rescue or Houdini trick. Jesus has *really died*, which leads to his *real burial* and *real resurrection* from the dead. This is not a stage show: it is deadly real. And the gospel of Jesus Christ depends on this physical, bodily reality. Paul puts it plainly: "I handed on to you as of first importance what I had received: that Christ *died* for our sins in accordance with the scriptures, and that he was *buried*, and he was *raised* on the third day" (1 Cor 15:3-4).

How does Mark characterize the key figure in Jesus's burial, Joseph of Arimathea? As with the Roman centurion at the cross, an air of ambiguity hovers around this Joseph (Lyons 2014, 1–20). His being "a respected member of the [Jewish] council" (15:43) that tried and convicted Jesus and recommended capital punishment (14:63-65; 15:1-4, 31) doesn't necessarily mean that Mark respects him. Joseph's solid reputation may simply make him the best choice to plead the Jewish case to Pilate for prompt burial of Jesus's body. The fact that Joseph approaches Pilate "boldly" (15:43) may simply be in the nature of the situation; as noted above, it took some moxie to seek Pilate's favor about anything, much more about an executed criminal.

Nonetheless, Mark's further distinguishing Joseph as one "who was also himself (*kai autos*) waiting expectantly for the kingdom of God" cannot be so easily explained by his position in the Jewish council. Many chief priests in this body were Sadducees with serious concerns about disrupting the status quo and narrow expectations about God's future messianic reign (see 12:18-27; Acts 4:1-2; 5:17-28; 23:6-8). Joseph seems to stand out from the council at this point and align more ("also") with Jesus's followers. Mark only uses the verb for "waiting expectantly" (*prosdechomai*) in this scene. Luke follows Mark's characterization of Joseph of Arimathea (Luke 23:51), while also associating him with the aged prophets Simeon and Anna who embraced the Christ-child Jesus in the temple as fulfilling their long-expected (*prosdechomai*) hopes for the "consolation/redemption of Israel" (Luke 2:25, 38). Although Joseph makes no direct confession of faith in Christ, he too takes Jesus's body into his arms, like Simeon and Anna in Luke, albeit shortly after his death rather than after his birth. Perhaps, then, Mark also intimates that Joseph entertains some measure of hope that this crucified Jesus will yet burst forth in new life.

A counterview of Joseph's disposition of Jesus's body in Mark sees it as a "hasty and perfunctory" gesture, since there is no indication of customary washing or perfuming of Jesus's corpse by Joseph. He "simply" wraps the body in a cloth and places it in a tomb. At the end of the day, "Jesus is hastily interred by a stranger" (Bond 2020, 218–19). This argument, however, derives from a minimalist interpretation of Mark's narrative that in a brief compass provides a detailed sketch of Joseph's actions, absent any anointing of Jesus's body. But recall that Jesus's body has already been pre-anointed for burial by the anonymous woman whom Jesus commended as a model witness (14:3-9). Moreover, Mary Magdalene and her women friends will visit Jesus's tomb on Sunday morning with spices in hand (16:1). Actual (14:3–9) or anticipated (16:1) anointing of the Messiah in Mark is the work of women disciples. As for Joseph's part, Mark unfolds his determined activity through a series of indicative verbs and participles (15:43-46).

- *Went to* (*eisēlthen*) Pilate, *showing boldness* (*tolmēsas*)
- *Asked for* (*ētēsato*) Jesus's body
- *Bought* (*agorasas*) a linen cloth
- *Took down* (*kathelōn*) Jesus's body from the cross
- *Wrapped* (*eneilēsen*) Jesus's body in a linen cloth
- *Laid* (*ethēken*) Jesus's body in a tomb
- *Rolled* (*lelatomēmenon*) a stone against the tomb's entrance

While these actions are carried out with all deliberate speed because of the approaching Sabbath deadline, they are hardly trivial or perfunctory. They involve considerable hands-on effort by Joseph (taking down, wrapping, placing Jesus's body; rolling the rock) and procurement of materials (cloth, tomb). Joseph's respectful, careful treatment of Jesus's body stands in marked contrast to the actions of Roman and (other) Jewish personnel and as a substitute for what Jesus's male disciples should be doing—as John the Baptist's did for their leader (Mark 6:29).

Joseph's purchase and placement of a "linen cloth" (*sindōn*, twice in 15:46) around Jesus's naked body stand out in particular because of the stark counterpoint with the "young man" who fled the arrest scene naked as the soldiers grabbed the "linen cloth" (*sindōn*, twice in 14:51-52) he was wearing, the only garment he had on. Recall that this escape typified the hasty desertion of all of Jesus's male disciples (14:50) even as the denuding recalled the stripping of Jesus's clothes by Roman soldiers (15:17, 20, 24). Whatever his precise motivations, the actions of Joseph of Arimathea demonstrate more faithful attention to Jesus's body than that shown by Jesus's male friends and foes and precipitate a fresh pattern of restoration—of re-dressing the weak and the naked (see below on 16:5).

But the Jewish councilman, Joseph, while the only man in the burial picture, is not entirely alone. The two Marys who witnessed Jesus's death from a distance (15:40) tracked Joseph's handling of Jesus's corpse and "saw where the body was laid" (15:47). Jesus's women disciples distinctively remain alert and attentive to Jesus to the very end.

Mary Magdalene, Mary the mother of James, and Salome come to Jesus's empty tomb (16:1-8a)

We have come to the end of Mark's story of Jesus (see below on 16:8b-20 as a late addition). All the players have exited except for three named women and an anonymous "young man" (16:5). Peter and the male disciples remain out of the picture, although the narrative anticipates that they will hear the women's witness (16:7). More surprising is *Jesus's absence* from the finale, although his risen state is affirmed and his reunion with his female and male disciples is expected (16:6-7).

Entering the tomb to serve (16:1-5a). Mark carefully sets the scene by time and place. Temporally, the Sabbath continues to prioritize events (16:1-2). Faithful Jews like Joseph of Arimathea (15:42-43), Mary of Magdalene, another Mary, and Salome restrict their activity on the sacred last day of the week (Saturday), especially in terms of corpse handling, even for their beloved Jesus. But as soon as possible, "very early on the first day of the week [Sunday], when the sun had risen," they come to Jesus's tomb for what they assume will be their last act of service for him: anointing his body with spices. Mark's time stamp reveals more, however, than chronological information and the women's eagerness to tend to Jesus's body. It suggests a fresh beginning, a new "first day" of creation, a "rising" again of Jesus's bright life (9:2-3), expelling the darkness of violence and injustice (15:33).

Yet the women are in no mood to entertain such hopeful thoughts. They have a somber service to perform on Jesus's cadaver in order to stem the stench of decay for a little while. And en route to the tomb site, they become consumed with a practical worry: "Who will roll away the stone for us from the entrance?" (16:3). Joseph seemed to manage the stone by himself, probably with the help of servants (15:46); but the heft of the "very large" rock poses a legitimate concern for the three women. This worry dissipates, however, when they arrive at the tomb and find the stone already removed, allowing them to go inside (16:4-5a).

They thus move into a limbo or liminal zone—a spooky threshold between life and death, open and closed space, freedom and bondage— which becomes spookier when they spot a "young man" already inside the tomb, "sitting on the right side," as if he parked there waiting on them! Their fretting over how they would gain entrance to the tomb ramps up to five-alarm fear once they get in. The term rendered "alarmed" (*ekthambeomai*) in 16:5, connoting emotional upheaval, elsewhere in Mark signals the crowd's being "overcome with awe" upon seeing Jesus after his transfiguration (9:15) and Jesus's own experience of being "greatly distressed" in Gethsemane at the prospect of his imminent death (14:33). It is an intense, frightening emotion teetering on the precipice of life and death, spiking even higher to "terror and dread" (16:7 CEB) after the "young man" speaks. He might as well have omitted his "Do not be alarmed" (16:6) introduction for all the good it does.

Encountering a "young man" in the tomb (16:5b-7). Who exactly is this mysterious figure, and what does he have to say? Each of the four Gospels identifies the messenger(s) at the tomb differently: Mark's "young man" becomes an "angel of the Lord" in Matthew 28:2, "two men" in Luke 24:4, and "two angels" in John 20:12. So was it one or two figures, angelic or human? As noted before, it's not unusual in the Bible for angels to take on human form and be called "men." But each descriptor needs to be interpreted in its narrative context. Mark's unique "young man" in Jesus's tomb evokes the "certain young man" in Gethsemane who fled naked from the arrest scene, leaving behind his clothes in the hands of policemen who tried to apprehend him (Mark 15:51-52). The current "young man" is also identified by his clothing and posture: "dressed in a white robe [not naked], sitting on the right side [not running away]" (16:5).

Since the shameful desertion of all the disciples (14:50) and the denuding of the young man and of Jesus himself (15:17, 20, 24), Mark's story has begun to turn a corner toward *re-dressing* Jesus's abject state and that of his failed, "fallible followers" (Malbon 2012, 492; cf. 2000, 41–69). As mentioned above, Jesus's body is enwrapped in a "linen cloth" (*sindōn*) matching the garment the young man left behind as a fugitive. Now in the very tomb where Jesus had lain, another "young man" (*neaniskos*) calmly sits inside, sporting a white robe, with no impulse to dash away through the opening in the rock cave. The narrative implies that he himself had removed the stone and chosen to enter the tomb to be where Jesus was, to identify with Jesus. It's as if the frightened, fleeing young man at Gethsemane has boldly *come back* to Jesus, despite the risk (if guards caught him inside the empty tomb, they would seize him and charge him with grave robbing [see Matt 28:11-15]). And the naked young man has been *received back* and *reclothed* with a fresh new robe (like the returning prodigal son in Luke 15:20-22). In Christological terms, the crucified-buried-risen Jesus Messiah incarnates the entire human experience and incorporates all human beings into his restored, resurrected body—the body of Christ.

The positive message that the young man delivers to the women is linked to three imperatives: "Look (*ide*). . . . go (*hypagate*), tell (*eipate*)." That is, "look" at the empty space where the body of "Jesus of Nazareth, who was crucified" (again certifying *this Jesus*'s death), had been placed. "He has been raised" from the dead (Mark 16:6)! And "go, tell" Jesus's disciples—Peter in particular—that he is waiting to be reunited with all of "you" (female and male followers) back home in Galilee, "just as he told you" (16:7). Jesus foretold this post-resurrection rendezvous during the Last Supper (14:28), right after he predicted his disciples would desert him (14:26-27) and right before Peter insisted he would never think of such disloyalty, followed by Jesus's insistence that Peter would deny him three times (14:29-31). Retrospectively, Mark implies that Mary Magdalene and company were also with Jesus and the Twelve at the Last Supper. The charge to tell Peter specifically about the Galilee reunion doubtless owes to his double role as deserter and denier. The risen Lord aims to restore even and especially this failed apostle. Bodily resurrection and community restoration go hand in hand (Crossan and Crossan 2018).

Even if the women disciples seem somewhat relegated to "errand girls" (Seim 1994, 749–50) for this young man on behalf of Peter and the male apostles, they nevertheless forever stand out as the first to learn that Jesus has been raised from the dead and to be charged with sharing that good news with the other disciples. They are the first witnesses to the resurrection, the first commissioned evangelists of the living Christ.

Fleeing the tomb in fear (16:8a). But the women's *actions* of fleeing the scene and speaking "nothing to anyone" and their *emotions* of "trembling and bewilder[ment]" (NIV) or "terror and dread" (CEB), along with being "afraid," appear to be jarring counter-responses to good news (Jesus is risen!) and happy assignment (spread the good word!). Why do they act and feel the way they do?

As noted above in commenting on Mark 14:37-42, emotions are prime drivers (e/motivators) of action, sparking "action readiness," shaping "action tendencies." Clearly the women respond as they do out of *fear*. More than that, their fear represents a dominant mood that Mark's narrative addresses or aims to instill in its audience. "Fear" literally has the last word in the Gospel—well, technically the next-to-last word: *ephobounto gar*, "they-were-afraid, for." The conjunction *gar* ("for") normally appears after the verb in Greek but *not* at the end of a sentence, still less at the end of an entire narrative. In English we naturally flip the conjunction before the verb, in this case: "for they were afraid." But either way, this is an awkward, cliffhanging ending, unmatched in the other Gospels (and undone by the added ending in Mark 16:8b-20). What exactly are the women afraid of, and why does Mark's Gospel leave their fear echoing in the ears and pulsing in the minds and bodies of its hearers?

Before proposing some answers to these emotive questions, we should try to clarify the women's actions—fleeing and not speaking—which their fear generates. We now have the entire foregoing narrative context to guide us. Although the "open-ended ending" (Malbon 2012, 492) looks out to the future, we must not lose sight of the fifteen chapters that have brought us to this point. The women's flight, a common response to fear (along with fight and freeze), readily recalls the male disciples' and young man's same "fugitive" reaction (*pheugō*) at Jesus's arrest (14:50, 52). But two earlier flight cases should also be considered in comparison with the women's actions and emotions.

In the *first flight case* (5:14-17), upon seeing their herd of two thousand pigs plummet to their watery demise following Jesus's exorcism of the Gerasene demoniac, the swineherds "ran off" or "fled" (*ephygon*) and broadcast the news of this tumultuous event "in the city and in the country" (5:14). When a crowd then arrived and noticed the (former) possessed man "sitting there, clothed and his right mind," they became "very afraid" (*ephobēthēsan*). In turn, these witnesses fanned out and further reported "what had happened," prompting people to pressure Jesus to leave their region (5:15-17).

Such responses by the Gerasenes markedly contrast as well as coordinate with the Galilean women's fearful flight from Jesus's tomb:

- Whereas the swineherds flee a mass death scene in a watery grave and tell everyone about the massacre, the women flee an individual resurrection scene from a rocky tomb and tell no one about it.
- Whereas the Gerasene people become afraid upon seeing the demoniac now seated, clothed, and sane, the Galilean women become afraid after seeing a seated, clothed young man in the last place they expect to meet such a person, and what he tells them seems crazy.
- Whereas the Gerasenes plead for Jesus—who had delivered the possessed man and drowned their pigs—to leave their land, the women flee from the empty tomb with instructions to meet Jesus—who has already left the scene!—with Peter and the other disciples in Galilee.

In the *second flight case* (13:14-17), from Jesus's prophetic discourse warning of ominous events on the near horizon, he urged his followers in Judea to "flee (*pheugetōsan*) to the mountains" when they see the "desolating sacrilege" of Roman imperial idolatry erected in the Jerusalem temple. Recall that Mark especially flagged this message for his audience ("Let the reader understand," 13:14). The situation will be especially dire for vulnerable pregnant and nursing women if they do not flee (13:17).

The fleeing women at the tomb do precisely what Jesus advised in chapter 13, although they are not specifically told to do so by the young man. He just says "go, tell"; they go in haste (flee) but tell no one, it seems (see more below). No sacrilegious image to Caesar has been placed in the tomb; the tomb is empty, except for the young man; and the tomb is no temple where Caesar can flaunt his divine aspirations. Yet this vacant tomb is the highest holy ground, the most sacred space in Mark's narrative. The curtain between heaven and earth has ripped open (15:38), revealing the "Holy One of God" (1:24), the "Son of the Most High God" (5:7), the true living Lord of the universe, infinitely greater than the petty rulers of this world—including Caesar! Mark dares to proclaim throughout his Gospel—with an exclamation point at the end—that this Jesus who was crucified on a Roman cross as a threat to the regime has overcome the powers of death and despotism. Such a claim to Christ's deity and dominance is sure to rile any Roman emperor: "Let the reader understand"—and beware and prepare to run, if necessary!

The *third flight case* (14:50-52) focused on the disappointing male disciples in Gethsemane: Peter, James, and John who failed to "keep awake" with Jesus (14:37-41); Judas who led the arrest party (14:43-45); and "all" who "deserted him and fled (*ephygon*)," including the anonymous "young man" who "ran off (*ephygen*) naked" (14:50-52). While their flight was not explicitly associated with fear, their fear of arrest was strongly implied.

Although in light of 15:40-41 we now know that women disciples came to Judea with Jesus and the Twelve, their presence with the men late at night in Gethsemane would be unlikely. In any case they do not utterly abandon Jesus and go into hiding; they stay in the vicinity of the cross and come into his tomb. Unlike the Twelve, Jesus's female followers seek to maintain connection with Jesus, a pattern of approach rather than avoidance. When they flee from the tomb and the white-robed young man, they do not flee *from Jesus* (he's not here!), and their flight complies with the young messenger's instruction: they "go," in a hurry!

In short, in view of previous flight information in Mark, the flight of the two Marys and Salome from the tomb contrasts with the flight from the exorcising Jesus by the Gerasene swineherds and from the arrested Jesus by his male apostles, even as the women's flight follows Jesus's marching orders during the coming political crisis (already engulfing Mark's audience). Accordingly, in this open ending, we should remain open to a positive assessment of the women's hasty getaway from the empty tomb.

But we still haven't accounted for the women's fear or their silence. Their deep-seated fear response is emphasized by multiple terms—*tromos* ("trembling," "trauma"), *ekstasis* ("beside oneself," "distraught"), and *phobeomai* ("being afraid," "phobic")—three of the last nine words in the Gospel, culminating a raft of preceding cases of fear.

Fear Case File #1 involves *antagonists of Jesus*. In addition to the Gerasene swineherds' fearful reaction, no doubt laced with anger, to Jesus's dispatching their herd into the sea (5:14), "Herod feared (*ephobeito*) John," Jesus's forerunner, because he sensed that John was a "righteous and holy man." But Herod's supposed desire to "protect" John (6:20) did not preclude the ruler from imprisoning John and having him beheaded! Even after John's death, however, Herod's anxiety persisted, as he fretted that Jesus might be an ominous reincarnation of John (6:14-16). Later, the chief priests and scribes in Jerusalem "were afraid of (*ephobouto*) [Jesus]," especially because of his popularity with the masses, thus jeopardizing their status to such an extent that these authorities plot to seize and kill Jesus (11:18; cf. 11:32; 12:12). They regard the powerful and influential Jesus as a personal threat to their social, economic, and political position, just as the Gerasene swineherds and Galilean ruler did.

If the women disciples at the tomb in any sense fear the risen Jesus or the prospects of meeting him in his exalted state, it would not owe to any angst about losing their status and would certainly not have any trace of desire to get him back in the tomb as a dead man!

Fear Case File #2 involves *women healed by Jesus*. The three "fear"-related terms in Mark 16:8 also cluster in the intertwined, "sandwiched" stories of the restored bleeding woman and the resuscitated daughter of Jairus (5:21-43). After the bleeding woman presses through the crowd and procures her healing by surreptitiously touching Jesus's clothing, she pulls back and says nothing until Jesus stops and insists that whoever drew his curative power must show him/her self. Then she is compelled to fall down before Jesus in "fear (*phobētheisa*) and trembling (*tremousa*)" (5:33), terrified about how this powerful man might punish her for her unauthorized contact—until he assuages her fear by addressing her as "Daughter" and affirming her faith (5:33-34).

But Jesus does not aim to be a fearsome, foreboding figure. As word comes from Jairus's house that his daughter has died, Jesus promptly tells the distraught father, "Do not fear (*mē phobou*), only believe" (5:35-36), and proceeds to the house to raise the little girl from the dead. Despite this "no fear" exhortation, however, the girl's father and mother, along with Peter, James, and John—the only people Jesus allows inside (5:37, 40)—become "overcome with [great] amazement (*exestēsan ekstasei megalē*)" when they see the girl restored to life (5:42). This juxtaposition of related verb and noun forms followed by the *mega-* adjective suggests an intense disorienting, disruptive "emotional experience to the point of being beside oneself" (BDAG 2000, 309; cf. 350). "Amazement" doesn't quite capture the volatile feelings of trepidation and perplexity mixed with awe and wonder. Jesus has done an incredible thing in bringing the deceased daughter back to life, a wonderful thing to be sure, but unsettling all the same in not simply resisting but *reversing* the ominous forces of death. The CEB aptly reads, "They were shocked!" (5:42). Who can blame them for this reaction? Jesus has taken his miracle-working to a whole new level.

Given the parents' and disciples' confusion, it's understandable that Jesus would give them "strict orders" *not* to broadcast what happened (5:43), as he tried to stifle reports of curing scaly skin disease and speech-and-hearing impairment. But remember that word gets out anyway (1:43-45; 7:35-37). News of extraordinary events is bound to get out and bound to be distorted to some extent in the telling.

The women who flee from the tomb have unquestionably been affected by Jesus, "touched" emotionally, if not physically, by his power and wisdom, persuading them to follow Jesus from Galilee to Judea, even to his cross and tomb; and while they've perhaps not always followed as closely as they should (witnessing the crucifixion from a distance), they've proved more supportive than the male disciples and have no reason to expect any reprisal from the risen Jesus. As for their tremulous "amazement" (*ekstasis*) over the announcement of Jesus's resurrection from the dead, confirmed by the empty tomb, they come to their traumatic "shock" as honestly as Jairus and company do after the little girl's revivification. And they follow Jesus's directive in Jairus's house (5:43) by saying nothing to anyone in their distraught state about the resurrection event.

The young man in the tomb has rescinded the previous gag orders and calls to secrecy. The resurrection of Jesus changes everything: it's the dawning of a new era when the "good news must . . . be proclaimed to all nations" (13:10), throughout "the whole world . . . in remembrance" of an anonymous woman's pre-anointing of Jesus for his burial (14:8-9)—anticipating its imminent obsolescence as Jesus will come alive again and leave the tomb. So do the two Marys and Salome fail to live up to that woman's example? Do these three miss the chance both to anoint Jesus's body and to announce the gospel of Jesus's death-burial-resurrection? Although they have no opportunity to perfume Jesus's body, they don't need to—because another had already done the job and because Jesus is no longer a corpse!

As for their reported silence at the end of the story, this need not be interpreted as final or "absolute" (Bauckham 2002, 289). Historically, word got out to Peter, other disciples, and a wider world across centuries. There would be no Gospel of Mark to read and study today if the women's experience at the empty tomb had not been shared. Stories of restoring skin health and hearing and of resurrecting deceased daughters and a crucified Messiah cannot be long concealed. A perfectly reasonable reading of Mark's ending is that in their state of shock the women do not *initially* or *indiscriminately* report Jesus's resurrection to anyone they happen to meet. They could scarcely explain what had happened and might well be judged as hysterical or mad if they tried to describe their experience (cf. MacDonald 1996). But this doesn't preclude the narrative's presumption that the women eventually bear witness, as instructed, to Peter and the other male apostles. The note about their initial silence may mean they kept the matter to themselves *until* they reported to Peter and company (Beavis 2011, 246).

Speaking of Peter and speculating how he and his cohorts might respond to the women's witness beyond Mark's narrative, we finally compare the men's previous responses of fear with the women's current reaction.

Fear Case File #3 involves *Peter and company on sea and mountain*. Recall that Mark's Jesus first recruited Peter and three fellow fishermen to follow him in a new vocation: he pledged to "make [them] fish for people" (1:17). The proclaimed gospel of God in Christ aims to captivate, as in a dragnet, many people throughout the world, to "catch" on with new believers. Mark's readers "know that [the disciples] go on to become revered missionaries" (Bond 2020, 252). But *within* Mark's narrative, the Twelve do not make the grade in mission training.

Consistent with the people-fishing goal, Jesus uses two turbulent sea crossings to test the mettle of his trainees. In both instances, however, they respond with more fear and trembling than faith and trust. In the first case, Jesus chides them for being "afraid" ("cowardly," *deilos*; L&N 1988, 318) they were going to perish in the storm (4:40), and even after Jesus tames the tempest they are "filled with great awe," literally, "frightened with great fear" (*ephobēthēsan phobon megan*), a volatile mix of wonder and terror regarding Jesus's identity ("Who then is this?" 4:41). In the second case, as they strained to steer their storm-wracked vessel, the disciples "were terrified" by the ghostly figure moving toward them across the water who turned out to be Jesus; but again, even after he identifies himself, tells them "Do not be afraid (*mē phobeisthe*)" (6:50), and stills the storm, they become "utterly astounded (*existanto*)" or "beside themselves" (6:51 CEB). This vast oceanic experience is beyond them, beside them, standing ominously outside (*ek-stasis*) their perceptual capability.

Peter, James, and John soon had another extraordinary, out-of-bounds revelation of Jesus, not as a misty, mysterious figure on the sea but as a dazzling, transfigured being on a mountain, accompanied by Moses and Elijah. Again "they were terrified" with extreme fear (*ekphobos*). But far from tongue-tying Peter, his terror made him blurt out a ridiculous building proposal because "he did not know what [else] to say" (9:6). Here he would have been better off to wonder and worship in silent awe.

The women at Jesus's empty tomb are assigned the task of bringing Peter and associates back on board with Jesus's mission and disclosing to them Jesus's new identity as the risen Lord, Christ, and Son of Humankind, as he had previously "told" them (16:7; cf. 8:31; 9:31; 10:34)—and they promptly dismissed. And like the Twelve at sea and on the mountain, the women at the tomb become frightened and thunderstruck by the perplexity and enormity of it all, joining the male disciples as finite "humans struggling to think the surprising things of God" (Malbon 2012, 492). Over the last forty-five or so hours (9:00 a.m. Friday to 6:00 a.m. Sunday), their senses have been stressed and stretched to the limit with overwhelming stimuli, particularly their sense of sight. Notice the torrent of "see" terms (forms of *theōreō*, *horaō*, and *anablepō*) applied to the women (Fowler 1991, 248–49):

- They were *looking on* Jesus's "dark" crucifixion (15:40; cf. 15:33).
- They *saw* where Joseph had placed Jesus's body (15:47).

- They *looked up* and *saw* the stone unexpectedly removed from the tomb entrance (16:4).
- They *saw* the shocking figure of a white-robed young man sitting inside the tomb (16:5).
- The young man invited them to *look* at the vacant place where they body had lain and informed them that the Jesus they seek was gone (16:6).
- The young man assured them that they *will see* him again live and in person in Galilee (with Peter and the apostles) (16:7).

All of this eye-popping perceptual experience in a short span of time at the very threshold of life and death proves too much for the women to take in. It naturally overloads their mental-emotional "carrying capacity," overcharges their neural-psychological circuitry (Deisseroth 2021, 64–98). As Jesus's mother and siblings had tried to "restrain" Jesus early in his ministry in light of increasing reports that "he has lost his mind (*exestē*)" (3:21)—that is, gone "out of his mind," "is beside himself"—his mother and her two women friends are now going out of their minds with fear (*ekstasis*, 16:8a) over the extraordinary event(s) of Jesus's crucifixion-entombment-resurrection. Identifying Jesus's mother by her relationship with another son—"Mary, the mother of James" (16:1)—may hint at her precarious relationship with Jesus: Who, then, is this Jesus (cf. 4:41)? Is this still the son I bore and raised in Nazareth, the boy who became a carpenter (6:3) (Fowler 1991, 244)?

In this perplexed, overwhelming state, it would be surprising if the two Marys and Salome were *not* overcome with fear, triggering both *flight* and *freeze* responses, both fleeing the tomb and freezing up, unable to speak to anyone. Again, these are *first responses* to the rapid buildup of traumatic sights (Spencer 2021, 13–15), not a permanent fugitive status or aphasic state. It will take a little time for the women to find their balance and their voice, to move from "ek-static" fear to ecstatic, expressive joy. Over two millennia later, we still struggle to apprehend the full mystery of Jesus's incarnation, crucifixion, and resurrection. We are in no position to deliver a blithe "Fear not" to these women, these distinguished women who, despite their terror and turmoil, showed up at the cross and tomb and became the first to receive the good news of Jesus's resurrection, which they eventually shared with Peter and the other apostles—and by extension with the whole world.

But what was the likely effect of this open "for-they-were-afraid" ending on Mark's first readers? Perhaps some felt like we feel when a suspenseful movie, play, or television show ends with a cliffhanger. We want to know more! It sets our minds to reeling about possible resolutions. But most, if not all, of Mark's primary audience already knew the outcome of Jesus's story: as believers in the risen Christ 60–70s CE, they themselves were living testimonies to the enduring power of the oral and written gospel. Yet their reality was also fraught with its own frightening dimension, as Roman armies moved to put down Jewish revolts in Galilee and Judea and became increasingly suspicious of a maverick Jewish sect devoted to a Messiah crucified by Rome. In Mark 13, Jesus warned his followers about these coming troubles.

Mark's Christ-believing audience would thus naturally respond to the past fear of the women at the tomb in light of their difficult present experience; they would read themselves back into the women's story and project the women forward into their story, sparking a swirl of mimetic emotions. As Michael Whitenton states, Mark's "audience members would likely exhibit a wide array of empathetic emotions, such as admiration, sympathy, antipathy, pity, hope, and fear based on how they made sense of the emotions of the women from their elevated perspective" (2016, 283; cf. Oatley 1994)—elevated, that is, by their later hindsight position and possibly by some sense of social superiority to the Galilean women. Alternately or compositely, Mark's original readers might draw comfort from the women's struggles, criticize the women's failures, or be challenged to pick up where the women left off and overcome their own fears about testifying to the risen Christ in a hostile world.

A less obvious reader response—for us, no less than first-century audiences—correlates with our narrative analysis above of the women's fear as a complex tremulous, tectonic shifting of worldview: an ek-static, out-standing, disorienting-and-reorienting ripping apart of the cosmic "curtain" between life and death, heaven and earth—an apocalyptic ("revealing," "unveiling") event of colossal magnitude. Unfortunately, however, believers can soon become inured to the ineffable sublimity of the gospel, taming its awesome-fearsome power to overcome death and tamping down its wild potential to break *out* (*ek/ex*) of stifling tombs and stagnant pools of thought, feeling, and action (on the "sublime," see Burke 2004 [1759], 49–199; Doran 2015; Verde 2020, 75). If familiarity doesn't breed contempt, it certainly breeds complacency. Mark's abrupt ending on the down note of fear aims to throw us back into the vortex of Easter morning with the fleeing, fearful women, to light a fire under our feet and jolt our hearts and minds to grasp new, boundary-breaking truths and generate fresh, life-giving stories.

Appearances and Commissions (16:8b-20)

At the risk of blunting the edge of this provocative ending, we must briefly consider a well-known longer, tidier, more upbeat ending. Although a strong consensus of modern textual scholars regards Mark 16:8b-20 as a later addition, this passage continues to be printed in modern English Bibles (though marked with double brackets in the NRSV and glossed with a footnote) and has been influential in some unconventional Christian circles. Only here does Jesus authorize snake-handling and poison-drinking as "signs" of faith in him and his powerful name (16:18). He links these two "signs" to three others that appear more often in the New Testament: casting out demons, speaking in tongues, and laying hands on the sick (16:17). Still, all five signs accentuate more exotic acts of ministry, "nothing short of stratospheric" manifestations, as Jack Levison writes, "brimming with the extraordinary and bordering on the bizarre" (2020, 176).

More in line with the other Gospel endings, though no less dramatic, the added material features the risen Jesus'

- *commissions* to his male apostles to preach the gospel and baptize believers throughout the world (Mark 16:8b, 15-16, 20; cf. Matt 28:19-20; Luke 24:47).
- *appearances* to Mary Magdalene (Mark 16:9-11; cf. Matt 28:1, 8-10; John 20:11-18), to two disciples "as they were walking into the country" (Mark 16:12-13; cf. the Emmaus road incident in Luke 24:13-35), and to "the eleven . . . as they were sitting at table" (Mark 16:14; cf. Matt 28:16; Luke 24:36-42; John 20:19-29; 21:9-14).
- *ascension* "into heaven" and enthronement "at the right hand of God" (Mark 16:19; cf. Luke 24:50-53).

In short, as Elizabeth Struthers Malbon puts it, this grand finale appendix "close[s] with a bang the story of Jesus on the way to renew his presence with his followers as they take up their lives again, substituting a majestic Jesus sitting at the right hand of God in heaven (16:19)" (2012, 492). This majestic, miracle-working (through his followers), settled (seated) Jesus substitutes for—or better put, subdues and suppresses, triumphalizes and trivializes—the mocked and killed Jesus painted in bold strokes at the end of Mark's story, giving way at the very last scene to an absent, elusive Jesus ("He is not here") still on the move ("to Galilee").

The critical "open" question Mark's Jesus leaves with his first followers, female and male, with the first hearers of this Gospel, and with us readers today is this: Will we take up our crosses and follow Jesus (8:34) wherever he leads through the barren deserts, across the stormy seas, and on the dizzying mountain heights to experience renewed embodied life on earth as it is in heaven and to share this new Christ-life with a battered and broken world?

Works Cited

Allison, Dale C. 1984. "Elijah Must Come First." *JBL* 103: 256–58.

Anderson, Gary A. 2009. *Sin: A History*. New Haven: Yale University Press.

Anderson, Janice Capel. 2008. "Feminist Criticism: The Dancing Daughter." Pages 11–43 in *Mark & Method: New Approaches in Biblical Studies*. 2nd edition. Edited by Janice Capel Anderson and Stephen D. Moore. Minneapolis: Fortress.

———, and Stephen D. Moore, editors. 2008. *Mark & Method: New Approaches in Biblical Study*. 2nd edition. Minneapolis: Fortress.

Arav, Rami. 1992. "Hermon, Mount." Pages 158–59 in *ABD*. Volume 3. Edited by David Noel Freedman et al. New York: Doubleday.

Arendt, Hannah. 2006 [1965]. *Eichmann in Jerusalem: A Report on the Banality of Evil*. Revised edition. London: Penguin.

Aristotle. 2007. *On Rhetoric: A Theory of Civic Discourse*. Translated by George A. Kennedy. 2nd edition. New York: Oxford University Press.

Avalos, Hector, Sarah J. Melcher, and Jeremy Schipper, editors. 2007. *This Abled Body: Rethinking Disabilities in Biblical Study*. Semeia Studies 55. Atlanta: SBL.

Bach, Alice. 1996. "Calling the Shots: Directing Salomé's Dance of Death." *Semeia* 74: 103–26.

Baden, Joel S., and Candida R. Moss. 2011. "The Origin and Interpretation of *ṣāra'at* in Leviticus 13–14." *JBL* 130: 643–62.

Balentine, Samuel E. 2002. *Leviticus*. Int. Louisville: Westminster John Knox.

Barrett, Lisa Feldman. 2017. *How Emotions Are Made: The Secret Life of the Brain*. Boston: Houghton Mifflin Harcourt.

BDAG. 2000. Walter Bauer et al. *A Greek-English Lexicon of the New Testament and Other Early Christian Literature*. 3rd edition. Revised and edited by Frederick William Danker. Chicago: University of Chicago Press.

Barclay, John M. G. 2018. "'Ιοδαιοϛ: Ethnicity and Translation." Pages 46–58 in *Ethnicity, Race, Religion: Identities and Ideologies in Early Jewish and Christian Texts, and in Modern Biblical Interpretation*. Edited by Katherine M. Hockey and David G. Horrell. London: T&T Clark.

Barnhill, Anne, Mark Budolfson, and Tyler Doggett. 2016. *Food, Society, and Ethics: An Introductory Text with Readings*. New York: Oxford University Press.

———, editors. 2018. *The Oxford Handbook of Food Ethics*. New York: Oxford University Press.

Bauckham, Richard. 2002. *Gospel Women: Studies of the Named Women in the Gospels*. Grand Rapids: Eerdmans.

———. 2010. *The Bible and Ecology: Rediscovering the Community of Creation*. Waco: Baylor University Press.

Baumgarten, A. I. 1984/1985. "*Korban* and the Pharisaic *Paradosis*." *JANESCU* 16/17: 5–17.

Beatty, Paul. 2015. *The Sellout: A Novel*. New York: Picador.

Beavis, Mary Ann. 1998. "From the Margin to the Way: A Feminist Reading of the Story of Bartimaeus." *Journal of Feminist Studies in Religion* 14: 19–39.

———. 2011. *Mark*. Paideia Commentaries on the New Testament. Grand Rapids: Baker Academic.

Bendoraitis, Kristian A. 2018. "The Parables of Enoch and Mark 1:14–2:12: The Authoritative Son of Man." Pages 48–54 in *Reading Mark in Context: Jesus and Second Temple Judaism*. Edited by Ben C. Blackwell, John K. Goodrich, and Jason Maston. Grand Rapids: Zondervan.

Ben-Ghiat, Ruth. 2020. *Strongmen: Mussolini to the Present*. New York: Norton.

Betsworth, Sharon. 2010. *The Reign of God Is Such as These: A Socio-Literary Analysis of Daughters in the Gospel of Mark.* Library of New Testament Studies. London: T&T Clark.

Betz, Hans Dieter, editor. 1986. *The Greek Magical Papyri in Translation, Including the Demotic Spells.* Chicago: University of Chicago Press.

Bird, Michael F. 2013. *Evangelical Theology: A Biblical and Systematic Introduction.* Grand Rapids: Zondervan.

———. 2018. "The Testament of Solomon and Mark 5:1-20: Exorcism and Power over Evil Spirits." Pages 77–83 in *Reading Mark in Context: Jesus and Second Temple Judaism.* Edited by Ben C. Blackwell, John K. Goodrich, and Jason Maston. Grand Rapids: Zondervan.

Black, C. Clifton. 1991. "An Oration at Olivet: Some Rhetorical Dimensions of Mark 13." Pages 66–92 in *Persuasive Artistry: Studies in New Testament Rhetoric in Honor of George A. Kennedy.* Journal for the Study of the New Testament Supplements. Edited by Duane F. Watson. Sheffield: Sheffield Academic Press.

———. 1994. *Mark: Images of an Apostolic Interpreter.* Studies in Personalities of the New Testament. Columbia: University of South Carolina Press.

———. 2011. *Mark.* Abingdon New Testament Commentaries. Nashville: Abingdon.

Black, C. Clifton, and Adela Yarbro Collins. 2006. Pages 1722–58 in *The HarperCollins Study Bible.* 2nd edition. Edited by Harold W. Attridge et al. New York: HarperCollins.

Blackburn, Barry. 1991. *Theios Anēr and the Markan Miracle Traditions: A Critique of the Theios Anēr Concept as an Interpretative Background of the Miracle Traditions Used by Mark.* Wissenschaftliche Untersuchungen zum Neuen Testament II/40. Tübingen: Mohr (Siebeck).

Blackwell, Ben C., John K. Goodrich, and Jason Maston, editors. 2018. *Reading Mark in Context: Jesus and Second Temple Judaism.* Grand Rapids: Zondervan.

Blenkinsopp, Joseph. 2011. *Creation, Un-creation, Re-creation: A Discursive Commentary on Genesis 1–11.* London: T&T Clark International.

Block, Daniel I. 2021. *Covenant: The Framework of God's Grand Plan of Redemption*. Grand Rapids: Baker Academic.

Bhabha, Homi K. 2004. *The Location of Culture*. Routledge Classics. Milton Park, UK: Routledge.

Bock, Darrell L. 2018. "The Parables of Enoch and Mark 14:53-73." Pages 231–37 in *Reading Mark in Context: Jesus and Second Temple Judaism*. Edited by Ben C. Blackwell, John K. Goodrich, and Jason Maston. Grand Rapids: Zondervan.

Boff, Leonardo. 1997. *Cry of the Earth, Cry of the Poor*. Ecology and Justice. Maryknoll, NY: Orbis.

Bond, Helen K. 2011. "Barabbas Remembered." Pages 59–71 in *Jesus and Paul: Global Perspectives in Honor of James D. G. Dunn for his Seventieth Birthday*. Edited by B. J. Oropeza, C. K. Robertson, and Douglas C. Mohrman. London: T&T Clark.

———. 2019. "A Fitting End? Self-Denial and a Slave's Death in Mark's Life of Jesus." *NTS* 65: 425–42.

———. 2020. *The First Biography of Jesus: Genre and Meaning in Mark's Gospel*. Grand Rapids: Eerdmans.

Bonner, Campbell. 1927. "Traces of Thaumaturgic Technique in the Miracles." *HTR* 20: 171–82.

Borg, Marcus J. 2003. *The Heart of Christianity: Rediscovering a Life of Faith*. New York: HarperSanFrancisco.

———. 2006. *Jesus: Uncovering the Life, Teachings, and Relevance of a Religious Revolutionary*. New York: HarperCollins.

Boring, M. Eugene. 2006. *Mark*. NTL. Louisville: Westminster John Knox.

Botha, Pieter J. J. 2012. *Orality and Literacy in Early Christianity*. Biblical Performance Criticism 5. Eugene, OR: Cascade.

Bowersock, G. W. 1995. *Fiction as History: Nero to Julian*. Berkeley: University of California Press.

Boys, Mary C. 2000. *Has God Only One Blessing? Judaism as a Source of Christian Self-Understanding*. Studies in Judaism and Christianity. Mahwah, NJ: Paulist.

Brady, Michael S. 2013. *Emotional Insight: The Epistemic Role of Emotional Experience*. Oxford: Oxford University Press.

Brewer, Douglas J., Terence Clark, and Adrian A. Phillips. 2002. *Dogs in Antiquity, Anubis to Cerberus: The Origins of the Domestic Dog*. Aris & Phillips Classical Texts. Liverpool: Liverpool University Press.

Brown, Raymond E. 1971. "Jesus and Elijah." *Per* 12: 85–104.

Brueggemann, Walter. 1997. *Theology of the Old Testament: Testimony, Dispute, Advocacy*. Minneapolis: Fortress.

Bruteau, Beatrice. 2005. *The Holy Thursday Revolution*. Maryknoll, NY: Orbis.

Burke, Edmund. 2004 [1759]. *A Philosophical Enquiry into the Origin of Our Ideas of the Sublime and Beautiful and Other Pre-Revolutionary Writings*. Edited by David Womersley. London: Penguin.

Burkill, T. A. 1967. "The Historical Significance of the Syrophoenician Woman (Mark vii: 24-31)." *NovT* 9: 161–77.

Cadbury, Henry J. 1920. *The Style and Literary Method of Luke*. HTS 6. Cambridge: Harvard University Press.

Cadwallader, Alan H. 2008a. *Beyond the Word of a Woman: Recovering the Bodies of the Syrophoenician Women*. Adelaide: ATF Press.

———. 2008b. "Out of Wordlock: Autobiography and the Syrophoenician Women." *Pacifica* 21: 257–84.

Camery-Hoggatt, Jerry. 1992. *Irony in Mark's Gospel*. SNTSMS 72. Cambridge: Cambridge University Press.

Caputo, John D. 2006. *The Weakness of God: A Theology of the Event*. Bloomington: Indiana University Press.

———. 2015. "The Weakness of God: A Radical Theology of the Cross." Pages 21–65 in *The Wisdom and Foolishness of God: First Corinthians 1–2 in Theological Exploration*. Edited by Christophe Chalamet and Hans-Christoph Askani. Minneapolis: Fortress.

———. 2019. *Cross and Cosmos: A Theology of Difficult Glory*. Bloomington: Indiana University Press.

Cardenal, Ernesto. 2010. *The Gospel in Solentiname*. Translated by Donald D. Walsh. Revised edition. Maryknoll, NY: Orbis.

Carey, Greg. 2006. "Arimathea." Page 259 in *The New Interpreter's Dictionary of the Bible*. Volume 1. Edited by Katherine Doob Sakenfeld et al. Nashville: Abingdon.

———. 2009. *Sinners: Jesus and His Earliest Followers*. Waco: Baylor University Press.

Carr, David M. 2014. *Holy Resilience: The Bible's Traumatic Origins*. New Haven: Yale University Press.

Carroll, Scott T. 1992. "Bethphage." Page 715 in *ABD*. Volume 1. Edited by David Noel Freedman et al. New York: Doubleday.

Carter, Warren. 2003. "Are There Imperial Texts in the Class? Intertextual Eagles and Matthean Eschatology as 'Lights Out' Time for Imperial Rome (Matt 24:27-31). *JBL* 122: 467–87.

———. 2013. *Seven Events that Shaped the New Testament World*. Grand Rapids: Baker Academic.

———. 2014. "Cross-Gendered Romans and Mark's Jesus: Legion Enters the Pigs (Mark 5:1-20)." *JBL* 133: 139–55.

———. 2019. *Mark*. Wisdom Commentary 42. Collegeville, MN: Liturgical Press.

CDC, Centers for Disease Control and Prevention. "Hansen's Disease (Leprosy)." cdc.gov/leprosy/index.html.

Chapman, David W., and Eckhard J. Schnabel. 2015. *The Trial and Crucifixion of Jesus: Texts and Commentary*. Tübingen: Mohr Siebeck.

Chilton, Bruce D. 2000. *Rabbi Jesus: An Intimate Biography*. New York: Doubleday.

Cohn-Sherbok, Dan M. 1979. "An Analysis of Jesus's Arguments concerning the Plucking of Grain on the Sabbath." *JSNT* 2: 31–41.

Collins, Adela Yarbro. 1994. "Rulers, Divine Men, and Walking on the Water (Mark 6:45-52)." Pages 207–27 in *Religious Propaganda and Missionary Competition in the New Testament World: Essays Honoring Dieter Georgi*. NovTSup 74. Edited by Lukas Bormann, Kelly Del Tredici, and Angela Standhartinger. Leiden: Brill.

———. 1996. "The Apocalyptic Rhetoric of Mark 13 in Historical Context." *BR* 41: 5–36.

———. 2004. "The Charge of Blasphemy in Mark 14.64." *JSNT* 26: 379–401.

———. 2007. *Mark: A Commentary*. Hermeneia. Minneapolis: Fortress.

Collins, Adela Yarbro, and John J. Collins. 2008. *King and Messiah as Son of God: Divine, Human, and Angelic Messianic Figures in Biblical and Related Literature.* Grand Rapids: Eerdmans.

Collins, John J. 2010. *The Scepter and the Star: Messianism in Light of the Dead Sea Scrolls.* 2nd edition. Grand Rapids: Eerdmans.

———. 2015. "The Transformation of Aseneth." Pages 93–108 in *Bodies, Borders, Believers: Ancient Texts and Present Conversations.* Edited by Anne Hege Grung, Marianne Bjeland Kartzow, and Anna Rebecca Solevåg. Eugene, OR: Pickwick.

———. 2016. *The Apocalyptic Imagination: An Introduction to Jewish Apocalyptic Literature.* Grand Rapids: Eerdmans.

Collins, Patricia Hill. 1998. "It's All in the Family: Intersections of Race, Gender, and Nation." *Hypatia* 13: 62–82.

Collins, Patricia Hill, and Sirma Bilge. 2020. *Intersectionality.* 2nd edition. Key Concepts. Cambridge, UK: Polity Press.

Combs, Jason Robert. 2008. "A Ghost on the Water? Understanding an Absurdity in Mark 6:45-52." *JBL* 128: 345–58.

Cone, James H. 2011. *The Cross and the Lynching Tree.* Maryknoll, NY: Orbis.

Corley, Kathleen E. 1993. *Private Women, Public Meals: Social Conflict in the Synoptic Tradition.* Peabody, MA. Hendrickson.

Cotter, Wendy. 1999. *Miracles in Greco-Roman Antiquity: A Sourcebook for the Study of New Testament Miracle Stories.* New York: Routledge.

———. 2010. *The Christ of the Miracle Stories: Portrait through Encounter.* Grand Rapids: Baker Academic.

Crenshaw, Kimberlé Williams. 1989. "Demarginalizing the Intersection of Race and Sex: A Black Feminist Critique of Antidiscrimination Doctrine, Feminist Theory and Antiracist Politics." *University of Chicago Legal Forum* 1: 139–67.

Cross, Anthony R., and Philip E. Thompson, editors. 2003. *Baptist Sacramentalism.* Studies in Baptist History and Thought. Milton Keynes, UK: Paternoster.

Crossan, John Dominic. 1991. *The Historical Jesus: The Life of a Mediterranean Jewish Peasant.* New York: HarperSanFrancisco.

———. 1994. *Jesus: A Revolutionary Biography*. New York: HarperCollins.

———. 1995. *Who Killed Jesus? Exposing the Roots of Anti-Semitism in the Gospel Story of the Death of Jesus*. New York: HarperCollins.

Crossan, John Dominic, and Sarah Sexton Crossan. 2018. *Resurrecting Easter: How the West Lost and the East Kept the Original Easter Vision*. New York: HarperOne.

Crossan, John Dominic, and Jonathan L. Reed. 2001. *Excavating Jesus: Beneath the Stones, Behind the Texts*. New York: HarperSanFrancisco.

Crouch, Stanley. 1995–1996. "The Afrocentric Hustle." *Journal of Blacks in Higher Education* 10: 77–82.

Culpepper, R. Alan. 2007. *Mark*. SHBC. Macon, GA: Smyth & Helwys.

———. 2011. "Mark 6:17-29 in Its Narrative Context: Kingdoms in Conflict." Pages 145–63 in *Mark as Story: Retrospect and Prospect*. Edited by Kelly R. Iverson and Christopher W. Skinner. Resources for Biblical Study 65. Atlanta: Society of Biblical Literature.

Damasio, Antonio. 2003. *Looking for Spinoza: Joy, Sorrow, and the Feeling Brain*. Orlando: Harcourt.

———. 2018. *The Strange Order of Things: Life, Feeling, and the Making of Cultures*. New York: Pantheon.

Danby, Herbert. 1933. *The Mishnah*. London: Oxford University Press.

Danker, Frederick W., and Kathryn Krug. 2009. *The Concise Greek-English Lexicon of the New Testament*. Chicago: University of Chicago Press.

Darwin, Charles. 2009 [1872]. *The Expression of Emotions in Man and Animals*. 4th edition. Edited by Paul Ekman. Oxford: Oxford University Press.

Davis, Ellen F. 2014. *Biblical Prophecy: Perspectives for Christian Theology, Discipleship, and Ministry*. Louisville: Westminster John Knox.

Deisseroth, Karl. 2021. *Projections: A Story of Human Emotions*. New York: Random House.

Deissmann, Adolf. 1978 [1927]. *Light from the Ancient East: The New Testament Illustrated by Recently Discovered Texts of the Graeco-Roman World*. 4th edition. Translated by Lionel R. M. Strachan. Grand Rapids: Baker.

Derrett, J. Duncan M. 1970. "ΚΟΡΒΑΝ Ο ΕΣΤΙΝ ΔΩΡΟΝ." *NTS* 16: 364–68.

———. 1971. "Law in the New Testament: The Palm Sunday Colt." *NovT* 13: 241–58.

———. 1973. "Salted with Fire: Studies in Texts: Mark 9:42-50." *Theology* 76: 364–68.

———. 1979. "Contributions to the Study of the Gerasene Demoniac." *JSNT* 2: 3–17.

———. 1983. "Why Jesus Blessed the Children (Mk 10:13 par.)." *NovT* 25: 1–18.

deSilva, David A. 2000. *Honor, Patronage, Kinship & Purity: Unlocking New Testament Culture.* Downers Grove, IL: InterVarsity Press.

DeSteno, David. 2018. *Emotional Success: The Power of Gratitude, Compassion, and Pride.* Boston: Houghton Mifflin Harcourt.

Dewey, Joanna. 2013. *The Oral Ethos of the Early Church: Speaking, Writing, and the Gospel of Mark.* Biblical Performance Criticism 8. Eugene, OR: Cascade.

Dibelius, Martin. 1935. *From Tradition to Gospel.* Translated by Bertram Lee Woolf. New York: Scribner's.

Donahue, John R., and Daniel J. Harrington. 2002. *The Gospel of Mark.* Sacra Pagina 2. Collegeville, MN: Liturgical.

Doran, Robert. 2015. *Theory of the Sublime from Longinus to Kant.* Cambridge: Cambridge University Press.

———. 2020. "'Salting with Fire' (Mark 9:49)." *NovT* 62: 361–74.

Douglas, Mary. 1993. "The Forbidden Animals in Leviticus." *JSOT* 59: 3–23.

Duff, Paul Brooks. 1992. "The March of the Divine Warrior and the Advent of the Greco-Roman King: Mark's Account of Jesus's Entry into Jerusalem." *JBL* 111: 55–71.

Dunn, James D. G. 1990. *Jesus, Paul, and the Law: Studies in Mark and Galatians.* Louisville: Westminster John Knox.

Eaton, John. 2005. *The Psalms: A Historical and Spiritual Commentary with an Introduction and New Translation.* London: Continuum.

Edwards, Douglas R. 1992. "Genessaret." Page 963 in *ABD*. Volume 2. Edited by David Freedman et al. New York: Doubleday.

Ehrman, Bart D. 2003. "A Leper in the Hands of an Angry Jesus." Pages 77–98 in *New Testament Greek and Exegesis. Essays in Honor of Gerald F. Hawthorne*. Edited by Amy M. Donaldson and Timothy B. Sailors. Grand Rapids: Eerdmans.

Ekman, Paul. 2007. *Emotions Revealed: Recognizing Faces and Feelings to Improve Communication and Emotional Life*. 2nd edition. New York: St. Martin's Griffin.

Epictetus. 2018. *How to Be Free: An Ancient Guide to the Stoic Life: Encheiridion and Selections from Discourses*. Translated with an introduction by A. A. Long. Ancient Wisdom for Modern Readers. Princeton: Princeton University Press.

Eusebius. 1965. *The History of the Church from Christ to Constantine*. Translated with an introduction by G. A. Williamson. Harmondsworth, UK: Penguin.

Evans, Christopher H. 2004. *The Kingdom Is Always but Coming: A Life of Walter Rauschenbusch*. Grand Rapids: Eerdmans.

———. 2017. *The Social Gospel in American Religion*. New York: New York University Press.

Evans, Craig A. 2003. "How Septuagintal Is Isa. 5:1–7 in Mark 12:1–9?" *NovT* 45:105–10.

———. 2012. *Jesus and His World: The Archaeological Evidence*. Louisville: Westminster John Knox.

Eve, Eric. 2008. "Spit in Your Eye: The Blind Man of Bethsaida and the Blind Man of Alexandria." *NTS* 54: 1–17.

Faerstein, Morris M. 1981. "Why Do the Scribes Say Elijah Must Come First?" *JBL* 100: 75–86.

Feldman, Louis. 1993. *Jew and Gentile in the Ancient World*. Princeton: Princeton University Press.

Ferris, Iain M. 2018. *Cave Canem: Animals and Roman Society*. Stroud, UK: Amberley.

Festinger, Leon, Henry W. Riecken, and Stanley Schachter. 1956. *When Prophecy Fails: A Social and Psychological Study of a Modern Group that Predicted the Destruction of the World*. Minneapolis: University of Minnesota Press.

Fiddes, Paul S. 2000. *Participating in God: A Pastoral Doctrine of the Trinity*. Louisville: Westminster John Knox.

Fitzmyer, Joseph A. 1985a. *The Gospel according to Luke X-XXIV: Introduction, Translation, and Notes*. AB 28a. New York: Doubleday.

———. 1985b. "More about Elijah Coming First." *JBL* 104: 295–96.

Foster, George M. 1965. "Peasant Society and the Image of the Limited Good." *American Anthropologist* 67: 293–315.

———. 1972. "A Second Look at Limited Good." *Anthropological Quarterly* 46: 57–74.

Fowler, Robert M. 1981. *Loaves and Fishes: The Function of the Feeding Stories in the Gospel of Mark*. SBLDS 54. Atlanta: Scholars Press.

———. 1991. *Let the Reader Understand: Reader-Response Criticism and the Gospel of Mark*. Minneapolis: Fortress.

———. 2008. "Reader-Response Criticism: Figuring Mark's Reader." Pages 59–93 in *Mark & Method: New Approaches in Biblical Studies*. 2nd edition. Edited by Janice Capel Anderson and Stephen D. Moore. Minneapolis: Fortress.

———. 2011. "In the Boat with Jesus: Imagining Ourselves in Mark's Story." Pages 233–58 in *Mark as Story: Retrospect and Prospect*. Edited by Kelly R. Iverson and Christopher W. Skinner. RBS 65. Atlanta: SBL.

Fowler, Stanley K. 2002. *More than a Symbol: The British Baptist Recovery of Baptist Sacramentalism*. Studies in Baptist History and Thought. Milton Keynes, UK: Paternoster.

France, R. T. 1987. *Matthew*. Tyndale New Testament Commentaries. Grand Rapids: Eerdmans.

———. 2002. *The Gospel of Mark*. NIGTC. Grand Rapids: Eerdmans.

Frayer-Griggs, Daniel. 2009. "'Everyone Will Be Baptized in Fire': Mark 9.49, Q 3.16, and the Baptism of the Coming One." *Journal for the Study of the Historical Jesus* 7: 254–85.

Francis, James. 1996. "Children and Childhood in the New Testament." Pages 65–85 in *The Family in Theological Perspective*. Edited by Stephen C. Barton. Edinburgh: T & T Clark.

Fredriksen, Paula. 2000. *From Jesus to Christ*. 2nd edition. New Haven: Yale University Press.

Freeman, Curtis W. 2014. *Contesting Catholicity: Theology for Other Baptists*. Waco, TX: Baylor University Press.

Fretheim, Terence E. 1994. "The Book of Genesis: Introduction, Commentary, and Reflections." Pages 319–674 in *NIB*. Volume 1. Edited by Leander E. Keck et al. Nashville: Abingdon.

Friberg, Barbara, Timothy Friberg, and Neva F. Miller. 2000. *Analytical Lexicon of the Greek New Testament*. Baker's Greek New Testament Library. Electronic edition. Grand Rapids: Baker.

Frijda, Nico H. 1986. *The Emotions*. Studies in Emotion and Social Interaction. Cambridge: Cambridge University Press.

———. 1988. "Laws of Emotion." *American Psychologist* 43: 349–58.

Furstenberg, Yair. 2008. "Defilement Penetrating the Body: A New Understanding of Contamination in Mark 7.15." *NTS* 54: 176–200.

———. 2021. "The Shared Image of Pharisaic Law in the Gospels and Rabbinic Tradition." Pages 199–219 in *The Pharisees*. Edited by Joseph Sievers and Amy-Jill Levine. Grand Rapids: Eerdmans.

Garroway, Joshua. 2009. "The Invasion of a Mustard Seed: A Reading of Mark 5.1-20." *JSNT* 32: 57–75.

Gellius, Aulus. 1927. *The Attic Nights*. Translated by John C. Rolfe. Loeb Classical Library. Cambridge: Harvard University Press.

Gench, Frances Taylor. 2004. *Back to the Well: Women's Encounters with Jesus in the Gospels*. Louisville: Westminster John Knox.

Geyer, Douglas W. 2002. *Fear, Anomaly, and Uncertainty in the Gospel of Mark*. American Theological Library Association Monograph Series, 47. Lanham, MD: Scarecrow Press.

Gieschen, Charles A. 2009. "Why Was Jesus with the Wild Beasts? (Mark 1:13)." *CTQ* 73: 77–80.

Goldstein, Rebecca Newberger. 2018. "What Really Matters: An Interview with Rebecca Goldstein." *IAI News*. September 3. iai.tv/articles/rebecca-goldstein-on-what-really-matters-auid-1141.

Goodacre, Mark. 2012. *Thomas and the Gospels: The Case for Thomas's Familiarity with the Synoptic Gospels*. Grand Rapids: Eerdmans.

Gould, Stephen Jay. 1989. *Wonderful Life: The Burgess Shale and the Nature of History*. New York: Norton.

Graver, Margaret R. 2007. *Stoicism and Emotion*. Chicago: University of Chicago Press.

Gray, Rebecca. 1993. *Prophetic Figures in Late Second Temple Jewish Palestine: The Evidence from Josephus*. New York: Oxford University Press.

Green, Joel B. 2008. *Body, Soul, and Human Life: The Nature of Humanity in the Bible*. Studies in Theological Interpretation. Grand Rapids: Baker Academic.

———. 2011a. *Practicing Theological Interpretation: Engaging Biblical Texts for Faith and Formation*. Grand Rapids: Baker Academic.

———. 2011b. "Healthcare Systems in Scripture." Pages 358–60 in *Dictionary of Scripture and Ethics*. Edited by Joel B. Green et al. Grand Rapids: Baker Academic.

———. 2013. "Transfiguration." Pages 966–72 in *Dictionary of Jesus and the Gospels*. 2nd edition. Edited by Joel B. Green, Jeannine K. Brown, and Nicholas Perrin. Downers Grove, IL: IVP Academic.

Greenblatt, Stephen. 2017. *The Rise and Fall of Adam and Eve*. New York: Norton.

Grindheim, Sigurd. 2018. "Sirach and Mark 8:27–9:13: Elijah and the Eschaton." Pages 130–36 in *Reading Mark in Context: Jesus and Second Temple Judaism*. Edited by Ben C. Blackwell, John K. Goodrich, and Jason Maston. Grand Rapids: Zondervan.

Gross, Aaron S., Jody Myers, and Jordan D. Rosenblum, editors. 2020. *Feasting and Fasting: The History and Ethics of Jewish Food*. New York: New York University Press.

Groody, Daniel G., and Gustavo Gutiérrez, editors. 2014. *The Preferential Option for the Poor Beyond Theology*. Notre Dame, IN: Notre Dame Press.

Grout, James. 2021. "Dogs in Ancient Greece and Rome." *Encyclopaedia Romana*. Retrieved August 10, 2021 from penelope.uchicago.edu/~grout/encyclopaedia_romana/miscellanea/canes/canes.html.

Guyon, Amélie J. A. A., et al. 2020. "Respiratory Variability, Sighing, Anxiety, and Breathing Symptoms on Low- and High-Anxious Music Students Before and After Performing." *Frontiers in Psychology*. doi.org/10.3389/fpsyg.2020.00303

Gundry, Robert H. 2004 [1993]. *Mark: A Commentary on His Apology for the Cross*. Volume 2. Grand Rapids: Eerdmans.

Gundry-Volf, Judith M. 2000. "'To Such as These Belongs the Reign of God': Jesus and Children." *ThTo* 56: 469–80.

———. 2008. "Children in the Gospel of Mark, with Special Attention to Jesus's Blessing of the Children (Mark 10:13-16) and the Purpose of Mark." Pages 143–76 in *The Child in the Bible*. Edited by Marcia J. Bunge, Terence E. Fretheim, and Beverly Roberts Gaventa. Grand Rapids: Eerdmans.

Gutiérrez, Gustavo. 1988. *A Theology of Liberation: History, Politics, and Salvation*. Translated by Caridad Inda and John Engleson. Revised edition. Maryknoll, NY: Orbis.

Haber, Susan. 2003. "A Woman's Touch. Feminist Encounters with the Hemorrhaging Woman in Mark 5.24-34." *JSNT* 26: 171–92. Reprinted in Haber. 2008. Pages 125–41 in *"They Shall Purify Themselves": Essays on Purity in Early Judaism*. Edited by Adele Reinhartz. SBLEJL 24. Atlanta: Society of Biblical Literature.

Hagedorn, Anselm C., and Jerome H. Neyrey. 1998. "'It Was out of Envy That They Handed Jesus Over' (Mark 15.10): The Anatomy of Envy and the Gospel of Mark." *JSNT* 69: 15–56.

Hanson, K. C. 1997. "The Galilean Fishing Economy and the Jesus Tradition." *BTB* 27: 99–111.

———. 2002. "Jesus and the Social Bandits." Pages 283–300 in *The Social Setting of Jesus and the Gospels*. Edited by Wolfgang Stegemann, Bruce J. Malina, and Gerd Theissen. Minneapolis: Fortress.

Hanson, K. C., and Douglas E. Oakman. 1998. *Palestine in the Time of Jesus: Social Structures and Social Conflicts*. Minneapolis: Fortress.

Harrington, Hannah K. 1995. "Did the Pharisees Eat Ordinary Food in a State of Ritual Purity?" *JSJ* 26: 42–54.

Harris, Steven Edward. 2019. "Greater Resurrections and a Greater Ascension: Figural Interpretation of Jesus and Elijah." *Journal of Theological Interpretation* 13: 21–35.

Harrison, J. R. 2012. "'Every dog has its day'." Pages 126–35 in *New Documents Illustrating Early Christianity*. Volume 10: *Greek and Other Inscriptions and Papyri Published 1988–1992*. Edited by S. R. Llewelyn, J. R. Harrison, and E. J. Bridge. Grand Rapids: Eerdmans.

Hays, Richard B. 1996. *The Moral Vision of the New Testament: A Contemporary Introduction to New Testament Ethics*. New York: HarperCollins.

Heath, Elaine A. 2019. *Healing the Wounds of Sexual Abuse: Reading the Bible with Survivors*. Grand Rapids: Brazos.

Heil, John Paul. 1992. *The Gospel of Mark as a Model for Action: A Reader-Response Commentary*. Mahwah, NJ: Paulist.

———. 2000. *The Transfiguration of Jesus: Narrative Meaning and Function of Mark 9:2-8, Matt 17:1-8, and Luke 9:28-36*. Analecta Biblica 144. Rome: Pontifical Biblical Institute.

Henderson, Suzanne Watts. 2006. *Christology and Discipleship in the Gospel of Mark*. SNTSMS 135. Cambridge: Cambridge University Press.

———. 2018. "The Gospel according to Mark." Pages 1829–64 in *The New Oxford Annotated Bible New Revised Standard Version with the Apocrypha: An Ecumenical Study Bible*. 5th edition. Edited by Michael D. Coogan et al. New York: Oxford Annotated Press.

Henderson, Thomas P. 2013. "Apocryphal Gospels." Pages 346–52 in *Dictionary of Jesus and the Gospels*. 2nd edition. Edited by Joel B. Green, Jeannine K. Brown, and Nicholas Perrin. Downers Grove, IL: IVP Academic.

Hengel, Martin. 1977. *Crucifixion*. Translated by John Bowden. Philadelphia: Fortress.

Herzog, William R., II. 1994. *Parables as Subversive Speech: Jesus as Pedagogue of the Oppressed*. Louisville: Westminster John Knox.

———. 2012. "Sowing Discord: The Parable of the Sower (Mark 4:1–9)." *RevExp* 109: 187–98.

Hock, Ronald F. 1995. *The Infancy Gospels of James and Thomas, with Introduction, Notes, and Original Text*. The Scholar's Bible. Santa Rosa, CA: Polebridge.

Hooker, Morna D. 2001 [1981]. *A Commentary on the Gospel according to St Mark*. BNTC. London: Continuum.

Hopkins, Gerard Manley. 2018 [1877]. "When Kingfishers Catch Fire." Page 45 in *The Poems of Gerard Manley Hopkins*. Edited by Robert Bridges. Digireads.com Publishing.

Hoppe, Leslie J. 2006. "Caesarea Philippi." Pages 517–18 in *The New Interpreter's Dictionary of the Bible*. Volume 1. Edited by Katherine Doob Sakenfeld et al. Nashville: Abingdon.

Horsley, Richard A. 2001. *Hearing the Whole Story: The Politics of Mark's Gospel*. Louisville: Westminster John Knox.

———. 2011. *Jesus and the Powers: Conflict, Covenant, and the Hope of the Poor*. Minneapolis: Fortress.

Horsley, Richard A., and John S. Hanson. 1985. *Bandits, Prophets, and Messiahs: Popular Movements at the Time of Jesus*. New Voices in Biblical Studies. New York: Harper & Row.

Hull, John M. 1974. *Hellenistic Magic and the Synoptic Tradition*. SBT. Second series. London: SCM.

Isasi-Diaz, Ada María. 2004. *La Lucha Continues: Mujerista Theology*. Maryknoll, NY: Orbis.

———. 2006. "Communication as Communion: Elements in a Hermeneutic of *Lo Cotidiano*." Pages 27–36 in *Engaging the Bible in a Gendered World: An Introduction to Feminist Biblical Interpretation in Honor of Katharine Doob Sakenfeld*. Edited by Linda Day and Carolyn Pressler. Louisville: Westminster John Knox.

Iverson, Kelly R. 2012. "Jews, Gentiles, and the Kingdom of God: The Parable of the Wicked Tenants in Narrative Perspective (Mark 12:1-12)." *BibInt* 20: 305–35.

Iverson, Kelly R., and Christopher W. Skinner, editors. 2011. *Mark as Story: Retrospect and Prospect*. SBLRBS 65. Atlanta: SBL.

Johnson, Elizabeth A. 2018. *Creation and the Cross: The Mercy of God for a Planet in Peril.* Maryknoll, NY: Orbis.

Johnson, Luke Timothy. 2010. *The New Testament: A Very Short Introduction.* New York: Oxford University Press.

Josephus, Flavius. 1999. *The New Complete Works of Josephus.* Translated by William Whiston. Commentary by Paul L. Maier. Grand Rapids: Kregel.

Just, Felix A. 1997. "From Tobit to Bartimaeus, from Qumran to Siloam: The Social World of Blind People and Attitudes toward the Blind in New Testament Times." PhD dissertation. Yale University.

Kahneman, Daniel, Olivier Sibony, and Cass R. Sunstein. 2021. *Noise: A Flaw in Human Judgment.* New York: Little, Brown Spark.

Kaiser, Walter C., Jr. 1994. "The Book of Leviticus." Pages 983–1191 in *NIB*. Volume 1. Edited by Leander E. Keck et al. Nashville: Abingdon.

Kaster, Robert A. 2010. "*On Clemency.*" Pages 131–76 in *Anger, Mercy, Revenge.* By Lucius Annaaeus Seneca. Translated by Robert A. Kaster and Martha C. Nussbaum. Chicago: University of Chicago Press.

Keener, Craig S. 2014. *The IVP Bible Background Commentary: New Testament.* 2nd edition. Downers Grove, IL: IVP Academic.

Kelber, Werner. 1979. *Mark's Story of Jesus.* Philadelphia: Fortress.

Kelley, Nicole. 2011. "'The punishment of the devil was apparent in the torment of the human body': Epilepsy in Ancient Christianity." Pages 205–21 in *Disability Studies and Biblical Literature.* Edited by Candida R. Moss and Jeremy Schipper. New York: Palgrave Macmillan.

Keltner, Dacher. 2009. *Born to Be Good: The Science of a Meaningful Life.* New York: Norton.

Kennedy, David. 1992. "Roman Army." Pages 789–98 in *ABD*. Volume 5. Edited by David Noel Freedman et al. New York: Doubleday.

Kirk, J. R. Daniel. 2012. "Time for Figs, Temple Destruction, and Houses of Prayer in Mark 11:12-25." *CBQ* 74: 509–27.

Kutsko, John. 1992. "Caesarea Philippi." Page 803 in *ABD*. Volume 1. Edited by David Noel Freedman et al. New York: Doubleday.

Kysar, Robert. 2007. *John, the Maverick Gospel*. 3rd edition. Louisville: Westminster John Knox.

Lakoff, George, and Mark Johnson. 2003. *Metaphors We Live By*. Chicago: University of Chicago Press.

LaCugna, Catherine Mowry. 1991. *God for Us: The Trinity and Christian Life*. New York: HarperCollins.

LaFrance, Adrienne. 2015. "A Cultural History of the Fever." *Atlantic* (September 15). theatlantic.com/health/archive/2015/09/running-hot-a-cultural-history-of-the-fever/405643/.

Lawrence, Louise J. 2013. *Sense and Stigma in the Gospels: Depictions of Sensory-Disabled Characters*. Biblical Refigurations. Oxford: Oxford University Press.

———. 2016. "Emotions of Protest in Mark 11–13: Responding to an Affective Turn in Social-Scientific Discourse." Pages 83–107 in *Matthew and Mark across Perspectives: Essays in Honour of Stephen C. Barton and William R. Telford*. Edited by Kristian Bendoraitis and Nijay K. Gupta. Library of New Testament Studies 538. London: T&T Clark.

Lazarus, Richard S. 1991. *Emotion and Adaptation*. New York: Oxford University Press.

Lazarus, Richard S., and Bernice N. Lazarus. 1994. *Passion and Reason: Making Sense of Our Emotions*. New York: Oxford University Press.

Leander, Hans. 2010. "With Homi Bhabha at the Jerusalem City Gates: A Postcolonial Reading of the 'Triumphant' Entry (Mark 11.1-11)." *JSNT* 32: 309–35.

———. 2013. *Discourses of Empire: The Gospel of Mark from a Postcolonial Perspective*. Atlanta: Society of Biblical Literature.

Levenson, Jon D. 1985. *Sinai and Zion: An Entry into the Jewish Bible*. New York: Harper & Row.

———. 1993. *The Death of the Beloved Son: The Transformation of Child Sacrifice in Judaism and Christianity*. New Haven: Yale University Press.

———. 2006. *Resurrection and the Restoration of Israel: The Ultimate Victory of the God of Life*. New Haven: Yale University Press.

———. 2016. *The Love of God: Divine Gift, Human Gratitude, and Mutual Faithfulness in Judaism*. Princeton: Princeton University Press.

Levine, Amy-Jill. 1996. "Discharging Responsibility: Matthean Jesus, Biblical Law, and Hemmorhaging Woman." Pages 379–97 in *Treasures New and Old: Contributions to Matthean Studies*. Edited by David R. Bauer and Mark Allan Powell. Society of Biblical Symposium Series. Atlanta: Society of Biblical Literature.

———. 2006. *The Misunderstood Jew: The Scandal of the Jewish Jesus*. New York: HarperSanFrancisco.

———. 2017. "Bearing False Witness: Common Errors Made about Early Judaism." Pages 759–763 in *The Jewish Annotated New Testament: New Revised Standard Bible Translation*. 2nd edition. Edited by Amy-Jill Levine and Marc Zvi Brettler. Oxford: Oxford University Press.

———. 2021. "Preaching and Teaching the Pharisees." Pages 403–427 in *The Pharisees*. Edited by Joseph Sievers and Amy-Jill Levine. Grand Rapids: Eerdmans.

———, and Marc Zvi Brettler, editors. 2017. *The Jewish Annotated New Testament*. 2nd ed. Oxford: Oxford University Press.

———, and Marc Zvi Brettler. 2020. *The Bible With and Without Jesus: How Jews and Christians Read the Same Stories Differently*. New York: HarperOne.

Levison, Jack. 2020. *An Unconventional God: The Spirit according to Jesus*. Grand Rapids: Baker Academic.

Lewis, Jordan Gaines. 2013. "Why Do We Sigh?" *Psychology Today*. psychologytoday.com/us/blog/brain-babble/201304/why-do-we-sigh.

Lieberman, Saul. 1994 [1965]. *Greek in Jewish Palestine/Hellenism in Jewish Palestine*. New York: Jewish Theological Seminary of America.

Liew, Tat-Siong Benny. 2008. "Postcolonial Criticism: Echoes of a Subaltern's Contribution and Exclusion." Pages 211–31 in *Mark & Method: New Approaches in Biblical Studies*. 2nd edition. Edited by Janice Capel Anderson and Stephen D. Moore. Minneapolis: Fortress.

L&N. 1988. Johannes P. Louw and Eugene A. Nida. *Greek-English Lexicon of the New Testament Based on Semantic Domains*. Volume 1: *Introduction and Domains*. New York: United Bible Societies.

Long, Thomas G. 2015. "Whose Work? Whose Healing? Mark 7:31-37." *Journal for Preachers* 38: 31–36.

Lyons, William John. 2014. *Joseph of Arimathea: A Study in Reception History*. Biblical Refigurations. Oxford: Oxford University Press.

MacDonald, Margaret Y. 1996. *Early Christian Women and Pagan Opinion: The Power of the Hysterical Woman*. Cambridge: Cambridge University Press.

Madigan, Kevin J., and Jon D. Levenson. 2008. *Resurrection: The Power of God for Christians and Jews*. New Haven: Yale University Press.

Maier, Paul L. 1996. "The Inscription on the Cross of Jesus of Nazareth." *Hermes* 124: 58–75.

Malbon, Elizabeth Struthers. 2000. *In the Company of Jesus: Characters in Mark's Gospel*. Louisville: Westminster John Knox.

———. 2002. *Hearing Mark: A Listener's Guide*. Harrisburg, PA: Trinity Press International.

———. 2008. "Narrative Criticism: How Does the Story Mean?" Pages 29–57 in *Mark & Method: New Approaches in Biblical Studies*. 2nd edition. Edited by Janice Capel Anderson and Stephen D. Moore. Minneapolis: Fortress.

———. 2012. "Gospel of Mark." Pages 478–92 in *Women's Bible Commentary*. 3rd edition. Twentieth Anniversary Edition. Edited by Carol A. Newsom, Sharon H. Ringe, and Jacqueline E. Lapsley. Louisville: Westminster John Knox.

Malina, Bruce J. 1994. "Establishment Violence in the New Testament World." *Scriptura* 51: 51–78.

———. 2001a. *The New Testament World: Insights from Cultural Anthropology*. 3rd edition. Louisville: Westminster John Knox.

———. 2001b. *The Social Gospel of Jesus: The Kingdom of God in Mediterranean Perspective*. Minneapolis Fortress.

Malina, Bruce J., and Richard L. Rohrbaugh. 1992. *Social-Science Commentary on the Synoptic Gospels*. Minneapolis: Fortress.

Marcus, Joel. 1992a. *The Way of the Lord: Christological Exegesis of the Old Testament in the Gospel of Mark*. Louisville: Westminster John Knox.

———. 1992b. "The Jewish War and the *Sitz im Leben* of Mark." *JBL* 111: 441–62.

———. 2000. *Mark 1–8: A New Translation with Introduction and Commentary*. AB 27. New York: Doubleday.

———. 2006. "Crucifixion as Parodic Exaltation." *JBL* 125: 73–87.

———. 2009. *Mark 8–16: A New Translation with Introduction and Commentary*. Anchor Yale Bible 27A. New Haven: Yale University Press.

Marshall, Christopher D. 1989. *Faith as a Theme in Mark's Narrative*. SNTSMS. Cambridge: Cambridge University Press.

———. 2012. *Compassionate Justice: An Interdisciplinary Dialogue with Two Gospel Parables on Law, Crime, and Restorative Justice*. Theopolitical Visions. Grand Rapids: Eerdmans.

Marshall, Mary, 2018. "Josephus and Mark 2:13–3:6: Controversies with the Scribes and Pharisees." Pages 55–61 in *Reading Mark in Context: Jesus and Second Temple Judaism*. Edited by Ben C. Blackwell, John K. Goodrich, and Jason Maston. Grand Rapids: Zondervan.

Mason, Steve. 2003. *Josephus and the New Testament*. 2nd edition. Peabody, MA: Hendrickson.

McCane, Byron R. 2003. *Roll Back the Stone: Death and Burial in the World of Jesus*. Harrisburg, PA. Trinity Press International.

McLaren, James S. 2008. "Inscription on the Cross." Pages 46–47 in *The New Interpreter's Dictionary of the Bible*. Volume 3. Edited by Katherine Doob Sakenfeld et al. Nashville: Abingdon.

McVann, Mark. 2008. "The 'Passion' of John the Baptist and Jesus before Pilate: Mark's Warnings about Kings and Governors." *BTB* 38: 152–57.

Meier, John P. 1994. *Mentor, Message, and Miracles*. Volume 2 of *A Marginal Jew*. Anchor Bible Reference Library. New York: Doubleday.

Merritt, Robert L. 1985. "Jesus Barabbas and the Paschal Pardon." *JBL* 104: 57–68.

Metzger, Bruce M., and Bart D. Ehrman. 2005. *The Text of the New Testament: Its Transmission, Corruption, and Restoration*. 4th edition. New York: Oxford University Press.

Meyers, Eric M., and Mark A. Chancey. 2012. *Alexander to Constantine: Archaeology of the Land of the Bible*. Anchor Yale Bible Reference Library. New Haven: Yale University Press.

Miller, David M. 2007. "The Messenger, the Lord, and the Coming Judgment in the Reception History of Malachi 3." *NTS* 53: 1–16.

Miller, Robert J., editor. 1994. *The Complete Gospels: Annotated Scholars Version*. Revised edition. Sonoma, CA: Polebridge.

Mishnah. *Sefaria*. sefaria.org/texts/Mishnah.

Moldenke, Harold N., and Alma I. Moldenke. 1986 [1952]. *Plants of the Bible*. New York: Dover.

Moloney, Francis J. 2002. *The Gospel of Mark: A Commentary*. Peabody, MA: Hendrickson.

Moltmann, Jürgen. 1993a. *The Crucified God: The Cross as the Foundation of Christian Theology*. Translated by R. A. Wilson, John Bowden, and Margaret Kohl. Minneapolis: Fortress.

———. 1993b. *The Trinity and the Kingdom: The Doctrine of God*. Translated by Margaret Kohl. Minneapolis: Fortress.

———. 2003. "*The Crucified God* Yesterday and Today: 1972–2002." Pages 69–85 in Jürgen Moltmann and Elisabeth Moltmann Wendel, *Passion for God: Theology in Two Voices*. Translated by Margaret Kohl. Louisville: Westminster John Knox.

———. 2004. *In the End—the Beginning: The Life of Hope*. Translated by Margaret Kohl. Minneapolis: Fortress.

———. 2015. *The Living God and the Fullness of Life.* Translated by Margaret Kohl. Louisville: Westminster John Knox.

Moore, Stephen D. 2008. "Deconstructive Criticism: Turning Mark Inside-Out." Pages 95–110 in *Mark & Method: New Approaches in Biblical Studies.* 2nd edition. Edited by Janice Capel Anderson and Stephen D. Moore. Minneapolis: Fortress.

Moors, Agnes. 2014. "Flavors of Appraisal Theories of Emotion." *Emotion Review* 6: 303–7.

Moreland, Milton. 2006. "Bethphage." Page 445 in *The New Interpreter's Dictionary of the Bible.* Volume 1. Edited by Katherine Doob Sakenfeld et al. Nashville: Abingdon.

Morgan, Teresa. 2015. *Roman Faith and Christian Faith: Pistis and Fides in the Early Roman Empire and Early Churches.* Oxford: Oxford University Press.

Moulton, James H., and George Milligan. 1930. *Vocabulary of the Greek New Testament.* London: Hodder & Stoughton.

Muddiman, John. 1992. "Fast, Fasting." Pages 773–76 in *The Anchor Bible Dictionary.* Volume 2. Edited by David Noel Freedman et al. New York: Doubleday.

Murphy, Frederick J. 2002. *Early Judaism: The Exile to the Time of Jesus.* Peabody, MA: Hendrickson.

Myers, Ched. 1988, *Binding the Strong Man: A Political Reading of Mark's Story of Jesus.* Maryknoll, NY: Orbis.

Myers, Ched and Elaine Enns. 2009. *Ambassadors of Reconciliation.* Volume 1: *New Testament Reflections on Restorative Justice and Peacemaking.* Maryknoll, NY: Orbis.

Myers, Ched, et al. 2003. *"Say to This Mountain": Mark's Story of Discipleship.* Edited by Karen Lattea. Maryknoll, NY: Orbis.

Myrick. C. Shinall. 2018. "The Social Condition of Lepers in the Gospels." *JBL* 137: 915–34.

NETS. 2007. *A New English Translation of the Septuagint.* Edited by Albert Pietersma and Benjamin G. Wright. New York: Oxford University Press. ccat.sas.upenn.edu/nets/ edition/.

Neusner, Jacob. 1984. *Judaism in the Beginning of Christianity*. Philadelphia: Fortress.

———. 1988. *From Testament to Torah: An Introduction to Judaism in Its Formative Age*. Englewood Cliffs, NJ: Prentice Hall.

Newell, John Philip. 2016. *The Rebirthing of God: Christianity's Struggle for New Beginnings*. Nashville: SkyLight Paths.

Neyrey, Jerome H., and Richard L. Rohrbaugh. 2008. "Limited Good: 'He Must Increase, I Must Decrease' (John 3:30): A Cultural and Social Interpretation." Pages 235–51 in *The Social World of the New Testament: Insights and Models*. Edited by Jerome H. Neyrey and Eric C. Stewart. Peabody, MA: Hendrickson.

Nickelsburg, George W. E., and James C. VanderKam. 2004. *1 Enoch: A New Translation Based on the Hermeneia Commentary*. Minneapolis: Fortress.

Novenson, Matthew V. 2017. *The Grammar of Messianism: An Ancient Jewish Political Idiom and Its Users*. New York: Oxford University Press.

Nussbaum, Martha C. 2001. *Upheavals of Thought: The Intelligence of Emotions*. Cambridge: Cambridge University Press.

———. 2013. *The Politics of Emotion: Why Love Matters for Justice*. Cambridge: Belknap/Harvard University Press.

Oakman, Douglas E. 2018. "The Biblical World of Limited Good in Cultural, Social, and Technological Perspective." *BTB* 48: 97–105.

Oatley, Keith. 1994. "A Taxonomy of the Emotions of Literary Response and a Theory of Identification in Fictional Narrative." *Poetics* 23: 53–74.

Obama, Barack. 2018. Nelson Mandela Annual Lecture (in partnership with the Motsepe Foundation), Johannesburg, South Africa. *Nelson Mandela Foundation*. nelsonmandela.org/content/page/annual-lecture-2018.

Omanson, Roger L. 2006. *A Textual Guide to the Greek New Testament*. Stuttgart: Deutsche Bibelgesellschaft.

Oord, Thomas Jay. 2015. *The Uncontrolling Love of God: An Open and Relational Account of Providence*. Downers Grove, IL: IVP Academic.

Ortlund, Dane C. 2018. "What Does It Mean to Cast a Mountain into the Sea? Another Look at Mark 11:23." *BBR* 28: 218–39.

Ossandón, Juan Carlos. 2012. "Bartimaeus' Faith: Plot and Point of View in Mark 10.46-52." *Bib* 93: 377–402.

Owens, Catherine. 2013. "'Hear, O Israel': Exegetical Blindness and Mark 7:31-37." *STRev* 56: 251–61.

Paffenroth, Kim. 2001. *Judas: Images of the Lost Disciple.* Louisville: Westminster John Knox.

Palmer, Parker J. 2011. *Healing the Heart of Democracy: The Courage to Create a Politics Worthy of the Human Spirit.* San Francisco: Jossey-Bass.

Pennington, Jonathan T. 2018. "The Parables of Enoch and Mark 13:1-37: Apocalyptic Eschatology and the Coming of the Son of Man." Pages 210–216 in *Reading Mark in Context: Jesus and Second Temple Judaism.* Edited by Ben C. Blackwell, John K. Goodrich, and Jason Maston. Grand Rapids: Zondervan.

Peppard, Michael. 2012. *The Son of God in the Roman World: Divine Sonship in Its Social and Political Context.* Oxford: Oxford University Press.

Perrin, Nicholas. 2018. "Psalms of Solomon and Mark 11:12-25: The Great Priestly Showdown in the Temple." Pages 182–88 in *Reading Mark in Context: Jesus and Second Temple Judaism.* Edited by Ben C. Blackwell, John K. Goodrich, and Jason Maston. Grand Rapids: Zondervan.

Peterson, Eugene H. 2005. *Christ Plays in Ten Thousand Places: A Conversation in Spiritual Theology.* Grand Rapids: Eerdmans.

———. 2008. *Tell It Slant: A Conversation on the Language of Jesus in His Stories and Prayers.* Grand Rapids: Eerdmans.

Philo. 1993. *The Works of Philo: Complete and Unabridged.* Translated by C. D. Yonge. Peabody, MA: Hendrickson.

Pilch, John J. 1981. "Biblical Leprosy and Body Symbolism." *BTB* 11: 108–13.

———. 2000. *Healing in the New Testament: Insights from Medical and Mediterranean Anthropology.* Minneapolis: Fortress.

Pixner, Bargil (Virgil). 1992. "Praetorium." Pages 447–49 in *The Anchor Bible Dictionary*. Volume 5. Edited by David Noel Freedman et al. New York: Doubleday.

Pliny the Elder. 1855. *The Natural History*. Translated by John Bostock. London: Taylor and Francis.

Pokorný, Petr. 1995. "From a Puppy to the Child: Some Problems of Contemporary Biblical Exegesis Demonstrated from Mark 7.24-30/Matt 15.21-28." *New Testament Studies* 41: 321–37.

Porter, Stanley E. 1994. *Idioms of the Greek New Testament*. 2nd edition. Sheffield: Sheffield Academic.

Powell, Mark Allan. 2018. *Introducing the New Testament: A Historical, Literary, and Theological Survey*. 2nd edition. Grand Rapids: Baker Academic.

Powery, Emerson B. 2007. "Gethsemane." Pages 561–62 in *The New Interpreter's Dictionary of the Bible*. Volume 2. Edited by Katherine Doob Sakenfeld et al. Nashville: Abingdon.

Price, Carolyn. 2015. *Emotion*. Key Concepts in Philosophy. Cambridge: Polity.

Rabinowitz, Isaac. 1962. "'Be Opened': Ἐφφαθά (Mark 7 34): Did Jesus Speak Hebrew?" *Zeitschrift für die neutestamentliche Wissenschaft* 53: 229–38.

Rauschenbusch, Walter. 1997 [1917]. *A Theology for the Social Gospel*. Library of Theological Ethics. Louisville: Westminster John Knox.

———. 2007 [1907]. *Christianity and the Social Crisis in the Twenty-First Century: The Classic that Woke the Church Up*. Edited by Paul Rauschenbusch. New York: HarperCollins.

Reaves, Jayme R., and David Tombs 2020. "#Me Too Jesus: Jesus as a Victim of Sexual Abuse." *Review & Expositor* 117: 202–21.

Reed, Jonathan L. 2000. *Archaeology and the Galilean Jesus: A Re-examination of the Evidence*. Harrisburg, PA: Trinity Press International.

———. 2007. *The HarperCollins Visual Guide to the New Testament: What Archaeology Reveals about the First Christians*. New York: HarperOne.

Reid, Barbara E. 1996. *Choosing the Best Part? Women in the Gospel of Luke.* Collegeville, MN: Liturgical Press.

———. 2007. *Taking Up the Cross: New Testament Interpretations through Latina and Feminist Eyes.* Minneapolis: Fortress.

Resseguie, James L. 2005. *Narrative Criticism of the New Testament.* Grand Rapids: Baker Academic.

Rhoads, David, Joanna Dewey, and Donald Michie. 1999. *Mark as Story: An Introduction to the Narrative of a Gospel.* 2nd edition. Minneapolis: Fortress.

Riesner, Rainer. 2009. "Praetorium." Pages 577–78 in *The New Interpreter's Dictionary of the Bible.* Volume 4. Edited by Katherine Doob Sakenfeld et al. Nashville: Abingdon.

Ringe, Sharon H. 1985. "A Gentile Woman's Story." Pages 65–72 in *Feminist Interpretation of the Bible.* Edited by Letty M. Russell. Philadelphia: Westminster.

———. 2001. "A Gentile Woman's Story Revisited: Rereading Mark 7.24-31a." Pages 79–100 in *A Feminist Companion to Mark.* Edited by Amy-Jill Levine and Marianne Blickenstaff. Sheffield: Sheffield Academic.

Ritmeyer, Leen. 1989. "Herod's Temple Mount—Stone by Stone." *BAR* 15: 23–53.

Robbins, Vernon K. 1989. "Plucking Grain on the Sabbath." Pages 107–41 in *Patterns of Persuasion in the Gospels.* Foundations and Facets. By Burton Mack and Vernon K. Robbins. Sonoma, CA: Polebridge.

Roberts, Robert C. 2003. *Emotions: An Essay in Aid of Moral Psychology.* Cambridge: Cambridge University Press.

———. 2007. *Spiritual Emotions: A Psychology of Christian Virtues.* Grand Rapids: Eerdmans.

Robertson, Donald. 2019. *How to Think Like a Roman Emperor: The Stoic Philosophy of Marcus Aurelius.* New York: St. Martin's Press.

Robin, Corey. 2004. *Fear: The History of a Political Idea.* Oxford: Oxford University Press.

Rohr, Richard. 2018. "Ascending and Descending Religions." *The Mendicant* 8: 1–6.

———. 2021. "This Is an Apocalypse." Pages 52–55 in *The Call to Unite: Voices of Hope and Awakening*. Edited by Tim Shriver and Tom Rosshirt. New York: Viking.

Rousseau, John J., and Rami Arav. 1995. *Jesus and His World: An Archaeological and Cultural Dictionary*. Minneapolis: Fortress.

Rowe, C. Kavin. 2009. *Early Narrative Christology: The Lord in the Gospel of Luke*. Grand Rapids: Baker Academic.

Sacks, Jonathan. 2005. *To Heal a Fractured World: The Ethics of Responsibility*. New York: Shocken.

Saldarini, Anthony J. 2001. *Pharisees, Scribes and Sadducees in Palestinian Society*. Biblical Resource Series. Grand Rapids: Eerdmans.

Salmon, Marilyn J. 2006. *Preaching without Contempt: Overcoming Unintended Anti-Judaism*. Fortress Resources for Preaching. Minneapolis: Fortress.

Sanders, E. P. 1985. *Jesus and Judaism*. London: SCM.

———. 1992. *Judaism: Practice & Belief 63 BCE–66 CE*. London: SCM.

———. 1993. *The Historical Figure of Jesus*. London: Penguin.

Sawicki, Marianne. 2000. *Crossing Galilee: Architectures of Contact in the Occupied Land of Jesus*. Harrisburg, PA: Trinity Press International.

———. 2001. "Making Jesus." Pages 136–70 in *A Feminist Companion to Mark*. Edited by Amy-Jill Levine with Marianne Blickenstaff. Sheffield: Sheffield Academic.

Saxby, Alan. 2015. *James, Brother of Jesus, and the Jerusalem Church: A Radical Exploration of Christian Origins*. Eugene, OR: Wipf & Stock.

Schottroff, Luise. 2006. *The Parables of Jesus*. Translated by Linda M. Maloney. Minneapolis: Fortress.

Schrenk, Gottlob. 1964. "εὐδοκέω, εὐδοκία." *TDNT* 2: 738-51.

Schüssler Fiorenza, Elisabeth. 1992. *But She Said: Feminist Practices of Biblical Interpretation*. Boston: Beacon.

———. 1994. *In Memory of Her: A Feminist Theological Reconstruction of Christian Origins*. Tenth Anniversary Edition with a New Introduction. New York: Crossroad.

———. 2009. "Introduction: Exploring the Intersections of Race, Gender, Status, and Ethnicity in Early Christian Studies." Pages 1–23 in *Prejudice and Christian Beginnings: Investigating Race, Gender, and Ethnicity in Early Christianity*. Edited by Laura Nasrallah and Elisabeth Schüssler Fiorenza. Minneapolis: Fortress.

Schwiebert, Jonathan. 2017. "Jesus's Question to Pilate in Mark 15:2." *JBL* 136: 937–47.

Scott, James C. 1990. *Domination and the Arts of Resistance: Hidden Transcripts*. New Haven: Yale University Press.

Seim, Turid Karlsen. 1994. "The Gospel of Luke." Pages 728–62 in *Searching the Scriptures. Volume 2: A Feminist Commentary*. Edited by Elisabeth Schüssler Fiorenza. New York: Crossroad.

Seligman, Martin E. P., Peter Railton, Roy F. Baumeister, and Chandra Sripada. 2016. *Homo Prospectus*. New York: Oxford University Press.

Seneca, Lucius Annaeus. 2010. *Anger, Mercy, Revenge*. Translated by Robert A. Kaster and Martha C. Nussbaum. Chicago: University of Chicago Press.

Shaw, Brent D. 2004. "Bandits in the Roman Empire." Pages 326–74 in *Studies in Ancient Greek and Roman Society*. Edited by Robin Osborne. Cambridge: Cambridge University Press.

Shiner, Whitney T. 2000. "The Ambiguous Pronouncement of the Centurion and the Shrouding of Meaning in Mark." *JSNT* 78: 3–22.

———. 2003. *Proclaiming the Gospel: First-Century Performance of Mark*. Harrisburg, PA: Trinity Press International.

Shively, Elizabeth E. 2012. *Apocalyptic Imagination in the Gospel of Mark: The Literary and Theological Role of Mark 3:22-30*. BZNW 189. Berlin: De Gruyter.

Shutt, R. J. H. 1985. "Letter of Aristeas." Pages 7–34 in *The Old Testament Pseudepigrapha*. Volume 2. Edited by James H. Charlesworth. London: Darton, Longman & Todd.

Siegel, Daniel J. 2017. *Mind: A Journey to the Heart of Being Human*. New York: Norton.

Sievers, Joseph, and Amy-Jill Levine, editors. 2021. *The Pharisees*. Grand Rapids: Eerdmans.

Sigal, Phillip. 2007. *The Halakhah of Jesus of Nazareth according to the Gospel of Matthew*. SBL Studies in Biblical Literature 18. Atlanta: SBL.

Smith, Abraham. 2006. "Tyranny Exposed: Mark's Typological Characterization of Herod Antipas (Mark 6:14-29)." *BibInt* 14 (2006): 259–93.

———. 2008. "Cultural Criticism." Pages 181–209 in *Mark & Method: New Approaches in Biblical Studies*. 2nd edition. Edited by Janice Capel Anderson and Stephen D. Moore. Minneapolis: Fortress.

Smith, Mitzi J. 2016. "Race, Gender, and the Politics of 'Sass': Reading Mark 7:24-30 through a Womanist Lens: Intersectionality and Inter(con)textuality. Pages 95–112 in *Womanist Interpretations of the Bible: Expanding the Discourse*. Edited by Gay L. Byron and Vanessa Lovelace. Semeia Studies 85. Atlanta: SBL Press.

Smith, Morton. 2014 [1978]. *Jesus the Magician*. San Francisco: Hampton Roads.

Snodgrass, Klyne R. 2008. *Stories with Intent: A Comprehensive Guide to the Parables of Jesus*. Grand Rapids: Eerdmans.

———. 2018. "4 Ezra and Mark 4:1-34: Parables on Seed, Sowing, and Fruit." Pages 69–76 in *Reading Mark in Context: Jesus and Second Temple Judaism*. Edited by Ben C. Blackwell, John K. Goodrich, and Jason Maston. Grand Rapids: Zondervan.

Solomon, Robert C. 2004. "Emotions, Thoughts, and Feelings: Emotions as Engagements with the World." Pages 76–88 in *Thinking about Feeling: Contemporary Philosophers on Emotions*. Edited by Robert C. Solomon. Oxford: Oxford University Press.

———, and Fernando Flores. 2001. *Building Trust in Business, Politics, Relationships, and Life*. Oxford: Oxford University Press.

Spencer, F. Scott. 1992. *The Portrait of Philip in Acts: A Study of Roles and Relations*, JSNTSup 67. Sheffield, UK: Sheffield Academic.

———. 1994. "Neglected Widows in Acts 6:1-7." *CBQ* 56: 714–33.

———. 2003. *What Did Jesus Do? Gospel Profiles of Jesus's Personal Conduct*. Harrisburg, PA: Trinity Press International.

———. 2004. *Dancing Girls, "Loose" Ladies, and Women of "the Cloth": The Women in Jesus's Life*. London: Continuum.

———. 2005. "'Follow Me': The Imperious Call of Jesus in the Synoptic Gospels." *Int* 59: 142–53.

———. 2010a. "Faith on Edge: The Difficult Case of the Spirit-Seized Boy in Mark 9:14-29." *RevExp* 107: 419–24.

———. 2010b. "Scripture, Hermeneutics, and Matthew's Jesus." *Int* 64: 368–78.

———. 2010c. "Feminist Criticism." Pages 289–325 in *Hearing the New Testament: Strategies for Interpretation*. 2nd edition. Edited by Joel B. Green. Grand Rapids: Eerdmans.

———. 2012. *Salty Wives, Spirited Mothers, and Savvy Widows: Capable Women of Purpose and Persistence in Luke's Gospel*. Grand Rapids: Eerdmans.

———. 2014. "Why Did the 'Leper' Get Under Jesus's Skin? Emotion Theory and Angry Reaction in Mark 1:40-45." *HBT* 36: 107–28.

———. 2015. "Son of God." Pages 308–16 in *The Oxford Encyclopedia of Bible and Theology*. Volume 2. Edited by Samuel E. Balentine et al. Oxford: Oxford University Press.

———. 2017a. "Getting a Feel for the 'Mixed' and 'Vexed' Study of Emotions in Biblical Literature." Pages 1–41 in *Mixed Feelings and Vexed Passions: Exploring Emotions in Biblical Literature*. Edited by F. Scott Spencer. Resources in Biblical Study 90. Atlanta: SBL Press.

———. 2017b. "'Your Faith Has Made You Well' (Mark 5:34; 10:52): Emotional Dynamics of Trustful Engagement with Jesus in Mark's Gospel." Pages 217–41 in *Mixed Feelings and Vexed Passions: Exploring Emotions in Biblical Literature*. Edited by F. Scott Spencer. Resources in Biblical Study 90. Atlanta: SBL Press.

———. 2019. *Luke*. Two Horizons New Testament Commentary. Grand Rapids: Eerdmans.

———. 2021. *Passions of the Christ: The Emotional Life of Jesus in the Gospels*. Grand Rapids: Baker Academic.

Stein, Bradley L. 1997. "Who the Devil is Beelzebul?" *BRev* 13: 43–45, 48.

Strange, W. A. 1996. *Children in the Early Church: Children in the Ancient World, the New Testament, and the Early Church*. Bletchley: Paternoster.

Strauss, Mark L. 2018. "Psalms of Solomon and Mark 12:28-44: The Messiah's Surprising Identity and Role." Pages 203–209 in *Reading Mark in Context: Jesus and Second Temple Judaism*. Edited by Ben C. Blackwell, John K. Goodrich, and Jason Maston. Grand Rapids: Zondervan.

Suetonius. 1914. *Lives of the Twelve Caesars*. Volume 2. Translated by John C. Rolfe. Loeb Classical Library. Cambridge: Harvard University Press.

Surowiecki, James. 2005. *The Wisdom of Crowds*. New York: Anchor Books.

Tavenner, Eugene. 1918. "Notes on the Development of Early Roman Religion." *Classical Weekly* 13: 97–102.

Tavris, Carol, and Eliot Aronson. 2020. *Mistakes Were Made (but Not by Me): Why We Justify Foolish Beliefs, Bad Decisions, and Hurtful Acts*. Updated edition. New York: Mariner.

Taylor, Joan E. 1997. *The Immerser: John the Baptist within Second Temple Judaism*. Grand Rapids: Eerdmans.

Teigen, Karl Halvor. 2008. "Is a Sigh 'Just a Sigh'? Sighs as Emotional Signals and Responses to a Difficult Task." *Scandinavian Journal of Psychology* 49: 49–57.

Theissen, Gerd. 1989. *The Shadow of the Galilean*. Philadelphia: Fortress.

———. 1991. *The Gospels in Context: Social and Political History in the Synoptic Tradition*. Translated by Linda M. Maloney. Minneapolis: Fortress.

Thiessen, Matthew. 2016. "The Many for One or One for the Many: Reading Mark 10:45 in the Roman Empire." *HTR* 109: 447–66.

———. 2020. *Jesus and the Forces of Death: The Gospels' Portrayal of Ritual Impurity within First-Century Judaism*. Grand Rapids: Baker Academic.

Thomas, D. Winton. 1960. "*Kelebh* 'Dog': Its Origin and Some Uses of It in the Old Testament." *VT* 10: 410–27.

Thomas, Dylan. 2003. *The Poems of Dylan Thomas*. Edited with an introduction by Daniel Jones. New York: New Directions.

Thorsen, Donald A. D. 1992. "Gethsemane." Pages 997–98 in *ABD*. Volume 2. Edited by David Noel Freedman et al. New York: Doubleday.

Thurman, Eric. 2003. "Looking for a Few Good Men: Mark and Masculinity." Pages 137–61 in *New Testament Masculinities*. Semeia Studies 45. Edited by Stephen D. Moore and Janice Capel Anderson. Atlanta: Society of Biblical Literature.

Tillich, Paul. 1957. *Dynamics of Faith*. New York: Harper.

———. 2005 [1955]. *The New Being*. Lincoln: University of Nebraska Press.

Toensing, Holly Joan. 2007. "'Living among the Tombs': Society, Mental Illness, and Self-Destruction in Mark 5:1-20." Pages 131–43 in *This Abled Body: Rethinking Disabilities in Biblical Studies*. Edited by Hector Avalos, Sarah J. Melcher, and Jeremy Schipper. Semeia Studies 55. Atlanta: SBL.

Tolbert, Mary Ann. 1989. *Sowing the Gospel: Mark's World in Literary-Historical Perspective*. Minneapolis: Fortress.

Tombs, David. 1999. "Crucifixion, State Terror, and Sexual Abuse." *USQR* 53: 89–109.

Treier, Daniel J. 2008. *Introducing Theological Interpretation of Scripture: Recovering a Christian Practice*. Grand Rapids: Baker Academic.

Twelftree, Graham H. 2009. "Jesus the Baptist." *Journal for the Study of the Historical Jesus* 7: 103–25.

———. 2013. "Feasts." Pages 270–78 in *Dictionary of Jesus and the Gospels*. 2nd edition. Edited by Joel B. Green, Jeannine K. Brown, and Nicholas Perrin. Downers Grove, IL: IVP Academic.

Vanderkam, James C. 1994. *The Dead Sea Scrolls Today*. Grand Rapids: Eerdmans.

Vegge, Ivar. 2017. "Not 'Hardened Hearts' but 'Petrified Hearts' (Mark 6:52): The Challenge to Assimilate and Accommodate the Vastness of Jesus in Mark 6:45-52." Pages 243–63 in *Mixed Feelings and Vexed Passions: Exploring Emotions in Biblical Literature*. Edited by F. Scott Spencer. RBS 90. Atlanta: Scholars Press.

Verde, Danilo. 2020. *Conquered Conquerors: Love and War in the Song of Songs*. Ancient Israel and Its Literature. Atlanta: SBL.

Vermes, Géza. 1999. *An Introduction to the Complete Dead Sea Scrolls*. Minneapolis: Fortress.

———. 2011. *The Complete Dead Sea Scrolls in English*. 7th edition. London: Penguin.

Vlemincx, Elke, et al. 2010a. "Respiratory Variability Preceding and Following Sighs: A Resetter Hypothesis." *Biological Psychology* 84: 82–87.

———. 2010b. "Take a Deep Breath: The Relief Effected of Spontaneous and Instructed Sighs." *Physiology & Behavior* 101: 67–73.

von Wahlde, Urban C. 1985. "Mark 9:33-50: Discipleship: The Authority that Serves." *BZ* 29: 49–67.

Waetjen, Herman C. 1989. *A Reordering of Power: A Socio-Political Reading of Mark's Gospel*. Minneapolis: Fortress.

Wallace, Daniel B. 1996. *Greek Grammar beyond the Basics: An Exegetical Syntax of the New Testament*. Grand Rapids: Zondervan.

Wardle, Timothy. 2016. "Mark, Jerusalem, and Jewish Sectarianism: Why Geographical Proximity Matters in Determining the Provenance of Mark." *NTS* 62: 60–78.

Wassen, Cecilia. 2008. "Jesus and the Hemorrhaging Woman in Mark 5:24-34. Pages 641–60 in *Scripture in Transition: Essays on Septuagint, Hebrew Bible, and Dead Sea Scrolls in Honour of Raija Sollamo*. Edited by Anssi Voitila and Jutta Jokiranta. Wissenschaftliche Untersuchungen zum Neuen Testament 2/5111. Tübingen: Mohr Siebeck.

———. 2016. "Jesus's Work as a Healer in Light of Jewish Purity Laws." Pages 87–104 in *Bridging between Sister Religions: Studies of Jewish and Christian Scriptures in Honor of Prof. John T. Townsend*. Edited by Isaac Kalimi. Brill Reference Library of Judaism 51. Leiden: Brill.

Watts, Rikk E. 2001. *Isaiah's New Exodus in Mark*. Grand Rapids: Baker.

———. 2007. "Mark." Pages 111–249 in *Commentary on the New Testament Use of the Old Testament*. Edited by G. K. Beale and D. A. Carson. Grand Rapids: Baker Academic.

———. 2018. "Rule of the Community and Mark 1:1-13." Pages 41-47 in *Reading Mark in Context: Jesus and Second Temple Judaism*. Edited by Ben C. Blackwell, John K. Goodrich, and Jason Maston. Grand Rapids: Zondervan.

Weren, Wim J. C. 1998. "The Use of Isaiah 5,1-7 in the Parable of the Tenants (Mark 12,1-12; Matthew 21,33-46)." *Bib* 70: 1–26.

Whitenton, Michael R. 2016. "Feeling the Silence: A Moment-by-Moment Account of Emotions at the End of Mark (16:1-8). *CBQ* 78: 272–89.

———. 2018. "Tasting the Kingdom: Wine-Drinking and Audience Inference in Mark 15.36." *JSNT* 40: 403–23.

Whittle, Sarah. 2018. "The Letter of Aristeas and Mark 7:1-23: Developing Ideas of Defilement." Pages 108–15 in *Reading Mark in Context: Jesus and Second Temple Judaism*. Edited by Ben C. Blackwell, John K. Goodrich, and Jason Maston. Grand Rapids: Zondervan.

Wilkins, Michael J. 1992. "Barabbas." Page 607 in *ABD*. Volume 1. Edited by David Noel Freedman et al. New York: Doubleday.

Wills, Lawrence M. 2017. "The Gospel according to Mark." Pages 67–106 in *The Jewish Annotated New Testament*. 2nd edition. Edited by Amy-Jill Levine and Marc Zvi Brettler. Oxford: Oxford University Press.

Wink, Walter. 1992. "Beyond Just War and Pacifism: Jesus's Nonviolent Way." *RevExp* 89: 197–214.

———. 1998. *When the Powers Fall: Reconciliation in the Healing of Nations*. Minneapolis: Fortress.

———. 2002. *The Human Being: Jesus and the Enigma of the Son of Man*. Minneapolis: Fortress.

Winn, Adam. 2014. "Tyrant or Servant? Roman Political Ideology and Mark 10.42-45." *JSNT* 36: 325–52.

Wolterstorff, Nicholas. 2011. *Justice in Love*. Emory Studies in Law and Religion. Grand Rapids: Eerdmans.

Wright, G. Addison. 1982. "The Widow's Mites: Praise or Lament?—A Matter of Context." *CBQ* 45: 32–43.

Wright, N. T. 1996. *Jesus and the Victory of God*. Volume 2 of *Christian Origins and the Question of God*. Minneapolis: Fortress.

———. 2008. *Surprised by Hope: Rethinking Heaven, the Resurrection, and the Mission of the Church*. New York: HarperOne.

Yanklowitz, Schmuly, editor. 2019. *Kashrut and Jewish Food Ethics*. Jewish Thought, Jewish History: New Studies. Boston: Academic Studies Press.

Yee, Gale A. 2020. "Thinking Intersectionally: Gender, Race, Class, and the Etceteras of Our Discipline." *JBL* 139: 7–26.

Yieh, John Y. H. 2009. "Simon." Page 260 in *The New Interpreter's Dictionary of the Bible*. Volume 5. Edited by Katherine Doob Sakenfeld et al. Nashville: Abingdon.

Young, Iris Marion. 2011. *Responsibility for Justice*. Oxford: Oxford University Press.

Zerwick, Max. 1993. *A Grammatical Analysis of the Greek New Testament*. Translated and revised by Mary Grosvenor. 4th edition. Rome: Pontifical Biblical Institute.

www.ingramcontent.com/pod-product-compliance
Lightning Source LLC
Chambersburg PA
CBHW052044220426
43663CB00012B/2434